RELIGION IN A REVOLUTIONARY AGE

U NITED S TATES C APITOL H ISTORICAL S OCIETY
Fred Schwengel, President

PERSPECTIVES ON THE AMERICAN REVOLUTION
Ronald Hoffman and Peter J. Albert, Editors

RELIGION

in a

REVOLUTIONARY
AGE

Edited by RONALD HOFFMAN
and PETER J. ALBERT

Published for the

UNITED STATES CAPITOL HISTORICAL SOCIETY

BY THE UNIVERSITY PRESS OF VIRGINIA

Charlottesville

THE UNIVERSITY PRESS OF VIRGINIA
Copyright © 1994 by the Rector and Visitors
of the University of Virginia

First Published 1994

Library of Congress Cataloging-in-Publication Data

Religion in a revolutionary age / edited by Ronald Hoffman and Peter
J. Albert.
    p.   cm. — (Perspectives on the American Revolution)
    Includes bibliographical references and index.
    ISBN 0–8139–1448–5
    1. United States—Religion—To 1800.   2. United States—Church
history—Colonial period, ca. 1600–1775.   3. United States—Church
history—19th century.   I. Hoffman, Ronald.   II. Albert, Peter J.
III. United States Capitol Historical Society.   IV. Series.
BR520.R45   1993
277.3′07—dc20   93–13544
                                                                    CIP

Printed in the United States of America

Contents

CONTENTS

Preface

IT IS A TRUISM to state that history cannot be comprehended
without taking into account the role of religion in human experience. From the beginnings of recorded time, human beings have engaged in a ceaseless quest for systems of belief
capable of explaining the world and of imparting meaning
and significance to their existence within it. As part of this
process, men and women have, throughout the ages, sought
the beneficent intervention of transcendent deities in behalf
of a vast array of individual and collective enterprises from
passing exams and getting into college to winning everything
from football games, beauty contests, and elections to wars—
including, of course, the American Revolution.

As the journals of the Continental Congress reveal, the
Founding Fathers understandably wished to secure the blessings of divine providence upon the dangerous course they
had undertaken. Thus, during the nine years of the War for
Independence, the delegates decreed eight annual days of
fasting and prayer, and, more happily, another eight of
thanksgiving. Moreover, while the Founders may not have
necessarily believed that Americans were God's chosen
people, they were not averse to using Old Testament language in their public pronouncements to define their cause
within the context of the Israelites. One of the most memorable uses of this kind of rhetoric occurred on May 8, 1778,
four days after Congress ratified the Franco-American alliance. Profoundly encouraged by this timely augmentation of
their military might, the delegates graciously overlooked the
despotic aspects of its origin and exhorted the American
people to

> arise then! to your tents, and gird you for the battle! It is time to
> turn the headlong current of vengeance upon the head of the
> destroyer. They have filled up the measure of their abominations,

ix

and, like ripe fruit, must drop from the tree. Although much is done, yet much remains to do. Expect not peace, whilst any corner of America is in possession of your foes. You must drive them away from this land of promise, a land flowing indeed with milk and honey. . . . if you exert the means of defence which God and nature have given you, the time will soon arrive when every man shall sit under his own vine and under his own fig-tree, and there shall be none to make him afraid. . . . It is to obtain these things that we call for your strenuous, unremitted exertions. Yet do not believe that you have been, or can be saved merely by your own strength. No! it is by the assistance of Heaven, and this you must assiduously cultivate, by acts which Heaven approves. Thus shall the power and the happiness of these sovereign, free and independent states, founded on the virtue of their citizens, increase, extend and endure, until the Almighty shall blot out all the empires of the earth.[1]

Neither an Old Testament prophet nor his modern cinematic counterpart could have said it better.

But, as Congress discovered, attempting to secure the favor of the deity they called variously "the Great Governor of the World," "the Supreme Disposer of all events," and "the ruler of the Universe," could be a tricky business. Consider, for example, the delegates' first experience in retaining the services of a congressional chaplain. During the very week in July 1776 when Congress voted for Independence, the members also instructed their president, John Hancock, to inform the popular Philadelphia Anglican clergyman Jacob Duché that his "Piety & Religion" as well as his "uniform & zealous Attachment to the Rights of America" had induced them to appoint him as their chaplain.[2] Mr. Duché's prowess in the pulpit was already well known to the Congress. Invited to pray before that body in September 1774, his performance had drawn what can only be called rave reviews. Connecticut

---

[1]Worthington C. Ford, ed., *Journals of the Continental Congress, 1774–1789*, 34 vols. (Washington, D.C., 1904–37), 11:478–79, 481.

[2]John Hancock to Jacob Duché, July [9], 1776, in Paul H. Smith et al., eds., *Letters of Delegates to Congress, 1774–1789*, 18 vols. to date (Washington, D.C., 1976–), 4:418.

delegate Silas Deane was moved to report effusively to his wife that Duché's words were "worth riding One Hundred Mile to hear." "So pertinently, with such Fervency, purity, & sublimity of Stile, & sentiment, and with such an apparent Sensibility of the Scenes, & Business before Us," did Duché pray, Deane continued, that "even Quakers shed Tears."[3] Similarly impressed, John Adams wrote to Abigail that Duché's "extemporary Prayer . . . for America, for the Congress, for The Province of Massachusetts Bay, and especially the Town of Boston" was the best he had ever heard and had "had an excellent Effect upon every Body here."[4]

But Mr. Duché's propitious beginning shortly took an unexpected turn. In October 1776, scarcely three months after his appointment, he resigned his post as chaplain to Congress, giving poor health as his reason. By the summer of 1777, however, it began to be obvious that whatever the state of his health, Mr. Duché's behavior had undergone a remarkable change. No sooner had the British taken Philadelphia than he appeared in his pulpit to pray for the royal family, and, on October 8, he wrote a fourteen-page letter to George Washington urging him to give up the war effort and repudiate the Declaration of Independence! Of the body that had formerly employed him, Mr. Duché had many unkind things to say, among them that most of its current members had been "chosen by a little, low faction" and that there were "few gentlemen . . . among them."[5] And he had even harsher words for the Adamses—Sam, who had first brought the reverend to Congress's attention, and John, who had complimented him so warmly. These two Mr. Duché now characterized as "Bankrupts, attorneys, [and] men of desperate fortunes!"[6]

Their affections quite curdled by these sentiments, the

[3]Silas Deane to Elizabeth Deane, [Sept. 7, 1774], ibid., 1:34.

[4]John Adams to Abigail Adams, Sept. 16, 1774, ibid., p. 74.

[5]Douglas Southall Freeman, *George Washington: A Biography*, vol. 4, *Leader of the Revolution* (New York, 1951), 4:543.

[6]Mark M. Boatner III, ed., *Encyclopedia of the American Revolution* (New York, 1966), p. 338.

members of Congress had a few choice phrases of their own for Mr. Duché—to John Harvie of Virginia he was an "Invidious Hypocrite," to Henry Laurens "the Ir-Revd. Jacob Duche . . . vain glorious insincere Man—in my estimation the worst Character in the world," and New Hampshire's Nathaniel Folsom called him a "Judas."[7] Unmoved by such opinions, Mr. Duché sailed for England in December 1777 and after his arrival was rewarded for his change of heart with an appointment as chaplain of the Asylum for Female Orphans of Lambeth Parish.[8]

If there is in this cautionary tale a moral about the perils of mixing politics and religion, there is also a subtle but equally valid warning against confining discussions of religion during the nation's formative period exclusively to the ideas and actions of the Founding Fathers. An unfortunate tendency to do just that in the ongoing public debate about the relationship between church and state has produced a contentious stalemate in which every assertion that the republic's creators were deeply religious is countered by another pointing out that God is not mentioned in the Constitution because, according to Alexander Hamilton, the Framers "forgot," or that in twenty volumes of personal correspondence, George Washington never once mentioned Jesus.[9] By contrast, the wider focus offered by the essays in this volume provides an enlightening opportunity to explore the rich variety and enormous complexity of the role of religion in America's Revolutionary age.

In the volume's opening essays, Jon Butler and Patricia U. Bonomi present contrasting assessments of the nature and consequences of the religious experience of the British North American colonies. Of fundamental significance in shaping

---

[7] John Harvie to Thomas Jefferson, [Oct. 25, 1777], Henry Laurens to Robert Howe, Oct. 20, 1777, and Nathaniel Folsom to Josiah Bartlett, Oct. 30, 1777, in Smith et al., eds., *Letters of Delegates*, 8:182–83, 150, 213.

[8] Boatner, ed., *Encyclopedia of the Revolution*, p. 338.

[9] Gordon S. Wood, "Ideology and the Origins of Liberal America," *William and Mary Quarterly*, 3d ser. 44 (1987): 637.

colonial religious institutions, Butler argues, was coercive authority—evidenced, for example, by the colonists' narrow conception of religious freedom, the establishment of state-supported churches in most of the colonies, the creation of denominational institutions that wielded coercive power over church members, and the destruction in the colonies of the religious systems brought from Africa by slaves. Paradoxically, despite this apparent acceptance of—even demand for—coercive authority, he finds that the colonies were generally marked by a diversity of religious expression and an increasing multiplicity of sects, the persistence of the occult and magical beliefs, widespread religious indifference and unbelief, and, among the elite, by the influence of Enlightenment rationalism, Deism, and skepticism. Nevertheless, Butler underscores the importance of church-state relations in colonial America and the institutional strength, sophistication, and authority of religious denominations.

Professor Bonomi also studies the colonial religious experience, and she goes on to evaluate the impact of this experience on the colonists' political outlook and to discover a quite different attitude toward authority from that described by Butler. The majority of Americans were Dissenters, she writes, and consequently their views and traditions were quite at odds with English values, politically as well as religiously, because Dissent promoted individualist and republican attitudes and the sharing of power between clergy and laity. Because the colonists, as an immigrant people, lacked established religious institutions, sufficient numbers of clergy, and adequate printed materials, their church polities were typically volatile, spontaneous, and nonhierarchical, and the ideal of a voluntary, gathered church was of fundamental importance to them. Lay members exercised considerable leadership, and the churches, founded as they were on voluntary association and majority rule, were less attached to the orthodox observance of traditional forms and doctrines than those in the Old World. As these tendencies became habitual over the course of the seventeenth and eighteenth centuries, Bonomi argues, this dissenting religious tradition merged easily with the emergent republicanism of the political radicals in the 1760s and 1770s.

The volume's next four essays study the religious experiences of women, blacks, workers, and evangelicals in Revolutionary America. Elaine Forman Crane focuses on Faith Robinson Trumbull and Mary Gould Almy in her exploration of the religious motivations and actions of women and their consequent impact on the political process. The influence of women in Revolutionary political affairs has been overlooked, she maintains, because historians have considered politics and religion in Revolutionary America to have been separate realms, with men active in the former and women restricted to the religious sphere. In reality, Crane argues, the women of the Revolutionary era acted as conduits of Revolutionary ideology from the pulpit to the community and, by making choices for themselves as well as by influencing others, they translated their religious beliefs and motivations into political actions.

Sylvia R. Frey then discusses the formative period of African-American Christianity in the South—the late eighteenth and early nineteenth centuries. In these years, she explains, the churches represented the only organized social existence for the slave population, a place where blacks could forge a separate cultural identity, assert traditional African patterns, and come together as a community of Christians. She traces the growth of the Baptist and Methodist churches among African Americans, outlines the role of black preachers, the development of black congregations, and concludes with an analysis of black religious practice in such areas as prayer, music, preaching, and discipline.

Ronald Schultz evaluates the role of religion among Philadelphia's working class in the years after the Revolution. The Revolutionary era was the formative period for the working class, he maintains, with the decline of small shop and craft production and the development of manufactories and the putting-out system. Encountering growing social stratification, dwindling economic opportunity, and a diminishing sense of their own worth as workers, Philadelphia's workers turned increasingly to religion as a source of legitimation and personal strength. Schultz describes the response of Methodism, Presbyterianism, and Universalism to the human costs of this disintegration of the craft economy, and he concludes with an analysis of the growing class and political consciousness of the workers and its expression in such organizations as the Democratic Society of Pennsylvania, the Mechanics' Union of Trade Associations, and the Workingmen's party.

Finally, Robert M. Calhoon studies evangelicalism in the South, particularly its impact on Revolutionary politics, its attempt to reconcile republicanism and Christianity, its congregational discipline, and its sermons. The evangelical impulse, he argues, was a product of the same processes that created the American republic, and he examines both its impact on the surrounding society and its eventual rupture in the face of the internal contradictions and conflicts generated by slavery.

The next essays deal with the relationship between religion and the political culture of the new nation. Stephen A. Marini analyzes the influence of religion on politics by focusing on the delegates to the state conventions called to ratify the new federal Constitution. Religious denominations experienced significant growth during the Revolutionary era, he points out, religion enjoyed a prominent place in the public culture, and religious affiliation was an important qualification for political leadership. Consequently, the delegates to the ratifying conventions represented the major churches of the day—Anglican, Congregationalist, Methodist, Baptist, and Presbyterian—and Marini's careful study of their votes indicates pervasive divisions between Federalist liberals and Antifederalist evangelicals and complex patterns of intradenominational religious influences rather than simple divisions along denominational lines.

Approaching the issue of religion and politics in the Revolutionary era from a different perspective, Edwin S. Gaustad outlines the provisions regarding religion in the state constitutions, the federal Constitution, and the Northwest Ordinance. He finds that while such state constitutions as those of Maryland, Pennsylvania, Massachusetts, and Tennessee endorsed religious liberty, they also retained a loyalty to Christianity and demanded religious tests for officeholders. The federal Constitution, on the other hand, provided a striking contrast in its prohibition of religious tests—the delegates at Philadelphia perhaps motivated, in Gaustad's view, by their desire to keep the new government free from ecclesiastical entanglements, their perception of the problem of unifying many local traditions, their conviction that the matter was, more properly, a state responsibility, or their reluctance to get into such a thorny issue at all.

M. L. Bradbury then discusses the creation of structures of governance by three denominations—Episcopalians, Presbyterians, and Baptists—in the decades of the Revolutionary era and after. He explores the use of federalist language and models—consciously derived, he argues, from the federal Constitution's response to the new nation's political diversity—and examines the effects on church polities of the creation of new national institutions by these denominations.

Paul K. Conkin's essay begins by considering the fact that the American political Revolution which resulted in Independence from Great Britain was not paralleled by a religious revolution or accompanied by an attack on the predominant forms and institutions of Christianity in the new nation. Conkin goes on to explore this by analyzing the religious philosophy of Joseph Priestley and its impact on the views of Thomas Jefferson. Priestley's influence notwithstanding, Conkin demonstrates that Jefferson retained a conviction that the survival of the republic depended on the adherence of its citizens to Christianity, and he refused to espouse a radical religious reformation in America.

In her essay that concludes the volume, Ruth H. Bloch begins by summarizing the debate in American Revolutionary historiography regarding the relative influence on Revolutionary ideology of community-centered civic humanism and individualistic classical liberalism. She argues that the influence of these two ideologies carried over into other aspects of American social life, and she studies the impact of these values on the cultural life of Revolutionary America, particularly the areas of religious and family issues. Her analysis of the religious, sentimental, and advice literature of the time reveals both communitarian (republican) and individualist (liberal) aspects and leads her to conclude that these were complementary rather than contradictory values.

The editors would like to acknowledge the valuable contributions made by the other participants at the U.S. Capitol Historical Society's symposium on religion in Revolutionary America, Philip F. Gura, Christine Leigh Heyrman, Donald G. Mathews, and Harry S. Stout. We would also like to acknowledge the help of Angeline Polites, Katherine Morin, R. Bruce Miller, Mary C. Jeske, Donald Stelluto, Jr., and Aileen Arnold for their assistance in the editing and typing of this manuscript.

JON BUTLER

Coercion, Miracle, Reason

Rethinking the

American Religious Experience

in the Revolutionary Age

WE USED TO THINK about two kinds of religion when we thought about the American religious experience in the Revolutionary age. The first was the rationalism, Deism, and skepticism found, most prominently, in Founding Fathers like Benjamin Franklin, Thomas Jefferson, and James Madison. The second was evangelical Dissent, meaning revivalist, born-again, witnessing Christianity, usually thriving outside the established government-supported churches and typified by George Whitefield, Jonathan Edwards, and the Tennents of New Jersey.

No more. The religion of the Founding Fathers has receded dramatically in importance to historians of eighteenth-century America. Its rationalism and spiritual coolness now seem unrepresentative of a tumultuous pre-Revolutionary society and unprophetic of antebellum America, where religious revivalism, moral reform, nativism, and a bombastic, self-aggrandizing expansionism proliferated in orgiastic fury.

Now, historians use dissenting evangelicalism to describe and explain eighteenth-century American religion and society. Whatever its vagaries in modern American politics, dissenting evangelicalism has clearly won the historians' nomination as America's most important religion. Indeed, it is the single most common explanatory device in contemporary

1

American history, outstripping such once powerful but now enfeebled predecessors as Puritanism, the rise of the middle class, industrialism, urbanization, or even the growth of democracy. In the current literature, dissenting evangelicalism explains in whole or in part the American Revolution, Jacksonian Democracy, antebellum reform, foreign conquest, the American family, women's rights, and even republicanism— meaning the ideology before 1820 and the party after 1975.[1]

The pendulum has swung too far, however. The rush to explanatory evangelicalism obscures historical realities of eighteenth-century America both before and after the Revolution. It distorts the substance of religious experience in the Revolutionary age and the dynamics of American religious development and change. Consequently, it is profitable to reassess the importance of three other characteristics that contemporaries themselves found important in their own changing society: authority and coercion in religion, the wide range of popular belief and unbelief, and the now discredited rationalism, Deism, and skepticism linked to the eighteenth-century Enlightenment. These traditions were central to the religious experience of the Revolutionary age; taken together, they help explain some (not all) of the distinctive tensions that underwrote and energized eighteenth-century American religious life and that, in attenuated and sometimes transplanted form, have continued even down to our own not-so-secular age.

---

[1]Henry F. May, *The Enlightenment in America* (New York, 1976), offers a more sophisticated study of the eighteenth-century Enlightenment than previous studies allowed and one whose complexities are necessarily obscured in this short piece. On the religion of the Founding Fathers, see, among others, Alfred O. Aldridge, *Benjamin Franklin and Nature's God* (Durham, N.C., 1967), Paul F. Boller, Jr., *George Washington & Religion* (Dallas, 1963), Daniel Boorstin, *The Lost World of Thomas Jefferson* (New York, 1948), Norman Cousins, *In God We Trust: The Religious Beliefs and Ideas of the American Founding Fathers* (New York, 1958), Edwin S. Gaustad, *Faith of Our Fathers: Religion and the New Nation* (San Francisco, 1987), Charles B. Sanford, *The Religious Life of Thomas Jefferson* (Charlottesville, Va., 1984). Much of the literature on evangelicalism is described and analyzed in Leonard Sweet, "The Evangelical Tradition in America," in Sanford, ed., *The Evangelical Tradition in America* (Macon, Ga., 1984), pp. 1–86.

Freedom fascinates historians of American religion. We believe that we know that coercive state-church establishments failed in America. As a result, we are sure that dissenting evangelical traditions created America's most enduring religious patterns. These views have limited explanatory and descriptive power, however. They buttress the erroneous notion that American religious patterns emerged from some singular creation, by most accounts from Puritan New England. They also tend to dismiss one of the most astonishing characteristics of American religiosity—its capacity for nearly constant creativity—by confining that creativity to a single stream with few tributaries. In fact, American religious patterns were made and remade in each century and in many places, complexity piling upon complexity, some patterns washing away, new ones appearing, frequently transcending, yet seldom wholly demolishing, the old.[2]

A complex, extended view of American religious creativity would recognize that authority, power, and coercion shaped religion generally throughout American history; they certainly did so in the Revolutionary era. British colonists did not flee the responsibilities, obligations, or even love of authority, power, and coercion in religion. Indeed, the eighteenth century witnessed their rise in new and powerful configurations, and these reshaped the seventeenth-century American religious experience. Some of these developments were energizing and enlivening; some proved devastatingly destructive. Taken together, they formed a distinctive and complex "American" religious moment—one of several moments that comprise the whole of the American religious heritage.

As late as the very eve of the Revolution, not a single American colony sanctioned religious freedom, meaning—as even contemporaries understood the term—freedom to worship any supernatural being. At best, the British colonial governments sanctioned freedom for Christianity. At worst, they lim-

---

[2]The emphasis on the failure of the European state-church pattern, which can at least be traced back to Robert Baird, obtained twentieth-century expression in the work of William Warren Sweet, especially his *Religion in the Development of American Culture, 1765–1840* (New York, 1952), and Sidney E. Mead, especially in *The Lively Experiment: The Shaping of Christianity in America* (New York, 1963).

ited that freedom not only to Protestant Christianity but to its state-supported varieties, meaning Congregational churches in New England and the Church of England in the southern colonies. Jews and Catholics worshiped in pre-Revolutionary America at the sufferance of legislators who perceived them as only a minor social, political, or religious threat, but who yet proved unwilling to transform practice into principle. No wonder, then, that in the 1740s and 1750s governments in New England and Virginia were still attempting to suppress alternate forms of Protestantism—"enthusiastic" Baptists and Presbyterians—even though they acknowledged that these groups proffered a religion no more esoteric than English Dissent.[3]

The colonial religious establishments were more than legal niceties. For many years they provided the only forms of public religious practice available to colonists in America. Through 1760, at least half the churches in the British mainland colonies were those that were sanctioned or mandated by law. They served well-defined areas and they utilized governmental coercive power to collect taxes to pay their ministers and maintain their buildings. Such patterns typified religious settings in nine of the thirteen colonies—New Hampshire, Massachusetts, Connecticut, New York, Maryland, Virginia, North Carolina, South Carolina, and Georgia. These colonies as well as the remaining four that lacked any kind of establishment—Rhode Island, Pennsylvania, New Jersey, and Delaware—used the law to uphold Christianity in general terms. For example, Quaker Pennsylvania forced officeholders to affirm their belief in Christ's divinity, banned blasphemy (defined simply as the derogation of Christianity), forbade Sunday labor, and urged settlers to attend church so

---

[3] Richard Bushman, *Puritan to Yankee: Character and the Social Order in Connecticut, 1690–1765* (Cambridge, Mass., 1967); Rhys Isaac, *The Transformation of Virginia, 1740–1790* (Chapel Hill, 1982). A contemporary work by the South Carolina chief justice, Nicholas Trott, *The Laws of the British Plantations in America, Relating to the Church and to the Clergy* (London, 1721), collected legislation passed to 1720. The most recent survey is Thomas J. Curry, *The First Freedoms: Church and State in America to the Passage of the First Amendment* (New York, 1986). Curry concentrates on church rather than on the broader issue of religion.

"looseness, irreligion, and Atheism may not creep in under pretense of conscience."[4]

On the eve of the American Revolution, most colonial religious establishments were eighteenth-century creations; they were not mere holdovers from the previous century of early settlement. Legislatures in South Carolina, North Carolina, Maryland, and New York enacted their first establishment laws between 1693 and 1710, and they refined and tightened them through the 1720s. Only in Virginia, Massachusetts, and Connecticut did lawmakers build on old establishments. Yet the tensions between establishment and Dissent after 1740 demonstrated how thoroughly the late seventeenth- and early eighteenth-century legislatures in each of these colonies worked to strengthen their established churches. Between 1690 and 1720, under the leadership of the much maligned James Blair, Virginia refurbished its establishment to create the single strongest Anglican church in the colonies. In the same period, Massachusetts and Connecticut restructured their town-church system to create a new, more supple, parish organization separate from the towns and better able to supervise religious activity in a larger, more bumptious society.[5]

The ubiquity of the colonial establishments dictated a variety that departed significantly from the European church-state tradition. Consequently, the established churches escaped the charge frequently leveled against them in both Europe and America that the coercive state-church tradition was inflexible and could not accommodate local variation. In fact, they accommodated all too well. Anglican authorities in the southern colonies continuously complained that their estab-

[4] Edwin S. Gaustad, *Historical Atlas of Religion in America* (New York, 1962), pp. 1–10, 13–16; Anson Phelps Stokes, *Church and State in the United States,* 3 vols. (New York, 1950), 1:168; Carl Zollman, *American Church Law* (St. Paul, 1933), pp. 2–6; Trott, *Laws of the British Plantations,* pp. 231–43.

[5] Georgia and New Hampshire also exemplified the push toward religious establishment in the eighteenth century. Georgia established Anglicanism in 1758, four years after its designation as a royal province, and New Hampshire adopted a pattern of local establishment, usually of Congregationalist societies. The laws with respect to religion for all the colonies, through 1720, are found in Trott, *Laws of the British Plantations.*

lishment allowed too much variety and heterogeneity. They blamed this on the lack of a bishop to preside over the colonies and on colonial establishment laws that gave too little power to Anglican commissaries and too much to parish ministers and vestries. In New England the state spoke with many mouths, frequently with contradictory results. Awakenings that upset the established order in one town were funded by the establishment in another. Jonathan Edwards invoked the state authority of his tax-supported ministry when he demanded conversion narratives from his Northampton congregants. But other state-supported ministers, ranging from Charles Chauncy of Boston to Timothy Walker of Rumford, New Hampshire, fulminated bitterly against revivalism. Still, however varied their experiences, Americans of the Revolutionary age usually encountered Christianity in a state-supported church, which provided the most readily available minister, services, and place of worship. They paid taxes to it irrespective of their actual relationship to the congregation, much less their personal views on religion.[6]

The "localist" character of eighteenth-century American state-church establishments bespoke another major contrast with England. The established church largely rested on its relationship with a dominant local elite. What contemporaries termed "connections"—the integration of economic and personal prestige, kinship, personal aspirations, and religious adherence into a working whole—proved more important in defining the character of tax-supported congregations than did formal rules of ecclesiology. In short, locality counted more than province, and familiarity more than theology. In New England, a Congregational state-church parish might be Calvinist, Arminian, or any reasonable combination. In the South, Anglican state-church parishes might exhibit similar heterogeneity. In addition, ministers in both regions often deliberately chose to blur rather than refine these distinctions.

[6]The most recent summary of the Anglican condition is found in John F. Wolverton, *Colonial Anglicanism in North America* (Detroit, 1984). On contradictory responses to revivalism in New England, see Edwin S. Gaustad, *The Great Awakening in New England* (New York, 1957), pp. 61–79.

As a result, the eighteenth-century parish, whether Congregationalist or Anglican, more often bespoke a local conformism than any clear proclamation of theological truth or ecclesiastical principle. The result could be as suffocating in the eighteenth as it demonstrably was in the nineteenth century. No one experienced it more dramatically than Jonathan Edwards. However brilliant, however evangelical, however apparently American he was, Edwards's Northampton, Massachusetts, parishioners stonewalled his emphasis on conversion and finally simply fired him. Whatever his genius, Edwards's theology was unfamiliar; at the least, it was unhistorical. Better to expound it in the wilderness among Indians.[7]

The creation of denominational institutions represented a second major expression of authority and coercion in eighteenth-century American religion. Colonists developed institutions to empower religion, and they did so most obviously in the region where the coercive European state-church tradition was weakest, the Delaware Valley of Pennsylvania and New Jersey. Between 1685 and 1710, an infant Philadelphia witnessed the formation of America's first major Protestant denominational institutions: the Philadelphia Yearly Meeting (1685), the Presbytery of Philadelphia (1706), and the Philadelphia Baptist Association (1707), followed by the Coetus of the Reformed, or German Calvinist, Church (1747) and the Lutheran Ministerium of Pennsylvania (1748). Similar institutions appeared elsewhere, as well, although not in the profusion that characterized their explosive development in the Delaware Valley. An association of Congregationalist ministers first met in Cambridge, Massachusetts, in 1690, and it was followed by additional associations organized elsewhere in Massachusetts and Connecticut after 1710, then by several presbyteries in the 1730s and 1740s. In the southern colonies,

---

[7] Patricia J. Tracy, *Jonathan Edwards, Pastor: Religion and Society in Eighteenth-Century Northampton* (New York, 1980), pp. 171–95. The problem of conformism and deviance informs the analysis of witchcraft accusations in John Demos, *Entertaining Satan: Witchcraft and the Culture of Early New England* (New York, 1983).

presbyteries and Baptist associations sprang up following the growth of significant proselytizing activity by both groups in the 1750s and 1760s.[8]

The name later given to these bodies—voluntary associations—belied their strength and, thereby, their importance. No one compelled "membership" in them. But claiming membership meant both exercising power and submitting to authority. Events solidified these principles. During the so-called Keithian Schism among Quakers in the 1690s, in the controversy about the Westminster Confession among Presbyterians in the 1720s, and in congregational and association disputes among Baptists between 1710 and 1730, leaders of all three groups found it difficult to agree on creeds but not at all problematic to demand adherence to their ecclesiastical authority.[9]

The denominations exercised coercive power over their members precisely because the colonists themselves valued authority. The denominations were hierarchical, not democratic, institutions. Authority in them flowed down from the top, not up from the bottom—from yearly to quarterly to monthly meeting to meeting for worship among Quakers, from synod to presbytery to congregation among Presbyterians, and from association to congregation among Baptists. Moreover, however differently each denomination defined "ministry," the ministers dominated denominational proceedings. Presbyterians, for example, allowed lay elders to attend only when the congregation's minister was present; elders never sat on committees and were not allowed to outnumber attending ministers. Ministering Quakers lost some authority to prominent lay elders in the 1710s and

---

[8]Sidney E. Mead, "Denominationalism: The Shape of Protestantism in America," in Mead, *The Lively Experiment*, pp. 103–33; Jon Butler, *Power, Authority, and the Origins of American Denominational Order: The English Churches in the Delaware Valley, 1680–1730* (Philadelphia, 1978).

[9]Butler, *Power, Authority, and Denominational Order*, pp. 33–39, 51–52, 62–64. For a more theological interpretation of the Keithian schism, see Barry Levy, *Quakerism and the American Family: British Settlement in the Delaware Valley* (New York, 1988), pp. 157–72.

1720s but regained it in a major Quaker reformation in the 1750s and 1760s.[10]

Denominational authority was not necessarily autocratic or even successful. The inability to produce statements of doctrinal orthodoxy often raised rather than lowered tension. The shortage of ministers frequently encouraged lenient treatment of wayward clerics. Still, the desire for authority remained. This became particularly obvious during the great Presbyterian schism of the 1740s. Usually interpreted as an attack on authority—indeed, as "antiauthoritarian" and perhaps even as a preface to the American Revolution—it was, instead, "proauthoritarian." Its instigators, Gilbert Tennent and the ministers of the evangelicals' so-called Log College, had long objected to the Philadelphia Synod's disciplinary laxness. The schism they created emerged from a carefully staged scenario designed to test the Synod's resolve. When the Synod refused the challenge, the Log College ministers walked out, not into the heady air of antiauthoritarian freedom but merely to New York. There, they created new presbyteries and, finally, another synod—the Synod of New York—to exercise effective coercive power over "true" Presbyterian ministers, ministerial candidates, and congregations.[11]

A third form of coercion demonstrated how law, social custom, and contempt for non-Christian religion could shatter traditional religious practice among already beleaguered groups and, ultimately, produce momentous change in religious affection. This was demonstrated in the wholesale destruction of the African religious systems brought to America

[10]Butler, *Power, Authority, and Denominational Order,* pp. 41–43, 55; Jack D. Marietta, *The Reformation of American Quakerism, 1748–1783* (Philadelphia, 1984), pp. 73–96. A democratic interpretation of Presbyterian development is found in Marilyn J. Westerkamp, *Triumph of the Laity: Scots-Irish Piety and the Great Awakening, 1625–1760* (New York, 1988).

[11]Leonard J. Trinterud, *The Forming of an American Tradition: A Reexamination of Colonial Presbyterianism* (Philadelphia, 1949), pp. 100–121, offers a reliable account of the proceeding, although it is tied too closely to Whitefield. For a more recent and more democratic interpretation, see Westerkamp, *Triumph of the Laity.*

by the half-million slaves transported to the mainland colonies between 1680 and the American Revolution. No other religious event during the entire colonial period or later, including the evolution of Puritanism or the emergence of American evangelicalism, so shaped a people's experience of religion as did the eighteenth-century African spiritual holocaust in Britain's mainland colonies.[12]

Not all African religious traditions perished in America. But the survival or importation of discrete religious practices and forms should not be confused with the prosperity of whole religious systems. By the 1760s the national religions that mainland colony slaves knew at home had been suppressed in their New World residences. Obeah and Myal men, and singular rites and customs survived in some places, such as Jamaica. But the *systems* within which these figures worked—systems at least as breathtaking in their spiritual expanse as Christianity—collapsed in the shattering destructiveness of British slaveholding.[13]

Social and demographic factors played a major role in destroying the African gods. Mainland slave settlements were dispersed, not dense, as in Brazil or Hispaniola. Death rates were extremely high among new slaves, especially before 1740; in many places, new slaves could expect to live less than five years. Death, the sex ratio (far more males than females), and the plantation system gave little impetus to procreation or to family life before 1740 and reduced incentives to sustain traditional national religious systems to hand on to successors.

[12]It has become impolitic and, certainly, unfashionable to speak of the destruction of African religions in America. It is said that emphasizing this destructiveness robs slaves of their collective and individual dignity. It also may call into question their subsequent conversion to Christianity. But historians, unlike politicians, cannot evade difficult questions, particularly where traditional African religious practices of entire peoples disappeared in British America but frequently survived elsewhere. The destruction of African religions in America likewise was a largely eighteenth-century phenomenon, not because it did not occur earlier but because the vast majority of slaves who came to British America were imported in that century.

[13]A convenient summary of work on African religions and their New World survival is contained in Albert J. Raboteau, *Slave Religion: The "Invisible Institution" in the Antebellum South* (New York, 1978), pp. 3–42.

The religious deselectivity of the slave trade worsened matters further. Unlike the Puritan emigrés, for example, Africans of special religious status and knowledge were not sought out for transport to the New World. If they were caught up in the slave trade, it was because of their capability for physical labor, and there is little evidence that owners changed this basis of evaluation once the slaves began working in the New World.[14]

Finally, labor discipline also contributed to the destruction of African religious systems in the colonies. Slaveholders could make few significant inroads on tightly held personal beliefs. But they could—and did—prohibit collective expressions of African religious practice. This often occurred indirectly as part of the campaign to increase field efficiency by controlling the slaves' collective lives. The law aided and abetted this trend. If it only tolerated variant forms of Protestant Christianity, it hardly protected Ashanti or Yoruba religion, particularly among people lacking legal standing in any case and wholly dependent upon others to invoke legal authority even in minor matters. Of course, for most English settlers, the law became an instrument of freedom. But for Africans, it became an instrument of oppression through both action and silence. Its use to enunciate slave codes gave slaveholding a powerful sanction among settlers long convinced that it articulated and upheld eternal principles. Its silence fostered an indifference and contempt for African religious practice not unlike the denominational silence that encouraged Nazi anti-Semitism in the 1920s and 1930s.[15]

Christianity played a major role in the eighteenth-century African spiritual holocaust by the way it shaped slavery. Between 1680 and 1740, Anglican clerics in the South articulated a doctrine of absolute obedience unparalleled in the English political tradition. Preaching in the 1740s, Maryland's

[14] Ibid., pp. 87–92.

[15] On colonial law and slavery, see A. Leon Higginbotham, Jr., *In the Matter of Color: Race and the American Legal Process. The Colonial Period* (New York, 1978). For descriptions of attempts to suppress African religious practice in South Carolina, see Frank J. Klingberg, ed., *The Carolina Chronicle of Dr. Francis Le Jau, 1706–1717* (Berkeley and Los Angeles, 1956), pp. 54, 61, 77.

Thomas Bacon—perhaps the Paul de Man or Martin Heidegger of American slavery—prescribed a regimen of unconditional obedience for slaves with consequent expectations for owners. Still grappling with the emerging terminology of American plantation life, Bacon called the owners "God's overseers." And since they were his direct representatives, God himself would punish slaves in the next world for disobeying their owners in this one. While slaves may have treated such doctrines with indifference or contempt, the words of Bacon and his ministerial colleagues had a profound impact on slaveholders. They deepened the direct Christian sanction of a religiously devastating labor discipline and rationalized the owners' real and threatened use of violence against slaves that soon typified British slavery everywhere in the mainland colonies.[16]

Amidst this spiritual holocaust, slaves faced an even more quizzical demand: conversion to Christianity and its consequent call to express—although not necessarily receive—Christian love. Thomas Bacon told slaves and their owners that Christianity not only obligated slaves to "do all service for them [that is, slaveholders], as if you did it for GOD himself," but to suppress stubbornness and sullenness and even love their owners as much as they loved the new Christian God they ought to be worshiping. Of course, those slaves who did become Christians frequently found a different God in the Christian scriptures, a God of compassion and, ultimately, a God of deliverance and even freedom. But this should not obscure the fact that their owners and colonial clergymen expressed doctrines of absolute obedience and obligation that far exceeded anything in the English political tradition and assumed both direct and indirect roles in the destruction of traditional African religions in America.[17]

The African spiritual holocaust appears all the more paradoxical, if not ironic, in contrast to the extraordinary diver-

[16]Thomas Bacon, *Four Sermons, Preached at the Parish Church of St. Peter, in Talbot County, in the Province of Maryland* . . . (1753) (Bath, 1783).

[17]Ibid., pp. 34–35.

sity of religious expression that arose in white, eighteenth-century America. This variety ranged from an expanding number of sects to a persistence of occult and magical supernatural traditions to an indifference to religion all the more remarkable when viewed from our own highly churched age.

Institutional Christianity bespoke that diversity in special, if sometimes misunderstood, ways. Despite what historians have sometimes written on the subject, it is doubtful that eighteenth-century American religious heterogeneity exceeded that found in Europe as a whole. But the combination of spiritual and national pluralism had no equal in any single European country. New England remained relatively homogeneous, of course. Yet elsewhere diversity seemed endless. Especially after 1710, colonists found English variety—Quaker, Baptist (Arminian, Calvinist, and Seventh-Day), Presbyterian, Rogerene, and Sandemanian—compounded by divisions stemming from the disagreements over revivalism and religious enthusiasm, then further compounded by the presence of French Huguenots, German mystical Pietists, and Jews, who had begun to arrive as early as the 1680s, and the German Lutherans, Pietists, German Calvinists (Reformed), Moravians, Mennonites, Swiss Protestants, and, finally, Roman Catholics, who became more numerous after 1720.[18]

Denominational deviations further tangled the American spiritual thicket. The doctrinal variety that simultaneously energized and plagued seventeenth-century Puritanism found heightened expression in the eighteenth century. Arianism (denial that Christ was consubstantial with God), Arminianism (denial of the Calvinist doctrine of predestination), Behmenism (attachment to the doctrines of the German mystical Pietist Jacob Boehme), Chiliasm (attachment to the importance of the thousand-year reign of Christ), Origenism (belief in universal salvation), Pelagianism (denial of the doctrine of original sin), Socinianism (denial of Christ's divinity), as well as diverse views on the resurrection of the body, hell, eternal

[18]Sydney E. Ahlstrom, *A Religious History of the American People* (New Haven, 1972), esp. chaps. 13–16.

13

punishment, and the validity of particular rituals all took root in eighteenth-century America. Sometimes disputants recognized their petty disagreements for what they were. Middle colony Baptists simply agreed in the 1720s to admit visitors from other congregations to the Lord's Supper despite their differences over the issue of "laying on of hands" in receiving new church members. But sometimes they did not. Certainly, the variety of religious opinion within the denominations could discourage membership. As the Anglican itinerant Charles Woodmason put it on the eve of the American Revolution, "By the Variety of Taylors who would pretend to know the best fashion in which [to wear] Christs Coat . . . none will put it on."[19]

Despite ridicule from Enlightenment skeptics, doctrines of supernatural intervention also found expression in eighteenth-century America. Chiliasm took several forms, all of them implying that God was about to change human history dramatically. Apocalypticism emphasized the earth's destruction in the coming millennium. Millennialism emphasized Christ's return to govern for a thousand years. Like the more esoteric heresies, these transcended denominational boundaries and were found among Baptists, Congregationalists, Presbyterians, Lutherans, German Reformed, and even Anglicans.[20]

A belief in miracles—rejected by most, if not all, Reforma-

---

[19]Charles Woodmason, *The Carolina Backcountry on the Eve of the American Revolution: The Journal and Other Writings of Charles Woodmason, Anglican Itinerant,* ed. Richard J. Hooker (Chapel Hill, 1953), p. 13. David S. Lovejoy, *Religious Enthusiasm in the New World: Heresy to Revolution* (Cambridge, Mass., 1985), traces many varieties of spiritual ecstasy in America, and Elizabeth W. Fisher, "'Prophesies and Revelations': German Cabbalists in Early Pennsylvania," *Pennsylvania Magazine of History and Biography* 109 (1985): 299–333, reassesses early German varieties.

[20]Millennialism has, of course, received enormous attention, beginning with Alan Heimert's controversial *Religion and the American Mind from the Great Awakening to the Revolution* (Cambridge, Mass., 1966) and continuing with Nathan D. Hatch, *The Sacred Cause of Liberty: Republican Thought and the Millennium in Revolutionary New England* (New Haven, 1977), James West Davidson, *The Logic of Millennial Thought* (New Haven, 1977), and Ruth H. Bloch, *Visionary Republic: Millennial Themes in American Thought, 1756–1800* (New York, 1985).

tion theologians—likewise took root in America. Small groups
like Rhode Island's Rogerenes, or individual clergymen, like
the Baptists' John Blount of Stockbridge, Massachusetts, and
Morgan Edwards of Philadelphia, engaged in divine healing.
An ecstatic religious radicalism surfaced among French Hu-
guenot refugees in South Carolina in the 1710s and 1720s.
These beliefs in miracles were not limited to obscure settlers.
Revivalist Presbyterians Gilbert, John, and William Tennent
portrayed themselves as far more than merely well-trained
Calvinist clergymen. They were holy men, charismatic figures
in Max Weber's original conception. Gilbert Tennent publicly
announced the resurrection of his brother William. John Tennent frequently wept when he held the Bible, and his congregants appear to have interpreted this weeping as well as his
regimen of fainting while walking in the woods as signs of
personal holiness. William Tennent, who had already been
raised from the dead, experienced other miracles. He was
saved from a perjury conviction by witnesses called to court in
their dreams. When he lost five toes during his sleep without
bleeding or pain, he interpreted that event as a miracle as
well, albeit one brought on by the devil. These events deeply
embarrassed nineteenth-century Presbyterian historians, who
sought to explain them as natural, but Tennent's contemporaries appear nonetheless to have been persuaded that this
five-toed, resurrected minister literally demonstrated God's
work in the modern world.[21]

---

[21]Clarke Garrett, *Spirit Possession and Popular Religion: From the Camisards
to the Shakers* (Baltimore, 1987); Lovejoy, *Religious Enthusiasm*, pp. 172–75;
Jon Butler, *The Huguenots in America: A Refugee People in New World Society*
(Cambridge, Mass., 1983), pp. 119–20. The Tennent episodes are recounted in Elias Boudinot, *Life of the Rev. William Tennent, Late Pastor of the
Presbyterian Church at Freehold, N.J.*, improved ed. (Trenton, 1833), and in
Archibald Alexander, *Biographical Sketches of the Founder and Principal Alumni
of the Log College* (Philadelphia, 1851), pp. 109–59, in which Alexander
downplayed the miraculous elements. On John Tennent, see Gilbert Tennent's introductory comments to John Tennent, *The Nature of Regeneration
Opened, and Its Absolute Necessity, in Order to Salvation, Demonstrated, in a Sermon
from Job. III.3* (Boston, 1735), pp. ii–x. One of the original letters on which
Boudinot based his account of William Tennent's life can still be found at
the New Jersey Historical Society, Newark (Thomas Henderson to Elias
Boudinot, undated, ms. group I, no. 11M7).

Occultism—secret quasi-Christian and non-Christian religious beliefs whose adepts were extremely eager to share their views with others—did not die with the seventeenth century even among intellectuals. In 1707, Nicholas Trott, South Carolina's chief justice, wrote an extensive defense of witch-hunting as a charge to a Charleston grand jury. In the 1730s the New Jersey Presbyterian minister Joseph Morgan, William Tennent's predecessor at Freehold, left the ministry to pursue occult speculation more fully. Previously a correspondent of Cotton Mather, seeker of membership in the Royal Society, inventor, author of a quasi-utopian novel, *History of the Kingdom of Basaruah* (1715), and member of the Synod of Philadelphia, Morgan resigned his pulpit, but not before performing astrological experiments to become what neighbors called a "philosopher." In 1744 he entertained the Maryland physician Alexander Hamilton with "a learned discourse concerning astrology and the influence of the stars, . . . the causes of the tides, the shape and dimensions of the earth, the laws of gravitation, and other physicall subjects." His neighbors, at least, including the local tavern keeper, considered him "the most conspicuous and notorious philosopher in all these American parts."[22]

Occult beliefs also persisted in the general population. They explained vagaries of life and offered ways to manipulate supernatural power. Witchcraft fears continued, Salem to the contrary. Fearsome reports appeared in South Carolina in 1707, in Connecticut in the 1740s, and in Pennsylvania in the 1750s and 1760s. What distinguished them from their predecessors was the refusal of magistrates to prosecute the accused. Salem's taint and the growing intellectual disparagement of witchcraft beliefs reduced most magistrates' willingness to become involved in witch-hunts, South Carolina's

[22]L. Lynne Hogue, "An Edition of 'Eight Charges Delivered, at So Many Several General Sessions . . .' [1703–7] by Nicholas Trott," Ph.D. diss., University of Tennessee, 1972, pp. 133–63; Carl Bridenbaugh, ed., *Gentleman's Progress: The Itinerarium of Dr. Alexander Hamilton, 1744* (Chapel Hill, 1948), pp. 35–36; Jon Butler, "Magic, Astrology, and the Early American Religious Heritage, 1600–1760," *American Historical Review* 84 (1979): 317–46.

Nicholas Trott to the contrary. Thus, as the Constitutional Convention gathered in Philadelphia in July 1787, fearful residents killed a suspected witch after city authorities refused to intervene. Their vigilante-style action demonstrated the persistence of popular witch beliefs and upset local newspapers whose editors, witnessing the creation of a new political order, worried that, veneer aside, the age of Enlightenment looked suspiciously like the age of superstition.[23]

Less dangerous and equally persistent supernatural beliefs appeared in popular literature. Almanacs regularly reprinted the "anatomy," a portrayal of a naked man surrounded by zodiacal signs designed to assist readers in practicing astrological medicine. Descriptions of "wonders," unusual events that did not violate natural law, and apparitions, which included visions of Jesus, were also reported with some regularity. Connecticut residents examined the body of a woman struck by lightning, looking to see if a cross had been burned into her flesh after they read that a cross had been burned into an English woman struck by lightning in a cathedral. Colonists also saw Jesus, dreamed about death, heaven, and hell, and told ghost stories. As often as not, these reports derived from churched rather than unchurched men and women, although ministers usually doubted them. Henry Melchior Muhlenberg expressed considerable irritation with a parishioner who still could not understand why ghost beliefs were blasphemous despite Muhlenberg's best efforts at explanation. In New England, a more phlegmatic Ezra Stiles simply called one Jacob Peebles "a visionary Man." Reputedly, Peebles experienced a "constant ministration of Angels." He saw them "in vast Multitudes, good and bad," and they "intimate[d] to him right and wrong course, not by Words, nor by inward Impression, but by passing to the left or right or

[23] Francis Le Jau to Philip Stubs, Apr. 15, 1707, in Klingberg, ed., *Carolina Chronicle of Francis Le Jau*, p. 25; Edward W. James, "Grace Sherwood, the Virginia Witch," *William and Mary Quarterly*, 1st ser. 3 (1894–95):96–101, 190–92, 243–44, and 4 (1895–96):18–22; autobiography of John Craig, ms. coll., Presbyterian Study Center, Montreat, N.C.

straight forward, and by causing radiances on the Lines of his hand."[24]

Yet amidst the belief in miracles and apparitions stood major signs of widespread indifference to religion. Given the nature of eighteenth-century evidence about church adherence, the precise level of this indifference may never be accurately known. But the contrast to modern America seems particularly marked. In the 1980s, about half of all adults regularly attended worship services and nearly two-thirds claimed church membership. Eighteenth-century English church adherence rates seem distinctly lower, although they varied considerably by time and place. In parishes in Yorkshire, even where no dissenting groups were active, Anglicans receiving communion varied from about half of village adults in parishes with fewer than 40 families to less than 10 percent in parishes of over 100 families. In Leeds, a city with about 15,000 adults and 40,000 persons, less than 5 percent of all eligible adults took communion. Similarly, critics in the 1780s complained that church attendance in London's Anglican parishes averaged fewer than seven persons per church each Sunday.[25]

In eighteenth-century America, between a quarter and a third of adults attended worship or claimed formal church membership. Even in New England, church membership rates in rural towns ranged from two-thirds to as low as one-fifth of all adults, and in 1780 Boston's Samuel Mather reported that "not *one sixth* attend publick worship." Ezra Stiles

[24]On the distinction between wonders and miracles, see D. P. Walker, "Valentine Greatrakes, the Irish Stoker, and the Question of Miracles," in *Mélanges sur la littérature de la renaissance à la mémoire de V.-L. Saulnier* (Geneva, 1984), pp. 343–56. Henry Melchior Muhlenberg, *The Journals of Henry Melchior Muhlenberg,* trans. and ed. Theodore G. Tappert and John W. Doberstein, 3 vols. (Philadelphia, 1942–58), 1:70, 89, 346–49. Muhlenberg also recorded the conversation of an occult adept, Simon Graf (*Journals*, p. 576). Franklin B. Dexter, ed., *The Literary Diary of Ezra Stiles*, 3 vols. (New York, 1901), 1:300–302.

[25]Derived from S. L. Ollard and P. C. Walker, eds., *Archbishop Herring's Visitation Return, 1743,* Yorkshire Archaeological Society, *Record Series,* 5 vols. (1928–31); the report on London congregations is contained in Dexter, ed., *Diary of Stiles,* 2:465.

counted some five hundred adults in his Newport, Rhode Island, congregation but seldom reported more than sixty communicants, the vast majority of them women. Indeed, during baptisms, Stiles sometimes had to hold the child himself because no male was in attendance to perform the duty.[26]

Colonial church adherence appears to have increased through the 1720s, then leveled off through the 1770s. A 1724 survey of Anglican congregations in America ordered by the bishop of London often reported between one hundred and two hundred attendants at Sunday services but only twenty or twenty-five communicants. Subsequent records of ministers working for the Society for the Propagation of the Gospel in Foreign Parts reveal similar patterns. At Apoquimminy, Delaware, Anglican clergymen reported that between 1743 and 1752 communicants accounted for no more than 10 to 15 percent of the area's eligible English-speaking residents. At New Castle, Delaware, Anglican communicants actually declined from 15 or 20 percent of those eligible to 8 or 12 percent between 1744 and 1776. In contrast, sectarianism at Radnor, Pennsylvania, probably increased nonsectarian church interest. The proportion of Anglicans receiving communion was higher at Radnor, where Quakers and Welsh Baptists were active, than in Delaware, where they were much less numerous. Roughly 20 percent of Radnor's four hundred to five hundred potential Anglicans participated in commu-

---

[26] My analysis of the data in Patricia U. Bonomi and Peter R. Eisenstadt, "Church Adherence in the Eighteenth-Century British American Colonies," *William and Mary Quarterly*, 3d ser. 39 (1982):245–86, is different from the authors'. They stress attendance figures, which are large and rounded off, while I stress communication figures, which are low and precise. On New England church adherence patterns, see Gerald F. Moran, "The Puritan Saint: Religious Experience, Church Membership, and Piety in Connecticut, 1636–1776," Ph.D. diss., Rutgers University, 1973, p. 130; Richard P. Gildrie, *Salem, Massachusetts, 1626–1682: A Covenant Community* (Charlottesville, Va., 1975), pp. 64, 163–64. Essentially there has been no systematic study of church adherence in eighteenth-century New England, but see Dexter, ed., *Diary of Stiles*, 1:28, 33, 106, 117. On feminization, see Richard D. Shiels, "The Feminization of American Congregationalism, 1730–1835," *American Quarterly* 33 (1981):46–62. For a recent study, see Roger Finke and Rodney Stark, *The Churching of America, 1776–1990: Winners and Losers in Our Religious Economy* (New Brunswick, N.J., 1992).

nion there between 1746 and 1775, although the rate still left 80 percent of eligible nonsectarian English settlers outside any known Christian group.[27]

The only thorough survey of the effect of revivalism on church adherence in the eighteenth century reports a temporary rise in church membership among the young, especially young males, followed by a quick leveling off and return to older patterns. Hence, there is little evidence to refute Crève-coeur's observation that in America "religious indifference is imperceptibly disseminated from one end of the continent to the other." Forgetful of the European heritage of lay indifference to institutional Christianity, Crèvecoeur too eagerly explained the American situation as stemming from sectarian pluralism and the spaciousness of the wilderness. "Zeal in Europe is confined; here it evaporates in the great distance it has to travel; there it is a grain of powder inclosed; here it burns away in the open air and consumes without effect." Still, Crèvecoeur remained fully cognizant of the paradox of so much popular religious indifference in a society that even he regarded as a religious asylum, at least for Europeans.[28]

Amidst coercion, lay religious heterogeneity, and simple indifference to organized religious practice, Enlightenment rationalism, Deism, and skepticism surely constituted a minority within a minority. Nonetheless, those convictions had both an immediate and a long-term impact on American religious patterns and practice. This influence derived from two sources—the nature of the adherents to these beliefs and their effect on public opinion about religion. Deists were not numerous, but they had the right numbers in the right places.

[27]The statistics regarding Apoquimminy and New Castle, Delaware, and Radnor, Pennsylvania, are based on the "Notitia Parochialis" scattered through the manuscript Records of the Society for the Propagation of the Gospel in Foreign Parts, ser. A, B, and C (microfilm).

[28]J. M. Bumsted and John E. Van de Wetering, *What Must I Do to Be Saved? The Great Awakening in Colonial America* (Hinsdale, Ill., 1976), pp. 127–40; J. Hector St. John de Crèvecoeur, *Letters from an American Farmer; and, Sketches of Eighteenth-Century America*, ed. Albert E. Stone (New York, 1981), p. 76.

Deism won a surprising following from the eighteenth-century elite, especially from the Republic's Founding Fathers. Franklin, Washington, Jefferson, Madison, and Hamilton all embraced Deist principles despite significant differences between them as individuals. In this regard, they capped a long, developing tradition of Enlightenment sympathy among the colonial political elite. Governors, colonial councils, upper houses of legislatures, and urban elites often espoused Enlightenment Deism, rationalism, and, sometimes, even skepticism.[29]

These Enlightenment beliefs shaped the perception of religion in eighteenth-century America in two very important ways. The first was through religious satire. Neither satire nor the anticlericalism that often accompanied it was exclusive to the Enlightenment elite. But from the 1720s on, satire was common in Enlightenment circles in America, and much of it was aimed at religion, both establishment and nonestablishment. The proceedings of Annapolis's Tuesday Club, of which the physician Alexander Hamilton was secretary, virtually centered on satire. Colonial newspapers printed satirical anticlerical and antireligious poetry and prose regularly. The biting humor of Ebenezer Cooke's *Sotweed Factor* (1708) and the anonymous "Dinwiddianae" letters of the 1750s attacking Virginia's established church punctured Christian pretensions and expanded its audience beyond narrow Enlightened circles. By comparison, criticism of religion in the next century turned far more bitter. William Dean Howells, Mark Twain, and Theodore Dreiser vented an anger toward religion that Enlightenment humor at least masked.[30]

Deism, rationalism, and skepticism also broadened contem-

---

[29]Deism has not won favor from historians in the past quarter-century. The most important new study is May, *The Enlightenment in America*. Henry Steele Commager's delightful *The Empire of Reason: How Europe Imagined and America Realized the Enlightenment* (Garden City, N.Y., 1977), offers a more traditional interpretation.

[30]On colonial satire, which is not frequently studied, see Richard Beale Davis, *Intellectual Life in the Colonial South, 1585–1763* (Knoxville, Tenn., 1978), esp. pp. 1344–1400. The "Dinwiddianae" texts are printed in Davis, ed., *The Colonial Virginia Satirist: Mid-Eighteenth-Century Commentaries on Politics, Religion, and Society* (Philadelphia, 1967).

porary conceptions of religion. Enlightenment authors did not discover non-Christian religions, nor were the rationalists, Deists, and skeptics the only eighteenth-century intellectuals fascinated by non-Christian religions. Roger Williams's interest in native American religions was justly famous in the seventeenth century, and in the eighteenth century Ezra Stiles demonstrated a near passion for Judaism. But where figures like Williams and Stiles studied these religions for the light they cast on Christianity, Enlightenment writers were interested in them on their own ground and tended to see all or most religions as essentially equal. Certainly they often described non-Christian religions dispassionately and nonpejoratively. When Jefferson criticized classical moralists like Epicurus or Seneca it was because their moral systems were not sufficiently comprehensive, not because they were not Christian. If Jefferson praised Christ, he did so because he found value in Christ's "universal philanthropy, not only to kindred and friends, but also to all mankind." Christian churches interested him little. Franklin felt the same. In his famous letter to Ezra Stiles of May 1790, Franklin described Christ's morals and religion as "the best the World ever saw, or is likely to see." But he doubted Christ's divinity and caviled about Christianity's many "corrupting changes." Indeed, even Franklin's compliment damned with faint praise. If there was "no harm" in Christianity's "being believed," it was because the belief generally had a "good Consequence." Not even in his old age did Franklin accept Christianity's claim to divine inspiration.[31]

Finally, it was the Enlightenment-drenched Founding Fathers who most systematically addressed the issue of religious coercion and persecution. Again, their attention was not exclusive. Before the Revolution, Dissenters protested plans to appoint an Anglican bishop for the American colonies, while

[31] Jefferson as quoted in Sanford, *Religious Life of Jefferson*, p. 39. Franklin's comments on religion, made to Stiles, are found in Dexter, ed., *Diary of Stiles*, 3:387; for Stiles's interest in Judaism and his reading habits, including his interest in Voltaire, see Edmund S. Morgan, *The Gentle Puritan: A Life of Ezra Stiles, 1727–1795* (Chapel Hill, 1962), pp. 48–57, 63–77, 142–45, 177–79, 393, 443, and Dexter, ed., *Diary of Stiles*, 1:105–6.

New England Baptists protested the taxes paid to Congregationalist towns and parishes. But protests against bishops and
church rates often proved at least as anti-Anglican as antiauthoritarian, more concerned with preserving Presbyterianism
than religious freedom or with freeing Baptists from church
rates than ending them altogether. In contrast, Enlightenment writers pursued relatively broad discussions of religious
coercion. They too proved indifferent to the destruction of
African religions in America. But where evangelicals complained about penalties suffered by their own groups, Enlightenment authors wrote about persecution as a general
problem. In fact, because they so customarily considered the
American experience in the general context of religious persecution, including episodes dating from ancient times, they
actually exaggerated the extent of religious persecution (if
not coercion) in the American colonies.[32]

Enlightenment writers also tended to support toleration for
a wide variety of groups under very broad principles. After
the Revolution, Jefferson, Washington, and Madison went out
of their way to support toleration for Jews not simply because
they saw Judaism as Christianity's necessary predecessor but
because they accepted Judaism's legitimacy as a religious system. If they were anti-Catholic, as they frequently were, their
antipopery also supported attacks on religious establishments. Essentially they treated religion as an issue of conscience untouchable by the state—hence their criticism of
both Catholic and Protestant intolerance. An Enlightenment
writer like New York's William Livingston (a nominal Presbyterian) was most likely to describe religion as an individual
and personal matter beyond the government's interest, while
evangelicals evidenced more concern for linkages among piety, morality, and society. As Livingston wrote in his *Independent Reflector* in 1753: "The religious Opinions and

[32]See Jefferson's comments on religious coercion and persecution in his
Notes on the State of Virginia, ed. William Peden (Chapel Hill, 1955), pp. 157–
61. For a discussion of the so-called Parsons' Cause in Virginia that empha-
sizes broad principles, see Rhys Isaac, "Religion and Authority: Problems
of the Anglican Establishment in Virginia in the Era of the Great Awakening
and the Parsons' Cause," *William and Mary Quarterly*, 3d ser. 30 (1973):3–36.

Speculations of the Subject, cannot be prejudicial to the Society, as a Society. . . . Matters of Religion relate to another World, and have nothing to do with the Interest of the State. The first resides in the Minds and Consciences of Men; the Latter in the outward Peace and Prosperity of the Public."[33]

Livingston's willingness to treat religion as a matter of conscience beyond government manipulation brings us full circle, back to settlers who had long experienced extraordinary diversity in religious matters and who also knew Christianity's intimate relationship with authority, power, and coercion even as it pushed past the Revolution and into the early national period.

Like the rumored death of Mark Twain, the alleged demise of the coercive state-church tradition and the spiritual lethargy of eighteenth-century America proved deceptive indeed. The vigor of both is, in fact, expressed in what passes for "colonial" church architecture in America. With fewer than five exceptions, the "colonial" churches that tourists now visit were wholly eighteenth-century constructions. Moreover, nearly all the surviving buildings constructed before 1740 and four-fifths of those built in the next thirty years were paid for largely by tax funds; they owed their existence to their favored position in the law. This includes large urban churches, like Philadelphia's Christ Church (begun in 1695) and Charleston's St. Michael's (1752), as well as the smaller but far more numerous rural churches, ranging from St. James Goose Creek in South Carolina (1708) to the better known ones in New England.[34]

[33] Leonard Levy, *The Establishment Clause: Religion and the First Amendment* (New York, 1986), pp. 38–41; Sanford, *Religious Life of Jefferson*, pp. 24–33, 118–19, 175–76. Sanford treats Jefferson's religious views statistically, so that it is not always possible to appreciate their development. *The Independent Reflector, or, Weekly Essays on Sundry Important Subjects . . . by William Livingston and Others*, ed. Milton M. Klein (Cambridge, Mass., 1963), p. 307.

[34] Dell Upton, *Holy Things and Profane: Anglican Churches in Eighteenth-Century Virginia* (Cambridge, Mass., 1986); James H. Smylie, *American Presbyterians: A Pictorial History* (Philadelphia, 1985); Peter Benes and Philip D. Zimmerman, eds., *New England Meeting House and Church, 1630–1850* (Boston, 1979).

Most of these surviving colonial church buildings represent the renascence of both organized Christianity and the state-church tradition in eighteenth-century America. Even their aesthetics bear the distinctive stamp of their eighteenth-century, state-church origins. New England buildings that seem lean and spare by modern standards actually exemplified a New England rococo by seventeenth-century standards. The concern for vaulted space, the attention to finished detail, the love of fine carving in the pews, the care expended on the design of magnificent pulpits, and, of course, the size—three to five times that of their small, crude, seventeenth-century predecessors—all demonstrated their builders' concern for place, hierarchy, social status, and propriety. We might understand, then, why so many colonists in New England and elsewhere flunked America's first historic preservation crisis. They simply demolished seventeenth-century church structures, leaving for successive generations the erroneous impression that the religious architecture of the Revolutionary age timelessly represented the religious architecture—and experience—of the colonial period itself.[35]

Colonial Christianity's association with authority likewise transformed the post-Revolutionary ecclesiastical landscape. Evangelicalism's burgeoning prosperity on the eve of the American Revolution occurred not only because of its theological appeal but also because of its institutional strength. The denominations embraced institutional authority and exercised expanding sinews of institutional power. Presbyterians, Baptists, and, later, Methodists won converts in late eighteenth-century America because they empowered denominational institutions. Rather than fleeing to a garden of evangelical individualism, they erected powerful institutions that channeled and expanded individual labor by establishing doctrinal boundaries, examining ministerial candidates, and laying out rules for congregations and ministers to follow in an increasingly complex religious world.

[35] Upton, *Holy Things and Profane,* p. 12, counts only eight churches actually constructed in Virginia before 1660 despite the establishment of more than fifty parishes there. On eighteenth-century New England churches, see Benes and Zimmerman, eds., *Meeting House and Church.*

The denominations' institutional sophistication only increased after the American Revolution. Denominations were "republican" not only in their love of virtue—actually in their love of Jesus, of course—but in their institutional sophistication. They tamed power so that they might exercise it, a tactic not unfamiliar to the creators of the federal government. Church members understood that their Presbyterian, Baptist, or Methodist identity hinged on institutional submission. That they might disagree about the substance of doctrine or ecclesiology and might fight vigorously and even rebelliously to gain or sustain one or another conception of either is not to suggest that they denigrated institutional authority or authority itself.[36]

The regard for authority and power in dissenting and established religious groups did not die with the passage of the First Amendment to the federal Constitution in 1791. As Thomas Buckley has demonstrated in his superb study of church and state in Revolutionary Virginia, evangelicals who supported Virginia's Statute for Establishing Religious Freedom (1786) soon agitated for "blue laws" to enforce their own moral convictions. Connecticut's Ezra Stiles, who once even claimed to be a "Jacobin," believed that government should take an active hand in guiding national religious development. Stiles and Virginia's Baptists argued that government ought to nourish religion—that is Christianity—so the new United States might *become* a Christian society because they knew it wasn't. Their successors in the antebellum period, especially those writing after 1840, tended to argue a different point: that government protection and support for Christianity reflected the fact that the United States *was* a Christian society. The difference was telling. It should remind us of how tenuously contemporaries in the Revolutionary age viewed Christianity's status in America. It also should point up important differences between colonial and antebellum views

[36]On the importance of institutional organization in the early national period see Donald G. Mathews, "The Second Great Awakening as an Organizing Process, 1780–1830: An Hypothesis," *American Quarterly* 21 (1969):23–43.

about the status of Christianity in their own and past societies.[37]

This creative embrace of authority and power as the means to establish both state-church and dissenting traditions in America further highlights the cause and character of the African spiritual holocaust in eighteenth-century America. At the most obvious level, that destruction constituted nothing less than cultural robbery of a particularly vicious sort. Assuming that African religions, like Christianity, were especially helpful in times of stress and danger, the loss was especially acute. Slaves not only were robbed of their lives but of their major traditional means of comprehending life and loss together. This destruction also precluded the development of the autonomous synthesis of African religions that occurred elsewhere in New World slavery. Such a synthesis would very likely have competed successfully for the spiritual loyalty of old and new slaves alike. At the least, it would have changed antebellum slavery, which so frequently took for granted a superficially common Christianity among slave and owner. At most, it would have accelerated black demands to end slavery by basing some of them on a quite different non-Christian or quasi-Christian slave religious system. Finally, to the extent that slaves chose to be religious, the destruction of African religions dictated their likely turn to Christianity—the most complete religious system available—and the consignment of discrete African religious practices to "survivals" within an African-American Christianity, some more important than others but still acting in the service of Christianity.[38]

[37] Thomas E. Buckley, S.J., *Church and State in Revolutionary Virginia, 1776–1787* (Charlottesville, Va., 1977), pp. 179–82; Morgan, *The Gentle Puritan*, p. 453. Among antebellum works arguing for America's Christian identity was Stephen Colwell, *The Position of Christianity in the United States . . .* (Philadelphia, 1854).

[38] Most any comparison in Christianity as practiced in modern Africa and in modern black churches in America will reveal profound differences between them. Foremost among the reasons for this, although not the only reason, is the English and Christian destruction of African religions in eighteenth-century America. For a particularly succinct statement of the

The suppression of traditional religions and religious diversity among Africans in America contrasted sharply with the continuing religious diversification among whites after the Revolution. At least in part, that diversity accounted for the founding and development of authoritative denominational institutions in pre-Revolutionary America and explains the capacity for schism in the next century. Like Gilbert Tennent and the New Side Presbyterians, those who found error within one religious body could not refrain from forming another, and in the next half century, the trickle of schisms descending from pre-Revolutionary society became a flood. For Americans generally, especially for religious Americans, the lure of wilderness individualism remained the stuff of novelists, not prophets.[39]

The acceleration of religious diversity before the Revolution measured the continuing Europeanization of pre-Revolutionary religion as thoroughly as cities, economic stratification, and the development of social and political aristocracies measured Europeanization in American society and politics. The arrival of Ann Lee and the subsequent development of the Shaker movement in post-Revolutionary New England demonstrated the continuing attraction of America to European religious radicals and was only one of several prophetic signs of the snarled, vexed, and utterly incomparable spiritual future that placed antebellum America on the veritable religious frontier of nineteenth-century Western culture.[40]

Finally, it was Enlightenment rationalism, Deism, and skepticism, which most directly determined that America's unique

---

contrary argument that African religious practices not only survived but operated almost independently of Christianity, see Sterling Stuckey, *Slave Culture: Nationalist Theory and the Foundations of Black America* (New York, 1987).

[39] On heterogeneity and diversity in nineteenth- and twentieth-century America, see R. Laurence Moore, *Religious Outsiders and the Making of Americans* (New York, 1986).

[40] On the interrelationship of American and European religious radicalism before and after the Revolution, see Garrett, *Possession and Religion*, and Stephen A. Marini, *Radical Sects of Revolutionary New England* (Cambridge, Mass., 1982).

antebellum religious future would *not* be shaped by the state, certainly not in ways recognizable in the Western church-state tradition. The two political statements that most profoundly shifted that relationship—Virginia's Statute for Establishing Religious Freedom and the First Amendment to the federal Constitution—enjoyed the obvious support of dissenting evangelicals. Indeed, the Virginia statute never could have been passed without it. But in conception and language, the statute and the First Amendment were Enlightenment creations. Both accepted the broadest Enlightenment conceptualizations about the evil of coercion in religion. The statute spelled these out in considerable detail. The First Amendment made the same point, but with elegant brevity. Equally important was their common Enlightenment understanding of religion. Neither limited their prohibitions merely to support of church or churches, and both referred to religion, not just to Christianity.[41]

Thus, the First Amendment meant what it said and said what it meant: "Congress shall make no law respecting an establishment of religion, or prohibiting the free exercise thereof." Its Enlightenment authors meant that Congress should not prescribe any of the numerous coercive establishments that the considered history of mankind demonstrated would directly or subtly manipulate and mangle popular religious opinion. They meant religion, not merely church. That is, they proscribed government activity in spiritual matters generally, not just formal support for one or many organized religious groups.

Of course, the Enlightenment faded, and evangelicalism and many other kinds of spirituality subsequently came to typify American religiosity in the nineteenth century. Jefferson himself subtly shifted the First Amendment's meaning in the most complex ways when, in his famous letter to Baptists in Danbury, Virginia, he described an ideal "wall of separation between the church and state," the term *church* inevitably nar-

---

[41] Jefferson's reconception of religion in the Virginia Statute or the conception of religion as understood in the First Amendment has drawn little attention from historians. Instead, most analyses center on the meaning of coercion and the limits of support for religion in each enactment.

rowing the meaning of an amendment concerned instead with religion and government. Evangelicals, happy that they had prevented aid to competing groups and, especially, to the old, persecuting, established churches, pushed ahead with their own legislative agendas, suggesting that, like Jefferson, they too were thinking about "church" and "state" rather than religion and government. Still, the words of the First Amendment—only sixteen—laid out the first boundaries of a relationship between religion and government in the new republic and established the fundamental tensions that would underlie the subsequent debate about religion and government in America. It may seem paradoxical that in a society where religion would continue to inform and distend the development of American society, these sixteen words of the eighteenth century would so shape the religious experience of the Revolutionary age and of so many subsequent decades.

PATRICIA U. BONOMI

Religious Dissent and the Case for American Exceptionalism

A NOTABLE SHIFT has recently occurred in the way historians view the relationship that existed in the pre-Revolutionary era between Great Britain and its North American colonies. At one time history books conventionally depicted the colonists as having begun their separation from England and English ways in the very act of crossing the ocean to settle in the New World. Compelled to build institutions anew on an untamed frontier, the settlers were seen to be fashioning political, religious, and economic forms that diverged from those of the Old World in ways uniquely American. This sense of cultural uniqueness—or of American exceptionalism, as it came to be called—seemed to explain, perhaps to make inevitable, the break from England in the American Revolution.

Lately, however, the notion of American exceptionalism has fallen out of favor. In its place we are urged to adopt a wider cultural scope, to think in terms of "Anglo-America" or the "Atlantic World," and to consider the process whereby culture was regularly transmitted from Old World metropolitan cores to colonial peripheries. Among historians there is at present a substantial acceptance of the idea that by the eighteenth century Americans were becoming "self-consciously English" while rejecting "the customary patterns of life which had evolved in the first century of settlement."[1] No longer can we assume that the political ideas of the American Revolution germinated in the soil of a democratic frontier; rather they were imported, if selectively, from the Old World. Similarly, we hear that colonial economic life did not strike off in a uniquely American direction but was closely bound to British merchant houses and imperial markets. The free market ideas that circulated in America came not so much from the colonials themselves as from English and Scottish theorists. The "Anglicization" thesis, as it is sometimes called, has come to touch every sphere of colonial society. Provincial family structures were not exceptional but reproduced the traditional patterns of England; legal practices and courts were by the eighteenth century increasingly modeled along English lines; high culture and patterns of consumption reflected English taste.[2]

Certainly this "neo-imperial" interpretation, as we might call it, which sees Old World culture rippling outward from metropolis to province, supplies a useful perspective. Like the old imperial school, it serves to correct our disproportionate emphasis on the specialness of American civilization. Yet it is, in another sense, a rather conservative standpoint from which to view the eighteenth-century British-American empire. Seeing everything through a veil of Anglicization may obscure some of the real differences and tensions that by 1776 motivated Americans to set off on their own. They did, after all, revolt. The energy and initiative for the first colonial revolution of modern times surely came, in some part, from within the American experience itself.

[1] John M. Murrin, "The Legal Transformation: The Bench and Bar of Eighteenth-Century Massachusetts," in Stanley N. Katz and John M. Murrin, eds., *Colonial America: Essays in Politics and Social Development* (New York, 1983), p. 540. See also the introductory discussion in Jack P. Greene and J. R. Pole, eds., *Colonial British America: Essays in the New History of the Early Modern Era* (Baltimore, 1984), pp. 14–16; and Jack P. Greene, *Peripheries and Center: Constitutional Development in the Extended Polities of the British Empire and the United States, 1607–1788* (Athens, Ga., 1987).

[2] For a review of all these themes, with far greater attention to their variations and nuances than can be attempted here, see the essays in Greene and Pole, eds., *Colonial British America*.

This essay will argue that in at least one aspect of colonial life—that of religion—we can discern an authentic area of American exceptionalism. Whatever we may make of Britain's preeminence in the formation of colonial culture, the fact remains that religion in America, subject to a particularly complex set of influences, made a pattern of its own.[3] In some cases the initial premise for settlement, and in all cases the experience, of religious groups in the colonies fostered ideals, practices, and habits of mind that made Americans different.

The single most important fact about colonial religion is that a majority of Americans were Dissenters. That is, they were adherents of churches or sects not in conformity with the religion of the mother country, as embodied in the established Church of England. After 1680 England was no longer the primary source of colonial immigration, having been displaced by the Continent, Scotland, and Northern Ireland. If in 1650 the ratio of Dissenters to Anglicans was roughly equal in America—with Nonconformists mainly in the North and Anglicans in the South—by the turn of the eighteenth century non-English immigrants had swelled the ratio of Dissenters to two-thirds, and by the time of the Revolution three-quarters or more of Americans did not conform to the Church of England.[4] Thus if the political and economic spheres were indeed becoming more closely aligned in England and America by the eighteenth century, as a number of writers have asserted, this was certainly not the case with religious life. As I will argue, the weighting of colonial religion toward Dissent helped shape a worldview that was in signifi-

[3] For a thoughtful discussion of those complexities, and of the issue of American exceptionalism, see David D. Hall, "Religion and Society: Problems and Reconsiderations," ibid., pp. 317–44.

[4] Edwin S. Gaustad, *Historical Atlas of Religion in America*, rev. ed. (New York, 1976); Sydney E. Ahlstrom, *A Religious History of the American People* (New Haven, 1972), p. 350; U.S. Bureau of the Census, *Historical Statistics of the United States, Colonial Times to 1970* (Washington, D.C., 1975), pt. 2, p. 1168. This does not mean that the Church of England was in decline, the number of Anglican congregations having grown from about 75 in 1690 to some 450 by 1776. But after 1680, immigration to the colonies was heavily weighted toward Dissenters.

cant ways at odds with English values, not only religious values but political ones as well.

To grasp the formative influence of dissent on American life, we must go back to the early years of each denomination's colonial experience—before the Great Awakening, before the growth of denominationalism, and especially before the organization of ministerial associations and centralized church governments. Historians have long recognized that certain characteristics of religious dissent promoted individualist and republican attitudes, as for example the localist autonomy of the Congregational churches, the voluntarist nature of the Quaker meeting, and the wider sharing of power between clergy and laity in all dissenting denominations.[5] In early America this initial disposition toward decentralized, popular forms was magnified by a critical shortage of clergymen. For the first century and a third of colonial life, only the Congregational churches had a sufficient supply of preachers. Other denominations fell woefully short in attracting ministers to the rough comforts of a provincial mission—a "frontier" influence of undoubted validity.[6] In the absence of clergymen there emerged in North America a purer form of voluntary, scripture-based church than had been seen perhaps since the Reformation. It is to the early years when churches were initially gathered that we may first turn in the search for American exceptionalism.

The ideal of the gathered church was drawn from scripture. Looking back to the primitive church of Christianity's first century, it involved a lay-initiated gathering of true be-

[5] A good recent example is F. D. Dow, *Radicalism in the English Revolution, 1640–1660* (Oxford, 1985), pp. 58–65.

[6] See, for example, Richard W. Pointer, *Protestant Pluralism and the New York Experience: A Study of Eighteenth-Century Religious Diversity* (Bloomington, Ind., 1988), p. 13; Patricia U. Bonomi, *Under the Cope of Heaven: Religion, Society, and Politics in Colonial America* (New York, 1986), chap. 3.

New England, so often thought to prefigure later American culture, is the least pertinent example for my argument, since after the first decade that section had plenty of clergymen.

lievers into a visible church. Once baptized into fellowship, the lay members chose some from among their number to lead the congregation—elders, deacons, a minister or exhorter—who then would admit new members and administer the sacraments. Quakers were the most radical of the gathered sects because they believed in neither sacraments nor ordained church leaders. Most other colonial dissenting groups—Calvinists, Lutherans, Baptists, and the pietistic sects—elected leaders for each congregation. Historians' attention has usually centered on the more mature stages of church development when the presence of a cohort of ministers facilitated the erection of consociations, presbyteries, synods, and the like.[7] Yet in the first years of each group's history, when clergymen were few, leadership of necessity fell to the lay members. The provincials' experience in building congregations—often the first organizations of any kind in newly settled areas—thus had a formative influence on how Americans came to conceive of all group relationships, not only those in local communities but those in the larger society as well.

We may look first at the middle and southern colonies, where congregations were gathered from the earliest days of settlement. In New Netherland the Dutch Reformed Church was officially sanctioned, yet so few clergymen came to America in the colony's early decades that the laity were thrown back on their own resources. Thus settlers at the Dutch West India Company's outpost on the Delaware River had no recourse on the Sabbath but to choose one among their number to "read every Sunday something out of the Apostiles."[8] Similarly a lay group of New Amsterdam Lutherans voluntarily formed a congregation in 1649; meeting in private houses they maintained a continuous existence over several decades though usually deprived of an ordained cler-

[7] Jon Butler, *Power, Authority, and the Origins of American Denominational Order: The English Churches in the Delaware Valley, 1680–1730* (Philadelphia, 1978); Sidney E. Mead, *The Lively Experiment: The Shaping of Christianity in America* (New York, 1963).

[8] E. B. O'Callaghan, ed., *The Documentary History of the State of New-York*, 4 vols. (Albany, 1849–51), 3:105.

gyman.[9] One of the fullest descriptions of a gathered church in early New York comes from the 1656 memoir of a visitor to a Westchester hamlet. There a group of migrants from New England assembled "on Sundays, to observe their mode of worship, as they have not as yet any clergyman. . . . I found a gathering of about fifteen men and ten or twelve women. Mr. Baly made a prayer, which being concluded, one Robert Basset read a sermon from a printed book composed . . . by an English minister in England. After the reading Mr. Baly made another prayer and they sang a psalm and separated."[10] Another such gathering was noted at Esopus, later Kingston, New York, where the newly settled Dutch community was said to "hold Sunday meetings and then one or the other of them reads from the Postilla." (The Postilla was a book of brief commentaries, or homilies, on the gospels.)[11] In heavily Dutch Kings County congregations assembled in houses, occasionally receiving visits from an ordained Reformed clergyman. It must have been one of these groups that in 1679 so crowded into Jan Theunissen's house in Flatlands to hear a visiting preacher that the auditors "could scarcely get in or out."[12]

In Pennsylvania it was the same, with Mennonites among the first of Penn's settlers "to have a meeting, although as sheep without a shepherd." (This phrase, heard frequently in

---

[9] Harry Julius Kreider, *Lutheranism in Colonial New York* (1942; reprint ed., New York, 1972), chap. 2. By 1656 so many such "conventicles" had formed in New Netherland that Peter Stuyvesant's government issued a directive forbidding all public or private religious meetings, except those of the Dutch Reformed Church, on pain of fines (E. T. Corwin, ed., *Ecclesiastical Records of the State of New York*, 7 vols. [Albany, 1901–16], 3:343–44).

[10] Journal of Brian Nuton [Newton] et al., in O'Callaghan, ed., *Documentary History of New York*, 3:923. For a full report on the colony's religious life in 1657, see ibid., pp. 69–72.

There is a striking similarity in the descriptions of these early congregations in all denominations and regions; each notes prayers, psalm singing, and the reading of a sermon by a lay leader.

[11] J. Franklin Jameson, ed., *Narratives of New Netherland, 1609–1664* (New York, 1909), p. 398.

[12] *Journal of a Voyage to New York by Jaspar Dankers and Peter Sluyter* (microfilm), p. 17.

colonial America, always referred to congregations that had no minister.) In 1690 this same Mennonite group was still gathering each Sunday in a private house, where one Dirck Keyser read from a book of sermons by Joost Harmensen. "Since they had no preacher, they endeavored to admonish one another." [13] In 1701, George Keith reported to the Anglican Society for the Propagation of the Gospel in London that in most New Jersey communities "there is no face of any publick Worship of any Sort." Yet in that same year some forty-five congregations in East and West Jersey gathered regularly for worship. Because many of them had neither meeting-houses nor permanent ministers, they were invisible to the likes of Keith. [14]

By the early eighteenth century German immigration was increasing, bringing to American shores an assortment of pietists and various churchpeople. Among the most interesting of these in Pennsylvania were the German Baptists, whose devotional life was described in some detail by the eighteenth-century Baptist historian Morgan Edwards and others. The custom in Pennsylvania, as in New York, was to meet in private houses where "every brother is allowed to stand up in the congregation to speak in a way of exhortation and expounding; and when by these means they find a man eminent for *knowledge* and *aptness* . . . they choose him to be a minister, and ordain him with imposition of hands, attended with fasting and prayer and giving the right hand of fellowship." The Baptists also chose "*deacons*; and ancient widows for *deaconesses;* and *exhorters;* who are licensed to use their gifts stat-

---

[13] J. C. Wenger, *The Mennonite Church in America* (Scottsdale, Pa., 1966), p. 58.

[14] A Letter from Mr. George Keith to the Secretary about the State of Quakerism in North America, n.d. [1701?], Journal of the Society for the Propagation of the Gospel in Foreign Parts, Appendix A, no. 4 (microfilm). For the locations of the New Jersey congregations, see the map at the front of Nelson R. Burr, *The Anglican Church in New Jersey* (Philadelphia, 1954).

Historians also tend to overlook congregations that met in homes or barns. Jon Butler equates the "sacralization" of the colonies largely with church building in *Awash in a Sea of Faith: Christianizing the American People* (Cambridge, Mass., 1990), chap. 4.

edly."[15] The first Baptist congregation at Germantown gathered on Christmas Day 1723, choosing one Peter Becker to serve as elder. Following prayers and an examination of the spiritual state of six unbaptized adherents, the little band of some twenty or so repaired with Becker to Wissahickon Creek, where after more prayer the new members were baptized by immersion. Returning to a member's house, the pious fellowship washed each others' feet and then, ranging themselves round a long table—sisters on one side, brothers on the other—celebrated communion, exchanged the kiss of charity, sang a hymn, and parted.[16]

A Baptist congregation was gathered at Coventry, Pennsylvania, in 1724 by six men and two women. And though it prospered, the society by 1770 still had no church but held its meetings "in a kind of rotation at five private houses."[17] The congregation at Great Swamp traced its beginnings to 1735, when four women and seven men formed a church.[18] Other Baptist groups had "united" or "coalesced" at White Oak Land, Oley, Little Conewago, and other places, a total of fifteen gathered churches in the region by 1770, with from twenty to fifty families per congregation. By that date there were "eight ordained ministers, . . . thirteen exhorters or probationers, and four meeting houses"—the last being few in number because "they choose rather to meet from *house to house* in imitation of the primitive Christians."[19]

Many Germans entering Pennsylvania in the eighteenth

[15] Donald F. Durnbaugh, ed., *The Brethren in Colonial America: A Source Book on the Transplantation and Development of the Church of the Brethren in the Eighteenth Century* (Elgin, Ill., 1967), p. 175.

[16] Ibid., pp. 62–63. All accounts of the Germantown Baptists are based in large part on the *Chronicon Ephratense.* The modern translation by J. Max Hark is titled *Chronicon Ephratense: A History of the Community of Seventh Day Baptists at Ephrata, Lancaster County, Pennsylvania, by "Lamech and Agrippa"* (Lancaster, 1889), see p. 11.

[17] Durnbaugh, ed., *The Brethren in Colonial America,* p. 178.

[18] Ibid., p. 177.

[19] Ibid., pp. 179–86; quotation on p. 186. Morgan Edwards continues: "We see also that their families are about 419, which contain about 2095

century, whether Baptists, Lutherans, or German Reformed, moved on to the southern backcountry, where gathered churches frequently provided their only community structure. When a circuit-riding clergyman first made contact in 1734 with a Lutheran congregation in Frederick County, Maryland, he found that "the settlers had gathered together almost to a man."[20] On his fifth annual visit in 1738, the minister held communion in a hayloft and formally ordained the elected deacons.[21] The first German Reformed clergyman to visit the area in 1747 found a large congregation "anxious after spiritual food" and listening with "tears of joy" to his every word. Forty-nine heads of families agreed to contribute support for a resident minister, if only they could find one.[22] Meanwhile, these congregations continued their services under the direction of devout laymen, or in the case of the Reformed church with the aid of a schoolteacher, who led the congregation "by means of singing, and reading the word of God and printed sermons on every Lord's

---

souls (allowing five to a family); whereof 763 persons are baptized and in communion" (p. 186).

English Baptists, though more quickly brought into church order, initially formed their congregations in a manner similar to the Germans (A. D. Gillette, ed., *Minutes of the Philadelphia Baptist Association, from AD 1707, to AD 1807* [Philadelphia, 1851], pp. 13, 16, 19).

[20] Elizabeth A. Kessel, "'A Mighty Fortress Is Our God': German Religious and Educational Organizations on the Maryland Frontier, 1734–1800," *Maryland Historical Magazine* 77 (1982):385 n. 15; Dieter Cunz, *The Maryland Germans: A History* (Princeton, 1948), p. 62. Elizabeth Kessel provides a detailed look at all of the early German congregations in Frederick County; she discusses the importance of lay involvement and compares church life on the American frontier with that in the German states. In her view, "Religious conviction initially brought these people together, and religious organization then sustained their bond" (p. 370).

For one German visitor's censure of the loose church organization of Pennsylvania compared with the more orderly ecclesiastical life of his home state, see Gottlieb Mittelberger, *Journey to Pennsylvania*, ed. and trans. Oscar Handlin and John Clive (Cambridge, Mass., 1960), esp. pp. 47–48.

[21] Cunz, *The Maryland Germans*, p. 63.

[22] Ibid., p. 68.

day."[23] By 1750 the German Reformed minister Michael Schlatter listed forty-six congregations—thirty-eight in Pennsylvania, two in New Jersey, four in Virginia, and two in Maryland. Thirty-two of these forty-six congregations had no resident minister.[24]

The German Baptists also moved south, gathering churches in Maryland, Virginia, and the Carolinas. Led by lay ministers and exhorters, and meeting in private dwellings, the Baptist congregations were serving at least 370 frontier families by 1770.[25]

These examples of the gathering of Reformed, Lutheran, and German Baptist churches in the middle and southern colonies are representative of the initial experience of every denomination and sect in colonial America. The earliest Puritans formed their first churches in a similar manner, as did the Quakers, the Presbyterians, and even the early Anglicans. Spontaneous and nonhierarchical in character, often poorly supplied with prayer books, psalters, and devotional literature, the early congregations were of necessity less firmly anchored to orthodox forms and doctrine than were their counterparts in the Old World.[26] To be sure, they were brought under more

[23] Henry Harbaugh, *The Life of Reverend Michael Schlatter* (Philadelphia, 1857), p. 177.

[24] Ibid., pp. 203–5. For more detailed information on the Reformed congregations, see *Minutes and Letters of the Coetus of the German Reformed Congregations in Pennsylvania, 1742–1792, Together with Three Preliminary Reports of Rev. John Philip Boehm, 1734–1744* (Philadelphia, 1903). For the Lutherans see *Reports of the United German Evangelical Lutheran Congregations in North America, Especially in Pennsylvania*, trans. Jonathan Oswald, 2 vols. (Philadelphia, 1880–81).

[25] Durnbaugh, ed., *The Brethren in Colonial America*, pp. 187–91.

[26] That innovation in formal church practice also started early is evident in a report from the first Dutch Reformed minister in New Netherland. He noted with pride that at the initial Reformed communion service in the colony in 1628, he had "fully fifty communicants—Walloons and Dutch." To qualify for the sacrament, a number of church members exhibited certificates from their Old Country churches. Some who had lost their certificates were admitted on the testimony of others regarding "their daily good deportment"; others had failed to bring them, "not thinking that a church would be formed and established here." Yet as the clergyman explained, "One cannot observe strictly all the usual formalities in making a beginning

centralized ecclesiastical regulation as communities stabilized and the number of ministers in North America rose. Yet the same impulse for lay association in voluntary churches we have just observed was repeated time and again as the colonial population expanded and new settlements formed, creating a kind of continuously unfolding religious frontier.

Thus when the Rev. David McClure visited transappalachian Pennsylvania in 1772, he found Presbyterian congregations springing up everywhere. He preached to them in private houses, log chapels, tents, and in the case of one big group "on a stage erected in a large shady grove."[27] McClure found the people to be neither ignorant nor superstitious in spiritual matters but "generally well indoctrinated in the principles of the christian religion"; when singing psalms, they used "the old Scotch version & all on the tenor."[28] Here was an immigrant people, bereft of preachers, adapting Old Country ways to new circumstances on the American frontier. The westerners begged McClure to stay with them and even drew up subscriptions for his salary. Clearly the visitor was impressed to find that in this near wilderness the people, as he wrote in his journal, were "forming themselves into something like ecclesiastical order."[29]

This phenomenon of lay initiative was repeated everywhere in newly settled regions throughout the seventeenth and eighteenth centuries—and for that matter throughout the nineteenth century as well. Once congregations gathered and chose leaders, moreover, ordinary lay members continued to exercise substantial authority in concert with the elders. Admission of new members often involved the entire congregation, as the Germantown Baptist Peter Becker acknowledged

---

under such circumstances" (letter of Rev. Jonas Michaelius, 1628, in Jameson, ed., *Narratives of New Netherland*, pp. 124–25).

[27] Franklin B. Dexter, ed., *Diary of David McClure* (New York, 1899), p. 37.

[28] Ibid., pp. 37–38.

[29] Ibid., p. 104. For another clergyman's similar experiences, see Guy Soulliard Klett, ed., *Journals of Charles Beatty, 1762–1769* (University Park, Pa., 1962).

when two newcomers applied to join the church. "If you can bear favorable witness concerning their lives," he told the congregation, "it is well, and we can baptize them with the greater assurance; but if you have any complaints to bring against them, we will not do it."[30] Similarly, at the Dutch Reformed Church of Philipse Manor, New York—which operated for nearly a century under lay leadership—newcomers were admitted only after "christian inquiry and admonition" by the congregation.[31]

In the Congregational churches of New England, despite the presence of permanent ministers, lay members once again had a voice in decisions about admission and discipline. An account of the disciplinary hearing of Richard Wayte, a tailor and member of Boston's First Church, reveals that when some of the brethren disagreed with their minister's recommendation to accept Wayte's confession of error, the proceedings could not go forward. Several parishioners, moreover, counseled privately with Wayte, taking "a greate deale of paynes" to reclaim the lost sheep—thereby asserting their own will in church matters. So commonly did New England congregations divide on such questions after the 1660s that the churches gradually stopped requiring unanimity for censures, settling instead for majority vote.[32]

Nor was such popular participation confined to formal church meetings only. Puritans often gathered in neighborhood devotional groups during the week, many of them under lay direction. There the members would "pray, and sing, and repeat sermons, and confer together about the things of God." It was just such a meeting—in this case a women's devotional group—that provided a stage for Anne Hutchinson. Still other societies, "fully under the control of women," continued their private meetings, as did a group of students at

[30] Hark, trans., *Chronicon Ephratense*, p. 26.

[31] David Cole, trans., *First Record Book of the "Old Dutch Church of Sleepy Hollow," Organized in 1697 . . . to 1791* (Yonkers, N.Y., 1901), pp. v–vii.

[32] James F. Cooper, Jr., "The Confession and Trial of Richard Wayte, Boston, 1640," *William and Mary Quarterly*, 3d ser. 44 (1987):310–32, 313n; quotation on p. 316.

Harvard, youth fellowships, and even a Society of Negroes at Boston.[33] We know less about such informal gatherings outside of New England, though there is no reason to doubt their existence.[34]

All of these activities demonstrate the authentically popular beginnings of religious life in the colonies as an immigrant people, finding themselves with few clergymen and no ready-made ecclesiastical structures, built their own congregations from the bottom up.[35] And because many of these societies were reluctant to "go to law" if they could settle disputes between members within the congregation, they found themselves taking on a number of civil responsibilities—resolving differences over lands, debts, breaches of contract, and of course moral infractions.[36] Not only did congregations serve a parallel function to the town meeting, in many early settlements they *were* the town meeting.

Another characteristic of Dissent was its structural fragility, the perennial tendency of its units to splinter and then to reassemble in new ways. As H. Richard Niebuhr has written:

[33]Charles E. Hambrick-Stowe, *The Practice of Piety: Puritan Devotional Disciplines in Seventeenth-Century New England* (Chapel Hill, 1982), pp. 12, 137–41. By the eighteenth century these New England groups were often organized by ministers (ibid., p. 141).

[34]See, for example, *Journal of . . . Jaspar Dankers and Peter Sluyter,* pp. xxxii n. 2, 134. Many among New York's more pious Dutch Reformed believed that conventicles brought them closer to God than did formal services based on the orthodox liturgy (James Tanis, "Reformed Pietism in Colonial America," in F. Ernest Stoeffler, ed., *Continental Pietism and Early American Christianity* [Grand Rapids, Mich., 1976]).

[35]For a sense of how ordinary people became involved in building institutions on the frontier, see Stanley Elkins and Eric McKitrick, "A Meaning for Turner's Frontier, Part I: Democracy in the Old Northwest," *Political Science Quarterly* 69 (1954):323–39. For the colonial period, see especially Timothy L. Smith, "Congregation, State, and Denomination: The Forming of the American Religious Structure," *William and Mary Quarterly,* 3d ser. 25 (1968):155–76.

[36]Durnbaugh, ed., *The Brethren in Colonial America,* pp. 200–210; Bonomi, *Under the Cope of Heaven,* p. 136.

"Between the polarities of order and movement, of structure and process, the Protestant finds himself and his communities always drawn toward the dynamic side." The Protestant pattern is one of "creation and fall and re-creation. . . . Everything . . . is movement; everything a becoming."[37] Niebuhr was contrasting Protestantism with Catholicism, but the same point may apply in contrasting the dynamic behavior of colonial Dissenters with the more orderly ideal of the Church of England, thereby shedding further light on the "exceptional" qualities of the Dissenters.

Many divisions within American Dissent arose over questions of doctrine. Such was the primary cause of the Keithian Schism in the Society of Friends, and of the late seventeenth-century split between Cocceians and Voetians in the Dutch Reformed Church.[38] The Baptists were notorious for hiving off into separate congregations, especially over the issue of when the Sabbath should be observed. In Pennsylvania one congregation of German Baptists embraced celibacy. Another was suspected of reviving Judaism when its members refused to eat pork and two of the brethren "circumcized each other after the Jewish manner."[39] But if rival denominations inveighed against such practices as fanatical and atheistic, their true source was the Bible—or at least each group's interpretation of the Bible. Having removed themselves from the more uniform procedures and authoritarian hierarchies of the Old World, the gathered congregations of early America, already wedded to the ideal of scripture as their primary source of authority, felt few impediments to split-

[37]H. Richard Niebuhr, "The Protestant Movement and Democracy in the United States," in James Ward Smith and A. Leland Jamison, eds., *The Shaping of American Religion* (Princeton, 1961), pp. 22, 24.

[38]Rufus M. Jones, *The Quakers in the American Colonies* (1911; reprint ed., New York, 1966), pp. 437–58; David Voorhees, "'In Behalf of the True Protestants Religion': The Glorious Revolution in New York," Ph.D. diss., New York University, 1988.

[39]A few members even "raised scruples against geese . . . because they supply man with their feathers for his luxurious indulgence" (Durnbaugh, ed., *The Brethren in Colonial America*, pp. 73–74).

ting hairs—and congregations—over conflicting interpretations of the Bible.[40]

Nor did differences over doctrine cease when ministers arrived in greater numbers. Indeed, it was frequently owing to clerical disputes about doctrine that the more churchly denominations fell to squabbling, as, for example, when evangelical Presbyterian and Congregational clergymen led parishioners out of the orthodox churches during the Great Awakening. Other divisions arose over the hiring of preachers, forms of psalm singing, and the location of church buildings.[41] Whatever the cause, church divisions provided further occasions for lay intervention as each separating congregation repeated the experience of creating itself anew.

The impression we gain, then, of the Dissenters in colonial America, especially during the founding years of each denomination, is one of high volatility. All is in motion as congregations gather, dispute, divide, and reconstitute themselves. And if ministers, synods, and associations eventually brought a kind of order to church government, it was an order that rested precariously on a foundation of voluntary association and majority rule. Clergymen frequently noted the fragility of church government, as when the Rev. Henry Muhlenberg observed that in a land where everything depended on the vote of the majority one could not "bend and force the people here . . . as in Germany."[42]

The word that came to be applied by the colonists them-

---

[40] For how a reliance on *Sola Scriptura* strengthened the laity in relations with the clergy, see Harry S. Stout, *The New England Soul: Preaching and Religious Culture in Colonial New England* (New York, 1986), pp. 14, 105–6.

[41] Bonomi, *Under the Cope of Heaven*, pp. 131–52. In some cases those living on the outskirts of parishes, especially mothers of young children, refused to travel long distances in bad weather to church. As towns grew, such pressures frequently led to the division of churches (Laurel Thatcher Ulrich, *Good Wives: Image and Reality in the Lives of Women in Northern New England, 1650–1750* [New York, 1982], pp. 217–19).

[42] Theodore E. Schmauk, *A History of the Lutheran Church in Pennsylvania (1638–1820) from the Original Sources* (Philadelphia, 1903), p. 534.

selves to the Dissenters' form of church government was *republican*. The German Baptists described their decentralized congregations as "purely republican"; the Rev. John Wise of Massachusetts even used the word *democracy* to characterize the Congregational polity.[43] Clearly those broadly based, elective church governments of the American Nonconformists stood in sharp contrast to the descending hierarchy of the Church of England. And if Anglican government by archbishop, bishop, and priest was increasingly seen to parallel the secular hierarchy of King, Lords, and Commons, the reverse parallel—between the Dissenters' republican church order and a far more popular form of secular government—could hardly be overlooked. As early as 1724 the high-Anglican governor of South Carolina, Francis Nicholson, warned of such a danger: "I think it no very Difficult thing to Prove that all the Dissenters here, in New England and other his Majestys Collonys and Provinces are of Common Wealth Principles both in Church and State and would be Independent to the Crown of Great Brittain if it were in their Power."[44] By the second half of the eighteenth century, fear that the Dissenters' republicanism might overflow from the religious realm to the secular was rising rapidly, leading some critics to charge that the Presbyterians, for example, favored "the Model of a Geneva Republic" in both church and state.[45]

Anglican ministers, on the other hand, believed that one of their primary responsibilities was to maintain the provincials in English ways. Thus, in their own words, they were "constantly instilling . . . into the People . . . the Principles of

[43] Durnbaugh, ed., *The Brethren in Colonial America*, p. 187; John Wise, *A Vindication of the Government of New-England Churches* (Boston, 1717), p. 64.

[44] Francis Nicholson to the bishop of London, Aug. 5, 1724, Fulham Papers, IX, p. 150, Lambeth Palace Library, London (microfilm). Almost twenty years earlier the Anglican governor of New York, Viscount Cornbury, had observed that the "Dessenters . . . are in no wise fond of monarchy" (Cornbury to Sec. Hedges, July 15, 1705, in E. B. O'Callaghan and Berthold Fernow, eds., *Documents Relative to the Colonial History of the State of New York*, 15 vols. (Albany, 1856–87), 4:1155.

[45] *A Looking-Glass for Presbyterians* (Philadelphia, 1764), in John R. Dunbar, ed., *The Paxton Papers* (The Hague, 1957), p. 250.

Submission and Loyalty."[46] The rector of King's Chapel in Boston, Henry Caner, admonished his congregants in 1761 to be "quiet and peaceable and obedient to their rulers, content with their respective stations, [and] reverent to the laws." New Jersey's Thomas Bradbury Chandler enjoined "reverence, respect, and obedience" to constituted authority.[47] The Anglicans never ceased supposing that their parishioners were the king's "best and most loyal Subjects in America."[48]

It was thus logical that Anglican clergymen, especially in the northern colonies, should frequently criticize the dissenting churches for instilling tendencies that were a challenge to orderly government. The Rev. Samuel Johnson of Connecticut, who had come to disdain Congregational church government "in which every brother has a hand," believed that a form so entirely popular must "crumble to pieces."[49] As the Revolution drew closer, Henry Caner saw ever more clearly the ominous connection between Dissent and the rebellious spirit. "We were lately the happiest people in the world," he wrote in 1775. "But a republican Spirit can never rest, the same levelling principles which induce them to withdraw from the wholesome establishment of the Church operate with equal force in throwing off the restraints of civil Government."[50] Northern Anglicans were particularly distraught when the Dissenters obstinately resisted their efforts to obtain a bishop for the colonies. How the Dissenters had got such a cramped

[46]A letter from the clergy in convention, Perth Amboy [New Jersey], Oct. 2, 1766, Records of the Society for the Propagation of the Gospel in Foreign Parts, Letterbooks, ser. B, XXIV, p. 314 (microfilm).

[47]Quoted in Robert M. Calhoon, *The Loyalists in Revolutionary America, 1760–1781* (New York, 1973), pp. 216–17.

[48]Henry Caner to Thomas Secker, archbishop of Canterbury, Oct. 20, 1766, Letterbook of the Rev. Henry Caner, University of Bristol, Bristol, England. (Transcriptions of these letters, made by the late Dr. Catherine S. Crary, are in the possession of the author.)

[49]Herbert Schneider and Carol Schneider, eds., *Samuel Johnson, President of King's College, His Career and Writings*, 4 vols. (New York, 1929), 1:12; see also ibid., p. 346.

[50]Caner to the bishop of London, July 22, 1775, Caner Letterbook; see also Caner to Archbishop Secker, Sept. 5, 1765, ibid.

view was no mystery to the Rev. Jonathan Boucher of Maryland. "Early prejudices, fostered by education and confirmed by religion, all conspire to cherish republicanism," he declared. "In America, literally and truly, all power flows from the people."[51]

Once the war began, Anglican leaders saw their worst forebodings confirmed. "It is a certain Truth," wrote the New York Anglican clergy to London in 1780, "that Dissenters in general, and particularly Presbyterians and Congregationalists were the active Promoters of the Rebellion," whereas most northern Anglicans were firmly for England. The reasons were inescapable: Anglicans "from their Infancy imbibe Principles of Loyalty, and Attachment to the Present State; and these Principles determine their Conduct." Dissenters "from their infancy, imbibe Republican, levelling Principles, which are unfriendly to the Constitution, and lead them to an opposite Conduct." Thus the ministers concluded: "Churchmen and Dissenters have only reduced to Practice the Principles in which they were educated."[52]

This is not to say that all Anglicans and Nonconformists fell into such neatly opposing patterns. Southern Anglicans, many of whose congregations were formed by lay leaders in the years when clergymen were in short supply, shared a number of attributes with the Dissenters—gathered congregations, low church tendencies, and above all government by elected vestries of local notables. These practices had crystallized in the seventeenth century, creating barriers to the im-

---

[51]Quoted in Calhoon, *Loyalists in America*, p. 232.

[52]Clergy of New York to [the Secretary?], Oct. 28, 1780, American Papers of the Society for the Propagation of the Gospel, X, pp. 190–91, Lambeth Palace Library, London (microfilm).

British officials concurred in this interpretation of the Revolution, as for example Ambrose Searle, who wrote to Lord Dartmouth on Nov. 8, 1776: "For, though it has not been much considered at Home, Presbyterianism is really at the Bottom of this whole Conspiracy, has supplied it with Vigor, and will never rest" (Benjamin Franklin Stevens, comp., *B. F. Stevens's Facsimiles of Manuscripts in European Archives Relating to America, 1773–1783*, 25 vols. [London, 1889–98], 24:no. 2042, cited in Leonard Lundin, *Cockpit of the Revolution: The War for Independence in New Jersey* [Princeton, 1940], p. 100).

position of Old World forms favored by the incoming eighteenth-century clergy—especially the appointment of a colonial bishop. Indeed, these very characteristics may help to explain why southern Anglicans behaved as they did in the Revolution, when from half to three-quarters of them—parishioners and clergy alike—supported the patriot cause.[53]

It is also true that by the mid-eighteenth century there were many leading Dissenters—especially in the cities—who appeared quite comfortable with an "English" outlook. The Boston ministers Jonathan Mayhew and Charles Chauncy carried on a brisk correspondence with learned circles in England and adopted many of the liberal attitudes of the metropolis. The New Yorker William Livingston was steeped in the popular literature of London and fancied himself as something of an American Addison.[54] These and other Dissenters of cosmopolitan inclinations are certainly good subjects for the "Anglicization" theorists. Yet it would take only the Anglican bishop question, as revived in the 1760s, to make such subjects rise

[53] David L. Holmes, "The Episcopal Church and the American Revolution," *Historical Magazine of the Protestant Episcopal Church* 48 (1978):267–68. The only anomaly was Maryland, where two-thirds of the clergy were loyalist, though the majority of the laity sided with the patriots (ibid., p. 267).

Northern Anglicans also had vestries but seem to have been far more influenced by their Society for the Propagation of the Gospel ministers, to say nothing of their Anglican or, as in the case of Thomas Hutchinson, Anglicizing governors. North of Pennsylvania, all but four of the Anglican clergy were loyal to England; "the 20 Connecticut clergy—all American born—were loyalists to a man" (ibid., p. 266).

More work must be done on individual northern Anglicans and specific congregations to refine our picture of ordinary lay members. Still, a recent investigation of New York assemblymen asserts that the most predictive element in their pre-Revolutionary behavior may have been their associations with Anglicanism or Dissent (James S. Olson, "The New York Assembly, the Politics of Religion, and the Origins of the American Revolution, 1768–1771," *Historical Magazine of the Protestant Episcopal Church* 43 [1974]:21–28). For a suggestive sampling of Anglican congregations in the Hudson Valley, see Philip Ranlet, *The New York Loyalists* (Knoxville, Tenn., 1986), pp. 141–46.

[54] Bernard Bailyn, *The Ideological Origins of the American Revolution* (Cambridge, Mass., 1967), p. 40; *The Independent Reflector, or, Weekly Essays on Sundry Important Subjects . . . by William Livingston and Others*, ed. Milton M. Klein (Cambridge, Mass., 1963), pp. 3, 20.

up and sniff the air for Stuart conspiracies. Their "Anglicization" was nothing if not selective; it included the mentality of
country rather than court, and prominent in it was the dread
of episcopacy. And thus it was that clergy and laity alike,
throughout the vast Nonconforming community, could rush
to the defense of what united them all.[55]

To be sure, religious differences alone did not bring on the
American Revolution. This same "republican" behavior was
to be observed in town meetings, colonial legislatures, cham-
bers of commerce, and voluntary associations of every sort.
But the striking thing about the dissenting mentality is how
easily it flowed in with the emergent republican understanding of the political radicals.[56] Habits inculcated over more
than 150 years by such Nonconformist practices as the gathering of congregations, electing of leaders, and then sharing
power with them under the principle of majority rule proved
far more congenial to republican forms than to the imperial
alternative. To Englishmen at home, on the other hand,
where religious Dissent in the mid-eighteenth century was at
low ebb and drew little sympathy, the tempest in the colonies
over bishops and rights and taxes could be seen as little more
than a Presbyterian conspiracy.[57]

[55] For more on how the bishop issue contributed to what I have called an
"ideology of dissent," see Bonomi, *Under the Cope of Heaven*, pp. 199–209.

The minority of Dissenters who did remain loyal to Great Britain came
largely from the more orthodox, conservative, and hierarchical side of their
denominations.

[56] Richard Buel, Jr., "Democracy and the American Revolution: A Frame
of Reference," *William and Mary Quarterly*, 3d ser. 21 (1964):165–90. For a
perceptive recent discussion of religion and politics, see Donald Weber,
Rhetoric and History in Revolutionary New England (New York, 1988).

[57] According to Caroline Robbins, the Dissenters' reputation in England
was associated with memories of "the Long Parliament, all innovations of
the Interregnum, and all intolerance manifested by Puritans at any time."
Moreover, "whatever dissent had gained in liberality and in comprehension
of different points of view, it had lost in fighting power" (*The Eighteenth-
Century Commonwealthman: Studies in the Transmission, Development, and Circumstance of English Liberal Thought from the Restoration of Charles II until the War
with the Thirteen Colonies* [Cambridge, Mass., 1959], pp. 225, 231). It is estimated that Dissenters constituted no more than 7 percent of the English

In their religious communities, majorities on either side of the Atlantic were now, very clearly, separate cultures. Whether Americans may have become in some ways increasingly "English"-minded in the course of the eighteenth century, they had not become so in the ways that mattered most. We may stop well short of proposing religious differences as the primary "cause" of the American Revolution. It may nonetheless be asserted that the state of mind in which American colonials moved toward separation is nowhere better seen than in the realm of religion.

---

population to 1740; when Methodists were counted among their number at the end of the eighteenth century, Dissenters still formed no more than 20 percent of the population (ibid., p. 230; Roland N. Stromberg, *Religious Liberalism in Eighteenth-Century England* [London, 1954], chap. 9).

ELAINE FORMAN CRANE

Religion and Rebellion

Women of Faith in the American War for Independence

OBSERVERS OF THE HISTORICAL PROCESS are well aware of the symbiotic relationship between religion and politics. Many would argue, in fact, that their intimacy is of such depth and duration that it is difficult to discuss one topic without at least a passing nod to the other. Yet to assert that one phenomenon has influenced the other is not to explain the *process* at work— that is, the means by which political decisions have been responsive to religious persuasion—or, for that matter, how the demands of practical politics have molded the practice of religion. It was only after much soul searching that Puritan orthodoxy reluctantly gave way to the Half-Way Covenant, and Quaker tenaciousness triumphed over the slave-trading hegemony, but in each case the intense concentration on the end

I would like to thank Dr. Irma B. Jaffe, Professor Emeritus of Art History, Fordham University, and author of *John Trumbull, Patriot Artist of the American Revolution,* for sharing her expertise with me in the preparation of the first part of this paper, and Dr. Yvonne Korshak, Professor of Art History, Adelphi University, for suggesting additional avenues of thought. I am also indebted (as usual) to Mrs. Gladys Bolhouse, Curator of Manuscripts at the Newport Historical Society, for helping me sort out the political and religious affiliations of various families in Newport, Rhode Island. Thanks also to Nicole Pelto, Lyman Allyn Museum, New London, Connecticut, for trying to establish the date of the Trumbull embroidery.

of the story has deflected attention from the intermediate chapters. Moreover, as a result of scrutinizing the end product rather than examining the ongoing process, acknowledgment for the deed itself has been limited to those who were only partially responsible for the outcome. In short, although both men and women have effected political-religious change, the contribution of women to that process has been overlooked, since their efforts were largely confined to the early and less well defined stages of the unfolding scenario.

This historical misinterpretation arose from an eighteenth-century worldview that linked politics or the political to male activities exclusively, thereby promoting and reinforcing female invisibility. Women neither held office nor voted, and thus only males were criticized or applauded—but in either event, credited—for decisions that ultimately affected the community, since the historical spotlight focused on their deliberations in civil assembly or on the precise moment at which a decision was ratified by voice, show of hands, or slip of paper.

It also took very little conscious effort to reach backward and connect that final, isolated, and decisive political moment to all those previous moments shared by men (in church committee, coffeehouse, or at street corners), which subsequently led to a resolution by assembled franchise holders. Collectively speaking, those activities were political, and conversely, what women did was apolitical. By virtue of their sexual identity and the gender roles attached to that identity, women were excluded from the political process. By definition and description (not to mention circular reasoning), they were neither political participants nor political beings.

At the same time, however, eighteenth-century gender roles permitted—indeed, encouraged—women to be motivated by, and act upon, religious principles. The paradox (for society then and historians now) was that women were not allowed by societal norms to translate religious stimuli—as men did—into political activism. In brief, permissible response was defined by gender role, and the gender role assigned to women arbitrarily separated the religious sphere from the political arena.

An acceptance of the traditional definition of what was political and of the assumption that women adhered to their assigned roles places women at the periphery of many of the world's significant events, among which is the American Revolution. In fact, however, neither women nor the world operates in such a manner. If politics had, or has, any association with principles, convictions, or opinions, if it refers to the art of persuasion, or relates to the decision-making process, if it may be said that political people take sides, lobby, and even scheme, or if they try to achieve power and determine policy, then certainly women must be accepted as political creatures and thus considered central to any event where they display these characteristics or engage in such activities.

As far as the American Revolution is concerned, religious convictions motivated many women to take sides in the struggle for Independence. They were strongly influenced by faith, just as many men were, but they reacted as women—in culturally determined gender roles to be sure, but roles that were no less political than the roles assumed by men. Thus, Faith Robinson Trumbull responded in one way, Mary Gould Almy in another, and women collectively in still other ways— but all the women discussed in the following pages made political decisions based on individual commitments to religious principles or orientation. By making choices, taking sides, and influencing others to do the same, they converted religious beliefs into political actions and, equally important, they did so unmindful of either contemporary opinion or historical perspective.

FAITH ROBINSON TRUMBULL:
THE ART OF REVOLUTION

To the casual observer scanning a map of Connecticut, Lebanon is in the middle of nowhere. Poised approximately ten miles northwest of Norwich and twenty-five miles southeast of Hartford, it is designated on one map as the site of the Jonathan Trumbull house rather than by its geographical name. Yet the bucolic simplicity of modern-day Lebanon masks its eighteenth-century significance—particularly in the era of the American Revolution. Indeed, it is an appropriate point from which to begin a discussion of women, religion, and revolution.

Lebanon was home to the Trumbull family, and the most prominent member of this family in the Revolutionary years was Gov. Jonathan Trumbull (1710–85). In office from 1769 to 1784, he was the only colonial governor to support the rebel cause when the weapons of warfare turned from pens to swords, and his vigorous stand for Independence can be traced as far back as 1770, when few people seriously demanded separation from Great Britain.[1] By that time he had been married to Faith Robinson of Duxbury, Massachusetts, for thirty-five years, a union that produced four sons and two daughters. One son, John (1756–1843), became the artist of the Revolution and one of the foremost painters of eighteenth- and nineteenth-century America.

This was a family that was bound firmly to the whig cause, one in which women were no less affected than men by the upheavals of those tumultuous decades. Yet if the Trumbull women and men shared similar concerns about their world, they nonetheless moved in separate spheres and reacted differently to the same provocations. Faith Robinson Trumbull (1718–80) left us a tangible reminder that the Revolution stirred her as much as it did the menfolk in her family, even though her response was shaped by the gender roles assigned to eighteenth-century women. Her statement, which uniquely blended religion, politics, and art, resulted from her education, the family she married into, and the church to which she belonged.

Sometime between the years 1765 and 1770, at the point on the Revolutionary calendar when her husband became increasingly committed to Independence, Faith Trumbull designed and executed a piece of needlework entitled "The Hanging of Absalom." The current owner of the piece, the Lyman Allyn Museum in New London, Connecticut, has no further information on its origin, nor has it evidence to date the embroidery with any greater precision. Indeed, we do not even know if it was Faith Trumbull or a subsequent admirer

[1]Jonathan Trumbull to William Samuel Johnson, Jan. 29, 1770, *The Trumbull Papers* (Boston, 1885), p. 403.

The Hanging of Absalom. (*Courtesy of the Lyman Allyn Art Museum, New London, Conn.*)

(or curator) who gave it that title, although the subject matter itself is unambiguous. It is possible to say with some certainty, however, that Mrs. Trumbull drew or outlined the design first on the black satin background, that the faces are painted rather than sewn (an artistic touch that corresponds to the latter half of the eighteenth century), and that the threads she used were both silk and metal, enhancements also more common after 1750 than before.[2]

[2]Susan B. Swan, *A Winterthur Guide to American Needlework* (New York, 1976), p. 31; Glee Krueger, *A Gallery of American Samplers: The Theodore H. Kapnek Collection* (New York, 1984), pp. 16, 20. See also Nancy Graves

In its simplest form, this embroidery represents the biblical story of King David, whose son Absalom led a rebellion against him.[3] In the course of a military engagement, Absalom rode a mule through a forest and his long thick hair caught on the boughs of an oak tree. When his mule rode out from under him, Absalom was left dangling, ensnared by the branches. Joab, David's commander, slew Absalom with his sword despite the king's express prohibition to the contrary, and although the insurrection was necessarily suppressed by force, David was distraught over his son's death.

Faith Robinson Trumbull was not the only person drawn to the story of David and Absalom, nor was she the only woman to demonstrate her creativity through this particular biblical scene. An English needlework Absalom panel survives from the reign of Charles II (or earlier), and both the Boston Museum of Fine Arts and the Currier Gallery of Art in Manchester, New Hampshire, hold pieces based on the same tragedy. The Winterthur Museum has another portrayal of the same theme, remarkably similar to Faith Trumbull's, stitched sometime between 1760 and 1785 by someone in Salem.[4] In this latter piece of needlework, there are at least four figures instead of three, but the configuration, animals, arch, and draperies under which King David sits with his harp are so reminiscent of Trumbull's that both pieces may have been inspired by a single source.

That source or inspiration was probably an engraving or print from the Bible. Various illustrated editions were published throughout the seventeenth and eighteenth centuries, and although we cannot be certain which Mrs. Trumbull was familiar with, depictions of King David's life in general and,

---

Cabot, "Engravings as Pattern Sources," *Antiques* 58 (1950):476–79, for a discussion of embroideries worked by three generations of Trumbull women.

[3] 2 Sam.13–19.

[4] Helen Bowen, "Tent Stitch Work," in Betty Ring, ed., *Needlework: An Historical Survey* (Pittstown, N.J., 1984), pp. 37–38; Susan B. Swan, *Plain and Fancy: American Women and Their Needlework, 1700–1850* (New York, 1977), pp. 64–65 (fig. 32).

more specifically, Joab killing Absalom, were common themes.[5] In addition, art books containing representations of biblical subjects suggest that David and Absalom frequently caught the imagination of the world's great artists.[6]

The argument made here—admittedly and unabashedly on the basis of circumstantial evidence—is that Trumbull's embroidery is an artistic expression of political sentiment based on religious symbolism, a metaphor that substituted King David of the Old Testament for King George of New England and Absalom, David's rebellious son, for the upstart colonies. Faith Trumbull was a member of a devout, educated, artistic family that was steeped in politics. Given her sex, her status, and the social codes by which she conducted herself, this work was a most natural way for her to express her deeply felt concerns about the civil war that would soon erupt around her.

Faith Robinson came by her religious credentials honestly. She was the youngest daughter of one John Robinson, a minister of Duxbury, Massachusetts, and the great-granddaughter of another, who was pastor of the Plymouth

[5] See, for example, the following illustrated English editions of the Bible: London, 1653–56; Cambridge, 1660, 1674; London, 1693, 1703; London [?], 1715; London, 1739, 1752; and Birmingham, 1769, 1770. The 1674, 1693, 1703, 1739, and 1752 editions include engravings related to the death of Absalom.

[6] "Absalom Caught in the Tree" (c. 1250), *The Bible in Art: Miniatures, Paintings, Drawings, and Sculptures Inspired by the Old Testament* (New York, 1956), pl. 173; "King David Playing the Harp," by Matthias Scheits (1625–1700), in *The Hebrew Bible in Christian, Jewish, and Muslim Art* (New York, 1963), pl. 81. The 1762 edition of the Bible published in Cambridge includes plates designed by Matthias Scheits, among other artists.

Furthermore, in an analysis of a fifteenth-century painting by Jan Van Eyck, one art historian notes that "the pavement tile which represents the *Death of Absalom* appears to have relevance to the theme of dynastic succession, for the story of Absalom, as the son of David, was interpreted in medieval exegesis as a parable on monarchy and monarchical succession" (Carra Ferguson O'Meara, "Isabelle of Portugal as the Virgin in Jan Van Eyck's Washington *Annunciation*," *Gazette des Beaux-Arts* 97 [1981]: 102). The author wishes to thank Andrea G. Crane, graduate student in art history, University of Chicago, for this citation.

Pilgrims during their residence in Holland.[7] Her husband, the governor, prepared for the ministry after graduating from Harvard in 1727 and was considering a call to a church in Colchester when a family crisis forced him to abandon his plans and enter the family's mercantile business instead. Nevertheless, Faith was surrounded by people of a religious bent from her earliest years, and it is likely that she was quite familiar with the story of David and Absalom as related in the second book of Samuel. According to the sermon preached at her death, she herself was "a serious professor of the religion of Jesus, a very constant attendant upon the worship of God's house, and the ordinances of the Gospel, which she attended with apparent pleasure and devotion."[8] Her son referred to her as an "Active Christian."[9] Rhetoric notwithstanding, faith was an essential ingredient of Mrs. Trumbull's mentalité.

Although fifty-two years old and a grandmother by 1770, Faith Trumbull probably spent a considerable amount of time in the Lebanon Meeting House, which was roughly four long blocks—but well within walking distance—from her home.[10] The minister who spoke at her funeral in 1780, the Rev. Timothy Stone (1742–97), suggested that he could not take credit for Mrs. Trumbull's exemplary life, given the shortness of his tenure at the Lebanon church, and thus it would have been the longtime minister of the First Society in Lebanon, the Rev. Solomon Williams (1700–1776), who molded Faith Trumbull's religious convictions. Equally important, it is likely that

[7] John Trumbull, *Autobiography, Reminiscences, and Letters of John Trumbull from 1756 to 1841* (New Haven, 1841), p. 2; Charles Royster, *A Revolutionary People at War: The Continental Army and American Character, 1775–1783* (Chapel Hill, 1979), p. 54.

[8] Timothy Stone, *Victory over Sin and Death, To Be Obtained, Only, Through Faith in Jesus Christ. A Sermon, Delivered in the First Society in Lebanon, May 31, 1780. At the Funeral of Madam Faith Trumbull, Wife of His Excellency, Gov. Trumbull* (Hartford, 1780), pp. 13–14.

[9] Trumbull, *Autobiography, Reminiscences, and Letters*, p. 5.

[10] *A Plan of the First Society in Lebanon, with the High Ways & Buildings Therein, with the Distance of Each House from the Meeting House; also the Center of Said Society . . . Surveyed Oct. & Nov. 1772 . . . A Plan of the Third Society in Lebanon, Called Goshen . . . Surveyed Nov. 1769 & Aug. 1770* (New York, [1912?]).

Solomon Williams had a hand in shaping Mrs. Trumbull's political proclivities as well, to the point where these two intellectual strands were almost inseparable.

Historians are in general agreement that a seditious pulpit influenced the outcome of the American Revolution.[11] By equating the colonies with Israel and the colonists with God's chosen people, the ministers frequently summoned the Old Testament to support their arguments in favor of natural rights and against oppression. And although less than 5 percent of the New England clergy "left a record of public performances on behalf of either Whig or Tory politics," Solomon Williams of Lebanon, Connecticut, was one of that small, select group who did.[12] Historian Alice M. Baldwin listed him among those who "preached resistance and gave strong arguments to the restless colonists." She called him "a zealous advocate of the colonial cause" from the outset of the struggle until his death in 1776. A pious woman like Faith Robinson Trumbull, whose constant attendance at church was noted in her funeral eulogy, could hardly have been unmoved by Williams's rhetoric. Besides, he was a close family friend, whose son married Faith's daughter Mary. Williams must have been a frequent visitor to the Trumbull home.[13]

---

[11]As William Fowler has noted, "The ministers of Connecticut taught the people their political rights" ("Ministers of Connecticut in the Revolution," in *Centennial Papers Published by Order of the General Conference of the Congregational Churches of Connecticut* [Hartford, 1877], p. 22). See also Richard D. Brown, "Spreading the Word: Rural Clergymen and the Communications Network of Eighteenth-Century New England," *Proceedings of the Massachusetts Historical Society* 94 (1982): 1–14; Harry S. Stout, "Religion, Communications, and the Ideological Origins of the American Revolution," *William and Mary Quarterly*, 3d ser. 34 (1977):519–41; Alice M. Baldwin, "Sowers of Sedition: The Political Theories of Some of the New Light Presbyterian Clergy of Virginia and North Carolina," *William and Mary Quarterly*, 3d ser. 5 (1948):52–76; idem, *New England Clergy and the American Revolution* (Durham, N.C., 1928).

[12]Brown, "Spreading the Word," p. 2; Alice M. Baldwin, *The Clergy of Connecticut in Revolutionary Days*, Connecticut Tercentenary Commission, publication no. 56 (New Haven, 1936), p. 11.

[13]Baldwin, *Clergy of Connecticut*, p. 13.

That home, according to John Trumbull, Faith's son, was tantamount to rebel headquarters, a place where John's father was "surrounded by patriots to whose ardent conversations [John] listened daily." John admitted that "it would have been strange if all this had failed to produce its natural effect."[14] Strange, too, if it had not produced the same effect on his mother, and there is reason to believe that she was, in fact, persuaded to the rebel cause. In his biography of her husband, Isaac William Stuart described Faith Trumbull (with true nineteenth-century flourish), as a woman "eminent . . . for her patriotism," who devoted herself "in every form in which a lady could" toward "the Revolutionary Struggle." The story of her splendid gesture when she placed a cloak given to her by the Count Rochambeau on the altar of the Lebanon Meeting House may be apocryphal, but, at the same time, it provides some assurance that she harbored no loyalist sympathies.[15]

Indeed, not only the Trumbull family but the wider Lebanon community reacted dramatically to British encroachments on their rights. On August 26, 1765, citizens demonstrated against the Stamp Act by dragging effigies through town in a cart. A distressed America played victim to a villainous Stamp Collector and both were depicted in a familial metaphor of an injured mother and an ungrateful, degenerate son. Moreover, the drama resonated with biblical imagery: the Stamp Collector was portrayed as a Judas who would betray America for a purse and office. Three years later, when British troops threatened Boston, the town of Lebanon resolved to "assist and support our American brethren at the expense of our lives and fortunes." Was Faith Robinson Trumbull one of the "vast concourse of spectators" to witness the Stamp Act demonstration? Was she among those at the "full meeting" of Lebanon "inhabitants" who unanimously agreed to assist beleaguered Boston? It is hard to

[14]Trumbull, *Autobiography, Reminiscences, and Letters,* p. 15.

[15]Isaac William Stuart, *Life of Jonathan Trumbull, Sen.* (Boston, 1859), pp. 513–15; Irma B. Jaffe, *John Trumbull, Patriot Artist of the American Revolution* (Boston, 1975), p. 8.

believe she could have remained aloof from the turbulence about her.[16]

It is fairly certain, then, that Mrs. Trumbull's religious and political background provided her with a conceptual framework within which she could produce "The Hanging of Absalom." Her upbringing also dictated the particular form she would choose as her means of expression. In his autobiography John Trumbull suggested that the female members of his family were particularly appreciative of art. He recalled that his sister Faith first awakened his own interest in drawing, and that her paintings hung in their mother's parlor. His sisters Faith and Mary were both taught embroidery at an excellent school in Boston, which says nothing about their mother's interest or proficiency but does confirm that needlework was an occupation appropriate to upper-class women in Revolutionary America.[17] Oil painting did not play the same role in the life of an adult woman.

Given Faith Trumbull's religious and political profile and the fact that if she were disposed to express herself artistically, the needle rather than the brush would be the medium of choice for a woman of her status, let us now consider the biblical story itself and see if it is reasonable to connect Old Testament political intrigues to events thousands of years later. In Jewish tradition, the story is a lesson about a rebellious and ungrateful child, and Absalom's punishment fit his crime. On its most elementary level, therefore, it is a heaven-sent argument in support of the loyalist position.

Since the wife of Gov. Jonathan Trumbull was not a loyalist, and since the colonists needed some incentive to applaud a

[16]The Lebanon demonstration is described in the *Boston Evening-Post*, Sept. 9, 1765. See Kenneth Silverman, *A Cultural History of the American Revolution* (New York, 1987), pp. 77, 85. *Boston Gazette*, Oct. 10, 1768 (supplement).

[17]Trumbull, *Autobiography, Reminiscences, and Letters*, pp. 4–5. Embroideries attributed to Faith and Mary Trumbull hang in the Connecticut Historical Society (see Cora Ginsburg, "Textiles in the Connecticut Historical Society," *Antiques* 107 [1975]:712–25). It should be noted that Cabot, "Engravings as Sources," and Ginsburg disagree as to which members of the Trumbull family worked the various pieces.

rebellious child, the story of David and Absalom required interpretation before it could be adapted to the Revolutionary cause. It was of some help that the Old Testament was conveniently filled with just and unjust kings, wicked and righteous children, and civil and uncivil wars, because during the Revolutionary era, the Bible inspired whig clergymen to compare those ancient monarchs with their own oppressive ruler. David Rowland, pastor at Windsor, Connecticut, drew a parallel between the tyrant Rehoboam and George III. Chauncey Whittlesey of New Haven used the same analogy and asked God to restore tranquillity by speaking to the king of Great Britain just as he had spoken to Rehoboam and the people of Judah so many eons before. John Adams wrote to Abigail that he had heard a minister compare "the Conduct of Pharaoh and that of George." In 1777 William Gordon, minister of the Third Church at Roxbury, Massachusetts, elaborated on "The Separation of the Jewish Tribes after the death of Solomon . . . applied to the present day." In the same year, Nathaniel Whitaker, pastor of the Third Church of Salem, Massachusetts, celebrated the victory of Deborah and Barak over Jabin, king of Canaan and Sisera.[18] In sum, it was not unusual for colonial ministers to weave biblical monarchs into the fabric of American liberty.

Moreover, by 1770 the story of David and Absalom had already been analyzed on several levels by both English and American ministers as well as by dramatists and composers. Sometimes Absalom was pictured as a thoroughly narcissistic young man who coveted his father's throne; at other times he was treated sympathetically, as a man trying to save a country brought to civil disorder by his father's immoral behavior and lack of virtue. One cannot be sure that Faith Robinson Trumbull ever heard a sermon that drew an analogy between the story of David and Absalom and the world as she knew it, but Trumbull, who had "an education answerable to her family

[18] Fowler, "Ministers of Connecticut," pp. 51, 62; John Adams to Abigail Adams, May 17, 1776, in Lyman H. Butterfield et al., eds., *The Book of Abigail and John* (Cambridge, Mass., 1975), p. 129; Frank Moore, ed., *The Patriot Preachers of the American Revolution* (New York, 1860), pp. 158–231.

and birth," might have been familiar with other literature applicable to the story.[19]

She realized, no doubt, that the confrontation between David and Absalom followed the establishment of the monarchy in Israel as set forth in 1 Samuel. Israel, like America, had struggled with incipient nationhood and had been equally ambivalent about a potentially abusive monarchical government. In choosing an earthly king, the ancient Israelites had offended God; under the circumstances, God could hardly be displeased with the Americans if they chose to reject one.

Mrs. Trumbull might also have known that, historically speaking, King David was intent on centralizing his administration and power—a policy that caused general disaffection. At the time, the leaders of the various Jewish tribes had become concerned over their loss of autonomy and authority, and they were reluctant to give up their independence in favor of imperial expansion. Elders who eventually supported Absalom did so because they had been deprived of their authority as judges. Absalom's coalition resisted the imposition of taxes, a permanent civil service establishment, and a regular army. They had misgivings about governmental leadership passing by inheritance within a single family. The men of Hebron were said to be insulted by the removal of the seat of the kingdom from Hebron to Jerusalem. Absalom's widespread support consisted of people who believed he acted to preserve their liberties. To Faith Robinson Trumbull, the story must have sounded for all the world like the controversy between the colonies and Great Britain—especially since she herself lived not ten miles from Hebron. Little did she know that King George, like the biblical king,

[19] East of Lebanon, Ezra Stiles, minister of the Second Congregational Church in Newport, Rhode Island, noted in his diary on April 3, 1769, that he had "Begun 2d Book of Samuel in Hebrew," and that on April 5 he "made a sermon." His sermons for that year have not survived, leaving one to wonder whether the minister presented the story of David and Absalom to his flock that week. If he did, the meaning of it would not have been in doubt (Franklin B. Dexter, ed., *The Literary Diary of Ezra Stiles*, 3 vols. [New York, 1901], 1:7–8; Stone, *Victory over Sin and Death*, p. 13).

would eventually hire foreign mercenaries to subdue the rebellion.[20]

Besides biblical commentary, there were more literary
sources from which Trumbull could have pieced together her
own interpretation of the historic contest between father and
son. Thomas Watson (1513–84) wrote *David and Absalom,* a
Latin tragedy in five acts, in the late 1530s. The play, which
portrayed Absalom as an ingrate with no redeeming values,
may have come to Mrs. Trumbull's attention.[21] Before the six-
teenth century was out, George Peele (1558?–97?) had written
The Love of King David and Fair Bethsabe (1599), a play that
dealt at length with Absalom's rebellion and placed the blame
for civil war not on Absalom but on David and his illicit love
affair with Bathsheba. Although its first edition is said to have
had an illustration of Absalom suspended from the tree as he
is stabbed by Joab, if Faith Trumbull read the play at all, it
was likely to have been its 1773 edition by Thomas Hawkins.
But no matter which edition, it was the lines themselves that
would have resonated so powerfully:

> Why should not *Absalom* that in his face
> Carries the final purpose of his God,
> That is, to work him grace in *Israel,*
> Endeavor to achieve with all his strength,
> The state that most may satisfy his joy,
> Keeping his statutes and his covenants pure?
>
> I am the man he made to glory in,
> When by the errours of my father's sin
> He lost the path that led him into the land
> Wherewith our chosen ancestors were bless'd.[22]

[20]*Encyclopaedia Judaica,* 1971 ed., s.v. "David"; P. Kyle McCarter,
Jr., *II Samuel: A New Translation with Introduction, Notes, and Commentary,* The
Anchor Bible, vol. 9 (New York, 1984), pp. 358–59.

[21]Thomas Watson, *David and Absalom* (London, 1535–40). The edition
examined for this essay is John Hazel Smith, ed., *A Humanists' "Trew Imitation." Thomas Watson's* Absalom: *A Critical Edition and Translation* (Urbana,
Ill., 1964).

[22]George Peele, *The Love of King David and Fair Bethsabe* (London, 1599),
in Thomas Hawkins, ed., *The Origin of the English Drama,* 3 vols. (Oxford,
1773), 2:123–93, esp. p. 169. The 1599 edition of this work is said to have

In one sense, then, David's marriage to Bathsheba was ultimately responsible for his political problems. David was not faithful to God's laws, and his private sexual lapses thus had unforeseen public consequences. Moreover, biblical commentary interpreted Deuteronomy 21:10–14 and 18 to mean that whoever married a beautiful captive woman would have a stubborn and rebellious son. In this interpretation, one could even argue that God directed Absalom's rebellion against his father as punishment for David's transgressions.[23]

This interpretation of David and Absalom was modified slightly by an English minister, Robert Harris (1581–1658), who preached a sermon entitled *Absaloms Funerall*, published in London in 1622. Harris acknowledged the treacherous and traitorous behavior of Absalom but noted at the same time that David was filled with grief at his son's death. Why, asked Harris, did God punish the king in this manner? Why was there such unrest in his household? Harris responded to his own question by pointing the finger at David: David had sinned, and David needed to be purged. God sent Absalom to absolve David of his sins.

This construction was also central to an eighteenth-century account of King David written by Patrick Delany. Delany did not exonerate the "miscreant" Absalom from treason and rebellion, nor did he acquit him of "vanity" and a "lying spirit." Yet, according to Delany's interpretation, God wrought this tragedy to punish David for adultery. So great was David's transgression *"that God had raised up this evil to him out of his own house."* Presumably, the worst punishment a father could suffer was the rebellion of his own son.[24]

---

included an illustration of Absalom suspended from the tree as he is stabbed by Joab, but none of the currently available reproductions of the edition contain that illustration.

[23]The preceding paragraph is derived from papers presented by professors Joel Rosenberg and Regina Schwartz at a symposium entitled "Stories of King David: The Hebrew Bible as Literature," Fordham University, New York, May 5, 1989.

[24]Robert Harris, *Absaloms Funerall. Preached at Banburie by a Neighbour Minister, or, The Lamentation of a Loving Father for a Rebellious Child* (London, 1622); Patrick Delany, *An Historical Account of the Life and Reign of David, King of Israel* (London, 1759), pp. 157–58, 161, 169, 193.

During the reign of Charles I, Thomas Fuller (1608–61) also seized on the David-Absalom analogy in his poetic trilogy and warned that just as David's sins were punished by the death of his sons and civil wars, so too would Charles suffer insurmountable hardships if he did not repent and reform. Although a supporter of King Charles, Fuller seems to have held him responsible for the civil unrest plaguing England and begged him to substitute "perfect peace" for the "bloody discords" and "long-lasting broyls" that spilled beyond English borders.[25]

It was John Dryden, however, who immortalized the story of David and Absalom during the reign of yet another Charles and whose poetry—if Faith Trumbull had borrowed schoolmaster Nathan Tisdale's copy—would have fired her imagination. Dryden's poem *Absalom and Achitophel* was published originally in London in 1681 with a preface that indicated he was unwilling to let the subtleties of the allegory go unrecognized by the reading public. The poem begins with a key to the characters that casts them in seventeenth-century garb: David as Charles II, Absalom as the duke of Monmouth, Achitophel (David's minister) as the earl of Shaftesbury. In this version David had mismanaged the government to the point where the people were factious and "Impoverisht and depriv'd of all Command / Their Taxes doubled as they lost Their Land." Achitophel (who convinces Absalom to rebel against his father) is the traitor in this version and "A name to all succeeding Ages curst / For close Designs and crooked Counsels fit." Achitophel duped and deluded Absalom into thinking that David was wasting the treasury, and in order to win people to his cause, Absalom argued that citizens were being exposed to arbitrary laws, their liberties made "a spoil," their trade intercepted, and their rights invaded. Would it have been so difficult for Faith Trumbull to imagine George III in place of Charles II?

As for Absalom, in this interpretation he may have been

<hr/>

[25] Raymond-Jean Frontain and Jan Wojcik, eds., *The David Myth in Western Literature* (West Lafayette, Ind., 1980), p. 6; Thomas Fuller, *Davids Hainous Sinne, Heartie Repentance, Heavie Punishment* (1631) (London, 1869), verse 67.

misguided, he may have overstated the case against David, but he acted as a "patriot." Clearly Absalom had been taken in by the crooked Achitophel, but in Dryden's version the former was not corrupt, malicious, or self-serving: "Never was a Patriot yet, but was a Fool." And David's only desire was for Absalom's repentence: "How easie 'tis for Parents to forgive / With how few tears a Pardon might be won."[26] In his introduction, Dryden said he would like the story to end with the reconciliation of David and Absalom—and in 1681 that was not an impossibility, metaphorically speaking, any more than it was in 1770.

Furthermore, the very scene Faith Trumbull chose to dramatize may have represented something even more specific to her. King David is off in the corner of the work, playing his harp, unaware that a soldier has just killed his son Absalom against the monarch's express wishes. How often did the colonists speak in familial terms vis-à-vis their relationship with King George? How often did they accuse the king's ministers of misleading the king with regard to the deterioration of colonial affairs? Indeed, how often did those acting in the name of the king do so without his consent?

The parent-child relationship was a recurrent theme in eighteenth-century Anglo-American literature, and Jay Fliegelman has demonstrated that the nature of that relationship underwent a dramatic transformation as the Revolutionary era approached. During the 1700s, a benevolent father who set a good example for his children replaced the seventeenth-century authoritarian, patriarchal parent, and the child, who at one time owed unquestioned obedience to the latter, became one who could challenge a parent who set a bad example—or even rebel against one who exhibited tyrannical behavior.

At the same time, the literature on the eve of the Revolution insisted that a child's first obligation was to God and God's laws. The first commandment (Thou shalt have no other gods

[26]Bruce P. Stark, "Personal Libraries in Lebanon, Connecticut, 1702–1789," *Connecticut History* no. 26 (Nov. 1985):8; John Dryden, *Absalom and Achitophel: A Poem* (London, 1708), pp. 5, 7, 18, 20, 23.

before me) took precedence over the fifth (Honor thy father and mother), thus legitimizing the behavior of both Absalom and his colonial counterparts. If Kings David and George were corrupt and immoral, Absalom and the colonists had no choice but to disavow them. The abuse of parental authority forced otherwise devoted children into resistance.

Parental authority was also a favorite subject of late eighteenth-century European artists who took increasing interest in the ambivalent relationship between father and son. According to Carol Duncan, in the three decades preceding the French Revolution, French salon painters focused heavily on elderly men whose ebbing power was often challenged by their male progeny. Engravings based on these paintings made their way to the marketplace and into the consciousness of an audience that may even have included some Americans.[27]

In the embroidery, Joab is sporting a red coat, eighteenth-century British style, while Absalom's is trimmed in a deep blue-green. In short, neither character is clothed in the garb of antiquity common to the engravings from which the embroidery was probably derived, although the color red was associated with ancient Roman sovereign power as well as with the British "lobsterbacks." Since the attire of the figures was in harmony with the decade of its reputed creation, it would have been a fitting memorial to either the Stamp Act repeal or the Boston Massacre—the more so, since the oak tree (from which Absalom's lifeless body hung) was sometimes considered a symbol of patriotism. In Connecticut, moreover, the oak tree had more than an abstract symbolic meaning. According to legend, a young member of the Wadsworth fam-

---

[27]According to Edwin G. Burrows and Michael Wallace, Americans and Englishmen "likened the empire to a family. . . . No other formulation of those ties came nearly so close to being the very *lingua franca* of the Revolution" ("The American Revolution: The Ideology and Psychology of National Liberation," *Perspectives in American History* 6 [1972]:168; see also Jay Fliegelman, *Prodigals and Pilgrims: The American Revolution against Patriarchal Authority, 1750–1800* [New York, 1982], pp. 5, 68). Carol Duncan, "Fallen Fathers: Images of Authority in Pre-Revolutionary French Art," *Art History* 4 (1981):186, 189.

ily saved the colony's charter in 1687 by hiding it in an oak tree when a royal governor threatened to revoke it.[28]

Indeed, the embroidery is rife with symbolism, most of which is religious and which may be decoded layer by layer, despite the absence of proof as to Trumbull's intentions.[29] If, on one level, the death of Absalom represents an assault on the American colonists, it may also portray the crucifixion of Christ, thus escalating, by imagery, the evil done by the king's minister. The synoptic Gospels (Matthew, Mark, and Luke) relate that on the day of the crucifixion, from noon until three in the afternoon, "there was darkness over all the land."[30] The black satin of the background may represent that darkness while other objects artistically symbolize aspects of the same scene. Both sun and moon were regular features of crucifixions in medieval art; usually they were both portrayed—one on either side of the cross. In this embroidery we cannot be certain which celestial orb Mrs. Trumbull chose to depict. Whichever it is, the glittering body is prominently displayed at the center of the cross, to the left of which and hovering directly over Absalom is an angel—one of God's messengers—who looks askance at the cross.

Christ, like Absalom, was pierced in the side with a lance carried by a soldier. The soldier in this however, is wearing a helmet to which is attached a curious appendage. It is not the plumage or quills usually associated with Roman military headgear, but rather looks more like sprigs from a cedar tree. What could give the piece more subtlety and contemporary meaning than the addition of branches from a cedar of Lebanon—especially since the cedar of ancient Leba-

[28]George Ferguson, *Signs and Symbols in Christian Art* (New York, 1966), p. 152: "English embroideries in the seventeenth century sometimes asserted patriotism by featuring oak trees." Also see Mary Gostelow, *Art of Embroidery: Great Needlework Collections of Britain and the United States* (New York, 1979), pl. 34; W. H. Gocher, *Wadsworth, or, The Charter Oak* (Hartford, 1904).

[29]The following interpretation relies heavily on James Hall, *Dictionary of Subjects and Symbols in Art*, rev. ed. (New York, 1979), pp. xv, 17, 81–85, 109, as well as Ferguson, *Signs and Symbols in Christian Art*, pp. 27, 29, 30, 37, 38, 39.

[30]Matt. 27:45.

non was a symbol of Christ himself? The soldier in the embroidery may even represent the centurion who, upon
witnessing the crucifixion, became convinced of Christ's divinity.

The dove, resting on a now dead limb of the tree to the left
of Absalom, frequently appears as the symbol of the Holy
Spirit in Christian art, as well as a symbol of good tidings and
peace. Moreover, a woodcut attributed to Paul Revere (c. December 1770), shows Britannia opening a bird cage to let a
dove fly out toward the town of Boston.[31]

By merging stories from the Hebrew Bible with the New
Testament, Mrs. Trumbull was only following a tradition developed by the Church fathers many centuries earlier. They
believed and encouraged the theory that people and events
in the Old Testament prefigured images in the New. Thus,
Abraham's sacrifice of his son Isaac foreshadowed God the
Father's sacrifice of Christ. Indeed, the Bible itself traces
Christ's ancestry back to King David, which strongly rein-
forces the familial image in the embroidery. A devout woman,
well aware of biblical history and devoted to the colonial
cause, would have no trouble portraying a triple-layered
scene that included the sacrifice of Absalom, Christ, and the
American patriot.

One might conjecture still further that the game in the fore-
ground of the embroidery contained a message as well. Faith
Trumbull chose her animal subjects as carefully as she chose
her human ones. No domestic animals like sheep or cattle
here. No dogs or cats are depicted either, but rather harts and
hares. They too may be considered on several levels. First,
both hart (or stag) and hare were at home in the forest where
Absalom was ensnared. They were equally at home in the
American wilderness. Both, like Absalom, were sought by
"hunters," and the hart, in particular, was eagerly pursued by
royalty. In the seventeenth century, a hart chased by a king
had a special name: "hart royal."

[31] Donald H. Cresswell, comp., *The American Revolution in Drawings and
Prints* (Washington, D.C., 1975), p. 262. Beginning with the issue of January 1, 1770, the *Boston Gazette and Country Journal* used this woodcut for
its masthead.

Second, it is probably not coincidental that there is a large stag and a little one, a large hare and a little one. If this embroidery is the story of several fathers and several sons, what could be more natural than to emphasize the parental theme by carrying it to the creatures of the forest? If the notions of spheres based on gender have any meaning at all, if women of Mrs. Trumbull's class were acculturated to believe that their world revolved around family, virtue, morality, and religion, then the symbols placed so strategically in the embroidery must have had particular significance for Faith Robinson Trumbull.

There is a third level on which the animals in the embroidery may be discussed, and for that it is necessary to return to the story of David and Absalom. When Absalom decided to rebel against his father, he sent for King David's counselor, Achitophel, who agreed to defect from David's service and ally himself with Absalom. Achitophel may therefore be called, with some legitimacy, an informer and a turncoat. In eighteenth-century slang, the word *stag* or the expression *to turn stag* referred to just such a person. Moreover, a *hare* was a person who played both sides, a double part or role. The Bible casts Hushai, David's companion, as such a character. At the king's request, Hushai pretended to serve Absalom, but his true allegiance belonged to David. Thus Hushai was a double agent. Since his double-dealings allowed King David to retreat and gather forces, the attitude of one colonial minister, at least, was hostile: "Happy should we be if all Hushais were banished from our councils, or their stratagems discovered and defeated."[32] Was Faith Trumbull aware of these interlocking interpretations, subplots, and allegories? Perhaps.

Mrs. Trumbull appears to have selected and arranged her flowers with the same care and precision she employed in choosing people and animals. Although it is difficult to distinguish the different varieties of flora, it is likely that they were invested with symbolic significance. All but one grow sturdily,

---

[32] *Oxford English Dictionary;* Nathaniel Whitaker, "An Antidote against Toryism, or, The Curse of Meroz," in Moore, ed., *Preachers of the Revolution,* pp. 214–15n.

and that exception wilts at the feet of the dying Absalom. Is that particular flower a rose, symbol of martyrdom? Or was Trumbull thinking of Thomas Fuller's lines?

> Then Crimson blades of grasse, whereon he bleeds
> Did Straitwayes dye, and in their roome succeeds
> A fruitful wildernesse, of fruitlesse weeds.[33]

And is the blossom just below the other fruit tree an anemone? Artists frequently depicted the anemone in crucifixion scenes with red spots on the petals—such as those in this needlework—to represent the blood of Christ. It was said that anemones sprang up on Calvary on the evening of the crucifixion, and in the early days of the Church the triple leaf of the plant, as portrayed here, symbolized the Trinity.

The puzzle pieces were all there to put together in whatever way Faith Trumbull chose, and it is altogether reasonable to assume that a virtuous, religious, politically motivated woman who lived in that time might express her feelings through an exquisitely designed needlework piece, just as her son expressed his sentiments in the form of heroic paintings. This was a woman who attended church regularly, who listened when ministers justified the rebel position in biblical language, and who was surrounded at home by people who expressed their frustration in political language. She merged both religion and politics and translated colonial grievances into a work of art that was acceptable from a person of her sex.

As a woman, the family analogy of the story of David and Absalom would have had special meaning for her, particularly since her mother died when she was four, and she was brought up by her father. And in the remote possibility that the embroidery was not made until 1775, Mrs. Trumbull would have had one further reason to find affinity—at least subconsciously—with that particular story. After the murder of Absalom the king's minister, Achitophel, committed suicide by hanging. Faith Robinson Trumbull would have taken more interest than usual in that passage because her daughter Faith

---

[33] Fuller, *Davids Hainous Sinne*, verse 48.

died by her own hand in 1775—when she too hanged herself.[34]

MARY GOULD ALMY:
CONSCIENCE AND CONFLICT

To anyone even casually acquainted with the North American colonies in the eighteenth century, Newport, Rhode Island, was in the middle of everywhere. It may be repeating the apochryphal to say that letters were addressed to "Mr. So and So, Merchant, New York (near Newport)," but it is certainly true that the town's merchants enjoyed a reputation for sharp trading, sophistication, urbanity, and culture that easily competed with that of their brothers in the larger seaports to the north and south.

Newporters were a factious lot, given to party politics that, fortunately, did not interfere with parties of a more genial nature where rum flowed profusely and men and women agreed to disagree about the various issues that affected their lives. And while they differed over the best political course to take, they were even less of a mind about religion. Congregationalists, Presbyterians, Baptists, Quakers, Anglicans, Jews, and probably a few Catholics competed for God's attention, each church member or congregant sure that he or she trod the true path. Competitive ideologies aside, however, neither politics nor prayers interrupted the pursuit of profit in the decades before the 1760s, although both had a decisive influence on the Revolutionary upheaval, with religious affiliation frequently determining political allegiance. Newport's ministers were extremely effective in keeping their flocks in line, and the Rev. George Bisset's Anglicans were as loyal to their king, when the final split came, as the Rev. Ezra Stiles's Congregationalists were not.

[34]Cabot, "Engravings," p. 476; Royster, *Revolutionary People at War,* p. 57. Since a controversy already exists with regard to the attribution of the needlework pieces stitched by the Trumbull daughters (and by a niece of Faith Trumbull, Jr.), it is remotely possible that "The Hanging of Absalom" was executed by young Faith, who would have been twenty-seven in 1770. On the other hand, the styles of the embroideries attributed to the younger women are markedly different from the Absalom piece.

What has gone unnoticed, however, is that many of Newport's families were as divided religiously as the larger community itself. Brothers, fathers, and sons often attended competing churches, as did wives, mothers, and daughters. And just as men found that theological persuasion influenced Revolutionary commitment, women learned that religious ties predisposed them toward political positions—some of which were incompatible with opinions held by other family members.

This phenomenon should surprise no one. Despite the invidious implications of female independence, Puritan doctrine guaranteed women the right to an individual conscience. Since God's words took precedence over those of a husband, a pious woman had some latitude as far as theological interpretation was concerned, at least to the extent that she was not required to belong to the same church as her spouse. The Great Awakening reinforced these patterns as New Light ministers emphasized individual rights and private judgment, while at the same time they legitimized factions, parties, and ultimately, secession (for the purpose of forming new churches).[35]

Mary and Benjamin Almy were among the many couples who reflected the liberal attitude toward church affiliation. Mary Almy, born Mary Gould in 1735, was married in 1762. Although both the Gould and Almy families had been counted in the Quaker ranks during the seventeenth century, by the time of the Revolution many of them were dispersed among the various churches in town. In the Revolutionary era, Mary Gould Almy was a member of Trinity Church, the only Anglican congregation in Newport, while her husband Benjamin, twelve years her senior, belonged to one of the two Congregational churches.[36] When war broke out and Independence was proclaimed, Benjamin Almy fought alongside the rebels. His wife remained a vigorous advocate for the crown.

According to notes made by the Rev. Ezra Stiles, Captain

[35]Patricia U. Bonomi, *Under the Cope of Heaven: Religion, Society, and Politics in Colonial America* (New York, 1986), pp. 147, 152–58, and chap. 7.

[36]Obituary of Mary Gould Almy in the *Newport Mercury*, Apr. 2, 1808.

Almy belonged to the First Congregational Church in 1760 but had moved to the Second Congregational Church by 1788, thereby abandoning the Rev. Samuel Hopkins in favor of the zealous whig preacher Ezra Stiles.[37] Although both Congregational ministers could count ardent whigs among their numbers, Stiles was clearly the more passionate rebel partisan, and he lost no opportunity to bring his congregation into the fracas with God's approbation and encouragement for incentive.[38] Benjamin Almy appears to have been convinced by either or both of these ministers.

The Rev. George Bisset of Trinity Church was no less firm in his commitment to the crown. Labeled as a four star loyalist by his antagonist Stiles, Bisset cautioned his congregation to beware of teachers who encouraged "lawless riots and disorders among men." He regularly prayed for the king and urged submission to legitimate authority. When Rhode Island proclaimed June 30, 1774, as a day of public fasting and prayer, "Mr. Bisset . . . took his Text—fast not as the Hypocrites—and preached a high tory Sermon inveiging (by allusions) against Boston and N. England as a turbulent ungoverned people."[39] Within a year, the members of Trinity Church showed their distaste for the whig cause by eschewing the designated day of fasting and prayer altogether. Mary Almy, sitting in pew number ten (which she shared with another woman), listened to Bisset and was swayed by his arguments.[40]

It is not hard to imagine the conversations between Mary and Benjamin Almy in the years before the outbreak of war, yet, in the end, both Mary and Benjamin found that the voices of their respective ministers resounded more powerfully than

---

[37] Mar. 28, 1770, Dexter, ed., *Diary of Stiles*, 1:44; Congregational Church Records, box 40, folder 4 (40-273), May 24, 1788 (list of pew holders Second Congregational Church), Newport Historical Society, Newport, R.I.

[38] For a discussion of the ways in which ministers in Newport related the Bible to their own civil unrest, see Elaine Forman Crane, *A Dependent People: Newport, Rhode Island, in the Revolutionary Era* (New York, 1985), pp. 129–32.

[39] June 30, 1774, Dexter, ed., *Diary of Stiles*, 1:447–48.

[40] George C. Mason, *Annals of Trinity Church, Newport, Rhode Island, 1698–1821* (Newport, 1890), pp. 126–27.

each other's. Their love for each other was undiminished by their political affections, but this was one woman, at least, who submitted herself to God's will (as interpreted by George Bisset), rather than to her husband's.

Mary Almy's account of the battle of Rhode Island, written in the form of a long letter to her husband, leaves little doubt of her political and personal affections.[41] In a reference to the French she asserted that "my dislike of the Nation that you call your friends, is the same as when you knew me," and, "I am for English government and an English fleet." Yet despite her political tendencies, which were shaped in some measure by her religious background, she leaned on that same faith to protect her husband from harm: "At last I shut myself from the family, to implore Heaven to protect you, and keep you from imprisonment and death. . . . Remember, in all your difficulties and trials of life, that when the All-wise disposer of human events thinks we have been sufficiently tried, then our patience in waiting will be amply repaid by a joyful meeting."[42]

Just as Faith Robinson Trumbull's unusual embroidery forces us to reconsider the art form a woman might choose through which she could express herself politically, so Mary Almy's story encourages a broad reevaluation of female political allegiance. There is little doubt that religious experiences, common to both men and women, motivated and shaped individual political affiliation. Yet political action differed from allegiance, since each specific response was likely to be determined by the sex of the respondent. Thus it was just as unlikely that Mrs. Trumbull's political leanings and artistic bent would combine to produce large oil paintings similar to those done by her son John as it was that Mrs. Almy would take up arms and join a regiment in defense of king and country— no matter how strong her sentiments might have been. As her diary reveals, however, she was no less politically motivated and no less determined to protect her home and children

[41] Mary Almy to Benjamin Almy, Sept. 2, 1778 (recounting the events of July 29–Aug. 31, 1778), in Elizabeth Evans, ed., *Weathering the Storm: Women of the American Revolution* (New York, 1975), pp. 245–70.

[42] Ibid., pp. 251, 260, 264–65.

than her husband, but her line of defense was with them, rather than in a distant field. She "boldly determined to keep possession" of her own house despite the possible consequences of the Franco-American assault on Newport in the summer of 1778. Frightened for her own safety and responsible for the lives of her children, she sustained herself with belief in the efficacy of prayer and the thought that "I have ever done to others as I wish they may do to me."[43] At the very least, Mary Almy refutes the whole notion of female timidity, submissiveness, and political dependence.

More important for our immediate perspective—that is, from a religious point of view—the story of the Almy family is probably more typical than we have imagined and thus raises new issues for further study of the Revolutionary era. The catalogue of parishioners compiled by Ezra Stiles for the year 1772 indicates that of the 176 names on his list, 22 belonged to women whose immediate families claimed other religious affiliations—or none at all. Thirty-two men fell into the same category. Thus, nearly one-third of Stiles's congregation were not, as he called them, "whole families." The missing members might have been safely ensconced with Samuel Hopkins, but they might also have been taking their cues from George Bisset at Trinity Church. As a result of these familial factions, individual members of the Coggeshall, Wanton, and Vernon families found themselves in opposing camps as hostilities spread from pamphlet to battlefield.[44]

Similarly, George Gibbs, who was a "principal and active tory," attended Newport's Anglican church, but the wife who shared his bed did not share his political principles. Mary Gibbs had been born a Channing. Her parents were members of the Second Congregational Church and she, along with her brothers and sisters, had been baptized in it. Mary and George were married at Trinity Church, but she remained a

---

[43] Ibid., pp. 260, 262–63.

[44] See Crane, *A Dependent People*, p. 135 and notes; the "Visiting Catalogue" of Ezra Stiles, Dec. 31, 1772, indicates the extent to which parishioners had wives or husbands who worshiped elsewhere (Dexter, ed., *Diary of Stiles*, 1:327–28).

faithful member of Stiles's congregation. Her father became one of the "warmest leaders" of the "Sons of Liberty." With this pedigree, Mary Channing Gibbs could hardly have become a loyalist.

Christopher Champlin and Margaret Grant Champlin followed the same pattern. Christopher was a member of Trinity Church. Margaret was baptized at Second Congregational. They, too, were married at Trinity. He was a suspected loyalist, she a proven supporter of the colonial cause, whose peacemaking efforts brought whigs and loyalists together after the British evacuation of Newport in 1779.[45]

In the end, there is a great paradox in how religious affiliation affected the Revolutionary movement in any community with a multiplicity of sects. On the one hand, the acceptance of religious differences may be seen as a step toward a more democratic, tolerant society. On the other, it is no less true that instead of acting as a catalyst for conciliation, religious diversity exacerbated discord and fostered hostility on the local level in a manner that had no comparison in the Civil War a century later. Nevertheless, as provocative as this issue is, and despite the questions it raises concerning family relationships in time of civil war, it will be no easy task to sort out the various components of this Revolutionary puzzle. In order to understand just how divisive religious affiliation became, it will be necessary to seek out church membership lists, trace families through different churches, and then determine political affiliation in the Revolution through family correspondence, diaries, or other sources. It is a worthwhile project, however, since it will present a different aspect of religious influence, offer a more gender-neutral picture of the American Revolution, and enhance appreciation for the intricacies of family networks.

WOMEN, RELIGION, AND REVOLUTION

If Faith Trumbull's religious persuasion stimulated a particular form of political expression suitable to her sex and station

[45] Mar. 1, 1777, Dexter, ed., *Diary of Stiles*, 2:131, 134; Dec. 31, 1772, ibid., 1:327; Mason, *Annals of Trinity Church*, pp. 126–27; Gibbs and Channing Family Records, box 2048, Newport Hist. Soc.; *Notes concerning the*

and Mary Almy's religious commitment dictated her political allegiance and response, it is also fair to say that ministerial exhortations motivated women as a group to contribute to the cause in a manner appropriate to eighteenth-century womanhood. This is not to argue, of course, that women were passive vessels, overwhelmed by ministerial majesty and unhesitatingly responsive to prescriptive advice from the pulpit. The fact that individual conscience played a role in church affiliation belies that assessment, as do the number of women who, for a variety of reasons (not the least of which was dissatisfaction with their ministers), requested dismissal to other churches. Yet even if female congregants could not be counted on to act as mere clerical conduits any more than their male counterparts, it is also true that the demographics of church membership strongly favored female involvement.

Although statistics relating to congregational size are difficult to find, available evidence indicates that by the end of the colonial period nearly 70 percent of those admitted to the church were female.[46] Edmund S. Morgan calculates that "the proportion of women to men in New England churches was seldom less than two to one and often, as at Newport, as high as three or four to one."[47] And even if the ratio of men to women appearing for worship on any given Sunday morning was less skewed than the full membership rolls suggest, it is still likely that far more women than men filled the pews.

As a result of this imbalance, the men of the rebel pulpit

Channing Family, collected by Edward T. Channing (Boston, 1895), p. 5; Grant, Champlin, Mason Papers, box 127, Newport Hist. Soc.; James M. Arnold, ed. *Vital Records of Rhode Island 1636–1850,* 1st ser. (Providence, 1892–1901).

[46]Richard D. Shiels, "The Feminization of American Congregationalism, 1730–1835," *American Quarterly* 33 (1981):46–50; Gerald F. Moran, "'Sisters' in Christ: Women and the Church in Seventeenth-Century New England," in Janet W. James, ed., *Women in American Religion* (Philadelphia, 1980), pp. 50–51; Mary Maples Dunn, "Saints and Sisters: Congregational and Quaker Women in the Early Colonial Period," in James, ed., *Women in American Religion,* pp. 35–36.

[47]Edmund S. Morgan, *The Gentle Puritan: A Life of Ezra Stiles, 1727–1795* (Chapel Hill, 1962), p. 188n.

could direct their seditious energies to the one audience that could best further the whig program through home manufacturing. By helping, as one woman recalled, "to form public opinion," the clergy simultaneously encouraged women to donate their time and skills in order to raise money for the provincial troops.[48]

During the nonimportation crisis of 1769, the Rev. Ezra Stiles of Newport recorded in his diary that he hosted a "Spinning Match" at his house. On that occasion, thirty-seven wheels hummed while the women spun ninety-four skeins, if not into gold, then into the next best thing—linen yarn. According to Stiles, the women not only brought their own flax, but "they made us a present of the whole. The Spinners were two Quakers, six Baptists, and twenty-nine of my own Society." That this was no minor event is attested to by the "six hundred Spectators" who visited the Spinners "in the course of the day."[49]

Each year for the next five, as the crisis escalated, Stiles held "a voluntary Bee" at his home. How his small house could have accommodated seventy wheels at one time defies imagination, but his reputation and penchant for quantifiable information renders his account above suspicion. In 1770, "ninety-two daughters of Liberty spun and reeled, respiting and assisting one another. . . . The Spinners were of all Denominations, Chh., Quakers, Bapt. & Congl. . . . Of the 70 stationed to the 70 Wheels, 41 or more were of my Meet., and of the 92 about 53 were mine."[50] According to his own "cursory Reckoning," those 53 represented about 40 percent of the total number of spinners in his congregation.[51]

We have no record of exactly what Stiles might have said to his congregation each year to elicit such a strong response,

[48] Fowler, "Ministers of Connecticut," p. 80.

[49] Apr. 26, 1769, Dexter, ed., *Diary of Stiles*, 1:8–9. See the discussion of spinning matches in Laurel Thatcher Ulrich, "'Daughters of Liberty': Religious Women in Revolutionary New England," in Ronald Hoffman and Peter J. Albert, eds., *Women in the Age of the American Revolution* (Charlottesville, Va., 1989), pp. 214–18.

[50] May 30, 1770, Dexter, ed., *Diary of Stiles*, 1:53.

[51] May 31, 1770, ibid.

but his surviving sermons are strongly political, couched in religious metaphors and allegories and clearly designed to ally his church with the whig cause. Thus, in response to Lexington and Concord, he alluded to Psalms 79 and 80 as he spoke of the heathen who shed the blood of God's servants "like water." In an attempt to engage the women of his congregation, perhaps he took his cue from the *Newport Mercury*, which offered the following advice: "Let your fingers embrace the needle, and the knitting kneedle be your Delight: then shall ye be praised, then shall it be said of you, *Many Daughters have done virtuously, but the Daughters of Newport excel them all.*"[52] These words were not the product of an editor's inventive quill but rather a paraphrase of Proverbs 31, where the attributes of a virtuous wife were spelled out in considerable detail. The newspaper advanced them in an attempt to foster a nascent clothing industry in the colonies at a time when trade had declined and home manufacturing was a volatile issue. By cloaking patriotism in religious garb, rebels won women to a spate of knitting parties where they were "determined to excite themselves, in a constitutional method, to support the cause of Liberty."[53]

The daughters of Newport were no more virtuous than their sisters elsewhere in the colonies, and the women of other congregations no less susceptible to the supplications of their spiritual leaders, once they were persuaded to take sides. In November 1775, the Rev. Judah Champion, minister at Litchfield, told his assembled group one Sabbath morning about the suffering of the American troops in Canada as the ill-clothed army was about to embark for Quebec. The women of the congregation reportedly questioned him further after the service and then subsequently spent the afternoon spinning or knitting.[54] Although performing such tasks on a Sunday would have been highly improper under normal circumstances, on this Sabbath there would be no recriminations. The work was done in God's service.

At the same time, there were other considerations that

[52] Apr. 23, 1775, ibid., p. 538; *Newport Mercury*, Dec. 28, 1767.

[53] *Newport Mercury*, Feb. 13, 1769.

[54] Fowler, "Ministers of Connecticut," pp. 57–58.

cannot be measured in terms of virtue or patriotism. Those skeins of yarn had economic implications. Dr. Stiles noted that the 172 skeins that were spun in May 1774 brought a profit of £4 sterling, which in the context of 1774 was considerably more than mere pocket change.[55] For £4 sterling one could buy a pew in the Old South Church in Boston, a chest of drawers, or a cart. Four pounds was the equivalent of a cow and calf, five acres of common in Northampton, Massachusetts, 491 pounds of pork, or two canoes. Since a very serviceable gun could be purchased for little more than £1 (and an old one for five shillings), the economic importance of the spinning bees in terms of home manufacturing and the eventual war effort was considerable.[56]

It is possible that the close relationship between women, religion, and revolution was enhanced in other ways by the disproportionate number of women who were either members or congregants of the New England churches. Since relatively few sermons survive from the Revolutionary era, we cannot say with any certainty whether the clergy tailored their messages to the composition of the audience. One might be tempted to think that each time a minister invoked the family analogy (Britain as mother, the colonies as children) or the idea of nurture (God as the force that planted and tended the colonial vine) he was sermonizing in a code that would appeal most directly to his female parishioners, but the evidence is far too sparse for such a conclusion. Moreover, these particular metaphors permeated the newspaper and pamphlet literature of the Revolutionary movement, and in that form were directed to anyone—male or female—who could read or hear. Surviving sermons suggest that ministers relied as heavily on whig ideology as they did on religious doctrine and familial allusions—the former arguments directed, no doubt, to male attendees, since strictly political matters were considered to be outside women's sphere of comprehension.[57]

[55] May 18, 1773, Dexter, ed., *Diary of Stiles*, 1:440.

[56] Alice Hanson Jones, *American Colonial Wealth: Documents and Methods*, 3 vols. (New York, 1977).

[57] In her study of southern Presbyterian ministers during the Revolution, Alice Baldwin noted that their political concepts were based on the Bible

Whatever the composition of the congregation, however, and no matter to whom the message was initially directed, surely the ministers intended that their passionate pleas in favor of Independence should reach as many additional people as possible. On the basis of numbers alone, women were best positioned to spread the word. More important, the focus of the message itself was one that women, in particular, could carry most convincingly. The clergy who supported separation from England argued with certainty that God could not condone the licentiousness, immorality, and lack of virtue exhibited by Great Britain. It followed then, that if the colonists did not abandon England, they themselves ran the risk of abandonment by God. Since late eighteenth-century rhetoric extolled both female virtue and the innate ability of women to help men achieve moral excellence, the equation of women = morality = resistance to Great Britain may have prompted an unconscious receptivity to arguments presented by members of the female sex.[58] By engaging in this process, women combined politics and religion in a way that was both unique and central to the Revolutionary experience.

The chain of persuasion that began with a sermon initially linked church to home. Yet the female world of the eighteenth century extended far beyond home and family, and most women were well situated to act as the intermediaries by which the ideology of rebellion passed from the pulpit to the community at large.

In towns and cities all along the seaboard, women were highly visible as purveyors of goods in the markets and in

---

and that they placed great emphasis on ideas relating to compact and inalienable rights that were God-given and therefore natural (Baldwin, "Sowers of Sedition").

[58]The importance of women as disseminators of information propounded by the clergy in the nineteenth century is discussed in Ann Douglas, *The Feminization of American Culture* (New York, 1977), pp. 97–99. For an excellent analysis of virtue and gender see Jan Lewis, "The Republican Wife: Virtue and Seduction in the Early Republic," *William and Mary Quarterly* 3d ser. 44 (1987):689–721, and Ruth H. Bloch, "The Gendered Meanings of Virtue in Revolutionary America," *Signs: Journal of Women in Culture and Society* 13 (1987):37–58.

shops along the harbor. In addition to the public contact they had as retailers, many women ran or worked in coffeehouses, inns, taverns, and boardinghouses. Mary Gould Almy was the proprietor of such an establishment, and her boarders could easily have received a second-hand dose of the Reverend Bisset's "high tory Sermon," whether they wanted to or not.[59] Sarah Osborn, also of Newport, held prayer meetings and taught school. A devoted member of Samuel Hopkins's First Congregational Church, her religious and political enthusiasm surely reinforced her minister's warnings and were, in turn, communicated to the people with whom she came in contact. In a letter to the Rev. Joseph Fish of Stonington, Connecticut, after the evacuation of Newport in 1779, she reported that the "deliverance of Newport" was due to prayer and hoped that she would be forgiven for praying so fervently for "the safety of God's little remnant."[60] She, at least, was convinced she had done her part as a religious patriot.

In the 1930s, Mary Dewson, a leader of the National Consumer League and a staunch New Deal supporter, urged female Democratic party workers to be the "mouth to mouth, house to house interpreters of the New Deal."[61] It is not unlikely that women of the Revolutionary era were encouraged to take on the same role. Each time a woman knocked on a neighbor's door to collect clothing for the rebel forces or money for the loyalist cause, she may have had to explain her position in order to win a donation. As a communal guardian of virtue, and because she was likely to have been motivated by what she heard in church, she probably did so in religious language.

Arguments have been made elsewhere for the connection between women, the Revolution, and a heightened sense of morality that extended into the post-Revolutionary era and

[59] Dexter, ed., *Diary of Stiles*, 1:447–58.

[60] Sarah Osborn to the Rev. Joseph Fish (n.d.), *Familiar Letters Written by Mrs. Sarah Osborn and Miss Susanna Anthony Late of Newport, Rhode Island* (Newport, 1807), p. 154.

[61] Quoted in William H. Chafe, *The American Woman: Her Changing Social, Economic, and Political Roles, 1920–1970* (New York, 1972), p. 40.

beyond.[62] That same morality would eventually link women—
as nurturers—with pacifism and the peace movement, but
when the North American colonies seceded from Great Britain, that association had not yet been formulated, much less
articulated. Thus women were intellectually free to be persuaded to take sides in the conflict and to persuade others to
do the same. That many women did so for what they perceived to be spiritual reasons, and that they were convincing
in that role, only disguises the political influence they wielded
in the name of religion.

[62]Rosemary Skinner Keller, "Women, Civil Religion, and the American
Revolution," in Rosemary Radford Ruether and Rosemary Skinner Keller,
eds., *Women and Religion in America*, vol. 2, *The Colonial and Revolutionary Periods* (New York, 1983), pp. 368–80; Martha Tomhave Blauvelt, "Women and
Revivalism," in Reuther and Keller, eds., *Women and Religion*, vol. 1, *The
Nineteenth Century* (New York, 1981), pp. 1–9; Robert Bellah, "The Revolution and the Civil Religion," in Jerald C. Brauer, ed., *Religion and the American Revolution* (Philadelphia, 1976), pp. 55–73; Elaine Forman Crane,
"Dependence in the Era of Independence: The Role of Women in a Republican Society," in Jack P. Greene, ed., *The American Revolution: Its Character
and Limits* (New York, 1987), pp. 269–70.

SYLVIA R. FREY

"The Year of Jubilee Is Come"

Black Christianity in the Plantation South in Post-Revolutionary America

Arise O zion! rise and shine.
  Behold thy light is come;
Thy glorious conq'ring King is near
  To take his exiles home;
His spirit now is pouring out
  To set poor captives free
The day of wonder now is come
  The year of Jubilee.

IN THE DECADES before the American Revolution a second revolution unfolded. The one, largely secular in origin, drew upon Enlightenment ideas to create a religion of humanity that set forth the guiding precepts of liberty and equality. The other, evangelical in nature, was profoundly influenced by transatlantic ideas and advanced similar notions of spiritual freedom and the brotherhood of man. Mutually supportive, their combined force produced revolutionary aspirations in black as well as white southerners, aspirations that for southern slaves were soon dashed on the shoals of reality raised by the war and the solidly entrenched slave system that emerged in its aftermath. The impulse for freedom persisted, however, kept alive by a dramatic upsurge of evangelical ardor and a

nascent, if short-lived, organized religious antislavery movement in the post-Revolutionary South. Constrained from exercising their full range of moral, intellectual, and emotional
powers in other ways, slaves pursued religion, which for them
became the chief—for most the only—way to define self
and discover community. The Afro-Baptist and Afro-Method-
ist churches that emerged thus represented a culmination
both of a search for faith and a quest for spiritual independence.

African-American Christianity is a product of white Protestantism, although from the very beginning it was Protestantism with a difference. Historical research has generally
identified four stages of development in the history of black
Christianity. The earliest was a complex mix, the roots of
which were found in the social environment of Africa where
clan life under the chief and the influence of the priest were
the dominating influences. The second, or formative, period
in the development of Afro-Christianity began in 1702, with
the first Christian efforts to convert slaves, and extended
roughly to 1829, when the South Carolina Conference of the
Methodist Episcopal Church launched the first plantation
missions. The third, a period of expansion and consolidation
that extended to the outbreak of the Civil War, was a time
when the plantation missions created black southern Protestantism, characterized principally by demographically biracial
churches. The final stage began in the postbellum period,
when religious autonomy and totally separate structures and
denominations emerged rapidly. This paper will concentrate
on the formative period, with appropriate references to African roots.

The slave ships that transported Africans to the British
mainland colonies, beginning early in the seventeenth century, carried not only human cargo, but also, as Roger Bastide
has observed, gods, beliefs, and lore.[1] Although the early slave

---

[1] Roger Bastide, *African Civilizations in the New World,* trans. Peter Green
(New York, 1971), p. 23. See also Charles H. Long, "Perspectives for a
Study of Afro-American Religion in the United States," *History of Religions*
11 (1971):57.

trade to the Chesapeake and, later, to the lower South, dealt mainly in slaves from the West Indies, that source declined over time, and slaves imported directly from various sites along the West African coast, especially Gambia, Sierra Leone, and Angola, came to dominate the market.[2] Inasmuch as they represented a cross-section of the African population, they brought with them a variety of culture forms, the most important of which was religion.

Although African culture was diverse, there was broad cultural unity among the West African societies from which most American slaves came. The basic features common throughout Africa centered on several concepts. Most African peoples recognized the existence of a cosmic power or supreme being who was both transcendent and immanent, omnipresent and omnipotent. Belief in the continued existence of ancestral spirits, who act as mediators between God and living members of society and therefore provide a vital link between the living and the spirit world, was also an important component of traditional African religion. This accounts in part for the African concept of humanity, which is defined in the context of the community and is dramatically articulated through music, dancing, and various other forms of artistic expression.[3]

The establishment of slavery severed the direct connection with Africa, but not with West African traditional religions. Torn from their religious moorings, slaves were temporarily left in a spiritual vacuum that, as a deeply religious people, they felt impelled to fill. To a large extent the survival of African culture in America, as in the Caribbean, was made pos-

[2]See for example Allan Kulikoff, "A 'Prolifick' People: Black Population Growth in the Chesapeake Colonies, 1700–1790," *Southern Studies* 16 (1977):391–414; Russell R. Menard, "The Maryland Slave Population, 1658 to 1730: A Demographic Profile of Blacks in Four Counties," *William and Mary Quarterly*, 3d ser. 32 (1975):29–54; Darold D. Wax, "'New Negroes Are Always in Demand': The Slave Trade in Eighteenth-Century Georgia," *Georgia Historical Quarterly* 68 (1984):193–220.

[3]John S. Mbiti, *African Religions and Philosophy* (New York, 1969); Newell Snow Booth, Jr., ed., *African Religions* (New York, 1977); Gwinyai H. Muzorewa, *The Origins and Development of African Theology* (Maryknoll, N.Y., 1985), pp. 10–18.

sible by the presence of Obeah men, African religious men who practiced a traditional African religion known as Obi. Although the plantation organization replaced the clan, it permitted the survival of the priest, whose enduring authority helped to create the first African-American institution, voodooism, which was derived from Obi. Through the practice of magic, witchcraft, and sorcery, slave society was able to perpetuate the existence and values of traditional religion. Passed from one generation to another through the oral tradition common throughout Africa, the beliefs, fears, and superstitions connected with those practices continued to play a prominent role in African-American life many years after contact with Christian teaching and education.

The persistence of West African religious beliefs and traditions, particularly monotheism, provided fertile ground for the seeds of evangelical Christianity, the first of which took root during a series of local awakenings that began east of the mountains in Hanover County, Virginia. The first direct effort to provide religious instruction for slaves was made by a young Presbyterian minister, Samuel Davies, who taught an estimated 1,000 blacks at the various places in Hanover, Henrico, Goochland, Caroline, and Louisa counties where he alternately officiated. The Rev. Robert Henry, the young Scottish pastor of Cub Creek, on the north bank of the Staunton River, and of Briery church, some twenty miles away, continued the work that Davies had begun. Henry's successors added about two hundred members to the Cub Creek church. Many of these black converts later became Baptists or Methodists, but the members of the Cub Creek church remained devout Presbyterians.[4]

The two main denominational groups that involved large numbers of blacks were, however, the Baptists and Methodists, both of which made tentative efforts to Christianize slaves during the First Great Awakening. In 1758 nine Baptist

[4]Benjamin Fawcett, *A Compassionate Address to the Christian Negroes in Virginia, and Other British Colonies in North-America* (London, 1756), pp. 33–37; William Pope Harrison, comp. and ed., *The Gospel among the Slaves: A Short Account of Missionary Operations among the African Slaves of the Southern States* (Nashville, 1893), pp. 51, 58.

churches were formed in Virginia. One of them, at Bluestone in Mecklenburg County, was composed principally of slaves from the estate of William Byrd. The breakup of Byrd's quarters scattered the congregation, but the church survived in a weakened form until 1772, when it was reconstituted and a white minister, John Marshall, was installed. In the meantime, the pious black converts continued to spread the gospel through the various neighborhoods into which they fell. Under the preaching of John Williams, a second, predominantly black Baptist church was founded about 1770 at Allen's Creek, also in Mecklenburg County.[5] In 1774 a black congregation formed in Petersburg. The first Baptist church in the city, it subsequently became the First African Church, the largest church in the Portsmouth Association.[6]

As Hanover was the center of the black Presbyterian revival impulse and Mecklenburg the center from which Baptist evangelistic activity among slaves radiated, so Baltimore was the early center of revivalism among black Methodists. In 1764 Robert Strawbridge founded the first Methodist society in America, at Sam's Creek in Frederick County, Maryland. A year later he visited Baltimore and preached in the streets from a homemade pulpit. Soon he organized a society and built Lovely Lane, the first Methodist meetinghouse in Baltimore, and shortly after formed Strawberry Alley. Both Lovely Lane and Strawberry Alley were integrated. During the Methodist revivals of 1773–76, which spread through fourteen counties in Virginia and two in North Carolina, hundreds of slaves were converted, thus establishing the first major beachheads in southeastern Virginia and in the area of Albemarle Sound in northeastern North Carolina.[7]

When the Revolution came, the effects of the First Great

[5] Robert B. Semple, *A History of the Rise and Progress of the Baptists in Virginia* (Richmond, 1810), pp. 222–23. The most complete listing of early black Baptist churches is Mechal Sobel, *Trabelin' On: The Slave Journey to an Afro-Baptist Faith* (Westport, Conn., 1979), pp. 250–356.

[6] David Benedict, *A General History of the Baptist Denomination in America* (New York, 1848), p. 664.

[7] Rt. Rev. James A. Handy, *Scraps of African Methodist Episcopal History* (Philadelphia, 1902), pp. 13–14; Harrison, *Gospel among the Slaves*, p. 53.

Awakening were still visible in the South. Baptists were established in Virginia, and the Methodists had effectively penetrated Maryland. The outbreak of the Revolutionary War, the British invasion of Virginia, and their amphibious raids on settlements on both sides of the Chesapeake Bay halted the process of church building and scattered some of the black congregations. Nonetheless, these early groups formed the nucleus of an Afro-Christian community in Virginia and Maryland that would increase numerically and spread geographically during the period of the Second Great Awakening—the central and defining event in the development of Afro-Christianity. The decline produced by the disruptions of war ended in Virginia in 1785. The creation of the Methodist Episcopal Church in 1784, followed by the extension of the itinerant system throughout the South, led to a period of revivalism that began on the banks of the James River and spread with astonishing rapidity over most of the state. During the seasons of revival that began in the Chesapeake in 1785 and continued until 1791–92, and in the great revival that spread from Canada to Georgia in 1796–97, both Baptist and Methodist denominations grew rapidly. Expansion thereafter waxed and waned until 1801, when the first camp meeting exploded on the Delmarva Peninsula, creating a great burst of religious frenzy that rolled unchecked across the southern prairies between 1801 and 1811.Out of its heaving tide, African-American Christianity was born.[8]

The process of propagating Christianity among southern slaves was complex and continuous and was set in motion under various auspices. During the Second Great Awakening, it was initiated by white itinerant preachers, who set Christian ideas in circulation among members of the slave community. From the beginning of the Methodist ministry, itinerants devoted special attention to slaves. Francis Asbury, Thomas Coke, Freeborn Garrettson, William Capers, Joseph Travis, James Meacham, and others all set aside special times to preach to slaves and adapted their instruction to the per-

---

[8]For details see William Henry Williams, *The Garden of American Methodism: The Delmarva Peninsula, 1769–1820* (Wilmington, Del., 1984).

ceived needs of these blacks. Asbury assembled them every morning at six o'clock for instruction and prayer and regularly conducted love feasts, which were "highly prized" by the slaves, perhaps for the opportunity it gave them to speak of their trials and sufferings.[9] Beginning in 1787 a policy of segregated instruction was formally adopted by the Methodist Conference, which approved a resolution calling on itinerants to supervise the instruction of slaves and "not suffer them to stay late and meet by themselves."[10]

The historical evidence suggests quite strongly that although many slaves learned about Christianity from white preachers, during the early phases of evangelization the majority of black converts may have first heard the Christian gospel from other blacks. White missionaries were the first to take the gospel to slaves during the First Great Awakening. They continued to play a major role in the Second Great Awakening and, after 1829, when the plantation mission movement was launched, probably did most of the work of evangelizing. In the period between 1776 and 1829, however, many of the black congregations that emerged in the South were led by black preachers, some of whom succeeded in establishing separate black churches that provided a physical structure for the expression of black aspirations for spiritual independence.

Appropriately enough, the trend was established in 1776 in Virginia, the seedbed of Afro-Christianity, when a black Baptist named Moses began preaching and holding meetings among the slaves in Williamsburg. Shortly after, a free black man, Gowan Pamphlet, arrived from Middlesex County, where he had been preaching for some time, and began to preach and baptize in Williamsburg and nearby James City County. Although he was ordered by the Dover Association to

[9]Elmer T. Clark, J. Manning Potts, and Jacob S. Payton, eds., *The Journal and Letters of Francis Asbury*, 3 vols. (Nashville, 1958), 1:56–57, 89, 222; 2:43–44, 70, 77, 424; Nathan Bangs, comp., *The Life of the Reverend Freeborn Garrettson* (New York, 1845), p. 60; Harrison, *Gospel among the Slaves*, pp. 141, 200; Thomas Osmond Sumners, ed., *Autobiography of the Reverend Joseph Travis* (Nashville, 1856), p. 55.

[10]*Minutes of the Methodist Conferences, Annually Held in America from 1773–1794* (Philadelphia, 1795), pp. 104, 147.

stop preaching on pain of excommunication, Pamphlet persisted, and he and a number of his followers were expelled
from the church. Pamphlet then formed his own church and,
without benefit of ordination, continued to administer the
sacraments. When the black Williamsburg Baptist Church was
admitted to the Dover Association in 1791, it had 500
members.[11]

After 1785 a number of Afro-Baptist churches sprang up in
the heavily black eastern corner of the state, from Portsmouth
and Norfolk to Petersburg and Richmond along both banks of
the James River. When the interracial church at Portsmouth,
founded in 1789, lost its founding minister, Thomas Ar-
misted, the congregation replaced him with Jacob Bishop, an
itinerant black preacher whose freedom had been purchased
by "brethren" in Northampton County.[12] Although Bishop
was soon forced out, black membership in the church continued to increase, and in 1805 most of the black members of
Portsmouth's Baptist church withdrew to join the Norfolk
Colored Baptist Church, formed in 1800. Another black
church was organized by a slave named Jack in Nottoway
County. A licensed Baptist preacher, Jack gained fame in a
public debate with a well-known black preacher named
Campbell, who advocated "noise and spirit" over the Bible.
In scoring a victory, Jack not only stopped a "heresy" but
won over Campbell's entire following. His church was known
simply as "Uncle Jack's."[13]

Although Gillfield, originally known as Davenport's
church, was an interracial church when constituted in 1788,
the great majority of its original 165 members were slaves
from Prince George County, and in 1797 it was organized as
a separate black church, the Second African Church of Petersburg. Around 1800 the Davenport church disbanded, and its
black members organized themselves as the Sandy Beach
church on the Appomattox River in Pocahontas. That site was

[11]Semple, *Rise and Progress of the Baptists*, pp. 97, 115.

[12]Lemuel Burkitt and Jesse Read, *A Concise History of the Kehukee Baptist
Association* (Halifax, N.C., 1803), pp. 253, 259; Semple, *Rise and Progress of
the Baptists*, p. 355.

[13]W. E. B. DuBois, ed., *The Negro Church* (Atlanta, 1903), p. 37.

also later abandoned and the congregation moved to Collier's Alley and organized as the Church of the Lord Jesus Christ of Petersburg.[14] In neighboring Charles City County preaching and prayer meetings were held as early as 1775 in a meetinghouse known as the "old log church." There was no organized church, however, and black Baptists had to travel to Petersburg—a three- to four-mile walk to Backhurst's Landing on Queen's Creek, then a short dugout trip on the creek followed by an eight-mile journey on the rough waters of the James, to the muddy Appomattox for the trip past Bermuda Hundred and City Point to Petersburg. In an 1809 revival, preachers from Petersburg spoke in the old log meetinghouse and converted Abram Brown, apparently a free black farmer of some substance. Brown led the movement to form an independent black church to provide a more accessible place of worship for the growing numbers of black Baptists. In August 1810 it was constituted as the Elam Baptist Church, and in 1813 it was admitted to the Dover Association.[15] A number of Afro-Baptist churches also sprang up in the fertile ground once tilled by the Reverend Davies. Shortly after Lord Cornwallis's surrender, the First Church of Richmond was formed. Between 1788 and 1808 its membership increased to 560. In 1820 seventeen members were sent out to form a separate church, the Second African Church.[16]

The creation of the Afro-Baptist church in Georgia was also largely the work of slaves and free blacks. As in Virginia, the seeds of Baptist faith and practice were planted by white preachers, but the tillers of the soil were slaves. George Liele, born a slave in 1750 in Virginia, was the founding father of the Afro-Baptist church in Georgia. Brought to Georgia in

[14]"History of the Gillfield Baptist Church," Records of Gillfield Baptist Church, 1827–1939, Alderman Library, University of Virginia, Charlottesville (microfilm); Semple, *Rise and Progress of the Baptists*, p. 361.

[15]*Organization and Development of the Elam Baptist Church, 1810–1910* (Ruthville, Va., 1976), pp. 10–13; see also *Minutes of the Dover Baptist Association for the Year 1813* (Richmond, 1798–1832), p. 5.

[16]Benedict, *History of the Baptist Denomination*, pp. 660, 662; *Minutes of the Dover Association*, 1821, p. 6.

1773 by his owner, Henry Sharp, Liele was converted by Matthew Moore, a Baptist minister in Burke County, and in 1774 he began to preach at various plantations along the Savannah River as far as Brampton. The first black Baptist in Georgia, Liele was ordained by the Buckhead Creek church on May 20, 1775, a date subsequently adopted by the First African Baptist Church as the official date of its birth, although it is not clear whether the church was fully organized.[17] During the Revolutionary War Liele remained at Tybee, devoting his ministerial activities to the church there. At the end of the war, perhaps fearing reenslavement, he fled with the British to Jamaica where he established the first Baptist church on the island. Before his departure, Liele baptized David George, a runaway slave from Essex County, Virginia, and Andrew Bryan, the slave of Jonathan Bryan. George and Jesse Peter, fellow slaves from the plantation of Thomas Galphin, formed a small church composed of eight members at Silver Bluff in Aiken County on the South Carolina bank of the Savannah River. In 1778 George led a group of about fifty fugitive slaves, presumably some of them members of the Silver Bluff church, to Savannah. At the end of the war, he evacuated with the British to Nova Scotia and there formed the first black Baptist church. Later George led his entire black congregation to Sierra Leone and established the first Baptist church there. In 1795 he baptized the first African-born person.[18] In 1791 Jesse Peter led 113 members of the Silver Bluff congregation to a site near Augusta and there established the Springfield African church. In 1802 it reported 220 members, and at Peter's death in 1809 membership stood at 505. By 1836 it had grown to 1,294.[19]

[17] Edgar Garfield Thomas, *The First African Baptist Church of North America* (Savannah, 1925), pp. 21–22.

[18] "An Account of the Life of Mr. David George, from Sierra Leone in Africa," *The Baptist Annual Register, 1790/93–1801/2,* 4 vols. (London, 1801–2), 1790, pp. 473–84; see also "Letters Showing the Rise and Progress of the Early Negro Churches of Georgia and the West Indies," *Journal of Negro History* 1 (1916):69–92.

[19] Sobel, *Trabelin' On,* pp. 314–15; Jesse H. Campbell, *Georgia Baptists: Historical and Biographical* (Macon, Ga., 1874), p. 64; Minutes of the Georgia

The man who brought the seeds of faith to full maturity and made the Christianization of slaves acceptable in Georgia was, however, Andrew Bryan. About a month after Liele's departure for Jamaica, Bryan began preaching to slaves in a rough wooden building on Edward Davis's land at Yamacraw in the Savannah suburbs. The rapid growth of Bryan's following alarmed some whites, and Bryan, his brother Sampson, and some fifty other church members were twice imprisoned and were severely whipped for defying a 1792 law that forbade the assembly of slaves for divine worship contrary to the patrol act. Befriended by Chief Justices Henry Osbourne, James Habersham, and David Montague, Bryan was allowed to resume preaching at Brampton, three miles from Savannah. In 1788 he was ordained by Abraham Marshall of Kiokee, who constituted Bryan's group of 80 followers as a Baptist congregation—the first formally organized Baptist church, black or white, in Savannah. Bryan's political talents and his ability to develop and lead an evangelical community led to the rapid growth of the Afro-Baptist church in Georgia. By 1792 the First Colored (later, African) Church of Savannah had 235 members plus an additional 350 converts whose masters would not consent to their baptism. By 1802 Bryan had converted enough people to form a second church of 200 members, and on January 1, 1803, Henry Cunningham was ordained to its pastorate. The next day 250 additional members were sent out from the First Colored church to form the Ogeechee Colored Baptist Church fourteen miles south of the city; Henry Francis, who was ordained May 23, 1802, assumed its pastorate.[20]

In South Carolina there was at least one flourishing center of Afro-Baptist faith, the Welsh Neck church on the Pee Dee River. Established as a church in 1737 by fifteen emigrants from Welsh Tract, Delaware, the church remained all-white until June 27, 1779, when Alingo, the slave of Aaron David,

---

Association, 1803–1905, Stetson Memorial Library, Mercer University, Macon, Ga., 1803, 1805, 1807, 1809, 1816 (microfilm).

[20]Benedict, *History of the Baptist Denomination,* pp. 740–41; Rev. Henry Holcombe, ed., *Georgia Analytical Repository,* 2d ed., 6 vols. (Savannah, 1802–3), 1:185–88.

and Plato, Stephen, Darien, and Susannah, slaves of Col. Alexander McIntosh, were baptized. Over the course of the summer, eighty-seven blacks were baptized under the preaching of the Rev. Elhanan Winchester, and on August 24 Winchester organized an independent church for blacks. Welsh Neck remained a separate black church until 1782 when, unable to find a pastor, they accepted the invitation of the Rev. Edmund Botsford to rejoin the white church. During the revival under Botsford's preaching in 1790, several hundred slaves were converted, many of them by black members of Botsford's church "who go to the plantations, and preach to their own colour on Lord-day evenings, and at other times when we have no services in the meeting house."[21]

From the earliest appearance of Methodism in the South, blacks shared largely in the labors of the ministry. Their proselytizing efforts resulted in the rapid rise of societies predominantly or exclusively black in membership. Among the most famous of the black preachers was Harry Hosier, one of the most powerful exhorters on the continent. Hosier traveled in turn with Asbury, Coke, Garrettson, Richard Whatcoat, Jesse Lee, and other distinguished Methodist preachers, principally to preach to the blacks. Asbury openly declared that the best way he knew to obtain a large congregation was to announce in advance that Hosier would preach.[22] Morris Brown, one of the leaders of the movement to organize the black Methodists of Charleston into an independent organization, regularly went out on Saturday nights to preach the gospel to slaves on plantations in surrounding parishes. There were scores of black preachers like Punch, who was converted by Asbury on one of his early tours of South Carolina and

[21] Minutes of Welsh Neck Baptist Church, Society Hill, S.C., 1737–1841, Baptist Historical Collection, Furman University, Greenville, S.C., June-Sept. 1779, Apr. 1782, Mar. 22, 1793, Apr. 21, 1798 (microfilm); the quotation is from Edmund Botsford to the Editor, Apr. 25–Aug., 1790, *Baptist Annual Register,* 1790, p. 105.

[22] Harrison, *Gospel among the Slaves,* p. 127; *Extracts of the Journals of the Reverend Dr. Coke's Five Visits to America* (London, 1793), p. 18; Clark et al., eds., *Journal and Letters of Asbury,* 1:403.

soon began holding prayer meetings at night in the slave quarters on a plantation in All-Saints Parish. By the time the Waccamaw Neck Mission was established, the "old bishop," as Punch was known to his followers, had between two and three hundred members in society.[23]

In parts of the South, Methodism was implanted first among the slave population. When William Meredith introduced Methodism in Wilmington, North Carolina, in 1784, his first congregations were entirely black.[24] New Bern, North Carolina, had a separate African Methodist society, which Asbury reported in 1796 was "about to build a place of worship," while to Asbury's disgust the white citizens were still only "full of good resolutions" to finish their meetinghouse. When he visited Edenton, North Carolina, in 1810, Asbury found eighteen whites and one hundred Africans in society and laid the foundations "for an African chapel."[25] In South Carolina the missionary efforts of Asbury, Travis, Henry Boehm, and others yielded results first among the slave and free black communities of Georgetown and Charleston. Georgetown was one of the focal centers of Methodism in South Carolina. When Asbury visited there in 1797, there were twenty whites and between three and four hundred blacks in society. Twelve years later when Travis preached there, the society consisted of three white males, a few white females, and "a goodly number of coloured people."[26] In Charleston, characterized by Asbury as "the seat of Satan, dissipation and folly," only "women and Africans" attended church services. The Cumberland Street church, the first Methodist meetinghouse in Charleston, had a mixed congregation of forty white members and fifty-three blacks when it was founded in 1787. Bethel church, completed in 1799 with

---

[23] Harrison, *Gospel among the Slaves*, p. 179; Daniel Alexander Payne, *History of the African Methodist Episcopal Church* (New York, 1969), p. 264.

[24] Payne, *African Methodist Episcopal Church*, p. 142; Sumners, ed., *Autobiography of Travis*, p. 71.

[25] Clark et al., eds., *Journal and Letters of Asbury*, 2:326, 628.

[26] Sumners, ed., *Autobiography of Travis*, p. 53.

contributions made by black and white members, was also predominantly black.[27]

Several of the predominantly black Methodist churches succeeded in establishing distinctive self-governing bodies. In 1817 Bethel's black membership attempted to take over the church on the grounds that they "had contributed largely to its erection." The failure of that effort, followed by a dispute over the building of a hearse house on the black burial lot adjoining Bethel church, led to the walkout of over 4,000 black Methodists and the creation of a separate church, the African Methodist Episcopal Church, which was admitted into full communion with Bishop Richard Allen's African Methodist Society in Philadelphia.[28] Harsh reprisals following the Denmark Vesey plot put an end to the separate existence of the African Methodist Episcopal Church in Charleston, however.

Sometime in 1785 the white membership of the Lovely Lane and Strawberry Alley meetinghouses in Baltimore decided to restrict black church members to pews in the gallery and forbade them to take communion with whites. Disturbed by their exclusion, black members withdrew from the two meetinghouses in 1786 and 1787, their secession anticipating by three weeks the withdrawal of Richard Allen and Philadelphia blacks from St. George Methodist Episcopal Church.[29] Led by Jacob Fortie, the separatists formed an independent prayer group that culminated eventually in the formation of a Colored Methodist Society. During a meeting with Asbury, the separatists discussed the possibility of forming a distinctly "African, yet Methodist Church." Disturbed by their demands

[27]Albert M. Shipp, *History of Methodism in South Carolina* (Nashville, 1883), p. 164; Clark et al., eds., *Journal and Letters of Asbury,* 1:535 n. 17, 2:119, 199, 414, 487.

[28]Rev. Abel McKee Chreitzberg, *Early Methodism in the Carolinas* (Nashville, 1897), pp. 156–57.

[29]The best general history of the Baltimore churches is Bettye C. Thomas, *History of the Sharp Street Memorial Methodist Episcopal Church, 1787–1920* (Baltimore, 1977). I am grateful to Phoebe Jacobson of the Maryland Hall of Records for calling this to my attention.

for "greater privileges than the white stewards and trustees ever had a right to claim," Asbury refused his approval, and the group remained under the governance of the white Methodist Episcopal Church until 1816.[30] Out of it, however, came the first two black Methodist churches in Baltimore, Sharp Street and Bethel, which in 1816 separated and joined Richard Allen's African Methodist Episcopal Church.[31]

These and other early sources were the centers from which evangelistic activity among the slave population radiated, giving to black Christianity by 1800 a definitive shape. Because they did not maintain racially distinctive records, there is no way to determine the number of black Baptists. According to John Asplund's *Universal Register,* there was a reported total of 38,922 Baptists in 1795, 22,500 of whom were located in Virginia, 5,135 in South Carolina, 7,625 in North Carolina, and 3,662 in Georgia. Asplund's estimate that nearly two out of every five southern Baptists were black suggests a rough approximation of about 15,500, the majority of whom were apparently in Virginia.[32]

Methodists did preserve separate returns of black and white members, and their reports offer the clearest picture of the dynamics of growth. In the beginning Maryland, "the heart of Methodism," was the major concentration of Afro-Methodism. In 1794 in five Eastern Shore counties, Cecil, Kent, Queen Anne's, Talbot, and Caroline, black Methodists numbered 1,821, or 43 percent of the Methodists. On the Western Shore, they numbered 2,611, almost 55 percent of the Methodists. The center of their strength in the state was Calvert County, which reported 1,102 black and 682 white members in society. In neighboring Virginia, where the Baptists were more firmly established, small black Methodist societies were spread throughout the state, most of them in

[30] Clark et al., eds., *Journal and Letters of Asbury,* 2:65.

[31] Handy, *African Methodist Episcopal History,* pp. 13–14; Thomas, *History of the Sharp Street Church.* This brief history is not paginated.

[32] John Asplund, *The Universal Register of the Baptist Denomination in North America, for the Years 1794 and 1795* (Hanover, N.H., 1796), pp. 68, 82.

such towns as Williamsburg, Portsmouth, Gloucester, and Norfolk in the heavily black southeastern portion of the state.[33]

The seeds of faith first planted in North Carolina by Joseph Pilmoor had also begun to bear fruit among the black population. In 1794 the Roanoke Circuit in the Albemarle Sound region had 800 Methodists, half of whom were black. In the Tar River Circuit, the only other area of significant Methodist strength, blacks represented slightly over 30 percent of the total membership of over 1,600. Although Pilmoor's journey had taken him through the heavily black Cape Fear region, only Bladen had a small number of blacks in society. In South Carolina barely 20 percent of the state's Methodists were black, and these were heavily concentrated in the slave-rich lowcountry. The center of black Methodism in the state was Charleston. Schisms and defections to the newly formed Trinity Primitive Methodist Church had stripped the Cumberland congregation of a third of its white membership, leaving it in 1794 with a substantial black majority of 220 and only 60 white members. The Primitive Methodist congregation in Georgetown, established around 1792, was over 30 percent black, and the society in Santee over 36 percent black.[34]

Despite a growing acceptance of religious proselytization of slaves, the rising demand of black southerners for spiritual liberty and equality, which manifested itself in the growing separate church movement, aroused dormant fears of the radicalizing effects of religion on slaves. The outbreak of Gabriel's Rebellion in Virginia in 1800 exacerbated those fears and resulted in the passage of a spate of laws prohibiting slaves from meeting, even in the company of whites, for instruction or religious worship before sunrise or after sunset. Once the crisis passed, the laws were modified to allow religious meetings provided that a majority of the worshipers were white. The effect was to arrest the progress of the sepa-

---

[33] *Minutes Taken at the Several Conferences of the Methodist Episcopal Church for the Year 1794* (New York, 1794), pp. 212–13.

[34] Ibid.

rate black church movement although, through their tactical skill and political adroitness, black leaders were able to preserve the major existing centers of church life.

After 1800 the growth of black Protestantism took place primarily within white churches, a development that was aided by the simultaneous rise of denominational organizations whose purpose was to forge a Christian community out of isolated congregations. Until 1796 Methodist congregations were served only by circuits, which ordinarily consisted of a number of preaching places. The decision of the General Conference to divide the church into six annual conferences, to further divide those into districts, and to dispatch hundreds of additional itinerants to areas throughout the South, initiated a great tide of religious revivalism that swept across the entire region beginning in 1802. Before its surging power was finally dissipated, the religious configuration of the South had been drastically changed.

As they had been from the beginning, black Christians were major participants in the shaping of southern religious life after 1800. For example, according to William Capers, subsequently bishop of the Methodist Episcopal Church, a free black Virginian named Henry Evans was "the father of the Methodist church, white and black, in Fayetteville" in North Carolina. Despite severe persecution, Evans continued to hold secret meetings with slaves in the woods, changing the location almost nightly to avoid detection. Persuaded at last of the social value of Evans's preaching, members of the white community not only dropped their opposition but soon began attending services and even applying for admission to the black church. Despite his church's newfound respectability, Evans, "as an humble, good Christian," transferred the church and congregation over to white preachers.[35]

In rural parts of South Carolina, where white Methodists were still regarded as agents of abolitionism, blacks supplied the energy and the faith for the growing missionary movement. In 1809 the first focused efforts to evangelize slaves had been made by the South Carolina Conference, which dis-

[35] Shipp, *History of Methodism*, p. 405; Sumners, ed., *Autobiography of Travis*, p. 101.

patched two white preachers—James H. Mallard as missionary to slaves in the area from the Ashley to the Cooper River, and James E. Glenn as missionary to those from the Cooper to the Santee—but planter hostility was so intense that the effort was abandoned in favor of black missionaries. Respected black Methodists from Charleston like Castile Selby, Amos Baxter, Tom Smith, Peter Simpson, Smart Simpson, Harry Bull, Richard Holloway, Alek Harlston, and others, were sent out to "hold meetings with the negroes."[36]

According to C. C. Jones, the Presbyterian plantation missionary, there were "a multitude of preachers and exhorters" among black Baptists in the southern states whose names never appeared on the minutes of the various Baptist associations but who preached on the plantations to "those of their own color." Their preaching, "though broken and illiterate," was regarded as "highly useful" by Baptists, who had no specific organization for evangelizing slaves.[37] Due in considerable part to their labors, black Christianity continued to develop with irresistible vigor and astonishing speed, producing a conspicuous Africanization of Protestantism in parts of the South.

Any attempt to deal with the Baptists or Methodists on a regional basis necessarily involves some distortion, for neither denomination was confined to a single area. Both made striking gains everywhere among blacks. At the turn of the century Maryland remained the center of Afro-Methodism, although a southerly shift was already apparent. In 1807 the newly organized Baltimore Conference, which extended from the Susquehanna River on the north to the Rappahannock River on the south and the Chesapeake Bay on the east, was over 26 percent black with 20,707 whites and 7,453 blacks. Despite the increase in numbers of blacks, black membership had slightly declined here as a percentage of the total. By contrast, Methodism had made impressive gains among blacks in the

[36]William Capers, *Autobiography,* in William May Wightman, *Life of William Capers, D.D.* (Nashville, 1859), pp. 138–39. Capers, subsequently bishop of the Methodist Episcopal Church, South, was a slaveholder.

[37]Harrison, *Gospel among the Slaves,* p. 65.

Virginia Conference—which included the Norfolk and Richmond districts in Virginia and the Salisbury and New Bern districts of North Carolina. The 5,668 blacks reported in society there represented nearly 32 percent of the total. The Southern Conference, which included the Oconee, Ogeechee, Saluda, and Camden districts, was 25 percent black with 13,484 whites and 4,432 blacks.[38]

By 1825 the geographical shift of the center of black Methodism to the lower South was complete. The disappearance of the pioneering Methodist antislavery leadership and the rise by 1815 of a new generation of proslavery southern leaders, represented by William Capers and Richard Furman in South Carolina, contributed to the erosion of planter opposition to Methodism and to the rapid expansion of the denomination among slaves in the lower South. By 1825 black membership in the Baltimore Conference had declined to slightly less than 30 percent of the total and, more striking, the numerical gain over a period of twenty-two years was less than 2,000. The Virginia Conference now reported 7,376 blacks, representing 25 percent of the total. Two North Carolina districts, Neuse and Roanoke, were the focal points of its black membership. With 3,812 black Methodists, the two districts accounted for over 51 percent of the total black membership of the conference. The South Carolina Conference reported 15,293 black members in society, or 35 percent of the total. Almost 65 percent of the Methodists in the Edisto District, which embraced the area from Charleston to Savannah, were black. Blacks made up over 86 percent of the Methodists in society in Charleston and nearly 40 percent of the total in the district. In the Pee Dee District they accounted for almost 30 percent of the total. The black membership of three predominantly black churches, Georgetown, Fayetteville, and Wilmington, alone accounted for over 43 percent of the total membership in the district. In the Broad River District, nearly 40 percent of all Methodists were black, and the Santee society remained predominantly black. In the three southern

[38]*Minutes Taken at the Several Annual Conferences of the Methodist Episcopal Church in the United States of America for the Year 1807* (New York, 1807), p. 15.

conferences combined, blacks represented almost 30 percent of the total.[39]

The fiercely guarded congregationalism of the Baptist tradition prevented the development of national Baptist organizations to unite adherents, but regional associations began to proliferate after 1800. Like the Methodist conferences, the Baptist associations were designed to foster a disciplined communion of churches united by common doctrine and standards of behavior. The development of ecclesiastical structures and the commitment of additional itinerants also contributed to a spate of revivalism, particularly among the black population, after 1802. Although Virginia did not have a single special slave mission until 1841, the state remained the center of black Baptist strength.[40] Before the Revolution the majority of Baptist churches in Virginia were located between the Blue Ridge Mountains and the Potomac River, an area of relatively light slave concentration.[41] During the Second Great Awakening this pattern changed considerably as Baptist strength grew dramatically in the populous eastern portion of the state, in the area extending south and east from the city of Richmond to the Chesapeake Bay and the southeastern corner of the state, traditionally an area of heavy slave concentration. By 1809 the Dover Association contained thirty-seven churches, including the predominantly black churches of Charles City, Goochland, Pocorone, Zoar, and Williamsburg, and had approximately 10,500 members.[42] The Portsmouth Association, which extended from Portsmouth and Norfolk to Petersburg and occupied the oldest Baptist ground in Virginia, contained several predominantly black churches, including the Portsmouth and Norfolk

[39]*Minutes Taken at the Several Annual Conferences of the Methodist Episcopal Church for the Year 1825* (New York, 1825), pp. 22, 26, 29.

[40]Harrison, *Gospel among the Slaves*, p. 189.

[41]Richard S. Dunn, "Black Society in the Chesapeake, 1776–1810," in Ira Berlin and Ronald Hoffman, eds., *Slavery and Freedom in the Age of the American Revolution* (Charlottesville, Va., 1983), p. 54.

[42]Robert B. Semple, *A History of the Rise and Progress of the Baptists in Virginia,* rev. and extended by G. W. Beale (Philadelphia, 1894), pp. 137, 140, 145, 163, 169, 148.

churches, Davenport's southeast of Petersburg in Prince George County, and the First African of Petersburg. Following the development of an organized missionary movement, the faith expanded dramatically. By 1845 three associations, Dover, Portsmouth, and Rappahannock, formed in 1843 from the Dover Association, contained over 34,000 members, well over a third of all Baptists in Virginia. Blacks comprised two thirds of the Rappahannock Association, the area extending roughly from the mouth of the York River to the Mattaponi, north in a line from Caroline County to King George County to the Potomac River, and east to the Chesapeake Bay.[43]

The burgeoning strength of the black Baptist movement in the lower South is also reflected in the composition of various lowcountry associations. Although the minutes of the various associations are not sufficiently complete for the development of a geography of black Baptist expansion, they suggest the patterns of growth. In Georgia the number of black Baptists multiplied phenomenally after 1802, the year of the first general revival, and except for a brief decline during the War of 1812 continued to expand through 1827.[44] The process began with the formation of the Savannah River Association in 1802. At first entirely a Georgia institution formed by the white Savannah and Newington churches and the two black Savannah churches, it was soon joined by a number of churches formerly belonging to the Charleston Association. In 1803 the twelve churches that formed the association reported 1,298 members. Three black churches, the First and Second Colored of Savannah and the Ogeechee Colored, represented 850 or 65 percent of the total membership of the Association. In 1813 the First and Second Colored churches of Savannah still accounted for 35 percent of the Savannah River Association's membership, exclusive of black members in interracial churches.[45]

[43] Benedict, *History of the Baptist Denomination,* p. 663.

[44] Campbell, *Georgia Baptists,* p. 15.

[45] Savannah River Baptist Association, S.C., 1803–29, Stetson Mem. Lib., Mercer Univ. (microfilm).

In 1818 the Savannah River Association agreed to divide the body, with the Savannah River to be the line of division. Those churches on the Georgia side of the river were united in the Sunbury Association, while the old Savannah River Association became a South Carolina institution. The constituent churches of the new association included the white Savannah Baptist, the First Colored with 1,712 members, the Second Colored with 536 members, Great Ogeechee Colored with 460 members, and Sunbury Baptist, a mixed congregation.[46] The black majority that characterized the Baptist movement in Georgia's lowcountry from the beginning was maintained through the antebellum period. By 1846 the Sunbury Association reported 4,300 members, less than 500 of whom were white. Approximately half of its twenty churches were entirely black and, with few exceptions, blacks constituted a majority of the interracial churches. The mother church, now known as the First African of Savannah, was the largest in the association.[47] Jesse Peter's African church of Augusta continued to be one of the largest churches in the Georgia Association. With an average of 500 members it alone accounted for approximately 15 percent of the total membership of the association before 1815.[48]

In South Carolina three lowcountry associations, Charleston, Welsh Neck, and Savannah River, contained about half the Baptists in the state. In the Charleston Association, the oldest, the black membership was twice that of the white. Out of a total of 1,643 members in 1846, all but 261 were black.[49] The Welsh Neck Association, formed in 1832 out of the northern portion of the Charleston Association, reported 477 members in 1846, only 83 of whom were white. Welsh Neck Church, the mother church of all Baptist churches in the Pee Dee River area, remained predominantly black. Although the

---

[46]Campbell, *Georgia Baptists*, p. 76; Benedict, *History of the Baptist Denomination*, p. 710; Thomas, *First African Baptist Church*, p. 45.

[47]Benedict, *History of the Baptist Denomination*, p. 742 n. 7.

[48]Minutes of the Georgia Association, State of the Church, 1803, 1805, 1807, 1815. Minutes for 1812–14, 1816, 1818–20, and 1822 are missing.

[49]Benedict, *History of the Baptist Denomination*, p. 710 n. 10.

Savannah River Association made no distinction between black and white members, it was from its creation heavily black.[50]

By the time the tide of revivalism was spent, three distinct types of black churches had emerged in the South. Autonomous or separate churches were primarily for blacks. Although some of these institutions traced their origins in part to an initiative from white Christians, the major factor in their development was the work of a black leader. Interracial churches—which on the whole were younger and represented a reaction to the growing strength of the independent black churches—and predominantly black churches with white pastors were linked in their origin to the white Christian community, although the initiative and general momentum often came from within. Distinctive as they were, the three were part of the same general movement and their members were very much alike in the values and ideas that attracted them to evangelicalism in the first place. On the other hand, because Afro-Christianity was designed for and adapted to the nature of slavery and its needs, it reveals some major dissimilarities when compared with white Christianity.

All churches, black, white, or interracial, shared four aspects in common: polity, worship, ethos, and doctrine. What distinguished one church from another was the fact that one aspect was usually emphasized as the starting point and focus for the others and was therefore the heart of the organism. In their formal organization, the separate black churches generally imitated forms found in white churches. The pastor presided, aided by exhorters, deacons, elders, a choir, and, later, missionaries. All black preachers, slave and free, were required to have the approval of the recognized group of their denomination. The Baptist form of organization into local congregations allowed blacks a degree of local autonomy not available in Methodist societies. Almost everywhere in the South, black Baptist churches were allowed to have black preachers. In Georgia, the African Baptist churches were largely independent. They purchased land and built their own churches, al-

[50]Ibid., pp. 706, 710 n. 1, 711.

though the deeds were executed to white trustees because as a black group they were not legally competent to hold title to property. They had their own pastors and deacons, and "sacraments and discipline all of their own."[51] By contrast, black preachers were not licensed to preach in the Methodist Episcopal Church until 1800, when the Third General Conference authorized bishops to ordain black preachers. Even then they were not given regular appointments. According to Daniel Coker there were eight black ministers in holy orders in Baltimore but none was in charge of a church; even the two African churches, Sharp Street and Bethel, continued to have white ministers until 1830.[52]

Almost all black churches, of necessity, maintained at least a tenuous connection with white polities—the Baptists with the association and the Methodists with the conference. At associational meetings the black Baptist churches were represented by their own delegates, some slave and some free. Their churches and their pastors' names stood in association minutes according to their seniority in the organization.[53] The black Methodists in Charleston held their own separate quarterly meetings, collected and disbursed church money, and were virtually autonomous, at least for a short period, but they were not admitted "to seats and votes" at the annual conferences of the Methodist Episcopal Church.[54] Like the African Methodist Bethel Church of Baltimore, the Charleston African Methodist Church separated from the Methodist Episcopal Church and affiliated with Richard Allen's African Methodist Episcopal Church.

[51]Shipp, *History of Methodism*, p. 426; see also "A Letter from the Negro Baptist Church in Savannah," Dec. 23, 1800, *Baptist Annual Register,* 1798–1801, pp. 366–67; Thomas, *First African Baptist Church,* p. 38.

[52]Daniel Coker, "A Dialogue between a Virginian and an African Minister," in *Negro Protest Pamphlets: A Compendium* (New York, 1969), p. 41. The rule permitting the ordination of black preachers was not, however, incorporated among the printed regulations of the discipline (Nathan Bangs, *A History of the Methodist Episcopal Church,* 2 vols. [New York, 1839], 1:97–98).

[53]Benedict, *History of the Baptist Denomination,* p. 739.

[54]Chreitzberg, *Early Methodism,* p. 156.

Although they adhered to the same formal organizations, the separate black churches generally exhibited certain common tendencies or special features that set them apart from the white Christian community. For one thing, within the black churches there was strong emphasis upon community life. Frequently black churches were organized around their founder in a way that reflected the traditional African organization of the community around the chief or religious leader. Each African community had sacred men of different kinds, recognized leaders whose duties were chiefly religious but whose presence symbolized the unity of the community.[55] Like African religious leaders, black preachers held a special place in slave society. As spiritual pastors of their communities, they were ritual leaders, moral advisors, and political leaders—which in the early church meant principally that they served as intermediaries between the slave and free communities—and were regarded with religious awe and respect.

A number of the early leaders of the black Christian community were recent arrivals or immediate descendants of traditional African societies. Uncle Jack, pastor of the Nottoway church in Virginia, was kidnapped from Africa and brought to Virginia where he was sold to a Nottoway planter. Later he was converted and licensed as a Baptist preacher.[56] Andrew Bryan, the father of the Baptist church in Georgia, was apparently of unmixed African descent. Andrew Cox Marshall, Bryan's nephew, was born in South Carolina of a pure African mother and an English father. Converted at about age fifty, Marshall became assistant pastor at his uncle Andrew Bryan's First Colored Baptist Church in Savannah; he served there from 1806 until 1815 when, following Bryan's death, he was called as pastor to the church.[57] David George, who formed one of the earliest Baptist churches in South Carolina and the

[55] Mbiti, *African Religions,* pp. 166–93.

[56] DuBois, ed., *The Negro Church,* p. 37.

[57] Clarence M. Wagner, *Profiles of Black Georgia Baptists* (Gainesville, Ga., 1980), pp. 6, 14.

first black Baptist churches in Nova Scotia and Sierra Leone, was born in Essex County, Virginia, of African parents.[58] In these early preachers was the continuity and essence of African religious life and thought. The visible symbols of national origin and unity, they were at one and the same time the propagators of traditional religious values and beliefs and the instigators of new cultural and religious ideas. The churches they created thus became the chief institutional carriers of African culture and the most dynamic area for the creation of new values, new identities, and a new self-consciousness.

Although white Protestantism gave black religious life its basic shape and substance, that black life developed its own distinctive ethos and character. Little is known about the actual practice of religion in the black churches, but the evidence that survives suggests a strong and enduring attachment to traditional African beliefs and practices as well as a conscious effort to adapt religious activities and worship to the nature and needs of slave life. Generally speaking, Christian liturgical forms, prayers, hymns, and symbols were freely borrowed by black Christians, although blacks made significant adjustments in religious concepts and practices and frequently drew upon African traditional religions. According to contemporary accounts, most of them left by white observers, singing, praying, and preaching were the primary elements in black worship. By all accounts slaves inherited the African fondness for singing. African peoples had no formal creeds to recite, but there were a number of prayer forms, either recited or sung, that were used to preserve and commemorate historical events—to mark births, marriages, or deaths, to ward off evil spirits, or to worship God. One African prayer form in wide use was the litany, a prayer or song form in which the leader made the invocation and the choir or congregation responded, either with a memorized formula or by repeating some of the words of the leader. Known as call and response, the technique was already in the slave work-song tradition and was apparently applied to the sa-

[58]"Life of David George," *Baptist Annual Register,* 1790, p. 473.

cred music slaves learned during the Second Great Awakening.[59]

Music played a major role in the great revivals of the late eighteenth century. John Leland, the great Baptist preacher, recalled groups of people singing to meeting and singing home, and singing in the fields, shops, and houses. Watts's hymns were the general standard although, as Leland wryly noted, many were original compositions "some of which have more divinity in them then poetry or grammer" and some "have little of either."[60] White preachers generally found that the easiest way to introduce Christian teaching to illiterate slaves was through music. Leland observed that they were "remarkable for learning a tune" and had "melodious voices." Edmund Botsford found them "remarkably fond of hymns" and thought that the black members of the Welsh Neck church "sing delightfully." James Meacham, an itinerant Methodist preacher in Virginia and North Carolina, recalled being awakened at night "in raptures of Heaven by the sweet Echo of Singing in the Kitchen among the dear Black people," who frequently continued to sing long after services were over. In a number of interracial churches blacks led the hymn singing and were often called upon to pray.[61]

Hymn singing was, of courses, an integral part of white church services. In black worship it was the primary element. The lyrics of camp hymns that swept the South during the

[59] John S. Mbiti, *The Prayers of African Religion* (Maryknoll, N.Y., 1975), p. 21; idem, *African Religions*, pp. 67, 86; Aylward Shorter, *Prayer in the Religious Traditions of Africa* (New York, 1976), pp. 20–21. In 1808 John Lambert traveled to Savannah by boat. He recalled slave oarsmen singing a "Boat-song of their own composing." A line was given out by one member, "We are going down to Georgia, boys," and the crew responded "Aye, Aye," etc. (Mills Lane, ed., *The Rambler in Georgia* [Savannah, 1973], p. 40).

[60] John Leland, *The Virginia Chronicle: With Judicious and Critical Remarks, Under XXIV Heads* (Fredericksburg, Va., 1790), p. 36.

[61] Ibid., p. 13; Botsford to the Editor, Apr. 25–Aug. 1790, *Baptist Annual Register,* 1790–93, p. 105; William K. Boyd, ed., "A Journal and Travel of James Meacham," Trinity College Historical Society, *Historical Papers*, ser. 9 (1912):88; Harrison, *Gospel among the Slaves*, p. 125.

Second Great Awakening struck a familiar experiential chord in black Christians. The simple, powerful songs thus became *their* music, made their own by the syncopating rhythms, the hand clapping, foot tapping, body swaying, and incremental leading lines typical of African prayer.[62] In Methodist meetinghouses, where rites and ceremonies could be adapted "to the diversity of countries, times, and men's manners," the ring dance, a "kind of spiritual *boulanger*," was a regular part of the service.[63]

Because singing preceded preaching in the black religious experience, it influenced both prayer and preaching in black worship. Very little is known about prayer in early black churches. One of the few surviving examples was composed by a black preacher for the ordination of a member of his church and was preserved by a Baptist missionary:

> Make he good, like he say,
> Make he say, like he good,
> Make he say, make he good, like he God.[64]

Addressed to God, the prayer asked that God make the young preacher as good as his doctrine, his doctrine as pure as his life, and both his doctrine and his life in the image of God. Although it was ridiculed as "gibberish" by whites, it is clearly an African blessing, a prayer form that plays an important role in the social and religious life of African peoples. Short, extemporaneous, and to the point, it has the easily memorized poetical form that had enjoyed long usage in Africa, where the oral tradition prevailed.[65]

The blending of prose sermon and music was perhaps unique to black worship and was apparently also derived from the African oral tradition. Few examples of black

---

[62] James L. Smith, *Autobiography* (Norwich, Conn., 1881), p. 27.

[63] Sir Charles Lyell, *A Second Visit to the United States of North America*, 2 vols. (New York and London, 1849):2:364.

[64] Ibid., p. 15.

[65] Mbiti, *Prayers of African Religion*, pp. 17, 21.

preaching survive, but those that do suggest that black preachers employed the same basic structural patterns used by early white Baptist and Methodist preachers, but with significant variations. First and foremost, the black sermon was oral, dynamic, and inventive. Harry Hosier, considered by Thomas Coke to be "one of the best Preachers in the world," was unable to read.[66] Venture Galphin was barely literate. Even literate slaves like Andrew Cox Marshall spoke without notes.[67] This was due in part to the influence of the African oral tradition, in part to the experience of slavery, the laws of which contained strict prohibitions against teaching slaves to read or write, and in part to the experiences many preachers gained as exhorters in early Christian churches.

Another distinguishing feature of black preaching was the tone and style of the language. The great revival of 1785, which added converts from the upper ranks of white society, produced major changes, most notably among Baptists, whose manner of preaching became less enthusiastic and whose piety became more rational.[68] Some Methodist preachers still used an affective preaching style, but their "whining" and "barking" contrasted markedly with the musical quality achieved by many black preachers, which derived perhaps from the African practice of singing almost everything. The descriptions of the "fine sonorous voice" of Andrew Cox Marshall and the "charming" voice of Jesse Galphin suggest the symbiotic roles of singing and preaching, unique to black worship.[69]

Although black sermons were usually based on scriptural

---

[66] *Journals of Coke's Visits*, p. 18. For general works on black preaching see Charles V. Hamilton, *The Black Preacher in America* (New York, 1972); Gerald L. Davis, *I Got the Word in Me and I Can Sing It, You Know: A Study of the Performed African-American Sermon* (Philadelphia, 1985); Bruce A. Rosenberg, *The Art of the American Folk Preacher* (New York, 1970).

[67] Lyell, *Second Visit*, 1:14.

[68] Benedict, *History of the Baptist Denomination*, p. 658.

[69] Lyell, *Second Visit*, 2:14–15; *Baptist Annual Register*, 1790–93, pp. 544–45.

authority and were replete with biblical imagery,[70] songs were a major source of sermon material. The barely literate Venture Galphin began his sermons with the words of hymns that were familiar to him. At one service attended by Adiel Sherwood, one of the principal figures of the Georgia revivals, Galphin preached a sermon based on the hymn "And Are We Wretches Yet Alive?" The sermon was, moreover, cast in the dialogue mode. Galphin began "without any tone." He then sang out a line of the hymn and the choir responded by re-singing the same line, a functional device used in the modern black church to promote interaction between the preacher and the congregation.[71] Part spiritual, part sermon, Galphin's style of preaching was apparently influenced by African prayer forms, which could be either recited or sung. The form was also perhaps influenced by exhortation, which by its very nature invites dialogue and response. Oratorical rather than literary, affective rather than intellectual, exhortation was intended to awaken an emotional fervor that generally found expression in an audible response.

In their sermons to black audiences, white southern preachers often theologically justified the oppression of black people in slavery. By contrast, black sermons commonly asserted the presence and power of God in black lives and promised that God would ultimately bring justice to the suffering race. A fragment of a sermon given by Andrew Cox Marshall in 1818 illustrates the point. After dwelling at length on "the gloom of the valley of the shadow of death," Marshall held out the hope of God's saving grace, comparing it to an eagle, who upon seeing her fledgling falling to the earth, darts "with the speed of lightening to save it before it reaches the ground."[72] Venture Galphin compared the plight of the sinner to that of the people of Israel at the Red Sea, with the water before them and Pharaoh's host behind, and with no

---

[70]Shipp, *History of Methodism*, pp. 405–7, Clark et al., eds., *Journal and Letters of Asbury*, 2:530.

[71]*Memoir of Adiel Sherwood* (Philadelphia, 1884), pp. 112–13.

[72]Lyell, *Second Visit*, 1:14.

way of escape apparent until God opened a way through the deep and made heaven accessible.[73] God's ultimate deliverance of the race was the theme of a sermon delivered by an itinerant black Methodist preacher in Baltimore. Using the text "Behold I come quickly," from the Book of Revelations, he told how John had avoided all attempts by his enemies to put him to death, how they had at last decided to throw him into a "kittle of Biling ile," and how God had baffled his enemies by taking him up alive.[74]

Because doctrine is bound up with material and psychological realities of daily existence, and because those realities were vastly different for blacks and whites, the doctrines of each group inevitably had distinctive attributes. The first black Christians were exposed to Christian teachings through contact with Christians, black and white. In fact, two different pedagogies existed, one of which developed in slave huts or in the makeshift pulpits erected in pleasant groves where slaves assembled for their own services in the afternoon or evening or between the services conducted in the white country churches. About this pedagogy little if anything will ever be known. The second pedagogy was provided by white preachers in interracial churches and schools and by black preachers in separate churches. Early Methodist societies formed their members into classes for purposes of religious instruction. The class meetings were conducted by a local class leader, whose responsibility it was to supervise the spiritual well-being of his charges. In their efforts to induce slaves to accept Christianity, white ministers relied heavily on the Bible. Many slaves learned to read the Bible before anything else.[75] Most, however, learned through oral instruction, the student repeating the answers after the teacher until the lesson was committed to memory. The method was popularized by the

[73] *Memoir of Sherwood*, p. 112.

[74] Ebenezer Davies, *American Scenes and Christian Slavery: A Recent Tour of Four Thousand Miles in the United States* (London, 1849), pp. 198–99.

[75] Edward Franklin Frazier, *The Negro Church in America* (New York, 1974), p. 11.

Rev. John Mines, pastor of a church in Leesburg, Virginia, who in 1822 published *The Evangelical Catechism* for use in sabbath schools and among slaves.[76]

Within the interracial Baptist churches, the preservation of doctrinal purity was the responsibility of white members. Although most Baptist churches had black deacons and exhorters to "guard" the black members and to "stir" their piety, their preaching was carefully controlled by the church. No one was allowed to "exercise" his gift unless approved by the church, which generally meant unless he demonstrated sound doctrine. Moreover, after 1800 increased control was thought necessary to suppress black preaching for fear of sedition and rebellion. Churches carefully scrutinized the conduct and the message communicated by exhorters and preachers. Before being allowed to take one of these positions, an individual was required to appear before the church to "exercise his gift." Those judged to be doctrinally sound were usually permitted to exhort "within the bounds of the church." Exhorters were frequently warned to "be careful in exercising their gifts at their meetings among themselves" and were repeatedly cautioned not "to take a text to preach from" without church authorization.[77]

No systematic course of instruction was provided for black churches, but they, too, "derived such assistance from their white brethren, ministers and others, as to establish and preserve them in the faith of the gospel."[78] Andrew Bryan, who was apparently a strict doctrinarian, relied on the Bible, the

---

[76]John Mines, *The Evangelical Catechism* (Richmond, 1822).

[77]This paragraph is based on the records of a number of interracial churches, including the following: Minutes of Big Creek Baptist Church, Williamston, S.C., 1801–1936, June 2, 1821, Aug. 1, 1809, and Records of Black Creek Baptist Church, Dovesville, S.C., 1798–1896, Sept. 6, 1829, Baptist Hist. Coll., Furman Univ. (both microfilm); Minute Book of Upper King and Queen Baptist Church, 1774–1816, June 19, 1790, Minutes of Berryville (Buck Marsh) Baptist Church, 1785–1803, Mar. 31, 1792, Oct. 6, 1804, Minutes of Wallers (Goshen) Baptist Church, 1799–1818, Aug. 2, 1800, and Minutes of Berryville Baptist Church, 1803–41, Jan. 5, 1805, Nov. 2, 1805, June 4, 1809, Sept. 3, 1809, Virginia Baptist Historical Society, Richmond.

[78]Campbell, *Georgia Baptists*, p. 90.

Baptist Confession of Faith, and some of John Bunyan's works to instruct his followers.[79] Despite Bryan's claim that "we enjoy the rights of conscience to a valuable degree," the First Colored Church of Savannah regularly held divine services three times on Sundays and performed the Lord's Supper quarterly, "without molestation, but in the presence and with the approbation and encouragement of many of the white people."[80] After the development of regional organizations, the association assumed responsibility for maintaining orthodoxy. When, for example, Andrew Cox Marshall invited Alexander Campbell, founder of the Disciples of Christ, to preach at Marshall's church after white churches had refused him their pulpits, the association refused to seat Marshall and recommended to his congregation that he be silenced. When the congregation persisted in keeping Marshall as its pastor it was condemned by the association for its "corrupt state" and its membership in the association was dissolved.[81]

What was taught was, moreover, not always necessarily received. Although the vast majority of black Christians relied on prayer to God to deliver them from fear, sickness, slavery, and a host of other evils, there is some evidence that slaves, at least in the lower South, where African infusions continued into the nineteenth century, did not easily reject either the spirits and deities of the traditional pantheon or the medicine man with his magical powers. When in trouble, some Afro-Christians still turned to these sources for protection against the host of evil forces surrounding them. The minutes of the Welsh Neck Baptist Church document the persistence of African beliefs and practices among South Carolina's black Baptists. In 1826 Jim, a member of the church, was arrested for the murder of Rachel, an elderly woman who was also a church member. Testimony heard by a special committee of the church set up to investigate the matter revealed that Jim thought Rachel was a

[79] *Baptist Annual Register,* 1790, p. 342.

[80] Holcombe, ed., *Georgia Repository,* 1:188; "A Letter from the Negro Baptist Church in Savannah," *Baptist Annual Register,* 1798–1801, p. 367.

[81] Thomas, *First African Baptist Church,* p. 50.

witch and had threatened "to draw blood to prevent her from doing him any more mischief." Two other church members, including Shine, Jim's wife, were also implicated. Upon the recommendation of the committee, all three were expelled from the church and the pastor was requested to "give such admonition and instruction to the black members of the Church as this Melancholy event seemed to require."[82]

Black Christianity was not, of course, a monolithic culture. Within the common culture there were diverse local practices. Nevertheless, surviving evidence, most of it from interracial churches, strongly suggests that when Christian teaching conflicted with inherited ideas and practices and with established social mores, black Christians adhered to their own rules. Although white churches struggled to implant the Christian ideals of marriage, they encountered opposition. Most slaves clearly preferred monogamy and most slave marriages were actually monogamous. A significant number of slaves, however, were involved in serial monogamy, if not polygamy. Disciplinary records from interracial churches in Virginia, Georgia, and South Carolina reveal that the most common and pervasive offenses against church discipline among slaves were adultery and "double marriage," as it was referred to in church records.[83] Although most offenders were male, female slaves like Anne, the property of William Holbert and a mem-

---

[82]Charles Ball, *Slavery in the United States: A Narrative of the Life and Adventures of Charles Ball, A Black Man* (Lewistown, Pa., 1836), p. 127; Sumners, ed., *Autobiography of Travis*, p. 71, Minutes of Welsh Neck Baptist Church, May 21, 1826, June 3, 1826.

[83]The high incidence of sexual offenses attributed to blacks might, in part, be due to what Donald G. Mathews describes as the evangelicals' preoccupation with the "voluptuousness" of Africans, and their desire to "subdue their sensuality" (*Religion in the Old South* [Chicago, 1977], pp. 71–72). Minutes of Big Creek Baptist Church, Jan. 2, 1812, Minutes of Turkey Creek Baptist Church, Abbeville County, S.C., 1785–1869, Jan. 9, 1808, Minutes of Big Stephen Creek Baptist Church, Edgefield District, S.C., June 1803–1901, June 1810, Aug. 1815, Feb. 1825, Minutes of Little Ogeechee Baptist Church, Screven County, Ga., 1797–1905, July 1829, Minutes of Society Hill (formerly Welsh Neck) Baptist Church, Jan. 19, 1822, Oct. 20, 1822, Sept. 3, 1823, and Minutes of Lower Fork of Lynches Creek (Gum Branch) Baptist Church, Oct. 1819, Baptist Hist. Coll., Furman Univ.; Minutes of Albemarle Baptist Church, 1773–1811, Nov. 1808, Minutes of

ber of the Big Creek Baptist Church of South Carolina, were also disciplined for "the sin of Adultery for mareing and having a former [husband] yet living."[84]

The explanation for these black marriage problems lies not in the number of marital problems among slave couples, but in the nature both of slave marriages themselves and the system of which they were a part. The white Christian ideal of monogamy clearly assumed a more or less equal sex ratio or the alternative of abstinence. By 1800 the sex ratio was equal in some parts of the South, but not in all. Numbers of slaves now lived on large plantation units, but many others still lived on small or middling units.[85] What this meant in practice was that many slaves had to find partners on neighboring plantations.[86] Some masters encouraged and promoted black family bonds, but because slave marriages were neither recognized nor protected by law, they could be, and frequently were, dissolved at the will of the master, usually as a result of sale or inheritance practices.[87] Lengthy separations created sexual desires that in some cases led to infidelity, in others to the

---

Broad Run Baptist Church, 1762–1872, May 18, 1774, Aug. 24, 1782, Mar. 22, 1783, July 7, 1805, Minutes of Carmel Baptist Church (Caroline County), 1779–1819, Oct. 2, 1811, Minutes of Lyles (Albemarle) Baptist Church, 1800–1835, Dec. 1811, Aug. 1812, and Minutes of Mill Swamp Baptist Church (Isle of Wight), 1774–1790, Apr. 19, 1794, Apr. 20, 1799, Va. Baptist Hist. Soc.

[84]Minutes of Big Creek Baptist Church, June 4, 1803, Minutes of Albemarle Baptist Church, Nov. 1808, Minutes of Mill Swamp Baptist Church, Apr. 20, 1799, Minutes of Tussekiah Baptist Church, 1784–1826, July 26, 1822, and Minutes of South Quay Baptist Church, 1775–1827, July 30, 1811, June 4, 1813, July 30, 1814, Va. Baptist Hist. Soc.

[85]Dunn, "Black Society in the Chesapeake," pp. 69–70; Philip D. Morgan, "Black Society in the Lowcountry, 1760–1810," in Berlin and Hoffman, eds., *Slavery and Freedom,* p. 93.

[86]Roughly half of the Georgia slave mothers studied by Betty Wood were living apart from their husbands (Betty Wood, "Some Aspects of Female Resistance to Chattel Slavery in Lowcountry Georgia," *The Historical Journal* 30 [1987]:606–7, 609).

[87]For evidence of the effect on slave family stability, see Jean Butenhoff Lee, "The Problem of Slave Community in the Eighteenth-Century Chesapeake," *William and Mary Quarterly,* 3d ser. 43 (1986):333–61.

selection of another partner. To many slaves, who had inherited from their African forbears a concept of sin that judged an act sinful by its consequences instead of in terms of a failure to conform to a set of a priori moral rules, these were sensible and moral solutions to a problem over which they had no control.[88]

Although interracial churches insisted that monogamy was the only acceptable form of marriage, they were powerless to help slaves implement this ideal in their lives. Some congregations, like the Little Ogeechee Baptist Church of Georgia, adopted rules forbidding slaves to remarry as long as one spouse remained alive.[89] Big Stephens Creek church decided to permit the remarriage of black church members providing that one partner was removed by a master "to a distant place," thereby rendering "their marriage void."[90] Unable to resolve the problem, most churches turned to their associations for advice, only to find them unable or unwilling to give guidance. For two years the Portsmouth Association debated the question of whether prolonged separation entitled a slave to remarry. Failing to reach a consensus, it ordered the query expunged from the record. The Strawberry Association refused either to recommend separation of the offending couple or to expel them from the church. The Goshen Association decided to leave the matter to the discretion of the individual churches.[91] Several associations eventually adopted forthright policies permitting couples who were involuntarily separated by their owners to remarry without penalty of exclusion.[92] Thus the sale of a

[88]Mbiti, *African Religions*, p. 207.

[89]Minutes of Little Ogeechee Baptist Church. The entry contains no date but precedes the minutes of 1827.

[90]Minutes of Big Stephens Creek Baptist Church, Oct. 1819.

[91]Minutes of the Portsmouth (Virginia) Association, 1791–1800, May 26, 1792, May 1794, Minutes of the Strawberry Association, 1787–1822, 1792, and Minutes of the Goshen Association, 1795, Oct. 1819, Va. Baptist Hist. Soc.

[92]Minutes of Accomac Association, 1815–24, 1825, Va. Baptist Hist. Soc.

slave or involuntary separation by inheritance was, by vir-
tual decree of the churches, recognized as tantamount to a
decree of divorce.[93]

In the meantime, the black churches were gradually evolv-
ing an officially monogamous system of marriage. Andrew
Bryan, for example, insisted upon monogamy for members of
the First Colored Church. In 1819 the black Gillfield Baptist
Church of Virginia adopted a rule requiring all members who
could marry under law to do so under pain of exclusion.[94]
The black churches also offered guidance on family matters
and even assumed certain family functions. Through the
creation of internal community structures of all kinds,
blacks attempted to assert their formative power over their
children's lives and to lay a claim to moral and social power
to control and to try to solve their own social problems.
One of the earliest examples is the Brown Fellowship Society organized in Charleston in 1790 by a group of free
black Methodists for the purpose of providing education
for children, assistance to orphans and widows, and support
for burial grounds for the dead.[95] The Minors Moralist Society, which made its appearance in Charleston in 1803, had
as its object the education of orphans and indigent children.[96] In cooperation with the white independent Presbyterian Church of Savannah, the First African Church
established the first Colored Sunday School in Savannah in
1825 and taught an average of two hundred students. A
number of Virginia cities with strong religious communities
also established schools and burial societies. John T. Ray-
mond ran a sabbath school under the auspices of the Beneficial Society of the Free People of Color of Petersburg. The
Burial Ground Society of the Free People of Color was
organized in 1815 in Richmond and a similar one was cre-

[93] DuBois, *The Negro Church,* p. 56.

[94] Minutes of Gillfield Baptist Church, Mar. 13, 1819.

[95] E. Horace Fitchett, "The Tradition of the Free Negro in Charleston,
South Carolina," *Journal of Negro History* 25 (1940):139–52.

[96] Daniel Alexander Payne, *Recollections of Seventy Years* (New York, 1968),
pp. 12–13.

ated in Petersburg.[97] The establishment of schools and the creation of an associational life underscored what the black Christian community deemed important and appropriate— family, community, and spiritual freedom.

Insofar as it represented the only organized social existence for the slave population, the black church was the place where slaves of diverse origins began to forge a separate cultural identity under the consolidating force of religion. Although they drew deeply from the wellspring of white Protestantism, the black churches and, to the degree that was possible, black members of interracial churches continued to exert traditional values through their strong emphasis on community life, through the preservation of traditional elements of worship, and through exuberance in services, all of which operated as assertions of traditional African patterns as opposed to those of the white churches. The growing consciousness of African Americans as members of a common community of black Christians, rather than as members of particular tribes, is apparent in the designation of their churches as "African"; the term stands as a public affirmation of their African origins and of the survival of African beliefs and customs.

[97]Thomas, *First African Baptist Church,* p. 48; Luther P. Jackson, "The Early Stirrings of the Negroes in Virginia," *Journal of Negro History* 25 (1940):25–34.

RONALD SCHULTZ

God and Workingmen

Popular Religion and the Formation of Philadelphia's Working Class 1790–1830

IN WAYS WE are only beginning to understand, the age of the American Revolution was also the formative age of America's working class.[1] Between the mobilization for Independence of the mid-1770s and the final political resolution of the Revolution in the 1820s, laboring-class Americans experienced a profound transformation in their personal and working lives.

The author would like to thank Gary B. Nash for his comments on an earlier version of this essay and the National Endowment for the Humanities for research support.

[1]The post-Revolutionary emergence of the American working class is surveyed in Sean Wilentz, "Artisan Origins of the American Working Class," *International Labor and Working Class History* 19 (1981):1–22. This should be supplemented by Wilentz, *Chants Democratic: New York City and the Rise of the American Working Class, 1788–1850* (New York, 1984), Bruce Laurie, *Working People of Philadelphia, 1800–1850* (Philadelphia, 1980), Howard B. Rock, *Artisans of the New Republic: The Tradesmen of New York City in the Age of Jefferson* (New York, 1984), Billy G. Smith, *The "Lower Sort": Philadelphia's Laboring People, 1750–1800* (Ithaca, N.Y., 1990), and Steven J. Ross, *Workers on the Edge: Work, Leisure, and Politics in Industrializing Cincinnati, 1788–1890* (New York, 1985). The colonial foundations of early working-class formation are discussed in Gary B. Nash, *The Urban Crucible: Social Change, Political Consciousness, and the Origins of the American Revolution* (Cambridge, Mass., 1979).

As the nation's economy turned from colonial dependence to embrace industrial independence, the give-and-take of the small shop and the uneven rhythms of craft production gave way to the increasing regularity and limited autonomy of manufactories and the putting-out system. In the process of confronting the rise of manufacturing and the declining fortunes of their unique way of life, American artisans and less-skilled workingmen forged a working-class movement from the raw material of craft traditions, popular politics, and rational religion.[2]

Religion has not played a large part in recent accounts of the rise of the American working class. In fact, before the arrival of the Second Great Awakening in America's urban production centers, it is hardly mentioned at all.[3] This neglect is due, in part, to a prevailing viewpoint that sees religion as either an inhibitor of working-class consciousness or as a quiescent alternative to working-class organization.[4] Yet as Herbert G. Gutman argued more than a decade ago, the American working class leaned heavily on religion, both as a source of moral legitimacy and as a reservoir of personal strength in times of adversity.[5] Gutman was writing generally about late nineteenth-century America, but his insights hold true in post-Revolutionary Philadelphia as well. For in the Quaker City, religion played a vital and unrecognized role in creating the nation's first working class.

[2]On this theme, see the works listed in note 1, above, as well as Ronald Schultz, *The Republic of Labor: Philadelphia Artisans and the Politics of Class, 1720–1830* (New York, 1993).

[3]Laurie, *Working People of Philadelphia*, and Wilentz, *Chants Democratic*, are partial exceptions; although they briefly mention religious influences on American artisans before the 1820s, they concentrate on the period of the Second Great Awakening.

[4]This is especially true of Laurie, *Working People of Philadelphia*, and Paul Johnson, *A Shopkeeper's Millennium: Society and Revivals in Rochester, New York, 1815–1837* (New York, 1978).

[5]Herbert G. Gutman, "Protestantism and the American Labor Movement: The Christian Spirit in the Gilded Age," *American Historical Review* 72 (1966):74–101.

Post-Revolutionary Philadelphia was a religious battleground. Responding to what the Rev. Robert Adair described as "a moral wilderness" of unchurched apprentices, journeymen, and poor working people, representatives of small sects and major denominations combed the city for laboring-class converts.[6] In meeting halls, on street corners, from storefront churches—even in an occasional tavern—urban itinerants preached, cajoled, and exhorted "plain and unlettered" Philadelphians to join the ranks of the pious.[7] City ministers embarked on this search for new souls because they were concerned and anxious. As they walked the back streets and alleys of laboring-class neighborhoods, they drew back from what they described as the "ignorance and vice" and the "moral degradation" of laboring-class parents and their "poor and ignorant children prowling the streets" without the "wholesome restraints" of religion.[8] For the new breed of itinerants, laboring-class Philadelphia was both a test of their moral courage and an unparalleled opportunity for redemption on a massive scale.

Philadelphia's urban itinerants shared with many of their clerical contemporaries a middle-class disdain for the unruliness of laboring-class life. Yet the rough-hewn lifestyles they witnessed on their daily rounds were stubbornly real and thriving, for post-Revolutionary Philadelphia was a city in the midst of enormous social change. To begin with, there were simply more people. On the eve of the Revolution the city was already the largest in America with a population of more than 25,000.[9] Postwar prosperity and the growth of cloth and iron manufacturing in the early nineteenth century brought thousands of new immigrants from Britain to join a flood of migrants from rural Pennsylvania and other seaboard states. By 1800 Philadelphia contained 81,000 inhabitants, nearly half

[6] Robert Adair, *Memoir of the Reverend James Patterson* (Philadelphia, 1840), p. 44. Adair's description of working-class Philadelphia refers to the 1810s.

[7] Ibid., p. 46; Abel C. Thomas, *A Century of Universalism in Philadelphia and New York* (Philadelphia, 1872), p. 76.

[8] Adair, *Memoir of Patterson*, p. 47.

[9] Nash, *Urban Crucible*, table 13, p. 408.

living in the rapidly growing laboring-class suburbs of the Northern Liberties and Southwark.[10] The 1810 federal census enumerated more than 111,000 residents, and when the workingmen's movement peaked in 1830, the city held nearly 189,000 people.[11]

This influx of people changed the scale of social relations in Philadelphia. No longer did craftsmen, merchants, and shopkeepers live side by side along the same street or lane as they had in the colonial city. Instead, by the turn of the nineteenth century, affluent and laboring-class Philadelphians lived in separate neighborhoods with their own distinctive ways of life. As a result, after 1800 the "better" and "poorer" sort saw and knew each other less well than at any previous time in the city's history. Increasingly isolated in their own neighborhoods, middle- and upper-class men and women gradually came to view their working-class counterparts with suspicion—as an alien and potentially dangerous people.

This growing distance between the everyday experiences and the diverse cultures of the city's upper, middling, and lower ranks ultimately became one of the engines of nineteenth-century urban evangelicalism and helped thrust Philadelphia into the forefront of post-Revolutionary benevolence. But if the growing rift in the city's class structure troubled urban itinerants, it was the changing nature of the city's work force that worried them more.[12] Throughout the colonial era Philadelphia's reputation as a manufacturing center rested on the output of hundreds of small shops housing a working master, one or two journeymen, and a like number of apprentices, indentured servants, or slaves. Only comparatively large enterprises like shipyards and ropewalks required a greater number of craftsmen and laborers, and the city never supported more than a handful of these highly capitalized establishments.[13]

[10]U.S. Census Office, Population Census for Philadelphia, 1800.

[11]Ibid., 1810, 1830.

[12]The following analysis is based on material in Schultz, *Republic of Labor,* chaps. 2 and 5.

[13]Carl Bridenbaugh, *The Colonial Craftsman* (Chicago, 1950), chap. 3.

By 1820, however, Philadelphia was no longer a craftsman's city. Now manufactories and putting-out concerns began to appear among the small shops that continued to dot the urban landscape. Employing young, half-trained apprentices and career-stalled journeymen, these early industrial enterprises divided tasks, increased hours, and, in the process, drove production up and prices down in ruinous competition with Philadelphia's small masters. The eclipse of the traditional craft system was evident as early as 1820 when more than a third of the city's workers labored in medium- and large-scale manufactories and uncounted others earned their livelihoods as dependent outworkers.[14]

Even in the remaining smaller shops work relations were vastly different from those of colonial times. By the end of the Revolution, lifelong journeymen and apprentices working on wage contracts had already begun to replace traditionally independent craftsmen.[15] This trend accelerated after the turn of the century, as mushrooming southern and western markets along with growing competition from larger and better capitalized manufacturers drove independent masters to cut costs the only way they could—by cheapening the price of labor. By hiring boys as laborers rather than apprentices, and by working them alongside journeymen increasingly trapped in a downward cycle of wage labor and dependence, small masters cut their costs and weakened craft traditions as well. By 1820 apprentice and journeyman had become nostalgic atavisms for what were, in fact, simply younger and older wage workers.[16]

[14]U.S. Census Office, Returns of the Industrial Census for Philadelphia County, 1820.

[15]The decline of apprenticeship and the rise of a wage-labor market in Philadelphia is discussed in Sharon V. Salinger, "Artisans, Journeymen, and the Transformation of Labor in Late Eighteenth-Century Philadelphia," *William and Mary Quarterly*, 3d ser. 40 (1983):62–84, idem, *"To Serve Well and Faithfully": Labor and Indentured Servants in Pennsylvania, 1682–1800* (New York, 1987), Billy G. Smith, "The Material Lives of Laboring Philadelphians, 1750–1800," *William and Mary Quarterly*, 3d ser. 38 (1981):163–202, and idem, *The "Lower Sort."*

[16]This is the argument of W. J. Rorabaugh, *The Craft Apprentice: From Franklin to the Machine Age in America* (New York, 1986).

Immigration added a final note of change to the city's burgeoning manufacturing economy. Soon after the postwar economy stabilized in the mid-1790s, low-paid Irish laborers, artisans, and handloom weavers flocked to Philadelphia, swelling the already substantial ranks of the city's laboring poor.[17] Coming at a time when even British- and American-born mariners, laborers, and tailors could support their families only by periodic resort to private and public poor relief, the arrival of the Irish only lowered already minimal wages and placed greater strain on a rudimentary relief system.[18]

Viewing the human costs of this rapidly disintegrating craft economy at close range, urban proselytizers set about the task of social reconstruction, armed with a mixture of religious zeal, personal determination, and a deep sense of moral righteousness. The Methodists were the first onto the field, attempting as early as the 1760s to revive the laboring-class enthusiasm that had lain dormant in Philadelphia since George Whitefield's enormously successful revivals of the 1740s and 1750s.[19] Directing their urban efforts from a sail loft along the Delaware riverfront, Thomas Webb, a British soldier turned itinerant, Edward Evans, a ladies' shoemaker, and James Emerson, a seller of orange-lemon shrubs, created Philadelphia Methodism with a distinctively plebeian cast.[20] The church retained this laboring-class identification during the uncertain years of the Revolution and into the 1780s and 1790s. By 1794 slightly more than half the city's white male

[17]The impact of Irish immigration on the composition of Philadelphia's working class is discussed in Schultz, *Republic of Labor,* chap. 4.

[18]The plight of Philadelphia's laboring poor is analyzed in Smith, "Material Lives," and Priscilla Ferguson Clement, *Welfare and the Poor in the Nineteenth-Century City: Philadelphia, 1800–1854* (Rutherford, N.J., 1985).

[19]The early history of Methodism in America is recounted in Frank Baker, *From Wesley to Asbury: Studies in Early American Methodism* (Durham, N.C., 1976), Emory Stevens Bucke, ed., *The History of American Methodism,* 3 vols. (Nashville, 1964), 1: chaps. 3–5, and John Lednum, *A History of the Rise of Methodism in America* (Philadelphia, 1859).

[20]Baker, *From Wesley to Asbury,* p. 32.

Methodists were workingmen, and by 1801 that proportion had grown to 68 percent.[21]

The rapid growth of American Methodism in the post-Revolutionary era owed much to the denomination's characteristic expectation that proselytes would confirm their conversion by becoming active bearers of their newfound faith. The Methodist discipline encouraged the creation of a lay ministry, and while only a handful might advance from class leader to full-fledged itinerant, many more took on missionary efforts closer to home.[22] In 1803, to cite but one example, a group of Philadelphia craftsmen, most of them cordwainers, created the Hospitable Society as a vehicle for missionary work among the city's laboring poor.[23] Traveling door to door, the visiting committee braved the "frequent insults and abuse" that greeted them at many laboring-class homes to bring a message of "relief" and personal salvation "to their fellow creatures."[24] Although apparently much more successful in converting wives than workingmen, the intensive campaign of the Hospitable Society did reap its share of male converts, some of whom spread the word among their mates.[25] In this way, Methodism expanded its laboring-class membership until, between 1830 and 1840, independent churches existed in each of Philadelphia's working-class suburbs and four of every five male members worked for his living. (See table 1.)

The success of the Methodists in attracting working-class members elicited two sorts of reactions from the city's other denominations. The Quakers, Anglicans, and Lutherans were for the most part comfortable with the social composition of

[21] See table 1.

[22] Baker, *From Wesley to Asbury*, pp. 199–201; *The Doctrines and Discipline of the Methodist Episcopal Church in America*, 8th ed. (Philadelphia, 1792).

[23] Philadelphia Hospitable Society, *The Nature and Design of the Hospitable Society* (Philadelphia, 1803). For an analysis of the social composition of the visiting committee, see Schultz, *Republic of Labor*, chap. 5.

[24] Philadelphia Hospitable Society, *Nature and Design*, p. 3.

[25] Ibid.

Table 1. Occupations of members of selected Philadelphia congregations

	Merchants		Manufacturers		Laboring class		Shopkeepers		Misc.	
	N	(%)	N	(%)	N	(%)	N	(%)	N	(%)
Universalist 1793	3	(12)	0	0	15	(63)	2	(8)	4	(17)
Universalist 1814–25	7	(4)	4	(2)	132	(78)	22	(13)	5	(3)
N. Liberties Presbyterian 1804	27	(34)	0	0	31	(39)	11	(14)	10	(13)
N. Liberties Presbyterian 1813	0		2	(15)	6	(46)	4	(31)	1	(8)
Methodist 1794	11	(24)*	—†		25	(54)	—†		10	(22)
St. George Methodist 1801	14	(16)*	—†		65	(75)	—†		8	(9)
Academy Methodist 1801	12	(40)*	—†		15	(50)	—†		3	(10)

Southwark Methodist 1830–40	16	(15)*	1	(1)	83	(81)	—†	3	(3)
Southwark Presbyterian 1830–40	2	(4)*	0		37	(77)	—†	9	(19)

Sources: 1793 Universalist: First Universalist Church, Subscription List, Historical Society of Pennsylvania, Philadelphia, 1793 City Directory; and 1789 Philadelphia tax list, Philadelphia City Archives; 1814–25 Universalist: First Universalist Church, Pew Book (1814–25), Hist. Soc. of Pa., and city directories for 1814–25; Presbyterian 1804: Second Presbyterian Church of the Northern Liberties, Subscription List, Presbyterian Historical Society, Philadelphia, 1804 City Directory; and 1798 Philadelphia tax list, Philadelphia City Archives; Presbyterian 1813: Presbyterian Church of the Northern Liberties, Original Communicants, November 1813, in Thomas James Shepherd, *The Days That Are Past* (Philadelphia, 1864), Appendix 3, pp. 180–81; Methodist: compiled from Doris Elisabett Andrews, "Popular Religion and the Revolution in the Middle Atlantic Ports: The Rise of the Methodists, 1770–1800," Ph.D. diss., University of Pennsylvania, 1986, table 4, p. 281; Southwark Methodist and Presbyterian: Bruce Laurie, *Working People of Philadelphia, 1800–1850* (Philadelphia, 1980), table 5, p. 47.

* Combines merchants and shopkeepers.

† Not applicable.

their existing congregations. Although Anglicans and Quakers were prominent among the city's many benevolent organizations, some of which touched the lives of the laboring poor, their churches made no direct attempts to recruit among working people. Other denominations were less complacent and organized themselves to follow the Methodist example. The Presbyterians, especially, trod close to the heels of the Methodists. Heirs, with the Methodists, of the Great Awakening, New Side Presbyterianism claimed a humble following through the Revolution and into the post-Revolutionary decades. In 1804, well before Methodist itinerants moved from the city into the laboring-class suburbs, the Presbyterians built a church in the Northern Liberties to accommodate the sailors and maritime craftsmen who were coming to dominate the district.[26] If they met with only modest success in the early years—the 1804 subscription listed nearly as many merchants as workingmen—within a decade almost half the membership of the Northern Liberties church came from the district's working class. (See table 1.)

The Rev. James Patterson was elected pastor of the Northern Liberties church in September 1813.[27] Finding that "the number that regularly attended upon religious instruction . . . was not very encouraging," Patterson borrowed a technique from local Methodists and began visiting door-to-door in the narrow streets and back alleys of the Liberties.[28] Unlike the reception accorded the members of the Methodist Hospitable Society a decade earlier, Patterson found the district more cordial, and before long his church was too small for his expanding congregation. Part of his success stemmed from his open distaste for deference and moralistic priggishness, attitudes he shared with many workingmen. As his successor in the Northern Liberties pulpit noted, Patterson possessed a "perfect disrelish of everything that savoured of affected dignity," and he frankly pitied any man who "had nothing but

[26] Thomas James Shepherd, *The Days That Are Past* (Philadelphia, 1864), pp. 180–81.

[27] Adair, *Memoir of Patterson*, p. 44.

[28] Ibid., p. 45.

his clerical robes to entitle him to the confidence and respect of men."[29]

Patterson was clearly the right man for his "plain and unlettered" congregation of workingmen and their families. His popularity was confirmed when, in January 1816, he inaugurated a seven-month-long revival. Preaching to overflow crowds, initially for seventy-six consecutive nights and then, after a brief respite, for another ninety, Patterson beat on the themes of Presbyterian doctrine: the total depravity of the heart, salvation through the sacrifice of the Son of God, and the dreadful doom awaiting those who rejected the gospel.[30] By the end of his spiritual marathon, Patterson lay ill and exhausted, but his Northern Liberties church counted 180 new communicants and many more were said to have joined neighboring congregations because of his preaching.[31]

The powerful effect of Patterson's preaching on his predominantly young working-class audience is preserved in a journal entry he made late in the revival. In it Patterson recounts the story of a young journeyman who experienced conversion the day after attending the revival. "While sitting on his work-bench," the entry begins, "he was powerfully convicted by reading the well known hymn, 'Alas, and did my Saviour bleed.' He fell upon his knees beside his work-bench, and cried aloud for mercy. This was the means of awakening four of his shop-mates to see and feel their danger as sinners, and to plead for salvation. They continued in supplication til mid-night, when they began to rejoice in hope, and to praise God for redeeming love."[32]

In James Patterson the Presbyterians had their best hope for victory in the competition for laboring-class souls. Yet neither Patterson's determined oratory nor the Methodists' self-

[29]Ibid., p. 50.

[30]Ibid., p. 74.

[31]Ibid., p. 75.

[32]Ibid., p. 73. It would be interesting to know the religious affiliation of the shop's master. Certainly not all employers would have countenanced this display of piety in the workplace or the disruption of production that it entailed.

expanding system of converts managed to capture more than a minority of Philadelphia workingmen for the militias of Christ. Even as he enjoyed the satisfaction of a successful revival, Patterson endured the street corner taunts of young journeymen and apprentices who called after him mockingly, "brimstone, fire and brimstone."[33] Nor could Patterson or the Methodists stop the growing number of masters and employers who worked their apprentices and journeymen on Sunday. And what could anyone do with the master baker who forbade his fourteen-year-old apprentice to read the New Testament, warning him that "it will fill your head with foolish freaks"?[34]

Working-class religiosity ran in many veins, and active proselytizing and enthusiastic revivals could not hope to tap them all. Again, it was the Rev. James Patterson who, unknowingly, demonstrated this. In an 1819 journal entry, Patterson considered his failure to convert a mariner whose wife was about to join the Presbyterian Church. Forcing his wife to accompany him on a country excursion the very Sunday she was to join Patterson's church, the mariner, apparently ill with tuberculosis, suffered a pulmonary lesion and was carried back to the city nearly dead. It was a weak and ashen-faced man whom Patterson confronted when he visited the couple's home shortly afterward. Realizing the gravity of the man's illness, the parson asked him whether he had made peace with God and was prepared to die. With that, the mariner flew into a rage and bellowed at Patterson, "I want no popish stuff, and no pope about me when I am going to die." Calming somewhat, he continued, "I am very weak, I don't wish you to talk to me." Undaunted, Patterson declined to leave and instead asked the mariner whether he believed the scriptures to be the word of God. By now incredulous, the sailor sprang from his sofa and turned to Patterson exclaiming, "I am astonished that you would ask any one such a question in an enlightened land." He then looked about the room for his pistols and threatened to shoot Patterson if he did not leave.

[33] Ibid., p. 97.

[34] Ibid., p. 77.

Patterson departed unharmed and the mariner died a few months later, but not before calling a Universalist minister to his side.[35]

This small glimpse of working-class life reveals another aspect of popular religion in the post-Revolutionary era. Like the beleaguered mariner, many workingmen viewed the missionary impulses of the Methodists and Presbyterians as an invasion of their world and an imposition on their way of life. This explains both the rough reception accorded the Hospitable Society's visiting committee in 1803 and the taunts that James Patterson endured fifteen years later. If they wanted religion, many laboring-class Philadelphians seemed to be saying, they would find it for themselves.

And so many did, finding a religion that fit with their views, often in surprising places. The dying mariner of Patterson's memoir found his religion with a Universalist minister. Likewise, Joe Holden, a New York blacksmith, thought that Universalism "may not be so bad after all" and undertook his own study of the matter.[36] Large numbers of Philadelphia craftsmen followed suit. As early as 1796, Benjamin Rush, an early convert to Universalism, noted the laboring-class appeal of Elhanan Winchester's Sunday evening lectures on universal salvation.[37] Rush's observation is confirmed by the 1793 subscription list of Winchester's First Universalist Church, in which nearly two-thirds of the identifiable signers were workingmen. If we add the 8 percent who were shopkeepers, grocers, and innkeepers—men with close ties to the city's craftsmen—fully 71 percent of the church's subscribers were members of Philadelphia's still amorphous working class. (See table 1.)

If Universalism was primarily a religion that attracted

[35] Ibid., pp. 79–80.

[36] Wilentz, *Chants Democratic*, p. 83.

[37] Benjamin Rush to Griffith Evans, Mar. 4, 1796, in Lyman H. Butterfield, ed., *Letters of Benjamin Rush*, 2 vols. (Princeton, 1951), 1:772–73. Elhanan Winchester was an ex-Calvinist minister who broke away from Philadelphia's First Baptist Church to found the city's premier Universalist congregation in 1781. The standard account of his life is Edwin Martin Stone, *Biography of Reverend Elhanan Winchester* (Boston, 1836).

craftsmen, small shopkeepers, and a handful of liberal intellectuals in the late eighteenth century, it was even more so during the first three decades of the following century. A tally of the surviving pew books for the years 1814–25 reveals a membership dominated by the city's *menu peuple*. In this crucial period of working-class formation, 91 percent of the identifiable members fell within this plebeian group, while fully 78 percent listed working-class occupations. Here, then, was a religion that spoke to the needs and desires of city workingmen. While the numerical strength of Universalism's plebeian appeal is remarkable in itself, it is made even more so by the fact that the Universalists, unlike the Methodists and Presbyterians, did not proselytize or mount revivals but attracted their following by simple lectures delivered in a moderate-sized church situated in Lombard Street, some distance from the city's largest working-class neighborhoods. That Philadelphia craftsmen and small shopkeepers were willing to tramp across the city on Sunday evenings to attend lectures and services speaks eloquently for the powerful attraction that drew the city's working classes to Universalism.

There were thus many paths that Philadelphia workingmen might walk in search of salvation. Some followed lay preachers into the Methodist connection and took their religion from the intimacy and fellowship of weekly class meetings. Others ran with open hearts to the message of emotional revelation that sputtered from fiery Presbyterians. Still others marked out their own path and moved with measured gait to embrace the democratic salvation offered by Universalism. But knowing the paths taken is not yet to understand the place of religion in the formation of Philadelphia's working class. What did Methodism, Presbyterianism, or Universalism offer workingmen? Was it hope for a better future, respite from the swift flow of social change, or strength to forge new collective identities in a rising manufacturing economy? An answer to these questions can only be found by placing the appeal of these plebeian denominations against the backdrop of Philadelphia's emerging working-class movement and the popular moral tradition that informed it.

Philadelphia's working-class movement developed over the course of a century, beginning with the political mobilization of city craftsmen during the 1720s and ending with the creation of distinctive working-class organizations at the close of the 1820s. In the course of this long and complex history, only the outlines of which can be sketched here, a unique set of popular intellectual traditions powerfully shaped the making of the city's working class.[38]

More a group of closely connected attitudes about work, community, and social justice than a fully articulated ideology, the small-producer tradition was the moral code by which artisans lived out their productive lives. At its core was a simple statement of the labor theory of value, or as it was more commonly rendered before the nineteenth century, the social value of labor. Beginning with the rise of urban guilds to political prominence in the twelfth century, English and European craftsmen asserted the linked claims that their labor alone was responsible for the transformation of nature into socially useful goods and that this social usefulness entitled them to respect and well-being within their communities.[39] By the time of the English Civil War, this simple idea had developed into what would become the typical artisan claim of the eighteenth and nineteenth centuries: that labor represented the basis of community life and the foundation of all collective wealth.

From the artisan's claim that civil society rested on the foundation of his labor, it was a short distance to the corollary notion that the craftsmen's collective contribution to the com-

---

[38]The rise and development of Philadelphia's working-class movement is the subject of Schultz, *Republic of Labor*. On artisan traditions of small-producer thought, see idem, "The Small-Producer Tradition and the Moral Origins of Artisan Radicalism in Philadelphia, 1720–1810," *Past and Present* 127 (1990):84–116, on which the following section is based.

[39]On the early use of the labor theory to justify guild formation, see Antony Black, *Guilds and Civil Society in European Political Thought from the Twelfth Century to the Present* (London, 1984), chaps. 1–2, Lauro Martines, *Power and Imagination: City-States in Renaissance Italy* (New York, 1980), pp. 180–83, and Mack Walker, *German Home Towns: Community, State, and General Estate, 1648–1871* (Ithaca, N.Y., 1971), chaps. 2–4.

monwealth placed them on an equal footing with other members of the community. Thus, it was no accident that artisans and small farmers were notorious advocates of democratic political reforms from at least the time of the English Civil War.[40] Claiming the rights of "freeborn Englishmen," small producers defended their rights to jury trial by their peers, to due process of law, and, if not the right to vote, then at least their right to be heard on the hustings. In the American context, artisan struggles during and after the Revolution would expand these rights to include manhood suffrage and the right of ordinary citizens to hold elective office.[41] Whether encountered in England or America, however, artisan notions of freeborn rights ran at odds with the prevailing notions of political rights and privileges propounded by large property holders and their political supporters. Against the claim that only the possession of substantial property provided a man with a true interest in society, artisans countered that the attainment of a skill and the social indispensability of productive labor combined to give all workingmen at least as great a stake in society as that claimed by the wealthy landowner or merchant.[42]

In the end, however, artisans derived their notion of equality from practice rather than high political theory. Since the Middle Ages, membership in a trade conferred upon craftsmen the right to voice their opinions, to vote, and to hold formal office or informal positions of authority within their

[40]The radical and democratic ideas of civil war England are analyzed in Christopher Hill, *The World Turned Upside Down: Radical Ideas during the English Revolution* (New York, 1972), and Brian Manning, *The English People and the English Revolution, 1640–1649* (London, 1976).

[41]On artisan suffrage struggles of the late eighteenth and early nineteenth centuries see, for New York City, Wilentz, *Chants Democratic,* and Rock, *Artisans of the New Republic;* for Baltimore, Charles G. Steffen, *The Mechanics of Baltimore: Workers and Politics in the Age of Revolution, 1763–1812* (Urbana, Ill., 1984); and for Philadelphia, Eric Foner, *Tom Paine and Revolutionary America* (New York, 1976), and Steven Rosswurm, *Arms, Country, and Class: The Philadelphia Militia and the "Lower Sort" During the American Revolution* (New Brunswick, N.J., 1987).

[42]On artisan "stake in society" theory see John Rule, "The Property of Skill in the Period of Manufacture," in Patrick Joyce, ed., *The Historical Meanings of Work* (London, 1987), pp. 99–118.

trade organizations. In short, it gave them the right to determine the affairs of their trade in conjunction with their fellow craftsmen. Thus, in drawing together popular notions of free-born rights with the rough democracy of the shop and informal trade society, artisans came to view themselves as equals, not only with other workingmen, but also with the wealthiest and most powerful members of society.

The third pillar of the small-producer tradition was competency. Few terms were as ubiquitous among artisans and other small producers as this. In its most basic form, competency was the lifelong ability of an artisan to provide a comfortable existence for his family through his own labor. A competency was the promise of moderate well-being and financial independence purchased through the early acquisition of a skill and the lifelong practice of a trade. For Anglo-American craftsmen, entry into a trade meant entering into a covenant with the community, a covenant in which the artisan offered a life of productive labor to the community in return for the respect of his peers and an independent life free from protracted want.

A sense of community-mindedness completed the small-producer tradition. Artisanal notions of community derived from the internal structure of the trades as well as from the local nature of craft production itself. Petty production in early America was typically production for a local market where producers and customers not only knew each other but were bound by intimate ties of custom and clientage. Under these conditions, in which artisans depended upon personal goodwill for their livelihood, the maintenance of community bonds was crucial to the smooth operation of the craft system.

But beyond the nature of small production itself, artisanal ideas about community developed from the communal organization of the craft workshop. Almost all artisans worked in small establishments with a handful of other craftsmen and apprentices. Even in larger enterprises like shipyards and metal works, craftsmen worked in gangs or crews that were seldom composed of more than a dozen men. Human relationships in these small-scale conditions were intimate and characterized by a norm of mutuality and cooperation. The shop was a little community where work rules, the pace of production, and personal relationships were governed to a considerable degree by the workers themselves. When artisans turned their attention to the larger community around them, they naturally referred to the daily operations of their shops as a guide. Much as earlier craft guilds looked to the operations of the workshop when they sought to create regulations for the conduct of their trades, artisans relied upon the world of the shop when they sought a model for the proper functioning of the community in which they lived.

Artisans, then, viewed community, like their craft, as an association of individuals who labored together for the benefit of all. A well-run society, like a well-regulated trade, required the subordination of individual self-interest and acquisitiveness to the collective well-being of its members. Just as artisans arranged shop tasks and the pace of production to ensure that there was work enough for all, so craftsmen saw a proper community as one in which labor and its rewards were shared with fairness and equality and in which no productive member lacked in essentials while others had a more than ample supply. What craftsmen could not abide was a society where a few men lived on the fruits of the workingmen's labor and deprived producers of their just recompense.

These qualities—the value of labor, equality, competency, and community—made up the small-producer tradition. Together they represented the intellectual and moral standard against which Philadelphia artisans measured the religious appeals of Methodist class leaders, Presbyterian evangelists, and Universalist ministers. As events were to prove, those appeals led city workingmen along two, very different, paths.

Blessed are the poor in spirit for they,
Towards heav'ns kingdom are far on the way.

In lowly rev'rence let me come,
And bow in heart before thy awful throne.[43]

The words are those of John Cox, a humble Philadelphia shoemaker, amateur poet, and ardent spokesman for working-class piety.[44] His seven hundred-odd lines of uneven verse represent one of the few direct statements of laboring-class religiosity that have come down to us and reveal the unmistakable accents of the evangelical appeal among the working classes.

In England, as E. P. Thompson noted long ago, Methodism and other evangelical confessions offered solace and spiritual recompense to the victims of industrial change, albeit at the price of a lifelong obedience and servility that extended well beyond the spiritual kingdom into the texture of everyday life.[45] In Philadelphia the evangelical message was more complex and equivocal, and the conditions of its auditors were altogether different. Unlike England, where the crushing weight of state repression joined with severe industrial dislocation to make of Methodism a "chiliasm of despair," laboring-class Philadelphians faced a more gradual industrial transformation with the power of manhood suffrage securely in their hands.[46] Accordingly, evangelical religion offered craftsmen a more positive, if ultimately limiting, message. In their simple theology as well as in their spontaneous and democratic style, urban itinerants appealed to a working class

[43] John Cox, *Rewards and Punishments, or, Satans Kingdom Aristocratical* (Philadelphia, 1795), pp. 14, 3.

[44] Cox's occupation and tax assessment are taken from the 1795 city directory and the 1798 city tax list. I am indebted to Billy G. Smith of Montana State University for the use of his computer-tabulated Philadelphia tax lists.

[45] E. P. Thompson, *The Making of the English Working Class* (London, 1963), chap. 11.

[46] On the industrial transformation of Philadelphia, see Laurie, *Working People of Philadelphia*, chap. 1.

that had successfully thrown off the bonds of colonial deference and had begun to demand a politics as plain and direct as their small-producer ethos. In this sense, evangelicalism was part of the larger cultural emergence of artisans and lesser workingmen into the public life of the post-Revolutionary era.[47]

But in the wider view, the evangelical appeal touched something deeper than the Revolutionary political experiences of ordinary men and women. In the postwar years, Methodist and Presbyterian evangelists opened the doors of Christian brotherhood to Philadelphia's working people. In its early stages, post-Revolutionary evangelicalism held forth the prospect of a religion that could encompass both searing emotionality and traditional notions of artisanal respectability. Under the cover of institutional legitimacy provided by their class meetings and shoestring congregations, workingmen and their families found the freedom to express the mutual release of emotion that was an essential part of working-class culture, a culture that the city's more established churches eschewed and condemned. Unlike the city's more staid clerics, urban itinerants exhorted their congregations to *feel* the power of God's grace and their own shared religiosity. At the same time they provided their parishioners with institutional channels—churches, class meetings, and love feasts—that cloaked their expressive emotionality with a measure of public respectability.

What ordinary Philadelphians sought in evangelical religion was collective commitment and shared experience, the mutual validation of belief and community that comes from rituals of collective catharsis and experiential piety. A nineteenth-century mariner described this evangelical appeal with great poignancy: "What I likes along o'preachin'," he told a traveling evangelist, is "when a man is a-preachin' at me I want him to take somert hot out of his heart and shove

---

[47]The emergence of artisans into eighteenth- and early nineteenth-century public life is the subject of a rapidly growing literature. Among the most important recent works are, Nash, *Urban Crucible*, Rock, *Artisans of the New Republic*, and Richard A. Ryerson, *The Revolution Is Now Begun: The Radical Committees of Philadelphia, 1765–1776* (Philadelphia, 1978).

it into mine,—that's what I calls preachin'."[48] It was by taking "somert hot" from their hearts and sharing it with their congregations that urban evangelists created the electric waves of piety that washed over their rough-hewn flocks. From the end of the Revolution until well into the next century, these plebeian proselytizers provided a respectable venue for those who thought, as did an anonymous Boston sailor, that "faith is suth'n like Tinder: shut it up and it will go out, but give it vent and it will burn."[49] Urban evangelicalism blew across a smoldering working-class piety that had long been ignored by more conventional churches and ignited flames of enthusiasm that would shape the lives of large numbers of working people for generations to come.[50]

The shared experiences of conversion, prayer, and public testimony built powerful and lasting bonds between preachers, class leaders, and rank-and-file believers. At the same time, the evangelical emphasis on the individual's responsibility for salvation, nurtured and confirmed within the circle of collective fellowship, conveyed a sense of self-worth and community esteem that paralleled traditional craft feelings and norms. For many craftsmen and deskilled workingmen, the competency and self-respect that was lost in the decline of the craft system might be redeemed in the class meeting and evangelical congregation. In the end, it was this combined search for secular redemption, personal recognition, and spiritual salvation that brought floods of working-class converts into Philadelphia's Methodist and Presbyterian churches in the years following the Revolution.

But for all its positive attributes—its democratic inclusiveness, its fostering of personal and collective worth, its promise of spiritual redemption—evangelicalism carried with it the heavy baggage of its Calvinist heritage. Despite its evident humanism and the genuine concern of street preachers

[48]Robert Collyer, *Father Taylor* (Boston, 1906), p. 39.

[49]Ibid., p. 43.

[50]The impact of evangelicalism on Philadelphia's mid-nineteenth-century working-class movement is analyzed in Laurie, *Working People of Philadelphia*, chaps. 7–9.

and class leaders to bring religion to the poor, urban evangelicalism was haunted by the notion of the depravity of man.
In the final analysis, urban itinerants brought religion to the
working-class as a way of tempering the sin and meanness
that they saw as inherent in human nature, especially as it was
manifested among the nation's lower orders. In the evangelists' eyes, mankind was by nature evil, and righteous living
was, for all men and women, the labor of Sisyphus. Once un-
remitting depravity was accepted as the essence of human
nature, asceticism and fear became the only pathways to salvation. Herein lay the central tension in the evangelical message
to the working class: accept God's love and you may regain
your competency and self-respect, but involve yourself too
much with worldly concerns and you face eternal damnation
from a wrathful, punishing God.

John Cox's *Rewards and Punishments* captures this tension
exactly, in its title as well as its verse. Cox begins by offering
the promise of restored competency and general prosperity
that would be God's reward to a regenerate Philadelphia:

> Filled with God's grace, our city will shine bright,
> And over the world will cast resplendent light;
> Our enemies shall never do us harm,
> For he will help us with outstretched arm.[51]

All that is required to achieve this urban millennium is for the
men and women of the city to bridle their passions and learn
the lesson of humility:

> Let us arise and shake ourselves from dust,
> And he will help us overcome our lust;
> His goodness he will extend to every soul,
> If they will subject be to his control.[52]

This is the message of a loving God, a God ever ready to "help
us with outstretched arm." But, let human pridefulness and

---

[51] Cox, *Rewards and Punishments*, p. 8.

[52] Ibid.

arrogance triumph, and the project fails. Here Cox's God takes on a more ominous countenance:

> With base ingratitude ye did despise
> My statutes, and from me did turn your eyes,
> And for this thing I on you will send terror,
> As long as you will still persist in error.[53]

The path is clearly marked: this way, reward; that way, punishment. Like Christian, John Bunyan's archetypal seeker, Philadelphians are offered choices and a moral road map. One path leads to the postmillennial Celestial City, all others lead to urban poverty and degrading dependency. Aware of the uncertainty of the human heart, Cox closes his promise with a characteristic evangelical warning wrapped within a threat: "If that we his blessed task forsake, / He'll on our heads his dreadful anger shake."[54]

For John Cox and workingmen who thought like him, the evangelical message of repressive deliverance promised the resurrection of a world of small producers, a world in which their labor would lead not only to competency but to simple respect. Most artisans in post-Revolutionary Philadelphia shared these aspirations and many spent their lives searching for a way to redeem what they saw as the lost promise of the American Revolution. Some, like Cox, found that way in an evangelical religion that traded laboring-class solidarity for the fellowship of the class meeting and, perhaps, a small measure of worldly success.

By rejecting the solidarity of the emerging labor movement for the consolation of faith, submission, not struggle became the center of Cox's religion:

> Let us with pleasure bear each dispensation,
> In ev'ry rank of life and ev'ry station;
> Let us become as clay in [a] potter's hand
> To mould in any form at his command.[55]

[53] Ibid., p. 4.

[54] Ibid.

[55] Ibid., p. 11.

In the end, it was submission rather than organization that would finally yield both temporal and spiritual rewards:

> Let us in all things to his will submit,
> With patience undergo all he thinks fit:
> And if unto the end we him adore,
> We will receive of him a heav'nly store.[56]

This was one side of working-class religion; restraint, repression, and self-denial operating through submission and fear to produce a life of satisfaction and self-esteem. All that was required was to reject the tavern, the Sunday excursion, the camaraderie of games and gambling, and, along with it, the journeymen's society and mutuality, the integument of working-class culture. What would be left in the end was not a working class but "respectable" workingmen indistinguishable in sentiment from their middle-class employers.

There was, of course, another side to working-class religion and it was, in many ways, the more important of the two. It was the side that empowered rather than diminished working-class life.[57] Unlike Methodism and evangelical Presbyterianism, both of which still bore the marks of Puritanical Calvinism in their message of denial and submission, this alternative to overweening piety offered democratic salvation as well as an open acceptance of the working-class way of life. In Philadelphia, this brighter side of working-class religion found its most forceful expression in the doctrines and organizations of the Universalist Church.

Part of a widespread reaction to predestinarian doctrines in the years following the Revolution, Universalism embraced

---

[56] Ibid.

[57] While evangelicalism may have ultimately diminished support for Philadelphia's growing white working-class movement, it functioned very differently for the city's black working class. See the important argument of Gary B. Nash, which presents Methodism as a positive force in building Philadelphia's black community in the years following the Revolution, in his *Forging Freedom: The Formation of Philadelphia's Black Community, 1720–1840* (Cambridge, Mass., 1988).

the notion of salvation for everyone.[58] Against John Cox's paradoxical image of a benevolent yet ultimately vengeful God, Universalists counterposed the God of pure love—a God who, in the end, understood human frailties and forgave human transgressions. The message of the Universalists was thus a simple but powerful one: all will be saved.

Translated from doctrine into practice, Universalism took on a distinctively laboring-class voice as early as the 1790s in the form of didactic hymns. Written to instruct as well as entertain, hymnody became the vehicle for Universalism's popular appeal.[59] Something of this plebeian appeal can be sensed in Abner Kneeland's "Invitation to the Gospel," with its imagery of plenty and social leveling:

> Hear ye that starve for food,
> By feeding on the wind,
> Or vainly strive with earthly good,
> To fill an empty mind.

> The Lord of Love has made,
> A soul reviving feast,
> And lets the world, of every grade,
> To rich provision taste.[60]

Universalist hymnody also contained more direct appeals, as in Elhanan Winchester's paean to "America's Future Glory and Happiness," which focused on the central theme of the craftsman's creed, a life of competency:

> No more the labour'r pines, and grieves,
> For want of plenty round;

[58] For the history of Universalism see Russell E. Miller, *The Larger Hope: The First Century of the Universalist Church in America, 1770–1870* (Boston, 1979), and Ernest Cassara, ed., *Universalism in America: A Documentary History* (Boston, 1971), chap. 1.

[59] On Universalist hymnody see Stephen A. Marini, *Radical Sects of Revolutionary New England* (Cambridge, Mass., 1982), pp. 162–66.

[60] Universalist Church in the U.S.A., *Hymns Composed by Different Authors* (Walpole, N.H., 1808), p. 80.

> His eyes behold the fruitful sheaves,
> Which makes his joys abound.[61]

Such working-class themes ran through many Universalist hymns, but their appeal to city workingmen ran deeper still. In their hymns and preaching, Universalists often spoke of a community of love in ways that echoed the solidarity of tight-knit journeymen's societies and the mutuality of the larger working-class community:

> How sweet is the union of souls,
> In harmony, friendship and love;
> Lord help us, this union to keep,
> In *union* God grant we may meet.[62]

This was written in 1808, a time when masters and journeymen were being relentlessly driven apart by the new manufacturing economy, a time during which the Democratic-Republican party was dividing itself into opposing manufacturing and working-class wings.[63] Reading these lines against the evidence of an emerging working-class movement, it would have been difficult for many Philadelphia workingmen to separate the union of Christian fellowship from early craft unions.

In the end, this was the most remarkable aspect of the Universalist–working-class connection. While the Universalist credo mirrored traditional artisan values better than the doctrines of any other denomination, it was not beliefs that ultimately mattered. It was organization. From its inception, the Universalist Church was a meeting ground for the leaders (and at least some of the rank-and-file) of Philadelphia's working-class movement.

---

[61] Elhanan Winchester, *Thirteen Hymns, Suited to the Present Times,* 2d ed. (Baltimore, 1776), p. 15.

[62] Universalist Church, *Hymns,* pp. 184–85.

[63] On divisions within Philadelphia's Democratic-Republican party see Roland M. Baumann, "John Swanwick: Spokesman for 'Merchant-Republicanism' in Philadelphia, 1790–1798," *Pennsylvania Magazine of History and Biography* 97 (1973):148–56. The formation of the working-class wing of the party is discussed in Schultz, *Republic of Labor,* chap. 5.

We can date the beginnings of the post-Revolutionary workers' movement from the formation of the Democratic Society of Pennsylvania in 1793.[64] Organized by old Antifederalists and a new generation of opposition politicians, the Democratic Society brought Philadelphia craftsmen into organized politics for the first time since the 1770s. The political connection of Philadelphia Universalism was evident the same year, when 39 percent of the church's subscribers were also listed as members of the Democratic Society.[65]

As the Democratic Society broadened into the Democratic-Republican party and, early in the nineteenth century, the party began to organize workingmen into neighborhood political clubs, the Universalist Church continued to play an informal organizing role.[66] Not only did the church count such Democratic-Republican luminaries as Alexander James Dallas and Matthew Clarkson among its members, but, more importantly, it also included two of the city's most prominent working-class leaders on its rolls. Anthony Cuthbert, a mastmaker and member of one of Philadelphia's most prominent artisan families, and Israel Israel, an innkeeper and political champion of the early nineteenth-century workingmen's movement, were both active Universalists from the 1790s through the 1820s.[67] Israel, who first earned his reputation among craftsmen for his selfless efforts in laboring-class neighborhoods during the yellow fever epidemic of 1794, became one of the most important popular leaders of the early nineteenth century.[68]

[64]Schultz, *Republic of Labor,* chap. 5.

[65]This figure was reached by comparing the 1793 Subscription List of the First Universalist Church with the Minutes of the Democratic Society of Pennsylvania. Both documents are held at the Historical Society of Pennsylvania, Philadelphia.

[66]On early working-class political organization, see Schultz, *Republic of Labor,* chaps. 4 and 5.

[67]These names were traced through the 1793 Subscription List of the First Universalist Church and the First Universalist Church, Pew Book (1814–25), Hist. Soc. of Pa.

[68]The public career of Israel Israel can be followed in John K. Alexander, *Render Them Submissive: Responses to Poverty in Philadelphia, 1760–1800* (Am-

The paucity of church records for the first two decades of the nineteenth century limits our understanding of the church's organizing role in those years, but the continued presence of popular leaders such as Cuthbert and, especially, Israel, coupled with the increasing working-class presence in the church itself, strongly suggests the church's importance to the emerging working-class movement. This importance was underlined when the workers' movement took on an institutional structure during the late 1820s.[69] The creation of the Mechanics' Union of Trade Associations in 1827 and the Workingmen's party the following year marked the formation of America's first working class. Led by William Heighton, a local shoemaker of English birth, the Mechanics' Union and the Workingmen's party forged artisan intellectual traditions and popular politics into a powerful working-class presence in Philadelphia. Universalism played more than a minor role in this process, for not only was Heighton a follower of Universalist doctrines, he also organized the Mechanics' Union through a series of meetings held in the city's Universalist churches.[70]

Religion played an important part in Heighton's ambitious and multifaceted plan to restore the producing classes—farmers, mechanics, and laborers—to their rightful place in American society. In an address delivered at the newly gathered Second Universalist Church, located near the working-class suburb of the Northern Liberties, Heighton outlined his plan. The cause of the continuing economic and social decline of Philadelphia's working classes, he declared, was the growing dominance of the "avaricious accumulators and ungenerous

---

herst, Mass., 1980), pp. 37–42, and J. H. Powell, *Bring Out Your Dead: The Great Plague of Yellow Fever in Philadelphia in 1793* (New York, 1965), pp. 188–99.

[69] On the institutionalization of Philadelphia's working-class movement, see Louis H. Arky, "The Mechanics' Union of Trade Associations and the Formation of the Philadelphia Workingmen's Movement," *Pennsylvania Magazine of History and Biography* 76 (1952):142–76.

[70] Several of William Heighton's speeches were printed. His most important discussion of religion is in *An Address, Delivered before the Mechanics and Working Classes . . . at the Universalist Church, in Callowhill Street* (Philadelphia, 1827).

employers" of the city.[71] This class of "aristocratic accumulators," Heighton told his working-class audience, consisted of social and economic parasites who obtained their livelihoods solely from the fruits of other men's labor.[72] The degraded condition of Philadelphia workingmen, he explained, came not from human moral failings or the wrath of a displeased God, but from the unrestrained greed of men who lived by exploiting the city's working classes.

In time, Heighton hoped to set the united working classes of the city against this growing class of accumulators. In the meantime, he maintained that it was the duty of Philadelphia's "legislative, judicial, and theological classes" to exercise "their influence to remedy [the workers'] degraded condition."[73] Yet, as Heighton painstakingly pointed out, none of these classes had thus far brought any degree of social justice to the workingman's door, and the clergy had failed most egregiously of all.

In the course of his public indictment of Philadelphia's reforming clergy, Heighton outlined the proper role of religion in a future republic of labor. As he saw it, the social and moral obligation of the clergy was not simply to "teach evangelical truths" but "to teach the absolute necessity of undeviating justice between man and man."[74] While he thought that true Christian ministers ought to be living "imitators of those primitive Christians who had 'all things in common,'" Heighton found instead that most Philadelphia clerics remained blind to the "legalized extortion" practiced on the city's working classes.[75] "Why do they not point out the enormous injustice of one class of men possessing legal authority to take advantage of the necessities of another?" he asked.[76]

[71] Ibid., p. 8.

[72] Ibid., p. 9.

[73] Ibid.

[74] Ibid.

[75] Ibid.

[76] Ibid.

And why had the denominational clergy not directed "the power of their reasoning, and the thunders of their eloquence against the unjust and vice-creating system of conflicting interest—a system so directly opposed to that adopted by . . . the Prince of Peace?"[77]

If the established clergy were shameless in their failure to speak out against this pernicious evil, the evangelists were, for Heighton, the most culpable of all. Taking aim at the city's Methodist and evangelical Presbyterian ministers, he pointed to the futility of their quest for working-class redemption in a world structured by industrial capitalism. With barely disguised contempt Heighton warned his listeners that "not all the fervent intercessions of prayer, not all the influence of pathetic exhortation, nor all the declarations of divine denunciation, can ever arrest the progress of sin while the system of individual interest and competition is supported."[78] For Heighton, the only hope for redemption lay not in working-class piety within the present system but in a united effort by clergy and workingmen alike to overturn that system in the name of social justice.

Religion, then, was closely bound up with Heighton's vision of a republic of independent producers; the competition and individual interest of the wage-labor market was a moral injustice, to be sure, but it was also a sin. The interest of the clergy and the interest of workingmen were consequently the same: the creation of a moral society founded in social justice. "If the clergy would arrest the fatal march of vice," Heighton advised, "let them direct their attacks on its fountain head."[79] "The grand nursery of sin must be destroyed," he added, "before they can cherish any reasonable hopes of a general and permanent reformation in our country."[80] Thus the republic of labor would be more than a society of loosely associated producers; it would be God's true community.

In the broadest sense, then, religion occupied a prominent

[77] Ibid.

[78] Ibid.

[79] Ibid.

[80] Ibid.

place in Philadelphia's working-class movement because that movement went well beyond a simple strengthening of workers' market capacities.[81] Heighton's aim, whether in the Mechanics' Union or the Workingmen's party, was to reform American society, to make America into the moral community that both clergy and workingmen saw as the nation's brightest promise. As husbandmen of public and private morality, the American clergy could do much to bring about this reformation, if only they would direct "their talents, their learning, and their influence . . . against the mainspring of all evil, and source of every crime."[82] If all of America's clerics would follow the example of their Universalist brethren and unite with the nation's working people in the project of labor reform, "religion [would] extend, and flourish in all its sublime and harmonious beauties" throughout the entire nation.[83]

Popular religion thus played an important role in the formation of Philadelphia's working class. While some workingmen retreated into the quiescence of evangelical piety and finally turned their backs on the working-class movement, many others turned to religion as a moral force that underwrote their own traditions and pointed toward a more hopeful future. While much, much more remains to be done before we can fully understand the place of religion in early working-class life, the case of the Universalists and Philadelphia's workingmen's movement suggests that religion could be a powerful ally in the workingmen's quest for economic and social justice.

[81] On the notion of working-class market capacities, see Anthony Giddens, *The Class Structure of the Advanced Societies* (New York, 1973), pp. 100–112.

[82] Heighton, *An Address*, p. 10.

[83] Ibid.

ROBERT M. CALHOON

The Evangelical Persuasion

SOMETIME IN 1762 or 1763 a backcountry North Carolina dandy named Elnathan Davis heard a delicious rumor. "John Steward . . . a very big man," was going to be baptized by the famous Separate Baptist preacher Shubal Stearns in the presence of the membership of the Sandy Creek Baptist Church, people who would come from miles around to participate in the creekside service. The spectacle of the short, wiry Stearns lowering Steward's heavy body into the muddy water promised "some diversion, if not drowning." Davis and eight or nine high-spirited cronies gathered on the bank above the creek to watch. Curious and troubled by the intensity of the feelings of the worshipers, Davis left his companions and joined the people at the water's edge. He peered into their trembling faces. Skeptical but moved, he touched the arm of one man to test whether he was dissembling; the man collapsed into his arms, pressing his face into Davis's shoulder, soiling his "new white coat." Davis fiercely shoved the man away and ran to rejoin his companions.

"Well, Elnathan, what to you think of these damned people?" one of them taunted him. "There is a trembling and crying spirit among them," the panting Davis replied, "but whether it be the spirit of God or the devil, I don't know." Dazed at the scene he had just witnessed and frightened by his own reaction to it, Davis listened, transfixed, to "the enchantment of Shubal Stearns's voice" until, shaking with anxiety, he collapsed. For several days he endured "dread and anxiety bordering upon horror" until, reflecting on Stearns's words, he "found relief by faith in Christ."[1]

[1] Robert M. Calhoon, ed., *Religion and the American Revolution in North Carolina* (Raleigh, N.C., 1976), pp. 51–52; Isaac Backus, *Church History of New England, from 1620 to 1804* (Philadelphia, 1839), pp. 227–28.

This event was emblematic of the spread of evangelical religion in the southern backcountry. Its depiction of tears and baptismal water, of trembling, sweaty bodies, transports modern readers into the physical reality of popular religion; its setting of stream bank and high bank from which the sons of privilege looked down with incredulity on humble, ecstatic ordinary folk helps readers visualize the way topography reinforced people's sense of social distance and human intimacy. And the "enchantment" of the preacher's voice reminds us that aural sensation surpassed the sight of the printed page as a social stimulus for ordinary people in eighteenth-century America.[2]

Evangelicals conceived of the world as organized into sacred space where the Holy Spirit came upon the bodies and into the consciousness of converts and surrounding secular terrains. Entering this space—crossing the threshold from mundane periphery to sacred center—could take minutes, days, or even years, and much of the process occurred imperceptibly. Only the conclusion of the encounter with the holy seized the attention of a convert, like the Virginian Edward Baptist, who noted in 1809 that his "conviction for sin became more deep and pungent every hour." Edward Baptist's conversion became a reality when he finally abandoned futile efforts to participate in his own moral reformation and then realized that "my guilt was gone, my conscience at rest, and my soul at liberty."[3] The propulsive power of this freeing, healing spiritual force, as one church covenant explained, was "faith" which "is not an act of man's free will and power but of the mighty, efficacious grace of God."[4]

Living within this sacred space—or more precisely, moving within this stream of perceived spiritual destiny—was, nonetheless, a struggle. Converts had to choose daily between the

[2]Robert M. Calhoon, *Evangelicals and Conservatives in the Early South, 1740–1861* (Columbia, S.C., 1988), chap. 1.

[3]Edward Baptist Diary (autobiographical memoir), typescript, Virginia Historical Society, Richmond.

[4]"Declaration of Faith in Practice, Being a Covenant, . . . November 7, 1773," John Corbly Memorial Baptist Church Records, Department of Archives and Manuscripts, West Virginia University Library, Morgantown.

arduous freedom of the new birth and the habit-encrusted, self-concerned inhibitions of their human nature. Nowhere was the struggle so sharply defined as in the preachers' complaints of being emotionally blocked and painfully inarticulate, complaints that were then followed by their celebrations of release from this malady. "My colleague seemed too much indisposed to officiate," Jeremiah Norman, a Methodist circuit rider, noted in his diary on June 1, 1796. "It consequently fell on me. I had not that sweetness and flow of the spirit that I have at some times. I was not able to account for it. I have often felt the effect of company, conversation, and the house where I am. . . . Lord bring me out of this dreadful lethargy." Several days later, he wrote, "I felt my soul as on the wing. I had lost my clog. I prayed and believed there would be some good done today." But it was not to be. Now it was the people to whom he preached that day who "appeared to be quite weary. . . . Many had gone away into the shades to talk. It was now out of my power to call up their attention onto the word. As stupid creatures they remained aloof."[5] Another North Carolina itinerant, Thomas Mann, noted in his journal in April 1805 that at a service at nine in the morning "I did not feel right. Things were not as they ought to be here," but at eleven "I preached under a red oak to a large congregation from Genesis 49:10, 'The sceptre shall not depart from Judah . . . until Shiloh come, and unto him shall the gathering of the people be,' with ease and liberty considering my ability, and the wind blew very fresh."[6]

The evangelical antidote to despair, fear, or emotional listlessness was twofold: the awesome realization that sin jeopardized each person's capacity to receive the spirit, and, still more searing, the discovery at the depth of estrangement from God that salvation had occurred and had healed the rupture. "Now he sees and feels that he is sold under sin, a bond slave to it and he sees no way in which God can give him grace," explained a Virginia preacher in July 1788; "now he is brought to think that the bond of his guilt lays God him-

---

[5]Calhoon, ed., *Religion and Revolution in North Carolina*, pp. 62–63.

[6]Thomas Mann Journal, Manuscripts Department, Duke University Library, Durham, N.C.

self under an obligation to inflict the whole of his vengeance upon him." Comprehending that reality—"the whole of God's vengeance"—and knowing it had been graciously withheld was the means by which the Spirit penetrated, transformed, and saved the sinner.[7]

Often these surprising intimations of God's grace came from ugly encounters with human cruelty and injustice. In Caroline County, Virginia, an unidentified Anglican clergyman, probably the Rev. Archibald Dick of St. Mary's parish, strode into a Baptist meeting in April 1771 during the singing of an opening hymn. Flicking the tip of his whip across the open pages of the hymnals and "running the end of his horsewhip in his mouth," he moved among the gathered worshipers. As the singing ended, the intruder "violently jerked" the Baptist minister, John Waller, "off the stage, caught him by the back part of his neck, beat his head against the ground," and dragged the half-conscious Waller outside. There, "a gentleman" administered "not less than twenty lashes with his horsewhip" and "the parson give him abominable ill language." Their point made, the parson, his curate, and the gentleman departed. Waller picked himself up, returned to the meeting "singing praises to God . . . and preached with a great deal of liberty."[8]

Two penetrating observations, one by Nathan O. Hatch and another by Gordon S. Wood, frame the problem of the social potency of evangelicalism in the new nation. "The right to think for oneself," Hatch declares, "became . . . the hallmark of popular Christianity" in post-Revolutionary America. "Visions, dreams, prophesyings, and new emotion-soaked religious seekings," Wood argues, "acquired a validity they had not earlier possessed. . . . Thousands of common people were cut loose from all sorts of traditional bonds and found themselves freer, more independent, more unconstrained than

[7]Manuscript sermon on Romans 8:9, Brock Collection, no. 120, Huntington Library, San Marino, Calif.

[8]John S. Moore, ed., "John Williams's Journal," *Virginia Baptist Register,* no. 17 (1978):798. For a different reading of this source, which places the handle of the whip in the victim's mouth, see Rhys Isaac, *The Transformation of Virginia, 1740–1790* (Chapel Hill, 1982), p. 162.

ever before in their history."[9] The powerful, democratic, largely evangelical impulse in American religious life recognized by Hatch and Wood was the product of the same processes of persuasion, intellectual competition, and application of theory to practice that undergirded the whole enterprise of creating the American republic.

The construct of a persuasion is appropriate to the study of early American culture. A persuasion is a view of reality, and a code of public conduct indicated by that view, that is normative for those who articulate it and respond to it. A persuasion assumes that truth exists in public affairs and that it activates the moral sense of individuals. Persuasions exist in flux. They arise from efforts to resolve paradoxes central to the life of the mind and spirit, and long before they die persuasions fray around the edges as new moral challenges call forth fresh language. Indeed, these stages of coalescence and deterioration in a persuasion can overlap as aging ideas provide the spur for revitalization of the message.[10]

Evangelical Christianity was, to be sure, more than a persuasion. It was a critical mass of spirituality, a stage in the development of the Protestant theological tradition, and a release of energy into a surrounding human environment. The immediacy of Christ's sacrifice brought ecstasy and the "indwelling of the spirit" into the consciousness of the convert;[11] evangelical Christianity combined Calvinist assumptions about human depravity and divine majesty with the Arminian appreciation of God's desire to flood all humanity

[9]Nathan O. Hatch, "In Pursuit of Religious Freedom: Church, State, and People in the New Republic," in Jack P. Greene, ed., *The American Revolution: Its Character and Limits* (New York, 1987), p. 391, and Gordon S. Wood, "Evangelical America and Early Mormonism," *New York History* 61 (1980):368, 361.

[10]Marvin Meyers, *The Jacksonian Persuasion: Politics and Belief,* preface to the Vintage edition (New York, 1960), pp. v–ix; Lance G. Banning, *The Jeffersonian Persuasion: Evolution of a Party Ideology* (Ithaca, N.Y., 1978), pp. 15–16, 274–90; and Robert Kelley, *The Transatlantic Persuasion* (New York, 1969), pp. xvii–xxi.

[11]George Whitefield, *The Indwelling of the Spirit, the Common Privilege of All Believers* (London, 1739), pp. 1–2.

with grace; evangelical converts felt and communicated a contagious desire to be bonded spiritually to others.

Evangelicalism is also shared public discourse. When Representative Fred Schwengel told his colleagues during the school prayer debate that "the persuasiveness of love" is the only function of religion appropriate in a republic, he identified the potency of spirituality in republican discourse, and he vindicated, historically and religiously, the separation of church and state.[12] This essay will examine the evangelical persuasion in four contexts: Revolutionary politics, attempts to reconcile Christianity and republicanism, congregational discipline, and sermon writing. Then it will observe the partial unraveling of evangelical citizenship as evangelicals grappled with issues of slavery and race.

The Revolution cut across a long-standing religious debate in America about the nature of authority and the intellectual and emotional links that connected individuals to their fellows and to their Creator. The dispute with Great Britain fed into and exacerbated this effort to know the extent and limits of personal and communal liberty. David Caldwell, Presbyterian minister in Guilford County, North Carolina, equated subjection to British tyranny with "the doom of the sluggard." "The Slothful shall be under tribute," declared his text from Proverbs 12:24, and slothfulness in Caldwell's call to political action and discipline was the natural, human inclination to inactivity, unreflectiveness, apathy, and to narrow and stupid concern with one's own comfort. "The sluggard, as a worthless being, destitute of merit and doing no good to himself or any body else is as really an object of reprobation as the miser, the spendthrift, or the highway robber; and the blessings which he foregoes and the evils which he brings on himself here are but forerunners of the heavier losses which he will sustain and the more insufferable woes which he will bring upon himself hereafter, . . . bound hand and foot, and cast

[12]Quoted by Ronald Hoffman in his introductory remarks at the U.S. Capitol Historical Society Symposium "Religion in a Revolutionary Age," Mar. 30–31, 1988.

into outer darkness where no ray of comfort can cast even a momentary radiance over the gloom."[13]

In Caldwell's view, the political and social implications of these tendencies in human nature were ominous. Throughout history "sloth," as a state of mind and body and as a moral condition, had tempted rulers to exercise tyrannical power. The slothful were people who seemed, to arrogant and unreflective rulers, to be fit objects of unbridled governmental coercion. The "ignorance, disregard of moral obligation, and supreme love of ease" of the groveling sluggard corresponded exactly with a tyrant's appetite and cynicism. "While [the sluggard] is spending or losing by his ignorance and sloth the inheritance handed down . . . through a number of generations . . . [of] his predecessors, . . . the ambitious and covetous, those tyrants of the human race and pests of society believing that his ignorance will screen them from his notice and that his indolence will make him perfectly submissive, . . . thus . . . are encouraged to make their experiment, and they too often succeed." Not only did the slothful encourage and facilitate oppression, their own "shame" and "sinking spirits," their own pitiful compliance and submission became self-made chains of slavery. The miraculous way in which God might intervene to preserve colonial liberty, Caldwell declared, would occur only as the Holy Spirit penetrated the encrustations of habit and lethargy and converted the soul, the conscience, the moral sense within the human frame into something graceful and swift and responsive.[14]

Addressing upwardly mobile, bookish Presbyterians, Cald-

[13]Eli W. Caruthers, *A Sketch of the Life and Character of the Reverend David Caldwell* (Greensboro, N.C., 1842), pp. 273–75. The pioneering study of this whole subject by Alice M. Baldwin, though published in 1947, was written as a seminar paper at the University of Chicago in 1921 or 1922; it dates Caldwell's sermon to 1767. Internal evidence strongly suggests that Caldwell wrote and preached it in 1775 or early 1776, and Baldwin's date is probably a typographical error in her manuscript carried over to the article ("Sowers of Sedition: The Political Theories of Some of the New Light Presbyterian Clergy of Virginia and North Carolina," *William and Mary Quarterly*, 3d ser. 5 [1948]:74, and Alice M. Baldwin Papers, Duke University Archives, Duke Univ. Lib.).

[14]Caruthers, *Life of Caldwell*, pp. 276–84.

well pushed to the utmost the search for political truth in history and the Bible. The Baptist minister Richard Furman addressed a different constituency when he appealed to backcountry settlers in South Carolina to close ranks with lowcountry planters in opposing British oppression. Furman displayed less erudition than Caldwell and frankly groped toward an understanding of colonial resistance as a moral crisis. "This alarming occasion," he explained, "concerns great numbers; . . . their lives, fortunes (and what is much greater) consciences being called into question." Furman felt constricted by the very paralysis of will and intellect that Caldwell had described. Promising his readers that he would speak from "a heart . . . influenced with the most tender and impartial concern for the good of the whole" society and that he would engage in "an impartial inquiry" into "the truth" behind "the unhappy disputes . . . between Great Brittain and America," Furman nonetheless admitted that "I find myself under difficulties (it is true) to go through this work because . . . so much [has been] called into question by people who have not the opportunity to inform themselves, who are prejudiced by false reports, carried about by men who wish well to neither King nor Country." "We are all liable," he warned, "to be imposed upon" by false, partial, and twisted information.[15]

Trying to cut through misinformation and ambiguity, Furman lapsed into the language of backcountry loyalists to define the issue: "If the above articles are believed by you, viz: the Congress being in rebellion against the King and designing to enslave and ruin the people, I shall . . . shew that they do not appear to be true." The truth, Furman countered, was the autonomy of individual conscience. "If a man tells me that he has a right to do with me or any thing I have got what he pleases, and therefore demands something of me, either of labour or of part of my estate, if I give it, I then submit to his unlimited power over me, and by my own consent he has a right to lay upon me what he pleases." British usurpation,

---

[15] [Richard Furman], "To the inhabitants of South Carolina who resided between Broad & Saluda Rivers at the time they were embodying in . . . opposition to the . . . American Congress," in James A. Rogers, *Richard Furman: Life and Legacy* (Macon, Ga., 1985), Appendix A, pp. 267–73.

Furman warned, was a threat to the moral autonomy of every American. Acquiescence "will be to bind yourselves under the unlimited sway of arbitrary power in the hands of men who, to make use of you for the accomplishment of their purposes, will smile upon you and promise you fair things, but once they have gotten their ends will make you and your posterity feel the heavy hand of their oppression."[16]

Furman's highly personalized version of evil—smiling hypocrites and tyrants pillaging all of a man's freedom and dignity—reflected the flinty individualism and combativeness that in isolated instances made Baptists intransigent loyalists in the Revolution. One of them was James Child, a Separate Baptist in Anson County, North Carolina, who warned his parishioners in 1776 not to bear arms in the War for Independence "either offensively or defensively" and threatened to excommunicate those who did. "Shew him a man with half moon in his hatt and liberty rote on it and his hatt full of feather [informal patriot insignia] [and] he would shew you a devil," one informant reported of Child; "the poor men was bowing and scaping [sic] to them," Child alleged; "they lead them down to hell and . . . he did not value the Congress or comitye no more than a passill of Rockoon dogs for he got his [commission?] from the king; the [patriot] field offessers got there [sic] comission from hell or the devil."[17]

Outright loyalism among Baptists may have been exceptional in North Carolina, but on the Delmarva peninsula, embracing Delaware and the Eastern Shore of Maryland and Virginia, disaffection from the patriot cause flourished among Methodist converts—black and poor white laborers and subsistence farmers. One newly arrived English Methodist itinerant, Martin Rodda, openly prayed a "long and full" prayer "for the King and a blessing on his arms" and fomented "the rage of the people" against patriot leaders. More frequently, Methodists simply saw the War for Independence as one

[16] Ibid.

[17] Jeffrey J. Crow and Paul D. Escott, "The Social Order and Violent Disorder: An Analysis of North Carolina in the Revolution and the Civil War," *Journal of Southern History* 52 (1986):389.

more travail of living in a sinful world. Patriot militia commanders complained that when young men "embrace the Methodist faith, they change their attitude toward the war." Methodist leader Thomas Rankin even heard reports in 1777 of recalcitrant Methodists "dragged by horses over stones and stumps till death put an end to their suffering," which, even if exaggerated, confirmed his conviction that "the people called Methodists do not take up arms as others have done and . . . suffer on this account . . . for conscience sake."[18] Their social marginality accentuated their sense of being suffering servants of the Lord.

These were the very conditions of violence and irregular warfare that prompted evangelicals to embrace republicanism, which was an alternative ideology to the Lockean concept of the ruler and the ruled. Based on the civic humanism of the Italian Renaissance, which in turn derived from Roman sources, and drawn into the English-speaking world in the late seventeenth and early eighteenth century by followers of James Harrington, republicanism taught Americans that virtue was fragile and that the forces of oppression lay just beneath the surface of political life. This pessimistic and communal strand of Revolutionary ideology appealed to patriot clergymen.

Samuel Eusebius McCorkle, in the spring of 1781, preached to the North Carolina legislature on "The Crime and Curse of Plundering" in the ugly irregular warfare accompanying and following Lord Cornwallis's invasion of the state. Like the "covetous" Israelite, Achan, who plundered the gold, silver, brass, and iron of the defeated Canaanites, North Carolina patriots who took advantage of conditions of war to plunder loyalist neighbors were guilty of "daring presumption, this sinning in the face of day" after waging war "under the auspices of heaven. . . . Precarious is property in peace, how much moreso it [*sic*] the waste of war. War has destroyed well-gotten wealth, and in war the plunderer has been plun-

---

[18] William Henry Williams, *The Garden of American Methodism: The Delmarva Peninsula, 1769–1820* (Wilmington, Del., 1984), pp. 40–41.

dered. War is a time to get privilege, not wealth." In fine republican pessimism, McCorkle saw economic enterprise, which usefully energized society in peace, reveal its corrosive underside; the line between rational self-interest and besotted greed and vengeance was perilously thin.[19]

Stephen A. Marini approaches this evangelical republicanism in a different way, in the context of the struggle over the ratification of the Constitution. There he finds evangelical Antifederalists basing their criticism of the Constitution on their experience of *conflict resolution* within autonomous church bodies while nationalists like James Madison drew on traditional sources like Calvinist theology and Scottish moral philosophy to praise the Constitution as a *conflict management* document.[20]

The important point to draw from evangelical political involvement during the 1780s is that Anglo-American Protestantism imparted to republicanism a paradoxical view of change. Theology and opposition political theory, transmitted across the Atlantic in part by evangelicals, held that conflict was endemic in human affairs; in America, the experience of congressional worship and the autonomy of dissenting preachers induced a simpler view that conflict was a manifestation of sin.

During the ratification debate, this paradox may have been stark and unresolved, but during the early national period evangelicals struggled to achieve a resolution of theory and practice—no one more so than David Ramsay, a South Carolina Presbyterian layman, physician, and historian. "Industry, frugality, and temperance are virtues which we should eminently cultivate," he proclaimed in a Fourth of July oration in 1794; "these are the only foundations on which a popular government can rest with safety. Republicans should be plain in their apparel—their entertainments, their furniture, and their equipage. Idleness, extravagance, and dissipation of every kind should be banished from our borders. The virtues

[19]Samuel McCorkle Papers, Manuscripts Dept., Duke Univ. Libr.

[20]Stephen A. Marini, "Religion, Politics, and Ratification," in this volume.

now recommended are those which prepared infant Rome for all her greatness."[21]

Not only was this a pure version of republican ideology—rooted in the classical polis, celebrated by Machiavelli, fashioned into prescriptive political vocabulary by eighteenth-century opposition polemicists in Britain, and put to work in the creation of the American republic. It also reflected Ramsay's personal situation and political experience. Born in Lancaster County, Pennsylvania, he graduated from the College of New Jersey in 1765—three years before the arrival of his future father-in-law, John Witherspoon—and studied medicine at the College of Philadelphia from 1770 to 1773. In 1775 he married Sabena Ellis, who died the following year, and in 1783 he married Frances Witherspoon, who also died after less than two years of marriage, in her case from scarlet fever following the birth of a son.

With its burgeoning commerce and self-conscious elite, Charleston, South Carolina, seemed to Ramsay a promising place to establish his career, although the slaveowner mentality that he found there offended him deeply. "White pride and avarice are great obstacles in the way of black liberty," he wrote his mentor, Benjamin Rush, in 1780. "Riches are not a blessing to a people," he had noted a few months earlier; "they induce an effeminacy of mind as well as of body. Why cannot a man live happy under the loss of a brigade of negroes and of a few thousands [of money to the British] when what remains is more than he can ever enjoy?"[22]

The 1790s saw an eclipse of Ramsay's political career—perhaps a backlash against his earlier antislavery opinions or perhaps because of his chronic financial embarrassments as he and his third wife, Henry Laurens's daughter, Martha, struggled to raise eleven children on a physician's income. Marriage into a South Carolina family made him a slaveowner and prompted a retreat from his earlier radical racial

[21] Robert L. Brunhouse, ed., "David Ramsay, 1749–1815: Selections from His Writings," *Transactions of the American Philosophical Society,* new ser. 55, part 4 (1965):195.

[22] Ibid., pp. 64, 66.

views. Just two years after his marriage to Miss Laurens, he wrote to a friend in Massachusetts that "you speak feelingly for the poor negroes. I have long considered their situation. . . . Experience proves that they who have been born & grow up in slavery are incapable of the blessings of freedom."[23]

Ramsay's religious beliefs and Stoic resignation may have insulated him for a time from the materialism and hubris of the South Carolina elite, but his evangelicalism primarily mediated between his leadership aspirations and his view of human and social intractability.[24] Ramsay's most explicit testimony on this point—a long letter informing John Witherspoon of Frances's sudden death—is difficult to interpret but nonetheless revealing. Ostensibly a letter about his departed young wife—about her piety, orthodoxy, and serenity in the face of death—and probably contrived to make the appropriate clinical, consoling impression on its recipient, Ramsay's letter to Witherspoon also transmuted private agony into public virtue in good republican fashion. "Had I been skeptical about . . . the great doctrines of religion which I have always been taught to revere . . . or about the gospel plan of salvation through the imputed merits of a Saviour," Ramsay confessed, then Frances's ordeal "would have convinced me of their reality." Her vulnerability and fragility taught him public fortitude and protected him from despair. Her completion of "the important business of life" reminded him of the existential and immediate requirements of personal virtue. The healthy condition of Frances's newborn—named John Witherspoon Ramsay and baptized in the presence of both parents just twelve hours before his mother's passing— prompted Ramsay to pray that "heaven may preserve his life and raise him up to *usefulness in his generation.*"[25] The son's *vitae* echoed the soundness and precariousness of those aspirations: A.B. and M.A., College of New Jersey, 1803 and 1806;

[23] Ibid., p. 123.

[24] Ibid., pp. 37–48.

[25] Ibid., pp. 84–85, italics added.

M.D., University of Pennsylvania, 1807; physician in Prince Edward's Parish, South Carolina, 1807–13; the father of one son; died in 1813.[26]

The peculiar mix of social imperative and individual volition in evangelicalism stimulated discourse in a republican culture. In 1816 Conrad Speece, an Augusta County, Virginia, Presbyterian minister, carefully copied and calendared his essays, poems, and letters published in various newspapers and magazines; they were models of republican admonition. The first, and longest, was a eulogy for George Washington given at Hampden Sydney College on February 22, 1800. It emphasized the qualities of Washington's "bravery," "fortitude," "perseverence," "patience," and "invincible love of country" that by example entered directly into the consciousness of his contemporaries and shaped the malleable collective moral character of a generation. "He delineates with a masterly hand the true interests of America," Speece explained; "demonstrates with incontestable clearness and essential dependence of social order on private virtue; and points with the nicest precision the path to national prosperity, glory, and happiness."[27]

Eleven years later Speece still brooded over the connection between private virtue and social order. "A Letter to a Young Friend Who . . . Lately Made a Public Profession of Religion" warned that republican virtue continually decomposed as it came into cultural contact with self-regarding human heedlessness: "We are lamentably prone to unbelief, to ingratitude under the reception of innumerable benefits, and to wandering from God, the only source of true rest and peace, and after a thousand trifles lighter than air, we are liable to be entangled with those vanities which we have again and again renounced."[28] Visiting the United States two decades later, Alexis de Tocqueville would find exactly this kind of psychic

---

[26] Ibid., p. 84 n. 2.

[27] Writings of Conrad Speece, vol. 1, pp. 3–20, Brock Collection, no. 81, Huntington Libr.

[28] Ibid., p. 54.

rootlessness, "a bootless chase of that complete felicity that forever eludes" Americans, the most persistent feature of life in a democracy.[29]

The corollary of personal salvation in evangelical thought was the individual convert's membership in a community of believers that cared for one another and practiced what Donald G. Mathews calls "loving discipline" as an antidote for the callous disorder of the world.[30] "We who desire to talk together in the fear of God, through the assistance of his holy spirit, do solemnly give up ourselves to the Lord and to one another . . . that he may be our God and we may be his people," declared a typical Baptist church covenant in North Carolina in 1790. The first two collective promises that each church member made were intended to establish the framework of vigor and constraint intrinsic to discipline in the church: "1st We do promise . . . to stir up one another to love and good wishes, to warn, reprove, rebuke, and admonish one another in meekness. . . . 2nd We do promise and engage in all true holiness to observe and practice all godliness and brotherly love . . . to render our communication acceptable to God, our Saviour and comfortable to each of us."[31] Discipline perpetuated the conversion experience, actualized its effect on the personality, and prefigured the kind of community an evangelical church ought to become.

The Kehukee Baptist Association in North Carolina in 1800 listened approvingly to a comprehensive explanation of discipline:

> As our Lord and Saviour has loved us and given himself for us, that he might deliver us from the curse of the law and the flames of devouring fire, and hath taken us from the wild stock of nature, made us to drink of the same fountain of his everlasting love, and so tempered our spirits as to unite us together . . . by

[29] Meyers, *Jacksonian Persuasion,* pp. 45–54.

[30] Donald G. Mathews, *Religion in the Old South* (Chicago, 1977), p. 42.

[31] Calhoon, ed., *Religion and Revolution in North Carolina,* pp. 56–57.

the sweetest bands of love and fellowship, declared us to be a select body by him chosen, and set apart from the world, it becomes our duty then to walk as people who are not of the world but chosen of God and bound for the heavenly Canaan.[32]

Evangelical discipline sought to reconcile respect for the complexity of human personality with stable, voluntarist notions of congregational governance. A striking example was the trial of Agnes Carr before a Session of the Fishing Creek, South Carolina, Presbyterian Church in January 1800 for public drunkenness. The difficulty arose on a Sunday morning when some travelers on their way to Georgia stopped in front of the Robert Carr home. While they were there Nancy (as Agnes Carr was apparently known) went into the house and "took a bottle of whiskey off the shelf, and handed it about the company." Later in the morning, a Mr. Ramsay arrived with a bottle of his own from which "she drank and gave the children some"—an act repeated from a Mr. Cain's bottle still later in the morning. By this time she was showing signs of not feeling well and "sat down upon a chair before the fire . . . put her hand behind her haunch" and complained of feeling sick; "her head began to hang to one side—the tears to run from her eyes." Two of the women present, one of them her mother-in-law, Margaret Carr, then tried to put Nancy to bed but she writhed violently and had to be restrained. She got up and laid down on the cold hearth, complaining of the cold but refusing cover. At this point the testimony revealed that Nancy Carr was pregnant; she began to talk wildly of her fear of a miscarriage and her belief that the child in her womb had been dead for a month. "She rolled and tumbled about and would not be held by us." Someone brought her a cup of tea and she seemed to revive. Without warning, she grabbed Margaret Carr "and said 'Mother, I'll shake you limb from limb, I'll leave you limbless.'" In cross-examination of the two women who testified against her, Nancy accused Margaret Carr of telling her the tea was spiked for medicinal purposes.

[32]"Circular Letter," Kehukee Baptist Association Minutes, October 1800, Baptist Collection, Wake Forest University Library, Wake Forest University, Winston-Salem, N.C.

"I said no such thing," Margaret retorted, "Did you not say my pains were the worst you had ever seen?" demanded Nancy; "I said I thought [you were] the maddest I ever saw," came the reply. The Session found her guilty and gave her a month to show repentance.[33]

Fragmentary though it is, this account is rich with implications about the larger phenomenon of church discipline and stresses its reconciling, healing role. Isolation, drink, difficult pregnancies, quarrelsome relations between neighbors who needed one another but resented intrusion into their privacy—all of these social conditions, which bulk large in the Fishing Creek church record of the Nancy Carr dispute, were endemic social conditions throughout the rural South in the early nineteenth century.

Containing within their own walls the seeds of contention, lacking institutional means to constrain internal dissension, and conscious of their own calling to foster harmony, evangelical churches stood at the vortex of community conflict. Article 4 of the constitution of the Mill Creek Lutheran Church in Botetourt County, Virginia—written in 1796 and dealing with the conduct of church council meetings—exemplifies this. It proscribed behavior that must have been widespread in backcountry communities and described tensions that lay just below the surface of church life:

> We shall be . . . impartial in giving advice [and] modest in behavior; when a matter is brought up . . . we shall diligently pay attention, ponder the matter silently and seriously with an impartial heart. When it is one or another's turn to speak, he shall state his opinion distinctly and openly . . . ; he shall not advise anyone either out of favor or rancor; not quarrel but with modesty and not always have the first word nor want to demand that everything must go according to his desire, even though he in his opinion might mean it well. Thus we want to ponder the matter together, . . . but . . . to avoid all tumult, disorder and confusion, only one shall speak at a time, and that without violence, not in

[33] Fishing Creek [S.C.] Presbyterian Church Records, Presbyterian Study Center, Montreat, N.C.

anger, not in love of power, nor like the quarrellers and impetu-
ous ones.[34]

Striking in this analysis of small-group dynamics was its
sensitivity to internal hierarchies of energy, ambition, and self-
confidence within the church and its use of decorum as an
antidote to these human proclivities. Also at stake in the Mill
Creek church was a democratic compact and republican polity that must have been in tension with hierarchies of wealth
and prominence within the parish: "No one shall presume
special privilege for himself even though he be older, richer,
or more distinguished." Citing Paul's injunction to "put away
from yourselves" the "fornicator, . . . covetous, . . . idolater,
. . . railer, . . . or a drunkard," the constitution required the
church officers to bring to the pastor's attention "anyone in
the congregation" who "leads an objectionable life or lives in
obvious sins and vices such as: quarreling, fighting, envy, glut-
tony, drinking, dancing, wild cavorting, gambling, lying,
cheating, whoring, adultery, false oath taking, swearing, curs-
ing, disregarding the Sabbath."[35] A "Union" church, which
shared a building with a German Reformed congregation, the
Mill Creek church's constitution reflected both Lutheran cor-
porateness and Reform pietist tradition.

As they confronted the Revolution, evangelicals had turned
outward to face the world; as they imposed discipline on
themselves, they turned inward toward a shared understanding of their fellowship. Evangelical homiletics yoked these two
elements of existential engagement and corporate identity.
This period was a transitional one in sermon writing, as in
other forms of enterprise and craftsmanship. Preachers developed, according to Daniel H. Calhoun, two strategies, an
older "calculating" style of stark simplicity and thematic unity
and a newer "personal" style that projected the personality of

[34]Guy A. Ritter, ed. and trans., Official Record Book of Brick Union
Lutheran Church, Howrytown (Greenville), Botetourt County, Virginia
(typescript), Roanoke College Library, Salem, Va.

[35]Ibid.

the preacher.[36] The calculating style echoed Lockean individualist assumptions about the capacity of individuals, protected
by the covenant, to make their own way in the world; the cha-
risma of the preacher was more a republican concept, which
depended on the virtuous community to affirm popular leadership.

Samuel McCorkle's exegetical notebook provides a rare in-
sight into the way the calculating approach laid the basis for,
and fed into, the projection of the preacher's own self.[37] In
June 1786 McCorkle preached for the first time on his favorite text, Job 14:14, a passage that allowed him to fuse theological analysis and personal conviction. Living before
Kierkegaard, McCorkle saw none of Job's anguished doubts
about the predictability of the Creator or the reality of life
after death. Instead he saw emblazoned the words, "If a man
die shall he live again? All the days of my appointed time will
I wait, till my change comes," a trilogy of stages in human
faith that he labeled *"belief," "waiting,"* and *"change."* He dealt
with belief quickly. It arose from the "power" of God and from
a human response called forth by God's willingness to suffer
for humanity. Citing the darkness and light imagery from 1
John, McCorkle declared that God creates belief "as a bridge
across the gulf of death." Belief further meant repentance,
what McCorkle called "mixt grace," created as the Spirit
flooded into the consciousness of the penitent and triggered
the response of "waiting," a faithlike activity.[38]

"To wait is to desire [the] event, Job VII," McCorkle noted.
That chapter announced the onset of Job's suffering—sleep-
lessness, "flesh clothed with . . . clods of dust, my skin . . . broken and . . . loathsome"—and its temporal dimension: "How
long wilt thou not depart from me nor let me alone till I can
swallow down my spittle. . . . And why dost thou not pardon
my transgression and take away mine iniquity?" Waiting was
to be engaged in, and effected by, the wearing out of physical

---

[36] Daniel H. Calhoun, *The Intelligence of a People* (Princeton, 1973), p. 312.

[37] Samuel McCorkle Notebook, Presbyterian Study Center, Montreat,
N.C.

[38] 1 John 1:4–5, McCorkle Notebook, ff. 40A-46B.

existence; it also meant "to be active." Here McCorkle cited Paul's exhortations to Titus to practice sober, conscientious behavior, 2 Timothy on the "crown of righteousness" awaiting the faithful, and Revelation on "rest from their labours."[39] At its deepest level, waiting meant "fortitude" in the face of immediate or eventual death. "I will not blaspheme a master I served 80 years," McCorkle quoted Polycarp, the early Christian martyr who died with these words on his lips, and Justin Martyr who faced his death saying "let fire consume my flesh, nerves shiver, twill but send me home."[40]

Just as "mixt grace" was the hinge between belief and waiting in McCorkle's scheme, fortitude was the hinge between waiting and "change." The most elaborate of his three states of faith, change occurred first in the body, then the body and the mind, next in the world of the spirit and the afterlife, and finally in inspiration, the "media by which the mind sees objects." It was the last of the dimensions that drew the sermon to its conclusion and answered Job's question about life after death. "We will not be unclothed II Cor. V, but clothed upon," McCorkle's notes explained; "[we] will be some medium, see I Cor. XIII, tongues of angels." The juxtaposition of these two Corinthians chapters emphasized McCorkle's Platonic understanding of the soul. The image of clothing in 2 Corinthians, chapter 5, was used to explain the progress of the soul toward perfection, and the "tongues of men and of angels" in 1 Corinthians, chapter 13, McCorkle reminded his listeners, could speak corruptly just as the gift of prophesy and knowledge could be empty vanity if the speaker and knower had no charity. These images gauged the distance between the ideal and the actual. Paul's "now we see through a glass darkly but then face to face" was the ultimate change in spiritual reality that began with belief, continued through repentance, gained shape and coherence in fortitude, and would come to completion only beyond the grave.[41] It was within this cosmic

---

[39]Titus 2:12; 3:18; 2 Tim. 4:8.

[40]Compare Robert M. Grant, *Eusebius as Church Historian* (Oxford, 1980), pp. 115–16.

[41]2 Cor. 5:2; 1 Cor. 13:12.

scheme, McCorkle concluded, that life and death, suffering and exultation, the unpredictable brevity of human existence and the eternal scope of divine creation could all be understood. He finished with a strenuous personal evocation: "Go then, try the world, cast around your arms and hug it to your bosom."[42]

Evangelical political thought, discipline, and use of the Bible—among other expressions of its activity and vision—formed a coherent whole and functioned as a persuasion in the early South. It was an electic, improvised mixture of intellectual assumptions, behavioral norms, and Scottish common-sense teachings about the interconnectedness of all knowledge and revelation. But the same processes that brought these elements together also triggered internal contradictions within evangelical social and political consciousness. The spread of religious consciousness across racial lines created the most obvious of these conflicts. As whites and blacks found themselves sharing grace and yet separated by the racial assumptions and practices of white society, they entered a new realm in which racial oppression began to enervate the fragile equipoise of Christianity and republicanism.

In 1838 the Cedar Spring Associate Reformed Presbyterian Church, Abbeville District, South Carolina, petitioned the state legislature to repeal a nullification era statute prohibiting whites from teaching blacks to read the Bible. The petition argued that the statute jeopardized the dual support of republicanism and Christianity in the body politic. They pointed to Article 8 of the South Carolina constitution allowing "free exercise of religious profession and worship" so long as religious activity did not promote "licentiousness" or appear "inconsistent with the peace or safety of this State." That reservation was, of course, an enormous potential infringement of free exercise, one that James Madison had with difficulty dissuaded Virginians from adopting in 1785. But the Abbeville petitioners argued vigorously that nothing licentious or contrary to public safety could possibly emanate

[42]McCorkle Notebook, f. 44A.

from slaves reading the words of God's injunction to be obedient to their masters "with fear and trembling in singleness of heart as unto Christ." If the quiet reading of Scripture was so dangerous, then why did the state not prohibit slaves from attending worship services where the Bible was read aloud, the petitioners demanded to know, and for that matter why did not the state exclude slaves from the far more contaminating influence of Fourth of July celebrations and militia musters? Set beside the whole range of social outlets for human energy and potential traps for the morally unwary, the petition argued, Bible-reading classes for slaves ranked very high as means of cultivating virtue and protecting public order.

Christianity had a unique capacity to protect society from the worst proclivities of human nature, the Abbeville petitioners declared, because Scripture was the word of God and, moreover, because "experience fully proves that those servants who live in religious families and have been taught to read and understand their duty from the word of God are, as a general rule, more trusty . . . than those . . . whose souls have been entirely neglected." To thwart the work of creating enclaves of peacefulness and piety within families and churches was to violate the public good and represented an "*unwarrantable interference* of the State in church affairs." What was most unwarrantable—literally, most presumptuous in substituting human for divine authority—was the sanction the law gave to "common informer[s]," the "most degraded of all characters," to spy upon, report, and cause to be prosecuted those persons who conscientiously taught their slaves to read the Bible. The petition came close to promising that the law would be broken, for the missionary principle in Christianity made efforts to convert the "heathen" an absolute imperative for believers; "to enact laws excluding that glorious light from a portion of our households" blighted the affection the petitioners had for their slaves, and affection was an impulse of the heart wholly separate from the "mere mercenary considerations" that were an unavoidable part of slaveowning.[43] The Abbeville petition was not memorable for its

---

[43] Petition to the South Carolina General Assembly, ca. 1838, ND 2822, South Carolina Department of Archives and History, Columbia.

moral grandeur, nor was it an apology for slavery. It redefined the politico-religious compact in South Carolina as a mission of families and communities to throw a cloak of devotionalism over their corporate selves.

Within the sanctum sanctorum of evangelical worship—the revival service—the evangelical persuasion most vividly exhibited its eclecticism and unpredictability. In the spring of 1828, a woman preacher, Zilpha Elaw—a free black born in Philadelphia in 1790 and converted at a Kentucky camp meeting in 1817—risked arrest and enslavement by conducting a preaching tour in Maryland and Virginia. "The Lord who sent me out to preach his gospel . . . in these regions of wickedness," she recalled, "preserved me in my going out and my coming in . . . during my sojourn on the soil of slavery." One of her most memorable experiences was delivering a sermon in a Methodist chapel at Mt. Tabor, Maryland, where the white "proprietors" of the church occupied the seats on the main floor and the slaves filled the gallery. Her text was Luke 2:10, "and the angel said unto them, fear not; for behold I bring you good tidings of great joy which shall be to all people," a passage of particular vibrancy when spoken by a black and a woman. Her account of what transpired kept its focus on the totality of the event, but also caught the racial variations in the responses of the people and the political and sexual dynamics of the situation involving the regular minister, a Mr. Beard, herself, and the people under the influence of what she was sure was the Holy Spirit:

> All were alike affected. Mr. Beard requested the congregation to restrain the expression of their feelings, but the powerful operation of the Holy Spirit disdained the limits prescribed by man's reason and bore down all the guards of human propriety and order. The presence of the Holy Spirit filled the place, and moved the people as the wind moves the forest boughs. Mr. Beard's cautions were unavailing; the coloured people in the gallery wept aloud and raised vehement cries to heaven; the people below were also unable to restrain their emotions; and all wept beneath the inspirations of the Spirit of grace.[44]

[44] William L. Andrews, ed., *Sisters in the Spirit: Three Black Women's Autobiographies of the Nineteenth Century* (Bloomington, Ind., 1986), pp. 98–99. See also Jean M. Humez, "'My Spirit Eye': Some Functions of Spiritual and

In characteristic evangelical fashion, Mrs. Elaw specified the stages of sanctification at work in this tumultuous scene: "mercy, love, and grace . . . streamed . . . into our little earthly sanctuary to staunch the bleeding heart, remove its guilt, reform its character, and give new impulse to its powers."[45] The same four-stage process had been depicted in evangelical preaching since George Whitefield's time.[46]

Evangelicals who distinguished between autonomy and freedom—between behavior and integrity—placed still more stress on the inner connections of the evangelical persuasion. Many slaves acquired, in this way, what Albert J. Raboteau calls "a sense of personal dignity and an attitude of moral superiority to their masters."[47] A striking example is a letter written in 1821 by an unnamed North Carolina slave to his former owner and minister, a Presbyterian named John Fort. "Master John," it began, "I want permation of you pleas to speak A few words to you—I hope you do not think me too bold Sir. I make my wants known to you because you are, I believe—the oldest and most experienced that I know of." The concerns that the slave called his "wants" came in the form of a series of penetrating questions: Why had Fort turned his back on slave worshipers and ignored their spiritual needs? Was there more financial gain in preaching to whites? Did white people know or even care about the salvation of blacks? How could the prayers of whites for the redemption of the world be answered, much less offered, when tainted by greed and racism? These questions were all the more thunderous for their calm, unacrimonious tone. And, like an Old Testament prophecy, the letter ended with a "thus saith the Lord" announcement of moral and ethical imperatives: "I now leave it to you and your aids to consider on I

Visionary Experience in the Lives of Five Black Women Preachers, 1810–1880," in Barbara J. Harris and JoAnn K. McNamara, eds., *Women and the Structure of Society* (Durham, N.C., 1984), pp. 133–43.

[45] Andrews, ed., *Sisters in the Spirit,* pp. 99–100.

[46] Calhoon, *Evangelicals and Conservatives,* pp. 32–33.

[47] Albert J. Raboteau, *Slave Religion: The "Invisible Institution" in the Antebellum South* (New York, 1978), p. 301.

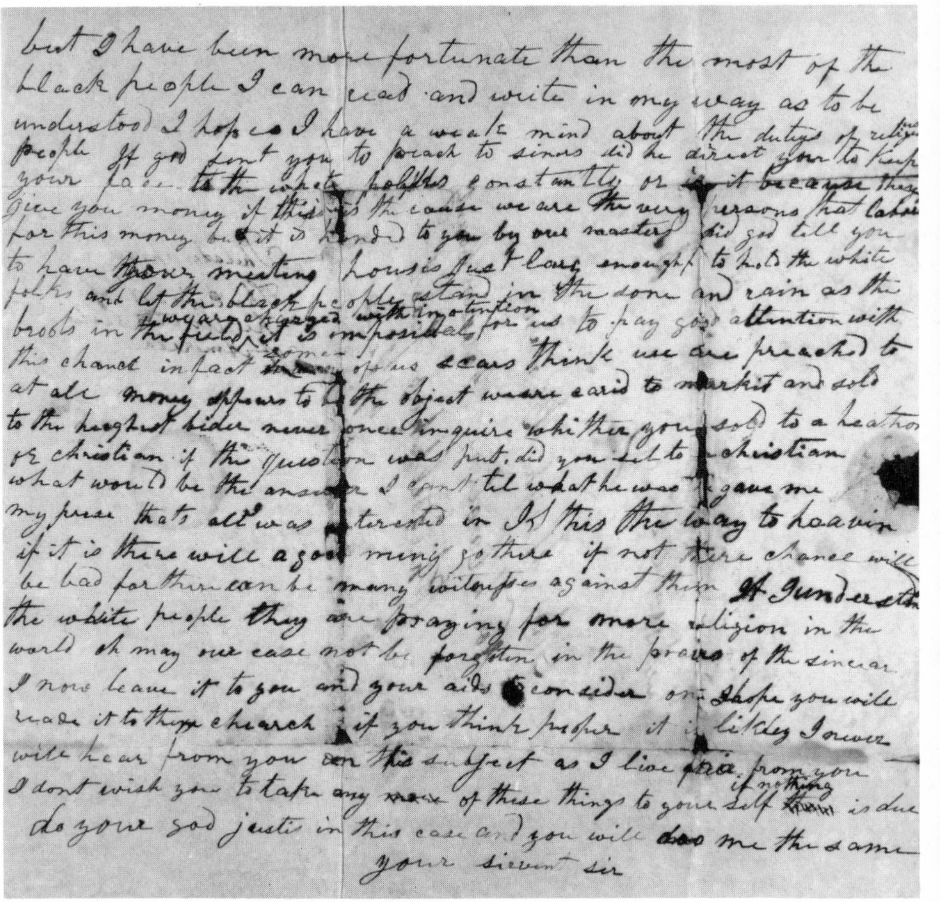

Figure 1. Extract of a letter from an unidentified North Carolina slave to John Fort, June 26, 1821. (Neill Brown Papers, Manuscripts Department, Duke University Library, Durham, N.C.)

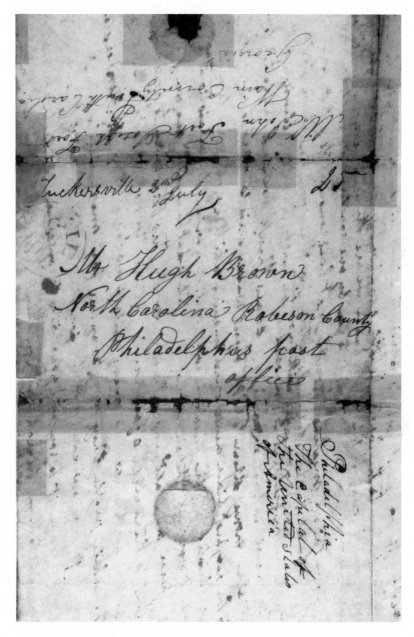

Figure 2. Reverse side of a letter from an unidentified North Carolina slave to John Fort, June 26, 1821. (Neill Brown Papers, Manuscripts Department, Duke University Library, Durham, N.C.)

hope you will read it to their church if you think proper it is
likely I never will hear from you on this subject as I live far
from you I dont wish you to take any of these things to your
self if nothing is due do your god justis in this case and you
will doo me to the same Your Sirvent Sir."[48]

In 1987 Isaac Kramnick spoke of the various political languages—republican, Lockean, Protestant, and statist—that
coexisted in the politics of the early republic. He concluded

---

[48][?] to John Fort, June 26, 1821, Neill Brown Papers, Manuscripts
Dept., Duke Univ. Libr. The full text of this letter, which corrects several
transcription errors in Calhoon, *Evangelicals and Conservatives,* p. 226, reads:
"Master John I want permation of you pleas to speak A few words to you—
I hope you will not think me too bold Sir. I make my wants known to you
because you are, I believe the oldist and most experienced that I know of.
in the first place I want you to tell me the Reson you allways preach to the
white folks and keep your back to us is it because they sit up on the hill we
have no chance a mong them then must we be for goten because we cant
get near enoughf without geting in the edg of the swamp behind you we
have no other chance because your stand is on the edg of the swamp. if I
should ask you what must I do to be saved, perhaps you would tel me pray
let the bible be your gide this would do very well if wei could read. I do not
think there is one in fifty that can read but I have been more fortunate
than the most of the black people I can read and write in my way as to be
understood I hopes I have a weak mind about the dutiys of religeus people
If god sent you to preach to siners did he direct you to keep your face to
the white folks constantly or is it because these give you money if this is the
cause we are the very persons that labor for this money but it is handed to
you by our masters did god tell you to have your meeting houses Just long
enoughf to hold the white folks and let the black people stand in the sone
and rain as the brook in the field we are charged with inatention it is impos-
ibal for us to pay good attention with this chance in fact some of us scars
think we are preached to at all Money appears to be the object weare carid
to markit and sold to the highest bider never once inquire whither you sold
to a heathon or christian if this question was put, did you sel to a christian
what would be the answer I cant tel what he was he gave me my price thats
all I was interested in Is this the way to heavin if it is there will [be] a good
many go there if not there chance will be bad for there can be many witnesses against them If I understand the white people they are praying for
more religion in the world oh may our case not be forgoten in the prairs of
the sincear I now leave it to you and your aids to consider on I hope you
will reade it to the chearch if you think proper. it is likely I never will hear
from you on this subject as I live far from you I dont wish you to take any
of these things to your self if nothing is due do your god justis in this case
and you will doo me the same Your Sirvent Sir."

by noting how the names of towns in his own part of up-state New York—Ithaca and Syracuse, Locke and Geneva—indicated the classical-republican and Calvinist-liberal traditions.[49] I will end this essay with a nomenclature story as well. The paper on which the slave known to us only as "Your Sirvent," penned his jeremiad was the blank portion of a discarded letter originally addressed to someone living in the Robeson County hamlet of Philadelphia, North Carolina. Next to that address the slave wrote—in a hand noticeably freer and more confident than the tense calligraphy of the letter proper—these words: "Philadelphia The Capital of the United States of America."[50] Whether this notation was a telling postscript or a deeply felt private reflection, we do not know. It was probably both. Here an evangelical Christian affirmed to a brother in Christ and for his own moral sense that the true seat of authority in America was not Washington, D.C., where compromises over slavery were fashioned, but rather Philadelphia, where all men were declared to be created equal.

[49] Isaac Kramnick, "The Discourse of Politics in 1787: The Constitution and Its Critics on Individualism, Community, and the State," in Herman Belz, Ronald Hoffman, and Peter J. Albert, eds., *To Form a More Perfect Union: The Critical Ideas of the Constitution* (Charlottesville, Va., 1992).

[50] Sydney Nathans, who by a fortunate coincidence was preparing to assign this document to Duke undergraduates learning the use of manuscript sources on the same day I consulted it in my own research, called my attention to this feature of the letter.

STEPHEN A. MARINI

Religion, Politics, and Ratification

As ELKANAH WATSON and Maj. John Murfree rode through Hertford County, North Carolina, one spring day in 1788, they found placards posted on the roads. The signs said: "Notice! On Wednesday next, at three o'clock, all persons desirous of hearing the new Constitution explained, by Elder Burkitt, are requested to attend his church in the Woodlands, 17th March 1788."[1] The meaning of the placards was instantly clear to Watson, a thirty-year-old merchant and planter originally from Plymouth, Massachusetts, who had located at Edenton in 1785, purchased a great estate on the Chowan River, and by 1788 enjoyed enough standing in Hertford County to run for election as a Federalist candidate to the North Carolina state convention on the proposed federal Constitution.[2] Watson's bitterly Antifederalist opponent, Elder Lemuel Burkitt, leader of the Separate Baptists in east Carolina, was agitating the citizenry again. The upstart Baptists were continuing their challenge to Watson's friends and customers, the planter elite that had traditionally controlled politics in Hertford County.

Watson and Murfree decided to face their opponents di-

Research for this essay was made possible by a 1987 Fellowship for College Teachers from the National Endowment for the Humanities under its Constitutional Bicentennial Initiative. I am grateful to the Endowment for its generous support.

[1] Louise Irby Trenholme, *The Ratification of the Federal Constitution in North Carolina* (New York, 1932), p. 110.

[2] *Dictionary of American Biography*, s.v., "Watson, Elkanah."

rectly and appeared at Burkitt's meetinghouse at the appointed hour. They found "a horse hitched to every tree about the church, and the interior of the building crowded." As befit their station, the planter and his military escort found seats near the pulpit, from whence Elder Burkitt addressed the assembly while casting "a suspicious and disconcerted eye" on the pair. The record preserves only one element of Burkitt's "exposition" of the new Constitution, a harangue against the idea of an autonomous federal district as an open invitation to military tyranny. "This, my friends, will be walled or fortified," he warned. "Here an army of fifty thousand, or perhaps, a hundred thousand men, will be finally embodied, and will sally forth, and enslave the people, who will be gradually disarmed."[3]

When Watson rose to oppose Burkitt, however, the people would not listen to the worldly newcomer, a man who, according to one account, was "amply occupied in social convivialities, wandering about the country; in deer hunting and other amusements."[4] An uproar ensued and the meeting broke up. The next day—election day—Watson counterattacked by "executing a caricature" of Burkitt and the Antifederalists and posting it on the door of Hertford County courthouse before the polls opened. Watson's caricature and its arrogant placement on public property incensed the Antifederalists gathering for the election, and they tried to tear it down. The subsequent melee disrupted the voting. During the scuffle, candles were extinguished inside the courthouse, and "both parties, in great confusion, were left in the dark, literally as well as politically." When the votes were finally counted, Elder Burkitt had won.[5] Elkanah Watson soon left for the North, where he found lasting fame as the founder of the county fair movement in America.

Political exchanges like this one reveal a new relationship between religion and politics provoked by the question of ratification. The Baptist elder's challenge to the planter elite in

---

[3] Trenholme, *Ratification of the Constitution*, p. 110.

[4] *Dictionary of American Biography*, s.v., "Watson, Elkanah."

[5] Trenholme, *Ratification of the Constitution*, p. 22.

the east Carolina Tidewater is just the sort of "dramatistic" act that marked the cultural insurgency of religious Dissenters in neighboring Virginia described by Rhys Isaac.[6] But there are other less familiar elements here as well. Burkitt's peroration did not address religious liberty, the constitutional issue historians have characteristically associated with Dissenters in Revolutionary America. Instead he raised an issue identified with the Harringtonian tradition of Anglo-American political thought, namely, the dangers of a standing army and centralization of power.[7] In Hertford County a dissenting religious leader crossed the boundary into the political arena and offered an apparently complete "exposition" of the federal Constitution in which we can glimpse a new religious appropriation and interpretation of political ideas. His followers, galvanized by his rhetoric and beliefs, wrought a local political revolution.

It would seem that during the late 1780s—at least in North Carolina—ways of being religious were associated with and powerfully informed ways of being political. Whether such a religious dimension can be identified in the larger national politics of ratification is the question I will address in this essay. I think there is enough evidence to answer that question affirmatively and to outline a tentative structure for the political roles of religion in 1787 and 1788.

Before proceeding, however, it is worth noting that such evidence is fugitive and dispersed, and that current historiographic opinion discourages its pursuit. Interpreters from Carl Becker to Adrienne and G. Adolf Koch, from Richard Bushman and Alan Heimert to Rhys Isaac and Patricia U. Bonomi, have made distinguished contributions toward understanding the interplay of religion and politics before

[6]Rhys Isaac, *The Transformation of Virginia, 1740–1790* (Chapel Hill, 1982), pp. 161–80.

[7]On Harrington see J. G. A. Pocock, "Machiavelli, Harrington, and English Political Ideologies in the Eighteenth Century," in Pocock, *Politics, Language, and Time: Essays on Political Thought and History* (New York, 1971), pp. 104–47, and Introduction to Pocock, ed., *The Writings of James Harrington* (Cambridge, 1977).

1776.[8] These writers have sought and found Revolutionary origins in such diverse sources as Enlightenment religious liberalism, evangelical Calvinism, and the Dissenters' struggle for equal civil and religious rights. For the Revolutionary era proper, however, the historiography generally still regards religion as secondary to politics. No less an authority than Sydney E. Ahlstrom saw the 1770s and 1780s as a period of "religious depression." Even important new work on the position of evangelicals in the South and on the significance of millennial speculation in Revolutionary thought has not altered that assessment.[9]

The recent scholarly recovery of an "ideology of republicanism" has in fact served to distance religion and religious thought still further from the intellectual center of the Revolution. Bernard Bailyn, Gordon S. Wood, and others have uncovered classical and Enlightenment underpinnings of the Revolutionary movement, but they have not detected any significant theological influences on the emergent ideology of republicanism. Such findings have led Bruce Kuklick to conclude that "it may be impossible to learn, in general, if and how politics influenced religion and if and how religion influenced politics" in Revolutionary America.[10] All this has con-

[8] Carl Becker, *The Declaration of Independence: A Study in the History of Political Ideas* (New York, 1942); Adrienne Koch, *Power, Morals, and the Founding Fathers: Essays in the Interpretation of the American Enlightenment* (Ithaca, N.Y., 1961); G. Adolph Koch, *Republican Religion: The American Revolution and the Cult of Reason* (Gloucester, Mass., 1964); Richard Bushman, *From Puritan to Yankee: Character and the Social Order in Connecticut, 1690–1765* (Cambridge, Mass., 1967); Alan Heimert, *Religion and the American Mind from the Great Awakening to the Revolution* (Cambridge, Mass., 1966); Isaac, *Transformation of Virginia;* Patricia U. Bonomi, *Under the Cope of Heaven: Religion, Society, and Politics in Colonial America* (New York, 1986).

[9] Sydney E. Ahlstrom, *A Religious History of the American People* (New Haven, 1972), pp. 365–66; Isaac, *Transformation of Virginia;* William Lee Miller, *The First Liberty: Religion and the American Republic* (New York, 1986); Nathan O. Hatch, *The Sacred Cause of Liberty: Republican Thought and the Millennium in Revolutionary New England* (New Haven, 1977).

[10] Bernard Bailyn, *The Ideological Origins of the American Revolution* (Cambridge, Mass., 1967); idem, *The Origins of American Politics* (New York, 1968); Gordon S. Wood, *The Creation of the American Republic, 1776–1787* (Chapel

tributed to a historiographic image of religion as weakened and confused, its institutions languishing and its intellectual resources depleted.

This image is inaccurate. Far from suffering decline, religion experienced vigorous growth and luxuriant development during the Revolutionary period. It occupied a prominent place in public culture and a disproportionately large number of religiously active men served in the new nation's constituent assemblies. In a host of ways, both practical and intellectual, the church served as a school for politics. In this essay I will draw some of the connections between religious and political culture during the 1770s and 1780s, using as a focal point the ratification of the United States Constitution.

DELEGATES TO THE RATIFYING CONVENTIONS

The delegates who attended the twelve state ratifying conventions during 1787 and 1788 were the largest group of elected representatives assembled during the Revolutionary era. These 1,420 men constituted the most direct representation of the people on a national question in American history. By their collective vote of 810 to 610 they made the Constitution the fundamental law of the United States. For these reasons they also comprise the ideal sample by which to identify and measure the many forces that brought about ratification. Our interest is religion, and solid evidence on the religious identity of the delegates can be assembled and analyzed. From an examination of their religious biographies, some suggestive patterns emerge that invite further exploration and consideration as elements in the political process of 1787–88.

Religion held a privileged position in the public culture of Revolutionary America. This fact is readily demonstrated by the new state constitutions of the 1770s and 1780s. Massachusetts and New Hampshire still required public instruction in "piety, religion, and morality," and South Carolina explicitly

---

Hill, 1969); Bruce Kuklick, *Churchmen and Philosophers* (New Haven, 1985), p. 60.

defined "the Christian Protestant religion" as the established religion of the state. These three, along with North Carolina, Maryland, Delaware, and New Jersey, also required profession of "the Christian religion" as a requirement for state office. Even the Virginia Statute for Establishing Religious Freedom, enacted in 1786, began its case with the theological claim that religious establishments "are a departure from the plan of the Holy author of our religion, who being Lord both of body and mind, yet chose not to propagate it by coercions on either, as was in his Almighty power to do." Pennsylvania's constitution of 1776, the most radical of the original thirteen, specifically provided that "laws for the enforcement of virtue, and prevention of vice and immorality shall be made and constantly kept in force, and provision shall be made for their due execution." [11]

In this context of public piety, religious affiliation became a qualification for political leadership. Religious organizations were the largest institutions in Revolutionary society. Hundreds of thousands of adult Americans held formal membership in religious congregations in 1787, and the denominations supplied influential colonial cultural networks. (See table 1.) Moreover, as many as two-thirds of the delegates to the ratifying conventions were church members. This fact indicates that, to the electorate of Revolutionary America, church membership was a strongly preferred quality in public leaders.

By any measure the delegates to the ratifying conventions were religious. Literally hundreds of them were Anglican vestrymen, Congregationalist deacons, and Presbyterian ruling elders. These were the highest church offices available to laymen, empowering them to maintain the financial health of the parish, to enforce the moral norms of the church, and often to choose the minister of the congregation. Many hundreds more of the delegates were loyal parishioners who held lesser church offices: trustees, wardens, tithingmen, assessors, teachers, moderators, commissioners, and committeemen. And another hundred or so were ordained ministers and

[11]Conrad Henry Moehlman, *The American Constitutions and Religion* (Berne, Ind., 1938), pp. 38–53.

Table 1. Major denominations in Revolutionary America:
estimated number of congregations by decade, 1760–90

Denomination	1760	1770	1776-A	1776-B	1780	1790
Congregational	550	625	663	800	700	750
Presbyterian	425	500	584	502	625	725
Anglican	315	356	488	408	150	170
Baptist	94	150	494	472	500	858
Methodist	0	20	62	16	106	712*

SOURCES: Denominational statistics and estimates based on the following: Congregationalists—Henry A. Hazen, *The Congregational and Presbyterian Ministry and Churches of New Hampshire* (Boston, 1875); Joseph S. Clark, *A Historical Sketch of the Congregational Churches in Massachusetts from 1620 to 1858* (Boston, 1858); Franklin B. Dexter, ed., *The Literary Diary of Ezra Stiles*, 3 vols. (New York, 1901), 2:412; Presbyterians—Guy Soulliard Klett, ed., *Minutes of the Presbyterian Church in America, 1706–1788* (Philadelphia, 1976), pp. 467–69; *A List of the Presbyteries, Ministers, Probationers, and Congregations, Both Settled and Vacant, within the Bounds of the Synod of New-York and Philadelphia* (Philadelphia, 1788); Anglicans—Charles C. Tiffany, *A History of the Protestant Episcopal Church in the United States*, American Church History Series, vol. 7 (New York, 1895); Baptists—Morgan Edwards, *Materials toward a History of the Baptists in America*, 2 vols. (Gallatin, Tenn., 1984); Isaac Backus, *A History of New-England*, vol. 3, *A Church History of New-England . . . from 1783 to 1796* (Boston, 1796), pp. 93–106; John Asplund, *The Annual Register of the Baptist Denomination in North America to the First of November, 1790* (Richmond, 1792); Methodists—*Minutes Taken at the General Conferences of the Methodist Episcopal Church in America* (Philadelphia, 1791).

Statistics for 1776, column A, are taken from Rodney Stark and Roger Finke, "American Religion in 1776: A Statistical Portrait," *Sociological Analysis* 49 (1988): 39–51, and Roger Finke and Rodney Stark, *The Churching of America, 1776–1990: Winners and Losers in Our Religious Economy* (New Brunswick, N.J., 1992). Statistics for 1776, column B, are derived from Frederick Lewis Weis, *The Colonial Churches and Colonial Clergy of New England* (Lancaster, Mass., 1936), idem, *The Colonial Churches and Colonial Clergy of the Middle and Southern Colonies, 1607–1776* (Lancaster, Mass., 1938), idem, *The Colonial Clergy of Maryland, Delaware, and Georgia* (Lancaster, Mass., 1950), idem, *The Colonial Clergy of Virginia, North Carolina, and South Carolina* (Boston, 1950), and idem, *The Colonial Clergy of New York, New Jersey, and Pennsylvania* (Lancaster, Mass., 1957).

*1791.

priests. In their religious commitments as well as in their political careers, the delegates undertook serious and long-term
responsibilities.

The delegates represented all the major churches, but the
legally established colonial religions, New England Congregationalism and southern Anglicanism, commanded the largest
blocs. For example, 75 of 114 religiously identified South Carolina delegates were Anglican; 44 of 70 New Hampshire delegates were Congregationalist. In the Middle States and the
South, Presbyterians were represented in significant strength.
Nearly a majority of the Pennsylvania convention was Presbyterian, and large numbers of coreligionists served in New Jersey, Virginia, and North Carolina. Baptists were scattered
through most of the conventions—13 in Massachusetts and
22 in North Carolina, for example—and small numbers of
Lutherans, Dutch Reformed, Huguenots, Moravians, Methodists, and Catholics could also be found among the delegates.

There has been virtually no detailed empirical research on
the correlation of these religious affiliations with the delegates' political positions on the Constitution, but there have
been some guesses. More than one historian has claimed that
the Baptists were virtually unanimous in their Antifederalism
or that Federalism predominated among Anglicans. While
there is some truth to these assertions, they are sufficiently
inaccurate to obscure more than they reveal. Such opinions
overgeneralize. They try to draw conclusions for an entire religious community and thereby assume, erroneously, that religion would somehow be immune to the divisions that
occurred in every other aspect of American culture in the
1770s and 1780s.

In actuality the correlation of religion to politics among the
delegates reveals a complex pattern not reducible to simple
denominational categories. Examples could be multiplied almost indefinitely to show that the political divisions of 1787–
88 passed through ecclesiastical communities rather than
between them. The religious character of the Federalist-
Antifederalist conflict was intradenominational, not inter-
denominational: not all Baptists were Antifederalist; not all
Anglicans were Federalists.

To make the problem more complex, these religio-political divisions were not uniformly distributed. Political divisions among coreligionists varied from state to state. Although Anglicans were by far the most Federalist of any denomination, their Federalism was more predominant in South Carolina, where identified Anglican delegates voted for ratification by a margin of 68 to 8, than it was in Virginia, where the tally was 41 to 21. Congregationalists were deeply divided in Massachusetts, but far more Federalist in New Hampshire and Connecticut. Presbyterian delegates reflected still less consistency, voting strongly for ratification in New Jersey, strongly against it in North Carolina (9–31), and dividing into more equal blocs in Pennsylvania, Virginia (7–10), and South Carolina (8–8). Even Baptists were not completely united against the Constitution, though they voted 2 to 12 in Massachusetts and 6 to 16 in North Carolina. In South Carolina, however, the only two Baptist delegates, Thomas Screven and Thomas Fuller, were Federalists.

While simple denominational analysis seems inconclusive, the religio-political alignments do fall into a clear geographical pattern. Anglicans, Congregationalists, and a significant Presbyterian contingent from older coastal communities inclined strongly toward Federalism, while most Presbyterian, Congregationalist, and Baptist delegates from the backcountry were Antifederalist. This differentiation follows a configuration familiar to interpreters of the Revolutionary era. Whether it is labeled court and country, cosmopolitan and local, urban and frontier, coastal and backcountry, old and new, or Federalist and Antifederalist, the phenomenon of conflicting subcultures fundamentally informs our understanding of Revolutionary America. Many sources of this difference have been identified—economic, political, ethnic, and demographic.

Religion should be added to that list as an important source of cultural differentiation in Revolutionary America, stemming from the struggle between prorevival New Lights and antirevival Old Lights in the Great Awakening of the 1740s and 1750s. By the Revolutionary decades the terms of this polarity had been redefined into the tension between evangelicals and Enlightenment liberals, but the religious geography of the earlier conflict was still clearly visible in the political contest for ratification. Evangelicals predominated in the northern hinterland and southern Piedmont, while liberals were ascendant in the coastal cities and the Tidewater South.

What mattered most in the religio-political alignment of the delegates was not simply their ecclesiastical identity but what kind of Anglicans, Congregationalists, Presbyterians, or Baptists they were. In the 1770s and 1780s these intradenominational tensions were neither latent nor in decline. To the contrary, they were increasing amidst the largest evangelical revival since the Great Awakening, the blossoming of urban religious liberalism, and an unprecedented period of ecclesiastical reorganization.

THE DECLINE OF ESTABLISHED RELIGION: ANGLICANS AND CONGREGATIONALISTS

While there were indeed some churches suffering Ahlstrom's "religious depression," it is more accurate to characterize the years from 1775 to 1790 as a Revolutionary revival. In broadest terms, the legally established colonial religions of Anglicanism in the South and Congregationalism in New England suffered severe institutional disruption during the Revolution even as they fostered a rich blossoming of Enlightenment religious liberalism. Meanwhile evangelicalism exploded in backcountry revivals that greatly increased the numbers of Methodists, Baptists, and Presbyterians, and stimulated the rise of new sects. This Revolutionary revival created a startling and important change in the shape of American religion. At the moment of ratification, the colonial configuration of religions had largely been replaced by a new and long-lasting pattern of evangelical dominance. In 1775 Congregationalists and Anglicans were the two largest religious groups in America, both suffused with Enlightenment theological optimism; by 1790 they were divided and diminished while the Baptists, Methodists, and Presbyterians had surged past them, bound for the evangelical empire of the nineteenth century.

During the Revolution more than half of America's Anglican priests honored their solemn oaths to the British crown, resigned their appointments, and left either for England or for other destinations in the British empire. In many locations, however, Anglican priests stood in the forefront of the patriot cause. In South Carolina, for example, only five of twenty Anglican priests were loyalists while in Charleston alone three were leading patriots.[12] Yet the combined effects of loyalism, warfare, and legal disestablishment devastated the Anglican church in America. In 1775 Virginia was the flourishing center of Anglicanism with 95 parishes, 164 churches and chapels, and 91 ministers and missionaries. By the end of the Revolution this establishment had been severely reduced. Only 72 parishes remained and 34 of them were vacant. Many church buildings had been destroyed, leaving about 35 active churches and chapels and only 28 priests to serve them. Aggregate national figures for Anglicanism during the Revolution are much less precise, but estimates of 450 churches served by 325 priests in 1775 compared to 160 churches and 100 priests in 1783 properly indicates the scale of the Anglican crisis.[13]

New England Congregationalists suffered from different but no less debilitating problems of ministerial supply, parish finances, and intellectual conflict. The war disrupted Harvard and Yale, the two main sources of learned Congregationalist clergy, and many ministers left their positions to serve in the Continental army either as chaplains or officers, creating vacancies in their parish pulpits. Ministers grew scarce as New Englanders fell prey to disastrous economic conditions that crippled their ability to pay their parish taxes and still stay free from debt. By the 1780s many simply could not afford their traditional and legally mandated religion. In 1780 Yale president Ezra Stiles counted an astonishing 245 parishes

[12] S. Charles Bolton, *Southern Anglicanism: The Church of England in Colonial South Carolina* (Westport, Conn., 1982), p. 79.

[13] Charles C. Tiffany, *A History of the Protestant Episcopal Church in the United States*, American Church History Series, vol. 7 (New York, 1895), p. 47.

without a minister, more than 35 percent of New England's Congregational churches. Still worse, he could identify only eighty qualified candidates to fill these pulpits.[14] To these institutional woes were added intellectual ones as well. During the 1780s the theological conflict between New Light Calvinists from the Connecticut Valley and the frontier and Old Light Arminians in Boston and other seaports that had ruptured Congregationalism during the Great Awakening flared again under the urging of a new generation of clerical leaders.[15]

Not surprisingly, the Revolution marked one of Congregationalism's slowest periods of growth, despite the fact that New England's population increased more than any other region's during the Revolution. In New Hampshire 25 parishes were organized between 1770 and 1775, but only 3 between 1780 and 1785 and just 9 more during the rest of the decade.[16] In Massachusetts an increase of 31 new churches in the 1760s was followed by the addition of just 16 in the 1770s, 22 in the 1780s, and 27 during the Revolutionary period as a whole. To place this performance in perspective, the 1770s represented the second smallest decennial increase of Congregational parishes in eighteenth-century Massachusetts.[17]

Yet despite these institutional weaknesses, it was primarily among Anglicans and Congregationalists and the political, economic, military, and literary elites they dominated that a movement of Enlightenment religious liberalism burst into full flower.[18] Thomas Jefferson, the Virginian who shared Vol-

[14]Stephen A. Marini, *Radical Sects of Revolutionary New England* (Cambridge, Mass., 1982), pp. 35–37.

[15]Joseph Haroutunian, *Piety versus Moralism: The Passing of the New England Theology* (New York, 1932); Conrad Wright, *The Beginnings of Unitarianism in America* (New York, 1955).

[16]Henry A. Hazen, *The Congregational and Presbyterian Ministry and Churches of New Hampshire* (Boston, 1875), pp. 65–66.

[17]Joseph S. Clark, *A Historical Sketch of the Congregational Churches in Massachusetts from 1620 to 1858* (Boston, 1858), pp. ix-x, 200–202.

[18]Wright, *The Beginnings of Unitarianism,* is the best survey of liberal theology in its most comprehensive New England Arminian form.

taire's theological skepticism yet penned passionate defenses of an innate moral sense and committed the sayings of Jesus to memory, Benjamin Rush, the Philadelphia physician who embraced Unitarianism and Universalism while campaigning passionately for temperance reform and the abolition of slavery, and Benjamin Franklin, the transplanted Bostonian who provided the new nation with a wealth of moral aphorisms and a model of toleration by contributing to all churches of Philadelphia, epitomized the sort of religious liberalism that swept through America's cultural elite during the late eighteenth century. To their names should be added those of clerical leaders like Anglican William White of Philadelphia, the priest and educator who transmitted English Arminianism to a generation of American Anglicans, and Congregationalist Charles Chauncy of Boston, the formidable opponent of Jonathan Edwards who advocated Universalism in *Mystery Hid from the Ages, or, The Salvation of All Men* (1783).

In its advocacy of a benign Creator, a benevolent cosmos, human reason and free will, and a thoroughgoing moral optimism, Enlightenment religious liberalism supplied a powerful theological and philosophical foundation for the cosmopolitan republican culture of the 1780s. But Deism, the extreme rationalist form of Enlightenment religious liberalism, proved generally unsuitable to mass organization. A religious persuasion that agreed with Thomas Paine's claim that "my mind is my own church" was bound to encounter such difficulties. While Universalism did grow quickly and had begun to organize successfully by the 1790s, and Congregationalist Arminians and Anglican liberals retained their parishes, the Deism of Paine and Ethan Allen failed dramatically to become the new American faith, especially after the French Revolution. In 1787, however, Enlightenment religious liberalism still flourished widely in America's urban churches, universities, and plantation parishes.[19]

[19] Koch, *Republican Religion*, pp. 74–116.

THE REVOLUTIONARY REVIVAL:
METHODISTS, BAPTISTS,
AND PRESBYTERIANS

Any one of a number of episodes might qualify as the beginning of the Revolutionary revival among evangelicals. Separate Baptists in Virginia promoted a successful revival during the early 1770s, for example, and chaplains everywhere in the Revolutionary army preached the need for a "spiritual purge" before taking aim at redcoats.[20] But the most notable event to signal the coming revival was a seven-county outbreak of Methodist piety in central Virginia in 1775–76 that eventually produced thirteen new circuits there and in North Carolina before breaking up under the pressures of war in 1778. This was the first large-scale success Methodists had enjoyed in America, and it came at the expense of the already weakened Anglicans, one of whose priests, Devereux Jarratt, provided essential help in launching the revival. Methodist revivals also occurred in 1781, and again from 1784 through 1790. They were concentrated in new settlements of the southern Piedmont but also spread to Maryland's Eastern Shore, New York, and New England.[21]

John Wesley's theology of free will, sanctification, and Christian perfection appealed to the Enlightenment sensibilities of many Anglicans, but his demand for spiritual rebirth and moral witness made early Methodism politically radical in the American South. Methodists condemned slavery, and some of them were also Christian pacifists. Yet so powerful was their appeal that from just twenty or so congregations in 1770, the Methodists had grown to be one of the largest religious bodies in the nation by 1790.

Spectacular as was Methodism's rise, it was not the only revivalistic success in the 1770s and 1780s. Baptists and Pres-

[20] Perry Miller, "From the Covenant to the Revival," in Miller, *Nature's Nation* (Cambridge, Mass., 1967).

[21] Wesley M. Gewehr, *The Great Awakening in Virginia, 1740–1790* (Durham, N.C., 1930), pp. 138–66; James Youngs, *A History of the Most Interesting Events in the Rise and Progress of Methodism in Europe and America* (New Haven, 1830), pp. 258–62, 267, 276–79, 332, 342–52.

byterians provided two powerful Calvinist varieties of evangelicalism that competed vigorously in the Revolutionary revival. In the South, Separate Baptist revivals counterpointed those of the Methodists. At the beginning of the war—and of Methodist growth—the Separate Baptists in Virginia were just completing their first large revival, which had spread from North Carolina. From 1785 to 1787, while the Methodist advance in the Piedmont was stalled, the Separates again seized the evangelistic initiative.[22]

The other center of Baptist expansion was New England, original home of the Separate Baptists after the Great Awakening. The revival there was sparked in 1779 by the preaching of army chaplain Hezekiah Smith in the Merrimack Valley of Massachusetts. It quickly spread north to New Hampshire, east to Maine, and west to the Berkshires. "The New Light Stir," as it was called, continued from 1780 through 1784. It brought the Separate Baptists to parity with Congregationalists on the northern frontier and collaterally spawned no less than three sects—the Freewill Baptists, the Universalists, and the Shakers—who drew their converts from the Separates.[23] Meanwhile, the Regular, or Particular, Baptists enjoyed solid growth in the Middle States. So widespread was their increase that by 1790 the new nation's combined membership of Calvinistic Baptists had surpassed that of the Methodists.

It was in the Middle States and the South that Presbyterians made their largest gains, riding a great wave of immigration from Scotland and Northern Ireland that settled in the frontier regions of Pennsylvania, Virginia, and North Carolina. Zealous preachers carrying forward the revivalistic traditions of the New Side party from the Great Awakening accompanied this mobile population and reaped a rich harvest of converts, especially in the Cumberland Valley of Pennsylvania and during the Hampden-Sydney revival of 1787 in Virginia. The best objective measure of this growth is the number of congregations reported by presbyteries. From roughly 340 churches in 1770, the Synod of New York and Philadelphia

[22] Gewehr, *Great Awakening in Virginia*, pp. 106–37, 173–77.

[23] Marini, *Radical Sects of New England*.

increased to nearly 500 congregations in 1788. Even more remarkably, the rate of Presbyterian growth during the Revolutionary decades was twice that of the 1760s. The effects of war were clearly evident, however, in a vacancy rate of nearly 50 percent, meaning that by 1788 more than two hundred new congregations had been organized but did not have a minister. By the end of the Revolution, Presbyterianism had emerged as a major national religious force, including not only the dominant Synod of New York and Philadelphia but also smaller groups like the Associate, Reformed, and Associate Reformed Presbyteries in Pennsylvania and the surprisingly strong independent presbyteries of New England.[24]

This, in roughest outline, was the denominational character of the Revolutionary revival. It had extraordinary long-range consequences. By establishing the Baptists and the Methodists as the new nation's largest Protestant denominations, it furnished momentum for the Second Great Awakening and formulated a powerful and permanent evangelical theological alternative to the liberalism of the Revolutionary elites. In the short run, however, the Revolutionary revival displayed the paradoxical character of all such movements by both increasing religious commitment and fostering ecclesiastical divisions. Doctrinal controversies and denominational rivalries flared to new heights: no fewer than five major sects— Shakers, Freewill Baptists, Universalists, Associate Reformed Presbyterians, and Republican Methodists—appeared during the 1780s. Virtually all American communions, stimulated by the opportunity to achieve national unity and their unique situation as Christian bodies in a democratic republic, rewrote their church constitutions. These developments raised important questions, not only about the proper relation of the churches to the state but more centrally about the ideal form of society to which both church and state aspired.

---

[24] *A List of the Presbyteries, Ministers, Probationers, and Congregations, Both Settled and Vacant, within the Bounds of the Synod of New York and Philadelphia* (Philadelphia, 1788); James Brown Scouller, *History of the United Presbyterian Church in North America,* American Church History Series, vol. 11 (New York, 1894), pp. 145–202.

THE RELIGIO-POLITICS OF RATIFICATION: ANGLICANS AND METHODISTS

If there was, as I have suggested, a rough correlation between the Federalist-Antifederalist political contest and the liberal and evangelical religious constituencies of the 1780s, then there should also have been intellectual linkage between Federalism and Enlightenment religious liberalism on the one hand and Antifederalism and evangelicalism on the other. In reviewing some examples of such reinforcement, however, it is necessary to remember that the constitutional crisis and the Revolutionary revival had altered the political and religious ideologies of 1775 and had fostered new configurations for the new national culture.

The full spectrum of religio-politics appeared in the Anglican community. Theologically this church, like its English parent, readily accommodated the Enlightenment's emphasis on religious rationalism and moral optimism, but it also followed Anglican tradition in its political conservatism and complex institutional structure. Surely it is more than mere coincidence that James Madison's cousin James Madison was the first Episcopal bishop of Virginia. The statesman and the churchman, along with their Anglican Federalist brethren, shared a vision of society ordered by carefully counterbalanced institutional mechanisms that rationally integrated the competing interests of constituent factions. The ecclesiastical dimension of this persuasion was most clearly revealed in the creation of a new constitution for the American church after the Revolution.

Though New England Anglicans agreed with the plan of Connecticut's Samuel Seabury to seek episcopal ordination in Scotland, church leaders in the Middle States and the South held a series of small state and general conventions—which included many of the Federalist delegates from the state ratifying conventions (seven from Virginia alone)—that produced a model for church government by 1785. The plan vested authority not in the bishops but in a unicameral general assembly that apportioned two lay delegates to every clergyman. The scheme was developed primarily by William White, rector of Christ Church, Philadelphia, whose "firm support of the contract theory of government" and "belief in the importance of natural as well as revealed religion" were influential among political elites from New York to Savannah. Eventually Seabury and White came to terms in a still more complex church constitution that more equally balanced the interests of elected bishops—now constituted in a separate house with veto powers—with those of the laity, whose house could override the bishops' veto by a three-fifths vote.[25]

This religio-political Federalism, however, did not represent all of the Anglican delegates at the ratifying conventions. A few joined Jefferson on the Deist extreme, opposing the Constitution because it did not honor human rights enough and it placed too many barriers to the will of a virtuous people. But most of the Antifederalist Anglican delegates came from the Virginia and North Carolina Piedmont where the Anglican church had virtually collapsed and been replaced by the Methodists. Until 1784 Methodist converts remained members of their Anglican parishes, and even after the formal organization of the Methodist Episcopal Church the two communions still permitted double membership. At the moment of ratification, the Methodists thus represented the evangelical wing of American Anglicanism.[26]

It was in the Methodist fellowship that evangelical Antifederalism was most clearly expressed. The focus of that persuasion was Elder James O'Kelly, leader of the Methodists in the Virginia and North Carolina Piedmont. O'Kelly dissented from two crucial decisions by the national Methodist leadership, the imposition of episcopal polity and the abandonment of excommunication for slaveholders. In 1780 he joined a group of Piedmont elders at Manakintown, Virginia, who challenged the authority of John Wesley's lieutenant Francis Asbury by ordaining new elders and assigning them to preach on Methodist circuits.

More than a decade of intense controversy followed this defiance, as Asbury removed some of these elders from southern

---

[25] Clara O. Loveland, *The Critical Years: The Reconstitution of the Anglican Church in the United States of America, 1780–1789* (Greenwich, Conn., 1956), pp. 9–10.

[26] Ibid., p. 248.

circuits and refused to acknowledge the ordination of others. At the 1784 Christmas Conference, O'Kelly argued against the election of Asbury and Thomas Coke as church superintendents and refused "to submit to John (Wesley) of England in matters of Church Government."[27] When Asbury and Coke were elected, O'Kelly and his followers demanded a "right of appeal" from the new superintendents' instructions to the General Conference—Methodism's legislative assembly of all ordained elders. At the 1792 General Conference in Baltimore, O'Kelly cited "the glorious liberty of the children of God" proclaimed by St. Paul in Romans 8:21 in support of the right of appeal. He and his followers believed that all who had experienced the New Birth possessed such liberty, and that church polity accordingly should reflect this egalitarian feature of "the Divine constitution" instead of Asbury's "tyrannical and unscriptural form of government." By a small majority the General Conference defeated the right to appeal, and O'Kelly, along with many of the Piedmont elders, withdrew to form the Republican Methodist Church.

For O'Kelly and many other Methodists, the "glorious liberty" of personal salvation also entailed an absolute moral prohibition of all forms of slavery, whether in the church or the state. During the 1780s O'Kelly denounced slavery as a corruption rooted in worldly "ease, honor, and self-interest." When the Methodist General Conference failed to enforce its 1784 ruling that all members would be excommunicated in one year if they did not manumit their slaves, O'Kelly added this capitulation to his bill of indictment. In his 1789 *Essay on Negro Slavery,* he declared that opposition to slaveholding was "a test of fidelity in the way of Jesus," and depicted "the true disciple of Christ" as "poor in spirit, meek in heart, thirsting after holiness, crucified with Christ, and dead to the world."[28] It is clear that deadness to the world, however, did not imply

[27] W. E. MacClenny, *The Life of James O'Kelly and the Early History of the Christian Church in the South* (Raleigh, N.C., 1910), p. 52.

[28] James D. Essig, *The Bonds of Wickedness: American Evangelicals against Slavery, 1770–1808* (Philadelphia, 1982), pp. 62–63.

indifference to politics. If true religion required egalitarian polity and a moral imperative against slavery, it was inevitable that O'Kelly would oppose a federal constitution that compromised on both counts and would counsel his followers to do likewise.

THE RELIGIO-POLITICS OF RATIFICATION: PRESBYTERIANS

Like the Anglicans and Methodists, the Presbyterian Synod of New York and Philadelphia also produced a new church constitution. Enacted in 1788, it was the product of more than three years of sporadic deliberation. The new Plan of Government created a unicameral General Assembly with equal representation of clergy and lay ruling elders and a system of checks and balances that permitted amendment only by vote of two-thirds of the constituent regional presbyteries.[29] In its laicization and localization of power the plan generally reflected the interests of the dominant and evangelical New Side party over those of the church's Old Side minority. But the debate on the new church constitution is so ill-documented that it does not shed much light on Presbyterian religio-political alignment. Theology and ratification politics furnish better evidence.

One of the most important Presbyterian Federalists was John Witherspoon, president of Princeton from 1766, tutor of James Madison (the future president, not the bishop), and signer of the Declaration of Independence. Witherspoon, like many of his Presbyterian contemporaries in England and Scotland, was an eclectic Enlightenment thinker whose Calvinism was less than completely orthodox and whose evangelicalism was not easy to detect. He insisted on the power of human reason to understand God and on a God whose actions are rational, not arbitrary. His moral thought was influenced most by Bishop Joseph Butler's theory of conscience, yet Witherspoon preserved a Calvinist distrust of human abil-

[29]Leonard J. Trinterud, *The Forming of an American Tradition: A Reexamination of Colonial Presbyterianism* (Philadelphia, 1949), pp. 279–306.

ity to do good. Politically he was a Lockean who embraced the whig contractual theory of government and who, like his most famous student, advocated checks and balances so that "when everyone draws to his own interest or inclination, there may be an even poise upon the whole." Witherspoon's political, educational, and ecclesiastical achievements made him the leading representative of Enlightenment Presbyterianism, and his influence was amplified, especially in the Middle States, by hundreds of graduates he sent forth during more than thirty years as Princeton's president.[30]

By 1787 this sort of political theology had spread to Presbyterian Federalists like James Wilson of Philadelphia, who used it in his heroic but vain effort to dissuade the largely Presbyterian Antifederalist minority of the Pennsylvania convention, led by Elder John Whitehill of Pequea.[31] The Witherspoon-Wilson position held sway primarily in the former Old Side areas of eastern Pennsylvania, Delaware, and New Jersey, and it reached through the Princeton educational network as far as northern Virginia.

The Presbyterian New Sides, concentrated in western Pennsylvania and the southern Piedmont, represented a different theological and political orientation. They were heirs to the fervent evangelical piety of the Great Awakening, associated with William Tennent's Log College and with Princeton before Witherspoon. Several generations of redoubtable New Side ministers had accompanied the Scots-Irish immigration south and west from Philadelphia after the Great Awakening, transmitting a vigorous evangelical Calvinism rooted in strict biblicism, regenerate morality, and political activism. These New Sides formed the backbone both of the Carolina Regulators, who demanded an explicit right to religious liberty, and of the Whiskey Rebels of western Penn-

[30] John Witherspoon, *An Annotated Edition of Lectures on Moral Philosophy*, ed. Jack Scott (Newark, Del., 1982), pp. 35–53.

[31] Elliot, Jonathan, ed., *The Debates in the Several State Conventions, on the Adoption of the Federal Constitution*, 2d ed., 5 vols. (Philadelphia, 1881), 2:438; Herbert J. Storing, "What the Anti-Federalists Were For," in Storing, ed., *The Complete Anti-Federalist*, 7 vols. (Chicago, 1981), 1:199–223.

sylvania, who defied the federal government four years after ratification.[32]

The New Sides also formed a large and vocal cohort of the Antifederalist delegates in the state ratifying conventions. Their religio-political orientation may be illustrated by the activities of three North Carolina clergymen, David Caldwell, William Graham, and Samuel Houston. Caldwell, longtime minister and educator, and an Antifederalist delegate from Chatham County, opened the North Carolina convention with a speech that defined government not as a pragmatic contract but as a covenant based on *a priori* principles: "I conceive that it will be necessary to lay down such rules or maxims as ought to be the fundamental principles of every free government," he said, "and after laying down such rules, to compare the Constitution with them, and see whether it has attended to them; for if it be not founded on such principles, it cannot be proper for our adoption."[33]

Caldwell proceeded to list six "fundamental principles," describing free government as a mutual "compact between the rulers and the people . . . lawful in itself, . . . lawfully executed, . . . plain, obvious, and easily understood," in which "unalienable rights ought not to be given up, if not necessary." By these criteria Caldwell and his New Side colleagues found the Constitution wanting.[34]

Caldwell's notion of fundamental law as a voluntary covenant grounded on explicit principles was derived, at least indirectly, from the Scottish Covenanter tradition and more directly from the biblical model of divine law so central to evangelical Calvinism. This habit of casting law in the form of general principles and mutual promises was familiar to the New Sides from their local church covenants as well as from their theology, and its impact can be seen not only in the rhet-

---

[32]Trinterud, *Forming an American Tradition*, p. 244; Robert E. Thompson, *A History of the Presbyterian Churches in America*, American Church History Series, vol. 3 (New York, 1902).

[33]Elliot, ed., *Debates*, 4:7.

[34]Ibid., p. 9.

oric of Caldwell but in the constitution-writing of two of his closest associates—William Graham, president of Liberty Hall Academy in Salisbury, North Carolina, and Samuel Houston, New Side minister from the transappalachian settlements of east Tennessee and uncle of the Texas founder.

Graham, like Caldwell, was a leading Presbyterian Antifederalist of the southern Piedmont, an educator, Revolutionary War chaplain, and active public figure. One of Graham's keenest interests was settlement and independent statehood for the new settlements west of the Blue Ridge. In 1785 he and Samuel Houston drafted a constitution for the proposed state of Franklin in present-day east Tennessee. Houston claimed that their constitution provided "principles, provisions, and restrictions which secure the poor and the ruled from being trampled by the rich and the rulers; also their property and money from being taken from them to support the extravagance of the great men . . . it is full of that which tends to free [the people] from prevailing enormous wickedness, and to make the citizens virtuous."[35] Houston's phrases were replete with the Antifederalist critique of the Philadelphia Convention and dictated a constitution quite different from the proposed federal instrument. The Franklin constitution indeed proposed a covenant, beginning with a twenty-four-article declaration of rights that presumed a virtuous citizenry and a unicameral legislature consisting "of persons noted for wisdom and virtue." It also provided for registrars whose task was to assemble the people periodically and at different locations in order to ascertain whether they consented to the laws passed by the assembly. The Franklin constitution also excluded from public office anyone who denied the existence of God, a future state of rewards and punishments, the inspiration of the holy scriptures, and the doctrine of the Trinity, or "who is of an immoral character, or guilty of such flagrant enormities as drunkenness, gaming, profane swearing, lewdness, Sabbath breaking, and such like."[36]

[35] "The Provisional Constitution of Frankland," *American Historical Magazine* 1 (1888):51–52.

[36] Ibid., pp. 51–55.

Here is a New Side political theology explicitly at odds with that of Witherspoon. It proceeded from a different set of assumptions that granted the possibility, through grace, of a regenerate majority and a state that would create public virtue from first principles, not from utilitarian consequence. The persuasion of Houston, Graham, and Caldwell was shared by thousands of New Side Presbyterians from Harrisburg to Spartanburg, who elected the largest religious bloc of Antifederalist delegates in the Middle States and the South.

THE RELIGIO-POLITICS OF RATIFICATION: CONGREGATIONALISTS AND BAPTISTS

In eastern New England, Arminian Congregationalist theologians like Charles Chauncy and Ebenezer Gay taught a "supernatural rationalism" that increasingly relied on the freedom of the will, the dictates of reason, and the order of nature as guides to religious truth.[37] Though highly optimistic about humanity's final end, these same liberals had by no means abandoned Congregationalism's traditional insistence on a hierarchic and disciplined social order. During the late 1780s they stood firmly for the religious establishment and the prerogatives of the state. From their center in and around Boston they invoked divine authority for the use of force against the "disordered" Shaysites—soon to be Antifederalists—of central and western Massachusetts. These metaphysical, moral, and political sympathies were shared by the Federalist political elite of eastern Massachusetts and coastal New Hampshire, and found characteristic embodiments in John Adams and the Langdon brothers, Samuel and John.

The evangelical New Light opposition within Congregationalism was focused in central and western Massachusetts and Maine. Jonathan Edwards's successors still demanded an individual experience of regenerating grace and moral reformation and the management of local church affairs by strict consensus—views in tension with the Federalist political and moral calculus of self-interest. Of especial importance here is

---

[37] Wright, *Beginnings of Unitarianism*, pp. 135–36, 246–48.

the political theology of Samuel Hopkins of Newport, Rhode Island, Jonathan Edwards's student and first biographer and the greatest systematizer of his thought. For Hopkins and Edwards a good ruler and a virtuous citizenry should be regenerate Christians, animated in their public as well as private activities by the moral principle of "disinterested benevolence," or good will for the whole of humanity under God's law.

In 1776 and again in 1790, Hopkins attacked the new nation's compromise with slavery in terms reminiscent of James O'Kelly.[38] Hopkins, however, added a potent apocalyptic note to the argument. He warned that preservation of domestic slavery after a successful revolution against England would constitute blasphemy against the very God to whom Americans had appealed for victory. The continuation of slavery, he taught, was a "national sin" that would bring swift and sure judgment on the United States by God the ruler of nations.[39]

Here again the evangelical sense of a God active in history and in individual lives stood in sharp disagreement with the expediency of the Federalist compromise on the slavery question. How far Hopkinsian radicalism extended is unclear. Central and western Massachusetts towns were generally Antifederalist and generally New Light Congregationalist, though not always Edwardsean or Hopkinsian. But Hopkins's antislavery may indeed help explain the controversial speech of New Light Congregationalist Joshua Atherton, leader of New Hampshire's Antifederalists, who proclaimed in the ratification debate at Concord that "if we ratify the Constitution . . . we become consenters to, and partakers in, the sin and guilt of this abominable traffic, at least for a certain period, without any positive stipulation that it should even then be brought to an end."[40]

In Massachusetts and Maine the most articulate Antifederalists came from towns where the Revolutionary revival had driven New Light fervor into religious sectarianism. These men and their towns—William Widgery of New Gloucester,

[38] Essig, *Bonds of Wickedness*, pp. 92–94.

[39] Samuel Hopkins, *Timely Articles on Slavery* (Miami, Fla., 1969).

[40] Elliot, ed., *Debates*, 2:203.

Maine, Samuel Thompson of Topsham, Maine, Samuel Nason of Sanford, Maine, John Taylor of Douglas, Massachusetts, and Phanuel Bishop of Rehoboth, Massachusetts—represented areas of greatest religious radicalism during the 1770s and 1780s, homes to consensual, covenantal, and localist religious dissent.[41]

Separate Baptists, Freewill Baptists, Universalists, and Shakers all had established congregations in William Widgery's New Gloucester by 1787. Samuel Thompson of Topsham was himself a Sandemanian, a Presbyterian sectarian who taught the absolute separation of church and state, footwashing as an ordinance, and a nearly Antinomian doctrine of the all-sufficiency of grace. Samuel Nason's town of Sanford was an early center of the Freewill Baptists, John Taylor's Douglas was the site of a very early Universalist community, and Phanuel Bishop's Rehoboth was the home of more Baptist congregations than any other Massachusetts town and a place where Mother Ann Lee successfully recruited Shaker converts in 1782.[42] All this activity suggests that Antifederalism in New England represented a religio-political association of New Light Congregationalists with the more libertarian and radical Separate Baptists and their related sectarian offshoots.

Certainly the Separate Baptists were overwhelmingly Antifederalist. The proposed Constitution's failure to protect the rights of religious conscience and freedom of the press and its rationale of countervailing self-interest clashed with the Separate Baptist vision of a religiously free nation in which Christian virtue and disinterested benevolence ruled the public as well as spiritual realm. Yet Massachusetts Separate Baptists were not united against the Constitution. In the close vote of 187 to 168 in the state's ratifying convention, rural

[41] Samuel Bannister Harding, *The Contest over the Ratification of the Federal Constitution in the State of Massachusetts* (Cambridge, Mass., 1896), pp. 63–66.

[42] Stephen A. Marini, "Evangelical Itinerancy in Rural New England: New Gloucester, Maine, 1754–1807," in Peter Benes, ed., *Itinerancy in New England and New York* (Boston, 1986), pp. 49–64; Marini, *Radical Sects of New England*, pp. 70–71, 90; Edwin Emery, *The History of Sanford, Maine* (Fall River, Mass., 1901), pp. 72–83.

Baptists were outraged at Boston's Samuel Stillman and Middleborough's Isaac Backus for supporting the new document. Backus was an especially difficult case. For more than two decades he had led the Separate Baptist campaign for religious liberty, and in 1779 he had prepared a bill of rights for the Massachusetts state constitution that contained virtually all the major points of the Antifederalist program, including the rights of assembly, petition, remonstrance, and amendment in order to guarantee "frequent recurrence to the first principles of government, and a firm adherence to justice, moderation, temperance, industery [sic], and frugality."[43] Backus's Federalist vote reflected his growing disappointment at the citizenry's greed and failure to curb its appetite for imported luxury goods—which he regarded as the cause of Shays's Rebellion—and his gradual incorporation into the Enlightened theological discourse of Boston, where Stillman's urbane preaching and personal style were often indistinguishable from those of his Congregationalist colleagues.[44]

Much the same differentiation appeared among Baptists in the Middle States and the South, where the Separate Baptists of the Piedmont were almost unanimous in their Antifederalism while the more cosmopolitan Regular Baptists of Philadelphia, Norfolk, and Charleston embraced the Constitution. Again there were crossovers, the most famous of whom was the popular Separate Baptist John Leland of Orange County, Virginia. Leland had been enlisted to run as an Antifederalist delegate, but he withdrew from the election when James Madison himself "fully and unreservedly communicated to him his opinions" in support of the Constitution. With Leland's support, Madison was elected from Orange County and provided vital leadership in the narrow Federalist victory in the Old Dominion.[45]

[43] William G. McLoughlin, ed., *Isaac Backus on Church, State, and Calvinism: Pamphlets, 1754–1789* (Cambridge, Mass., 1968), pp. 487–89.

[44] Isaac Backus, "An Address to the Inhabitants of New England, Concerning the Present Bloody Controversy Therein," in McLoughlin, ed., *Isaac Backus*, pp. 439–46.

[45] William Buell Sprague, *Annals of the American Pulpit*, 9 vols. (New York, 1857–69), 6:177.

This Baptist focus brings us back full circle to Separate Baptist Lemuel Burkitt of Hertford County, North Carolina, with whose successful Antifederalist campaign against Elkanah Watson we began. Burkitt was not only politically active, he was the religious leader of the Kehukee Separate Baptist Association as well. In the latter role he had presided over delicate negotiations from 1775 to 1786 that finally united the Separates and the Regular Baptists of North Carolina. A similar union took place in Virginia during the 1770s and 1780s, but in Carolina the issue was the practice of the Regulars to baptize persons who were simply "willing, whether they had an experience of grace or not."[46] The Separate majority refused to hold communion with Regulars who had been "baptized in unbelief" and demanded that they abandon such a liberal criterion for church membership.

One of the Regulars slow to capitulate was Elder Henry Abbot of Camden County. Son of John Abbot, Anglican canon of St. Paul's London, Henry had been "baptized in unbelief" in 1758; he, in turn, baptized Burkitt as a Regular Baptist in 1771. Burkitt was soon won to the rigorous evangelicalism of the Separate Baptists, but Abbot continued to adhere to a more cosmopolitan and liberal theology. Eventually Abbot joined in ecclesiastical union with Burkitt, but the two remained culturally and politically estranged. When Antifederalist Burkitt attended the North Carolina ratifying convention he found Henry Abbot across the aisle representing the Federalists of Tidewater Camden County.[47]

FEDERALIST LIBERALS AND ANTIFEDERALIST EVANGELICALS

Of such fine distinctions and shifting loyalties were the religio-politics of ratification composed. From the distance of two centuries it is all too easy to forget that the aphorism "all politics is local" was at least as true then as now. In many ways

[46]Lemuel Burkitt and Jesse Read, *A Concise History of the Kehukee Baptist Association* (Halifax, N.C., 1803), p. 43.

[47]George Washington Paschal, *History of North Carolina Baptists* (Raleigh, N.C., 1930), p. 149.

it is also true that all religion is local, and any effort to general-
ize about either politics or religion must first honor this wisdom. Yet the patterns of religio-political activity surrounding
ratification do seem broad and substantial enough to warrant
a hypothesis about why and how so many Federalists were
religious liberals, while Antifederalists were overwhelmingly
evangelical.

The most significant recent attempt to essay the religio-
politics of the Revolution is Alan Heimert's *Religion and the
American Mind* (1966), a sophisticated reading of theological
and sermonic texts that divides eighteenth-century American
religious thought into Calvinist and liberal categories and as-
signs to the former primary responsibility for Revolutionary
political theology. The alignment of delegates to the state ratifying conventions suggests a different approach, however,
one that focuses on moral theology and the crucial link between political theory and religious thought and proposes a
different typology, already used in this essay, between evangelical and liberal.[48] Heimert's argument is learned and complex and cannot be treated in detail here. His Calvinists move
from Revolutionary ardor in 1776 to a pessimistic Federalism
by 1800—at least in New England—in which, ironically
enough, they joined erstwhile Federalist liberals. My argument suggests that the political lines of 1787 cut across Heimert's categories: evangelical Arminians like O'Kelly and
evangelical Calvinists like Caldwell and Graham were Antifederalist; liberal Arminians like the Langdons and liberal Calvinists like Witherspoon and Wilson were Federalists.

In *Federalist* No. 10, James Madison placed the origin of
politics in the laws of nature and proceeded to an assessment
of how citizens by nature will behave. His famous analysis of
faction turned on the inevitable temptation of the human will

---

[48] My approach to the problem of religion, morality, and political thought
here is methodologically informed by the work of J. G. A. Pocock, particularly the essays in his *Politics, Language, and Time* and his *Virtue, Commerce,
and History: Essays on Political Thought and History, Chiefly in the Eighteenth Century* (New York, 1987); and Quentin Skinner, *The Foundations of Modern Political Thought*, vol. 2, *The Age of Reformation* (Cambridge, 1978), and idem,
Philosophy in History: Essays on the Historiography of Philosophy (New York,
1984).

by the passions and the consequent inability of citizens to pursue anything but their own self-interest in public affairs. Hence an intricate public contract of rational checks and balances was necessary to prevent factions from gaining control. Such a constitution, he argued, was to be achieved by pragmatic compromise on certain issues of principle like representation or slavery, and it did not require a specific declaration of rights.[49]

It might seem paradoxical to associate this rather grim and utilitarian political philosophy with Enlightenment religious liberalism. After all, the religion of the Enlightenment extolled the essential goodness and rationality of human beings, not their tendency to pursue their passions and self-interest. Yet religious liberals were clearly aligned with the new Constitution. How can this pattern be explained? In the 1780s most American religious liberals were Arminians of some sort, Christian believers who agreed with seventeenth-century Dutch theologian Jacobus Arminius that human will was free and Christ died for all. But by 1787 American Arminianism thus defined had itself become divided into evangelical and liberal wings, the former including the Methodists and the sects of the Revolutionary revival, the latter comprised of the more familiar New England Unitarians, Middle States Deists and Presbyterians, and southern Anglicans so prominent among the Founders. The liberals fully absorbed the Enlightenment's philosophies of reason and sentiment. They confidently endorsed reason's ability to determine the truth of revelation and, during the heady early 1780s, some high Arminians even went so far as to posit, with Scottish philosopher Francis Hutcheson, a universal and innately benevolent moral sense.

This ontological optimism had definite limits, however, and American events in the mid-1780s tested them. For more than a year after the Peace of Paris, American optimism remained at its zenith. But when the celebrating was over, the hard realities of economic disorder, political rivalry, and insurrection assaulted all Americans including religious liberals. They pos-

[49]Jacob E. Cooke, ed., *The Federalist* (Middletown, Conn., 1961), pp. 56–65.

sessed the theological means, however, to respond to this unhappy turn of events. No American liberal had ever denied the reality of human sin and most of them held conservative social and political views during the Revolutionary period. Alan Heimert observed that liberal "interpretations of the social contract . . . were careful and methodical arguments for holding in check a populace that was by no means conceived to be a community of natural equals. Even in the Revolutionary period, when the Liberal spoke on public affairs, his ideas were so phrased, and presented in such a form, as to keep 'the multitude' from involving itself in matters of state." Even Universalists like Charles Chauncy taught that sin would be punished in the afterlife, if not necessarily by eternal damnation. In the Revolutionary crisis it had been liberals like the Rev. Samuel Langdon, Harvard president and later a Federalist delegate from New Hampshire, who took the lead in denouncing the vice and corruption of the British ministry.[50]

When the sins of disorder and corruption made their sudden and devastating reentry into post-Revolutionary America, liberals used the same vocabulary of the jeremiad to exorcise them. They portrayed Shaysites and other rural debtors and dissidents as guilty of covetousness for consuming a flood of British imports, ignorance in blaming their problems on their government, and disordered passions by their resort to insurrection.[51] By the late 1780s American religious liberals had moved to a more chastened understanding of human nature and politics than their earlier theological assumptions might have warranted. Nonetheless they, like Madison, affirmed the ability of reason to cure the public moral diseases of covetousness, ignorance, and disorder.

Most American religious liberals were Anglican, Congregationalist, or Presbyterian, members of communions that shared the Reformation tradition of utilizing the complex

---

[50] Heimert, *Religion and the American Mind*, p. 17; Edmund S. Morgan, ed., *Puritan Political Ideas, 1558–1794* (Indianapolis, 1965), pp. 352–72.

[51] See especially two Massachusetts election sermons: Joseph Lyman, *A Sermon, Preached before His Excellency James Bowdoin, Esq., Governour . . .* (Boston, 1787), and David Parsons, *A Sermon, Preached before His Excellency John Hancock, Esq., Governour . . .* (Boston, 1788).

mechanisms of the state to enforce the moral teachings of the church. These establishmentarian traditions led them to agree again with Madison that the only viable, rational strategy for the American nation was to construct powerful instrumentalities of law and government that would produce the greatest good for all by preventing any disordered minority from taking power.

Antifederalists did not produce quite as succinct or eloquent a case as Madison had for Federalism, but their political program sought to maintain a national federation of the several state republics that was minimal in structure, strictly limited in authority by the guaranteed, enumerated rights of the people, and animated by a spirit of consensus and a virtuous regard for the common good.[52] If the new federal Constitution had to be adopted, Antifederalists demanded amendments in the form of a Bill of Rights to check the corrupting and tyrannical potential of an energetic central government. In sharp contrast to Federalism, this political theory posited the existence of intrinsic virtue, manifested both in principled rights and in the moral nature of the people at large. Antifederalist government presumed the existence of moral and political consensus in principle and therefore advocated a constitution for consensus management, not conflict resolution.

Many of these Antifederalist political imperatives were shared by evangelicals. To be sure, an undeniable element of self-interest informed evangelical demands for religious liberty. Baptists and Presbyterians had suffered political, financial, and physical abuse under the religious establishments of the Anglican South and Congregationalist New England. Important as their advocacy of the separation of church and state was, however, it should not obscure the deeper constructive dimension of evangelical political theology. At the heart of that theology was "the necessity of the New Birth," the requirement that all true Christians experience an episode of conscious spiritual regeneration modeled on the accounts of the New Testament. Evangelicals drew a number of theological inferences from the New Birth that had important political

[52]Storing, "What the Anti-Federalists Were *For*."

implications as well. First and most fundamental was the principle of spiritual equality. They believed that any person, of whatever station in life, could be converted by the Holy Spirit. Women, children, and blacks, along with white males of every rank throughout the new nation, found saving grace and joined evangelical congregations as spiritual equals.

Evangelicals organized their congregations by drawing up and signing mutual covenants. These agreements typically bound members to follow the Bible as "the only rule of faith and practice" and spelled out specific rights and duties each member was responsible to observe. Underlying these church covenants were the assumptions that through saving grace the regenerate had received the moral ability to carry out their covenant obligations and that lay and local enforcement of them was the best form of church government. In the classic formulation of Jonathan Edwards, this gracious gift of individual and community virtue derived from the principle of "disinterested benevolence"—defined as "good will to being in general"—implanted in the converted soul by the Holy Spirit.[53]

Disinterested benevolence empowered believers to observe the biblical lifestyle mandated by evangelical moral theology, especially its demand for "separation from the world." By this phrase they meant a series of moral stances that prohibited worldliness in all its forms and committed the saints, among other things, not to sue one another in secular courts, to observe the Golden Rule in business practice, and in most cases to free their slaves. When collective congregational decisions became necessary, evangelicals characteristically invoked the principle of consensus. Since the same Holy Spirit had created all saints spiritually equal, evangelicals claimed that "the Spirit cannot be divided against itself" in church politics. In crucial matters like calling a minister, altering the covenant, or prescribing discipline for a church member, evangelical polities demanded unanimity, not majority, as the sign of divinely guided decision making.

[53]Jonathan Edwards, *The Nature of True Virtue*, ed. William K. Frankena (Ann Arbor, 1960), and Norman Fiering, *Jonathan Edwards's Moral Thought and Its British Context* (Chapel Hill, 1981).

Evangelical theology and ecclesiology thus provided a quite different cluster of religio-political norms than did religious liberalism. Instead of reason, conflict resolution, contractual legal principles, and utilitarian warrants for submission to government, evangelicals emphasized grace, consensus, local covenants grounded in popular consent, and intrinsic moral principles that good government, sacred or secular, must serve.

Evangelicals also, of course, held a Manichaean worldview in which only the regenerate were capable of such virtuous activity. Transferring their closely held norms to a distrusted public realm was at best problematical. But it is precisely here that the impact of the Revolutionary revival may be seen. The 1770s and especially the 1780s had substantially altered the religious world of America's backcountry from Maine to the Carolinas. Evangelicals there had swiftly and unexpectedly moved from the periphery to the center of religio-political influence. Though denominationally divided, they had become the preponderant political and cultural majority by 1787 in places like the southern Piedmont, western Pennsylvania, and the northern frontier of New England. There they caught their first glimpse of majoritarian power and the possibility that the new nation's government could embody their agenda.

The Constitution, however, did not meet their requirements. Accordingly evangelicals helped to elect hundreds of Antifederalist delegates in opposition to what they perceived as the conspiratorial origin and corruptible provisions of the proposed federal Constitution. They instructed their representatives to demand a Bill of Rights as a covenantal counter-constitution if all else failed. They did indeed fail to halt the adoption of the federal Constitution and in defeat had to risk trusting Federalist promises to join them in passing a Bill of Rights after ratification had been secured. The Federalist liberals proved true to their word and Antifederalist evangelicals honored the outcome. Thereby began a momentous national dialogue of religion and politics that has neither slackened nor ceased for two hundred years.

EDWIN S. GAUSTAD

Religious Tests, Constitutions, and "Christian Nation"

IN 1788 AN ANTIFEDERALIST using the pseudonym of William Penn declared that the actions of the several states with respect to religion violated the explicit premises set forth by those states. "These facts," he noted, "will no doubt afford an interesting page in the history of the contradictions of the human mind."[1] It is this interesting page that I would like to examine more closely, not only with respect to the states but in regard as well to the federal government's search for consistency and, even more, for acceptance in 1787 and 1788.

Following the Declaration of Independence in 1776, most states moved quickly to bring their own charters or constitutions into conformity with the new political realities. And so closely identified in the minds of many colonists were the twin goals of civil and religious liberty that no state failed to endorse the freedom of religion and the liberty of conscience—up to a point. The language of New York's 1777 constitution finds a rough parallel in most other state documents: "The free exercise and enjoyment of religious profession and worship, without discrimination or preference, shall forever hereafter be allowed, within this State, to all mankind." Such ringing words carried with them the expected and uncontroverted cavil that liberty in religion must never be used as an excuse for licentiousness nor as a threat to the peace and safety of the state. Thus far, no painful contradictions, no tor-

[1] Herbert J. Storing, ed., *The Complete Anti-Federalist*, 7 vols. (Chicago, 1981), 3:174–75 (3.12.18).

tuous logic. But the states for the most part did not stop there, as they struggled to be loyal to two ideals: religious liberty, as they understood it, and Christianity, as they had inherited it.

The religious history of colonial Maryland, for example, almost guaranteed that its adjustment to the revolutionary change in religion would come more slowly than in some of the other states. Beginning as an English Catholic colony, Maryland early in the eighteenth century had become an Anglican one; its Anglicanism, moreover, had a special defensiveness to it. Finding themselves (or at least imagining themselves) besieged by "enthusiasts" (by which they meant Quakers), by "idolaters" (by which they meant Roman Catholics), and by "atheists" (by which they meant all other non-Anglicans), the tiny knot of Anglican clergy begged for a bishop who could "lay a firm foundation" for England's own church in Maryland.[2] No bishop came, but missionaries of the Society for the Propagation of the Gospel did come in sufficient numbers so that Maryland by mid-century was second only to Virginia in its number of Anglican parishes. Having labored so hard and so recently for its privileges, Anglicanism in Maryland was determined not to let them go.

Maryland's 1776 constitution, therefore, while granting liberty to "all persons, professing the Christian religion," provided specifically that taxes could be levied for the support of Christianity and that all "churches, chapels, glebes, and all other property now belonging to the Church of England, ought to remain to the Church of England forever." Unlike its neighboring state of Virginia, which moved quickly to dislodge Anglicanism from its favored position, Maryland tried to build a protective wall around its once established church. Moreover, it also tried to maintain close ties between the civil and ecclesiastical estates by providing that officeholders be required to declare their loyalty to the state *and* their belief in the Christian religion. To demonstrate that this demand was made in no spirit of intolerance or sectarian bigotry, the constitution carefully exempted Quakers, Mennonites, and German Baptists from the necessity of swearing an oath of

---

[2] William S. Perry, ed., *Historical Collections Relating to the American Colonial Church* (1878; reprint ed., New York, 1969), pp. 11–13.

allegiance, even permitting them to be witnesses in a court of law in "all criminal cases not capital." [3]

In that same year of 1776, the citizens of Pennsylvania, inheritors of a tradition quite different from that of Maryland, adopted a Declaration of Rights that offered the expected guarantees of religious liberty. After all, Penn's colony had been a haven and a refuge for religious dissent for nearly a century when the American Revolution began. No surprise, then, that Penn's political descendants would assert that "no man ought or of right can be compelled to attend any religious worship, or erect or support any place of worship, or maintain any ministry, contrary to, or against his own free will." Somewhat of a surprise, perhaps, was the next sentence, which limited liberties to those who acknowledged "the being of a God," though such a limitation had been specified in Penn's own first set of laws published in 1682. But even more surprising to many friends of liberty, both at home and abroad, was Pennsylvania's religious test for all officeholders, a test more restrictive than had been the case under the proprietary government. In 1776 the new state declared that all legislators, before taking their seats, must first solemnly make the following declaration: "I do believe in one God, the creator and governor of the universe, the rewarder to the good and the punisher of the wicked. And I do acknowledge the Scriptures of the Old and New Testament to be given by Divine inspiration."

Such a "religious test" proved embarrassing to the resident libertarians and onerous to those so summarily barred from holding office. In England Richard Price, Unitarian minister and eloquent British defender of American rights, complained vigorously in 1778 against Pennsylvania's restrictions in a constitution that was "in other respects wise and liberal." He predicted that this religious test would have a short life; even so, it reflected unfavorably upon a whole people engaged in war for liberty, *all* liberty. Religious tests, Price

[3] For these and all other quotations from state constitutions, see Francis Newton Thorpe, ed., *The Federal and State Constitutions, Colonial Charters, and Other Organic Laws of the United States, Territories, and Colonies*, 7 vols. (Washington, D.C., 1909). Also see James Quayle Dealey, *Growth of American State*

added, "do inconceivable mischief by turning religion into a trade, by engendering strife and persecution, by forming hypocrites, by obstructing the progress of truth, and [by] fettering and perverting the human mind." Price could not pass up the opportunity, moreover, to register his strong disagreement with the archbishop of York who, in a sermon delivered the previous year, had avowed the propriety, indeed the necessity, of government for its own safety inquiring into the religious opinions of its citizens and its officials. Christianity requires such civil assistance, the archbishop affirmed. Nonsense, Price scoffed; politicians and statesmen have truly helped Christianity only when they opposed it, never when they supported it. Political friendship had, in fact, invariably "been almost fatal to it."[4]

In 1783 the synagogue in Philadelphia made obvious by public petition what might be too quickly glided over, namely, that Jews by this religious test were barred from rendering the services that other citizens could be called upon to give. True, Jews in Pennsylvania were few, as the petitioners noted, but, they maintained, many were still fleeing the restraints of Europe for the enlarged freedoms of America. How unfortunate it would be if such a religious test would turn them away from Pennsylvania to some other state where "there is no such like restraint laid upon the nation and the religion of the Jews." Jews were as fond of liberty as their fellow citizens, the petitioners noted, and merely for doctrinal dissent they should not be "excluded from the most important and honourable part of the rights of a free citizen."[5] Philadelphia's physician-patriot, Benjamin Rush, could only agree that such a constitutional limitation blighted the liberality of the new nation in general and of the Quaker colony in particular. The accession of Benjamin Franklin to the governorship of the state would add, Rush noted in a 1785 letter to Price, "the

---

Constitutions from 1776 to . . . 1914 (1915; reprint ed., New York, 1972), chap. 10.

[4] Bernard Peach, ed., *Richard Price and the Ethical Foundations of the American Revolution* (Durham, N.C., 1979), pp. 54–55n, 200, and Appendix 5.

[5] Anson Phelps Stokes, *Church and State in the United States*, 3 vols. (New York, 1950), 1:288.

weight of his name to yours to remove such a stain from the American Revolution." Then, just a few months later (April 1786), Rush happily reported to Price that "the test law was so far repealed a few weeks ago in Pennsylvania as to confer equal privileges upon every citizen of the state." One more step had been taken, Rush observed, toward that grand effort "to enlighten and reform the world."[6]

Before Pennsylvania managed to take that welcomed step, Massachusetts had held its constitutional convention in 1780; much of the labor that occurred there bore the stamp of John Adams. The Bay Colony had come a long way from the days of jailing, fining, cropping, exiling, or hanging those who dissented from or defiantly opposed the Congregational way. But Massachusetts had not come so far in 1780 as to be prepared to abandon its commitment to "the support and maintenance of public Protestant teachers of piety, religion, and morality." If Protestant denominations were strong enough and diligent enough to meet this public necessity on their own, well and good. But if not, then the towns themselves must levy taxes to provide what was not offered voluntarily. Public officials, moreover, must swear that they "believe the Christian religion, and have firm persuasion of its truth." Franklin felt compelled to apologize to Richard Price for this illiberality, even if it did not occur in his own state. One must consider, Franklin observed, that Massachusetts had over the years taken significant strides so far as religious liberty was concerned. This gives us reason to hope, Franklin continued, "for greater Degrees of Perfection, when their Constitution, some years hence, shall be revised."[7] Adams, on the other hand, thought that the vestige of establishment in his state was such a "slender thing" that it would endure as long as the

---

[6]Lyman H. Butterfield, ed., *Letters of Benjamin Rush*, 2 vols. (Princeton, 1951), 1:371, 385–86. At this point, however, Pennsylvania had retreated only to the extent of not requiring a declaration of belief in both the Old and the New Testaments. Belief in the existence of God and in cosmic rewards and punishments after death still remained.

[7]Leonard S. Labaree et al., eds., *The Papers of Benjamin Franklin*, 28 vols. to date (New Haven, 1959–), 8:153–54.

solar system itself.[8] Franklin's prediction, as things turned out, was somewhat closer to the mark.

One final example from this "page of contradictions" with respect to the states is drawn from Tennessee. Adopting its constitution long after the federal document had been ratified, long after the First Amendment had been added, Tennessee in 1796 declared on the one hand that "no religious test shall ever be required as a qualification to any office or public trust under this State." But in the very same document at the very same time (and almost in the very same breath), the state of Tennessee stated that "no person who denies the being of God, or a future state of rewards and punishments, shall hold any office in the civil department of this State." Such clear contradiction can be explained only in terms of the pervasive conviction that public trust could be granted exclusively to those who acknowledged a cosmic scheme of justice that made human justice both plausible and enforceable. Here was civil religion at its purest: not ceremony, not creedal loyalty, but the irreducible minimum without which public morality and civic responsibility could not survive. Or, at least, so many believed in the concluding years of the eighteenth century.

Tennessee, like several of the original thirteen states, wished, nonetheless, to ensure that this irreducible minimum did not open the gates to undue religious influence nor permit any return to the status quo ante bellum in America or to the continuing status quo in England. To that end, Tennessee declared in 1796 that "no minister of the gospel, or priest of any denomination whatever, shall be eligible to a seat in either house of the legislature." So also declared Delaware, Georgia, Kentucky (in 1799), New York, and North and South Carolina. Ecclesiastical and civil tyranny had been made the more tyrannical by the fatal and familiar combination that permitted each to work in concert with the other. To prevent that pattern from obtaining in the future, one useful precaution

[8]Charles Francis Adams, ed., *The Works of John Adams*, 10 vols. (Boston, 1850–56), 2:398–99. In 1833 disestablishment at last came to Massachusetts. While Franklin did not live to see it, the solar system did.

was to preclude active clergymen from also being active politicians. Tennessee's prohibition was not unique; what is remarkable is that it took a United States Supreme Court decision in 1978 to strike it down. In *McDaniel* v. *Paty* (435 U.S. 618), the Court quoted with approval James Madison's rhetorical question: "Does not the exclusion of Ministers of the Gospel as such violate a fundamental principle of liberty by punishing a religious profession with the privation of a civil right?" And in a concurring opinion, Justices William Brennan and Thurgood Marshall argued that "a law which limits political participation to those who eschew prayer, public worship, or the ministry as much establishes a religious test as one which disqualifies Catholics, or Jews, or Protestants."[9]

So the specter of religious tests came in yet another guise in the constitutions of those states comprising or admitted to the Union by the end of the eighteenth century. The issue of religious tests also confronted the delegates who gathered in Philadelphia in May of 1787 to draft a federal or national frame of government. But before coming to Article VI of that document, one must note the utter absence of the sort of religious language with which the state constitutions and state declarations of rights are filled. The preamble to the Constitution, for example, is remarkably free of any "God-talk" whatsoever—remarkable when compared not only with state constitutions of the day, but remarkable as well when compared with the Declaration of Independence that preceded it or the inaugural addresses that followed it. The religious silences of the Constitution proper were even more impressive than its assertions.

These silences were impressive, or singularly depressing, according to one's point of view. A mathematics instructor at the College of Philadelphia found himself totally bewildered by them. The only logical explanations that occurred to him were that either all the delegates were indifferent to religion or else that all were of the same religion and were "determined to compel the whole continent to conform" to a single religious standard. But knowing full well that neither per-

---

[9]Robert T. Miller and Ronald B. Flowers, *Toward Benevolent Neutrality: Church, State, and the Supreme Court* (Waco, Tex., 1987), pp. 172–79.

fectly logical proposition was valid, he concluded in some confusion and despair: "For my own part, I really think that their
conduct in this instance is inexplicable."[10]

How do we account for a "secular Constitution" drawn up
and approved by a "Christian nation"? At least four factors
help to explain these Constitutional silences. First, as a matter
of principle, many delegates believed that religion was an issue most properly left to the states. Second, as a practical matter, many delegates recognized that distinctive historical
traditions, colony by colony, region by region, even decade
by decade, made any unifying assertion highly problematic.
Third, confronted by a larger task than many had bargained
for, the delegates would gladly avoid, even ignore, the one
area sure to delay and perhaps fatally damage the main business at hand. And fourth, a few delegates, highly suspicious
of the power-seeking so characteristic (in their view) of institutional religion, envisioned a newly created central government emancipated from all priestly politicians or clerical
lords. Thus there was no acknowledgment even of a benevolent creator or overarching providence, no invocation of divine blessing or prayer for divine favor, no appeal to a
Christian majority or a Christian morality, no explicit assumption of an essential connection between Christianity and common law, between the foundations of this ancient religion and
the stability of this modern civil government. Long after ratification, these Constitutional silences so rankled and worried
many citizens that repeated efforts were made to see that the
federal Constitution read more like those of the states that it
had joined together. As Congregationalist Samuel Austin
warned in 1811, the separation of the Constitution from
Christianity, its one "capital defect," would inevitably lead to
that document's destruction and to the nation's as well.[11]

Sins of omission were bad enough, but there was a sin of
commission too. In Article VI, clause 3, the delegates declared
that "no religious Test shall ever be required as a Qualification
to any Office or public Trust under the United States." Not

[10]Storing, *The Complete Anti-Federalist*, 1:107–8.

[11]Quoted in Morton Borden, *Jews, Turks, and Infidels* (Chapel Hill, 1984),
p. 59.

only did the Constitution proceed without religious affirmation or petition, it seemed determined that the nation itself would be insulated from any pervading influence arising from the denominations. While many would complain in the ratification debates about the absence of guarantees for religious liberty (and they would be heeded), others would complain about the absence of language that preserved religion in the public sphere forever (and they, for the most part, would be ignored).

In the Massachusetts ratifying convention several delegates argued that such strict religious neutrality represented a departure from the principles of that state's forefathers. Moreover, they asserted, the language of Article VI would permit even "deists, atheists, &c." to enter the general government, with the inevitable consequence that all public virtue would soon be at an end.[12] In New Hampshire, an Antifederalist pointed out that under these all too indiscriminate terms "we may have a Papist, a Mohomatan, a Deist, yea an Atheist at the helm of Government." Unlike any other civil government known to the Western world, the United States would not cherish its religious heritage, but totally abandon it. Is it "good policy to discard all religion?" inquired the aggrieved delegate. Public servants who had no regard for the laws of God "will have less regard to the laws of men, or to the most solemn oaths or affirmations." And so the New Hampshire polemic of 1788 concluded with the unspoken premise with which it had begun: "Civil governments can't well be supported without the assistance of religion."[13]

This central assumption was even more elegantly stated and persuasively argued in the pages of the *Massachusetts Ga-*

[12] Philip B. Kurland and Ralph Lerner, eds., *The Founders' Constitution*, 5 vols. (Chicago, 1987), 4:642–43.

[13] Storing, *The Complete Anti-Federalist*, 4:242 (4.23.3). Also ibid., 1:22, where Richard Henry Lee is quoted as explaining to James Madison the compelling public necessity of maintaining religion as "the guardian of morals." A Massachusetts writer in 1787 asserted that only in three ways can the "turbulent passions of mankind" be controlled: by punishment, by reward, and "by prepossessing the people in favour of virtue by affording publick protection to religion." Of the three, the last was the most important.

zette as the moment for ratification drew near. The people of this state, the author proudly noted, have stood for and fought for liberty. But it is just this love of liberty "that has induced them to adopt a religious test," for it is religion that "secures our independence as a nation." All nations acknowledged the need of religion; all, or almost all, instructed both old and young in those religious principles that had "a direct tendency to secure the practice of good morals and consequently the peace of society." Just as governments had a right to instruct their citizens in the arts of defense in order to promote external peace, so they had a right to instruct their citizens "in such principles as tend to secure internal peace." At an absolute minimum, the Constitution should be amended to exclude both "Papists and Atheists" from ever holding public office, the former because they acknowledged a foreign power, the latter "because they have no principles of virtue."

If all this argument did not persuade, then the Massachusetts author played his trump card. We have an example immediately beside us, he pointed out, of a society that required no affirmation of or allegiance to religion: namely, the state of Rhode Island. There, as we all know, people "do whatever they please without any compunction. . . . they have no principles of restraint but laws of their own making; and from such laws may Heaven defend us." How sad it was, this writer concluded, that here we are trying to create a new nation, trying to "build an elegant house," yet we deny ourselves the necessary tools to work with by trying to "establish a durable government without the publick protection of religion."[14] Maryland's Luther Martin, no friend to strong central government, sarcastically observed that in the Philadelphia Convention, some were "*so unfashionable* as to think . . . that in a Christian country it would be at *least decent* to hold out some distinction between the professors of Christianity and downright infidelity or paganism."[15]

A Pennsylvania critic pointed out in the fall of 1788 that all the world had found it necessary for the survival and strength

[14] Ibid., 4:247–48 (4.24.3–6).

[15] Ibid., 2:75 (2.4.108).

of government to maintain some religious foundation. His words dripping with sarcasm, he then commented: "What the world could not accomplish from the commencement of time till now, they [the Philadelphia delegates] easily performed in a few moments." What he had in mind, of course, was the provision against any religious test. "This is laying the ax to the root of the tree," he added, "whereas other nations only lopped off a few noxious branches." But his objection was not so much to the religious test provision itself as to the removal of religion as one possible check upon too strong a central government. His Antifederalist bias comes through clearly when he slyly notes that it must be only weak and feeble governments that require the sanction of religion. The proposed Constitution, on the other hand, envisions an "energetic" government; as such, it "disdains such contemptible auxiliaries as the belief of a Deity, the immortality of the soul, or the resurrection of the body, a day of judgment, or a future state of rewards and punishments." The aggrieved writer from Carlisle concluded that "the grand convention hath dexterously provided for the removal of every thing that has ever operated as a restraint upon government in any place or age of the world." [16] Wise men, liberty-loving men, will simply not vote for such an unchecked elevation of power, for such a frame of government that knows no law higher than itself.

In New York, Cincinnatus found even darker motives behind the provision for no religious test. Since the Constitution made no mention of liberty of conscience and since the only allusion to such liberty lay in this single sentence of Article VI, then we must conclude that no other such liberty was protected or would be respected. We must assume that all other conscientious behavior, religious and otherwise, could be regulated by the new federal government. "For, though no such power is expressly given, yet it is plainly meant to be included in the general powers, or else this exception would have been

---

[16] Ibid., 3:206–7 (3.16.14–15). The writer who adopted the pseudonym of "Aristocrotis" aimed his remarks especially at James Wilson, "political hackney writer to the most lucrative order of the bank" and "patronee" of Robert Morris (ibid., p. 196).

totally unnecessary."[17] Cincinnatus began his discussion by declaring that if men intended to vote for this document, they should at least make some effort to understand it. His understanding of what powers were reserved to the new government would, if widely shared, lead many to oppose ratification with all their might.

If persuasive arguments on behalf of religious tests could be offered, more persuasive arguments could be offered against such tests. And even in a nation so largely Christian and so self-consciously Protestant, such arguments prevailed. In the fall of 1787 Tench Coxe, Philadelphia merchant and later friend to Thomas Jefferson, contrasted the liberality of the United States with the religious restrictions applied abroad. "In Italy, Spain, and Portugal," he wrote, "no protestant can hold a public trust." And in England, no Dissenter from the established church can be elected or appointed to office. The Constitutional Convention "has the honour of proposing the first public act, by which any nation has ever divested itself of a power, every exercise of which is a trespass on the Majesty of Heaven."[18]

Connecticut's representative to the Constitutional Convention, Oliver Ellsworth, reviewed the way that religious tests had operated in England since Charles II, their baleful effect, their deceitful character (the law was imposed on the pretext of excluding "the papists, but the real design was to exclude the protestant dissenters"). When one sees how such laws have been used and abused elsewhere, one can only conclude, Ellsworth noted, that Americans would find religious tests "useless, tyrannical, and peculiarly unfit for the people of this country." Just as we would not submit to a test that would be in favor of Congregationalists or Episcopalians, of Baptists or Quakers, neither should we submit even to the most general kind of religious test. The first would be "indignity" and the second a sham. In England, Ellsworth reported, "the most abandoned characters partake of the sacrament, in order to

[17]Ibid., 6:14 (6.1.19).

[18]Paul Leicester Ford, ed., *Pamphlets on the Constitution of the United States* (1888; reprint ed., New York, 1968), p. 146.

qualify themselves for public employments." The only people excluded by religious tests were the honest and the conscientious, those who on principle would "rather suffer an injury, than act contrary to the dictates of their consciences." Religious test laws were mere "cob-web barriers," not to be relied upon, not to be erected simply for show. Happily in Connecticut, Ellsworth concluded, we have no such laws; neither should the nation employ such a potential "engine of persecution."[19]

Writing in the *American Mercury* in February 1788, William Williams, who had helped frame the Articles of Confederation, admitted that he would vote for the Constitution not because of its prohibition against religious tests but in spite of it. He would have much preferred that the preamble of the Constitution begin with "an explicit acknowledgment of the being of a God, his perfections and his providence." Then, Article VI could say that "no *other* religious test should ever be required," and he would have been happily content. Of course, one can argue that religious tests encourage hypocrisy or duplicity, but the same can be said of all oaths, Williams declared, either at the state or federal level. Nevertheless, oaths of office were widely employed, experience demonstrating that they were both useful and "a security to mankind." Williams, however, would not propose a new preamble at this time, the Constitution as written being "too wise and too necessary to be rejected."[20] Without question, the kind of pre-

---

[19] Paul Leicester Ford, *Essays on the Constitution of the United States* (1892; reprint ed., New York, 1970), pp. 167–71.

[20] Ibid., pp. 207–9. Williams suggested that the introductory words of the Constitution follow these lines: "We the people of the United States, in a firm belief of the being and perfections of the one living and true God, the creator and supreme Governour of the world, in his universal providence and the authority of his laws; that he will require of all moral agents an account of their conduct; that all rightful powers among men are ordained of, and mediately derived from God; therefore in a dependence on his blessing and acknowledgment of his efficient protection in establishing our Independence, whereby it is become necessary to agree upon and settle a Constitution of federal government for ourselves, and in order to form a more perfect union &c." (ibid., p. 208).

amble that Williams proposed would have pleased many citizens (perhaps a majority of them), not only in 1788 but for at least a century thereafter.

Neither the successful ratification of the Constitution nor the subsequent ratification of a Bill of Rights closed the deep fissure that the debate over religious tests revealed. Throughout the nineteenth century, proposals kept cropping up to rewrite at least the preamble of the Constitution to make it clearly religious if not explicitly Christian. And over the same century, state as well as federal courts vacillated in their understanding both of Christianity's relationship to common law and of the religious or Christian character of the country as a whole. Cases dealing with blasphemy, polygamy, and education clearly revealed this persisting bifurcation.[21]

One aspect of Maryland's uniqueness has already been noted, but a second deserves comment as well. Maryland moved more slowly than others to soften or expunge its requirement of a religious and, in the earlier years of statehood, a Christian oath for all officeholders. In 1867 the requirement was further modified to specify no religious test "other than a declaration of belief in the existence of God." That stipulation remained in effect for almost another century until the U.S. Supreme Court in 1961 (*Torcaso* v. *Watkins*, 367 U.S. 488) unanimously agreed that such a statement did indeed amount to a religious test. To avoid having to decide whether Article VI, clause 3, applied to the states, however, the Court decided the issue on First Amendment grounds. Roy Torcaso, who had been appointed as a notary public, could not assume office because, as an atheist, he declined to take the long-standing oath of office. The court concluded that Maryland's test "unconstitutionally invades the appellant's freedom of belief and religion and therefore cannot be enforced against

[21]See, for example, the 1811 New York case against blasphemy (*The People* v. *Ruggles*) and the 1838 Massachusetts case (*Commonwealth* v. *Kneeland*). On the broad theme, consult H. Frank Way, "The Death of the Christian Nation: The Judiciary and Church-State Relations," *A Journal of Church and State* 29 (1987):509–29; Borden, *Jews, Turks, and Infidels,* chap. 3; and Jon C. Teaford, "Toward a Christian Nation: Religion, Law, and Justice Strong," *Journal of Presbyterian History* 54 (1976):422–37.

him."[22] Tradition dies hard; it also dies slowly. It was not until nearly two hundred years after the drafting of the Constitution that all the states had at last fallen into line.

To return to 1787, however, one finds yet another significant symbol of the young nation's uncertainty regarding its proper stance toward religion. As the Constitutional Convention was busy with its important labors, the Continental Congress was busy setting long-range policy for the western territories and the subsequent admission of new states. The document that ultimately emerged from these deliberations, the Northwest Ordinance of 1787, had far-reaching significance in many areas, of course, but examination here is limited to the single facet of religion. We are still looking at constitutions, but now constitutions for a territory and for states yet to be created. These constitutions, moreover, concerned an untamed West where, in the eyes of so many easterners, the civilizing, disciplining force of religion was not a mere option but an urgent necessity.

In Jefferson's 1784 draft of the ordinance, religion was conspicuous by its absence. Always reluctant to mix the language of religion into instruments that had the force of law, Jefferson—like so many of the framers of the Constitution—preferred to avoid even naming the word. But this draft of Jefferson's, like his draft years earlier of the Declaration of Independence, fell into the hands of a committee of the whole. In 1785 Congress began to rework the Jeffersonian document that had temporarily been set into law. In March of that year the Continental Congress recommended that the central section of every township be reserved for the support of education and the section just to the north of it, for the support of religion. Charles Pinckney of South Carolina then proposed to substitute for the phrase "support of religion" this broader one: "for the support of religion and charitable uses." To some of the legislators this looked like an improvement, to others like a dodge. That troublesome word "religion," some argued, should simply be dropped altogether. Whereupon Pinckney withdrew his amendment, and Congress started over again. How about setting aside a section of

[22]Miller and Flowers, *Toward Benevolent Neutrality,* pp. 170–72.

land that would be used just for "charitable purposes"? Four states were willing to support that proposition, but four votes were not enough.

But wasn't religion necessary in the West? Yes, most agreed. Well then, wasn't government obligated in some way to promote and support religion in the West? The answer to that more difficult question turned out to be "yes and no," with the "no" votes sufficient in number to prevent that additional section of land from being set aside, even for "charitable uses." But the "yes" votes, or at least the sentiment behind those votes, nonetheless won a partial victory in the final language of the ordinance. Article III begins in this manner: "Religion, Morality and knowledge being necessary to good government and the happiness of mankind . . ." Thus far a victory for those forces wishing to provide some governmental endorsement of and perhaps assistance to religion. If they had been unopposed, no doubt this sentence in Article III would have concluded in quite logical fashion by declaring that "schools and churches shall forever be encouraged." But too many delegates to the Congress were nervous about or baldly opposed to such a commitment on the part of the central government. So that famous sentence, though setting forth in its premise religion and morality and education as a trinity of essentials, concluded much more lamely that "schools and the means of education shall forever be encouraged." The ordinance, of course, also provided for the protection of religious liberty, but that occasioned no protracted discussion, no complex parliamentary maneuvering. In 1787 religious liberty was not the issue. Religious affirmations were an issue, and assistance to religion, even of a generalized, nonsectarian sort, was still more a matter of controversy, debate, and ultimate defeat.[23]

A single sentence in the Northwest Ordinance thus summarizes the nature of a people divided on the question of what their government could or should do concerning religion in general or Christianity in particular. Religion and morality

---

[23] For a more detailed summary of these negotiations, see Edwin S. Gaustad, *Faith of Our Fathers: Religion and the New Nation* (San Francisco, 1987), pp. 151–56.

were necessary to good government and human happiness. Therefore ... what? Responsible authorities found themselves trapped in a cruel dilemma, or traveling down a passage that offered no exit. Older states had a special responsibility for and special anxiety concerning newer states, but so far as Christian nurture or Christian virtue went, severe limits bound these states and frustrated them.

In the state constitutions, one found much more readiness to affirm a faith, require an oath, preserve a tradition. Yet one did not find uniformity in the faith affirmed or protected, nor did one find all citizens resting easily with doctrinal tests and creedal assumptions. Nonetheless, if the union consisted mainly of states that declared their Christian faith, was not the entity that resulted from the combination of states properly called a "Christian nation"? Many thought it only axiomatic, self-evident if you will, that the whole was equal to the sum of its parts.

The Constitution's framers, on the other hand, knew they walked a tightrope. They knew that the religious diversity represented by, say, Connecticut, New York, and South Carolina, could not readily be encompassed in language of sufficient generality as still to permit some meaning. They knew further that consciences were tender, often rubbed raw by the practiced cruelties of earlier times. They also knew that dissenters against America's own ecclesiastical establishments stood ready to protest at the first sign of governmental favor or privilege. And, finally, they knew that some in their midst believed that religion did not need and perhaps did not deserve any constitutional endorsement. The delegates even declined to offer public prayers, though the patriarchal Franklin tried to shame them into doing so after they had spent four or five weeks groping "in the dark to find Political Truth." Without divine assistance, Franklin observed, "we shall succeed in this political Building no better than the Builders of Babel." Franklin, of course, spoke only of those weeks spent in drafting a political document, but many throughout the nation thought his words equally applicable to the charter itself. We prayed for God's help in this very room during the Revolution, Franklin noted; we should pray for it now. And the Constitution itself, many would later argue, should also indicate its reliance upon that same "superintending Providence," that God who, as Franklin declared, "governs in the Affairs of Men."[24]

Thus the irony, the paradox, the page of contradictions with which the fundamental charters of states, of territories, and of the nation are filled. Our pseudonymous Antifederalist of 1788, after reviewing the contradictions and confusions, concluded that perhaps the only safe path was to rely more on principles than on precedents. Madison would have heartily agreed. "It is safer to trust the consequences of a right principle," he wrote in his retirement at Montpelier, "than reasonings in support of a bad one." Precedent and tradition pointed to a "Christian nation." Principle, on the other hand, pointed to a land that would be, to quote Madison again, "an Asylum to the persecuted and oppressed of every Nation and Religion."[25]

[24]Albert Henry Smyth, ed., *The Writings of Benjamin Franklin*, 10 vols. (New York, 1905–7), 9:600–601.

[25]Elizabeth Fleet, ed., "Madison's 'Detached Memoranda,'" *William and Mary Quarterly*, 3d ser. 3 (1946):554–56; Madison wrote this undated piece in retirement. Also see his "Memorial and Remonstrance," ca. June 20, 1785, in William T. Hutchinson et al., eds., *The Papers of James Madison*, 19 vols. to date (Chicago and Charlottesville, Va., 1962–), 8:298–304.

M. L. BRADBURY

Structures of
Nationalism

To CLAIM THAT the Revolutionary era was a period of significant change in the institutional life and development of
American religious groups is hardly a startling assertion.
From the Revolution onward, no one has disputed that the
achievement of political freedom and the resulting separation
of church and state involved them in organizational change,
though there might be disagreement about its particulars.[1]

[1] Standard bibliographies of the period include Nelson R. Burr, *A Critical
Bibliography of Religion in America*, 2 vols. (Princeton, 1961), and Ronald M.
Gephart, comp., *Revolutionary America, 1763–1789: A Bibliography*, 2 vols.
(Washington, D.C., 1984), 2:922–62. Also useful are Robert deV. Brunkow,
ed., *Religion and Society in North America: An Annotated Bibliography* (Santa
Barbara, Calif., 1983); Nathan O. Hatch, "In Pursuit of Religious Freedom:
Church, State, and People in the New Republic," in Jack P. Greene, ed., *The
American Revolution: Its Character and Limits* (New York, 1987), pp. 388–406;
and the bibliographies in the relevant articles in Charles H. Lippy and Peter
W. Williams, eds., *Encyclopedia of the American Religious Experience*, 3 vols.
(New York, 1988).
   The effect of the Revolution on the institutional structure of religious
groups can be followed in any number of works, most obviously in the standard histories of the various denominations. See in addition, however, Edward F. Humphrey, *Nationalism and Religion in America, 1774–1789* (Boston,
1924), and William P. Trent, "The Period of Constitution-Making in the
American Churches," in J. Franklin Jameson, ed., *Essays in the Constitutional
History of the United States in the Formative Period, 1775–1789* (Boston, 1889),
pp. 186–262. For an effort to understand institution-building in America's
churches as an attempt to replace a shattered sense of community, see Timothy L. Smith, "Congregation, State, and Denomination: The Forming of
the American Religious Structure," *William and Mary Quarterly*, 3d ser. 25
(1968):155–76. For a related argument, see Donald G. Mathews, "The Second Great Awakening as an Organizing Process, 1780–1830: An Hypothesis," *American Quarterly* 21 (1969): 23–43. Discussions of community in
religious terms can sentimentalize the reality, whose historical expressions
are filled with acts, individuals, and situations as mean, devious, self-

For reasons sometimes internal to their history and other times not, many religious bodies found the institutional arrangements persisting from the colonial period no longer adequate or relevant after Independence. For some, separation from Great Britain eliminated obstacles equivalent to those imposed on the development of the Anglo-American empire by British reluctance to legitimate colonial participation in its workings during the course of the eighteenth century. It is no coincidence, then, that many churches celebrated the 200th anniversary of their founding at the same time as that of the American republic.[2] Those that organized into national bodies in the 1780s and 1790s were constrained by their chronology, if nothing else, to imitating in varying ways the federalism that finally prevailed as the solution to America's political diversity. Together with their doctrines and traditions, it provided them with language and models in constructing their structures of governance. This essay will focus on the uses of this federalism in the building of national institutions by three bodies—the Episcopalians, the Presbyterians, and the Baptists.

In a curious way this act of political imitation by America's churches has caused historians to pass over many of its details and to look instead at its role in making possible later religious growth. If one examines most historical surveys of American religion that have appeared since Robert Baird invented the genre in *Religion in America* (1844), one finds that

---

aggrandizing, and psychologically destructive as any to be found in American society.

[2] As part of its bicentennial observance, for example, the Presbyterian Church forewent few opportunities in 1988 and 1989 to have individuals portray John Witherspoon, its chief Revolutionary luminary, in various of the acts that created American Presbyterianism. Perhaps fortunately, few other groups sought to imitate this example in their national celebrations. For another example of such celebratory activities see the Episcopal Church's *This Nation under God: A Book of Aids to Worship in the Bicentennial Year 1976* (New York, 1976). For the religious context of the years 1776–1826, see Edwin S. Gaustad, *Faith of Our Fathers: Religion and the New Nation* (San Francisco, 1987). Also valuable is Nathan O. Hatch, *Democratizing American Christianity* (New Haven, 1989).

the institution-building of the Revolutionary era has typically been seen as a venture in political adaptation that linked the religious freedom won in the Revolution and ratified in the Constitution with the Second Great Awakening or, more generally, with the religious expansion of the 1800s. The religious history of the early nation is, of course, obsessed with revivalism and expansion, perhaps rightly so. But one source of the persisting interest in these subjects represents the residue of an earlier point of view that saw past, present, and future as joined in advancing the coming of the kingdom of God. Thus, this formulation defines the significance of the creation of parallel religious and political institutions in ways that divert attention from its ambiguities and contradictions. At one level it permits conceiving the religious history of the new nation in terms that confer political legitimacy on the churches and religious legitimacy on the republic, without violating the constitutional requirement that church and state be kept separate.[3]

The list of surveys that one might consider in any effort to validate this argument is long. It stretches from Baird to Martin Marty's *Pilgrims in Their Own Land* (1984) or the latest edition of Winthrop S. Hudson's textbook, also named *Religion in America* (1992).[4] Yet even a cursory encounter with the titles on such a list reveals that, although they differ in tone, em-

---

[3]This apologetic function helps to explain why historical accounts of groups that arrived after the Revolution often exhibit very similar lacunae. Although their authors pay attention to institution-building and its relation to indigenous patterns of religious freedom—usually under the rubric of Americanization—the detailed implications of Americanization for the life of these churches characteristically remain obscure. For example, Hasia Diner has written of the Americanization process in nineteenth-century Judaism that, in spite of the extensive attention paid to it, "little is known about how it occurred, what it meant, and what was implied by the reformulation of Judaism along specifically American lines." Although not limited to organizational change, her remarks are valid for the history of many groups that arrived after the Revolution ("From Covenant to Constitution: The Americanization of Judaism," in M. L. Bradbury and James B. Gilbert, eds., *Transforming Faith: The Sacred and Secular in Modern American History* [Westport, Conn., 1989], p. 12).

[4]Martin Marty, *Pilgrims in Their Own Land* (Boston, 1984); Winthrop S. Hudson, *Religion in America* (New York, 1992).

phases, and, to some extent, on matters of fact, they are remarkably consistent in most respects in their definitions of the significant issues of the Revolutionary period and demonstrate surprising fidelity to the formulation of Robert Baird, who made the first serious attempt to make sense of America's religious diversity. Baird, of course, wrote in what in many respects was the formative period of American religious history, when individuals such as Joseph Belcher, Israel Daniel Rupp, and William Buell Sprague were trying to recover and give order to the nation's religious past. The conventions then established continue to influence historical scholarship more than is sometimes appreciated, a persistence that must to some extent qualify one's reaction to periodic announcements that yet another "new" church history is being written, or that portray this enterprise as necessarily involving growth in historical sophistication and complexity. Four issues predominate in Baird's account of the Revolutionary years, which is scattered in various places in his book: the support of the Revolutionary cause by religious groups, the establishment of religious freedom in the new nation, the state of religion at the time—were the churches gaining or losing members?—and the organizational changes in religious bodies that were the product principally of the first three.[5]

Baird's successors remained surprisingly faithful to this analytical framework. For example, Leonard W. Bacon in his *History of American Christianity* (1897) regarded the years after Independence as "the period of the lowest ebb-tide of vitality in the history of American Christianity" but also argued that the period contained the seeds of renewal. The nativism that was fashionable in many intellectual and religious circles when he wrote slipped out in his observation that, happily for America's religious future, "the tide of foreign immigration . . . was stayed" during the Revolution, and the church had the opportunity to gather strength "for the immense task that

[5] Robert Baird, *Religion in the United States of America* (Glasgow and Edinburgh, 1844), pp. 221–53, 498–599, 612–51. For a guide to the historiography of America's religious past, see Edwin S. Gaustad, *Religion in America: History and Historiography* (Washington, D.C., 1973), pp. 37–43. Also useful is Burr, *Bibliography of Religion in America*, 1:55–61, and, for more recent writers, Hatch, *Democratizing Christianity*, pp. 220–26.

was presently to be devolved upon it." As a result of the impetus provided by religious freedom and freedom from foreign interference, churches reorganized and rebuilt—in short, did the preparatory work that was necessary for the outpouring of religious zeal in the Second Great Awakening of the early nineteenth century.[6] William Warren Sweet was arguably the most important student of American religious history from the 1920s to the 1940s, the result partly of his prolific output and partly of his location for much of the period at the University of Chicago Divinity School. His classic one-volume account of American religious life, *The Story of Religions in America* (1930), was perhaps more optimistic in tone than Bacon's *History of American Christianity* and less inclined to emphasize religious decline after Independence. However, his theme was essentially the same: religious groups supported the patriot cause, and their consequent acceptance of the separation of church and state and institutional reorganization produced the religious renewal of the Second Great Awakening. To a greater degree than most, however, Sweet saw an explicit connection between the creation of a nation state and national churches. Just as political unification in the Revolutionary period made possible later western expansion, those churches that converted themselves into genuinely national bodies in the 1780s and 1790s were in the best position to profit later from the opportunities offered by the westward movement.[7] Sydney E. Ahlstrom's *Religious History of the American People* (1972) has been in the 1970s and 1980s the most influential single-volume interpretation of American religious

[6]Leonard W. Bacon, *A History of American Christianity* (New York, 1897). The book was part of the thirteen-volume American Church History Series edited by Philip Schaff, Henry C. Potter, and Samuel M. Jackson. Published from 1893 to 1897, the series was the first systematic professional effort to write the religious history of America and that of its leading churches (Henry W. Bowden, *Church History in the Age of Science* [Chapel Hill, 1971], pp. 64–65, and George H. Schriver, *Philip Schaff: Christian Scholar and Ecumenical Prophet* [Macon, Ga., 1986], pp. 94–97).

[7]William Warren Sweet, *The Story of Religions in America* (New York, 1930), pp. 303, 250–97. For Sweet as a historian, see Sidney E. Mead, "Prof. Sweet's Religion and Culture in America: A Review Article," *Church History* 22 (1953):33–49.

history, in many ways rivaling Sweet's *Religions in America* in its impact. Yet for all the originality of Ahlstrom's work, his themes in the Revolutionary period are familiar ones: the religious support of Independence, changing church-state relations, the decline of church membership in the years after Independence, and the possibility of eventual revival. "All religious groups were provided with new opportunities for increased vitality and growth by important adjustments of church and state relationships, adjustments which they, in turn, had helped to bring about." In short, the Second Great Awakening was the culmination of the Revolutionary era.[8]

Admittedly, the quantitative aspects of the adoption of religious federalism in the Revolutionary era have often been chronicled. Many churches now held regular gatherings, variously called presbyteries, synods, conferences, conventions, assemblies, or yearly meetings, and composed in different ways of lay and clerical representatives, that formed a superstructure above the local churches. By 1820 John Pintard, a New York businessman and founder of the New-York Historical Society, could celebrate an extraordinary manifestation of

---

[8]Sydney E. Ahlstrom, *A Religious History of the American People* (New Haven, 1972), pp. 364, 387. On Ahlstrom, see Gaustad, *Religion in America*, pp. 40–41, 58 n. 36, 59. One must point out what would surely be a provision in any Truth-in-History law, if such a statute existed. To discuss some specific aspect of the past in terms of its treatment in such survey accounts runs the danger of creating a straw man, whose principal purpose may well be to make the writer discussing the historical development seem a more profound and original student of the past than is, in fact, the case. Looking at monographic literature rather than surveys often provides a more nuanced and detailed view of the past. But the monographic literature most likely to notice institutional change is composed principally of denominational studies, whose narrative and analytical imperatives for the Revolutionary era have been essentially the same as the surveys reviewed above—to demonstrate how a particular religious group used the Revolution to fit into the American mainstream—in effect, to complete the process of Americanization and adapt to the separation of church and state. Thus, even this literature skimps on organizational matters because they are regarded as lacking significance as a source of change.

For the effect of attitudes about church-state relations and religious voluntarism on the writing of surveys of American religion, see R. Laurence Moore, *Religious Outsiders and the Making of Americans* (New York, 1986), pp. 3–21. His discussion applies equally to most denominational histories.

this phenomenon. He reported to his daughter that the third week of May was to be "an ecclesiastical week" in Philadelphia where all was "life and animation" as the "General Assembly of the Presbyterian and Associate (Scotch) Reformed Churches, of the Baptist Church, and the triennial convention of the Episcopal Church" assembled in the city at the same time. Without Independence such a week could never have taken place.[9]

But the creation of national institutions involved far more than simply redrawing lines on an organization chart. For example, it meant that for the first time some churches had to deal as well with the consequences of having a political existence lived at local, state, and national levels. This, of course, was not necessarily the same political life as that of the new nation. For both religious groups and the American people to create bodies that operated at local, state, and national levels does not imply that these necessarily functioned in precisely the same way. Structural mimesis does not inevitably produce complete functional equivalence. A participant at some church conventions could occasionally hear a variant of the cry "no politics," by which was meant that the separation of church and state required that religious groups not meddle in the affairs of government. In 1795 Isaac Backus doubted that the Baptist churches of Massachusetts ought even to incorporate under the laws of the state, for such joining them to the world "tends to hinder the church from being governed wholly by the laws of Christ, which is essentially necessary for her acting as a chaste virgin to him." Yet the separation of church and state could also be used as a cloak to disguise what by any standard were highly partisan political activities. Nehemiah Dodge was an ardent Jeffersonian and a leader in the struggle for religious disestablishment in Connecticut. At a celebration to honor Thomas Jefferson's 1804 election to the presidency he argued the duty of his fellow Baptists to support Jefferson. Through Jefferson and like-

[9]Dorothy C. Barck, ed., *Letters from John Pintard to His Daughter, Eliza Noel Pintard Davidson: 1816–1833*, New-York Historical Society *Collections* 70 (1940):291.

minded politicians, Dodge asserted, Baptists could overcome the widespread belief in infant baptism, which served as the "middle link between church and state, the swivel they both play upon." Regardless of their attitudes about participation in secular affairs, however, religious bodies are just as concerned with power—its legitimation, allocation, and maintenance—as any others. Therefore, some developed in the Revolutionary period the beginnings of a political life that was different from any they had known in the colonial period, one concerned with the exercise of power within the group and, to a lesser extent, without.[10]

What these developments implied in a qualitative way, however, is less clear. James Madison in *Federalist* No. 51 argued that "a multiplicity of sects" in a federal republic would provide the best guarantee of religious freedom. But might not the argument of *Federalist* No. 10 be coupled with that of No. 51? In the former essay Madison was concerned with the question of the survival of large republics. He insisted that those with large territories and populations were more stable and better guardians of liberty than small ones. In large republics the number of self-interested factions was greater, so the chances of any of them dominating government and destroying liberty were consequently less. Is this analysis valid for the churches in the Revolutionary era? If churches had factions in a Madisonian sense—as they most certainly did—what were they composed of? Did they line up clerical versus lay interests, sectional against sectional, ethnic against ethnic, or theological versus theological? Or were the interest groups more complex in formation and subtle in operation than these questions imply? Obviously Madison's eighteenth-century rendition of the vocabulary of power does not fix the boundaries of relevant questions. In addition, it seems legitimate to ask how the political life of churches with greater lay

[10]William G. McLoughlin, ed., *The Diary of Isaac Backus,* 3 vols. (Providence, 1979), 3:1387–88 n. 1. Nehemiah Dodge, *A Discourse Delivered at Lebanon in Connecticut* (Norwich, Conn., 1805), p. 40. For Dodge, see McLoughlin, ed., *Diary of Backus,* 3:1278 n. 2. For church-state matters in general, see Thomas J. Curry, *The First Freedoms: Church and State in America to the Passage of the First Amendment* (New York, 1986).

participation differed from those with less or without any at all. If doctrine, tradition, and political federalism influenced choices about governing institutions—which they did—and if structures of governance to some extent define political behavior—which they do—then how did their interaction affect the decision-making process in specific bodies, as well as the way individuals acquired and used power in them? Fully to answer these questions would require detailed and individual consideration of all the important religious groups of the Revolutionary era, an undertaking beyond the scope of this essay. However, it can at least begin to answer these questions by examining some of the effects of creating national organizations on the life of the three churches whose coincidental assembling in Philadelphia in 1820 so attracted John Pintard's attention—the Episcopal, Presbyterian, and Baptist. Because their Revolutionary histories begin in different places and proceed at a different pace, each is considered separately for analytical convenience.[11]

When Episcopalians took up the task of constructing a national church in the 1780s, the obstacles left over from the colonial past posed problems in many respects greater than those newly created by the Revolution. Obviously the latter—prominent among them suspicion of political loyalty and the loss of privileged status in those states where the Church of England had been established by law—affected this effort to a considerable degree. Yet from the 1780s to the early 1800s, many of the political energies of the Episcopal Church were expended internally in erasing the colonial past by resolving issues that had earlier appeared insoluble. Before Independence the Church of England had existed in America under a set of ill-defined and largely ad hoc arrangements and had been beset, among other matters, by sectional differences, antagonism between clergy and laity, and divisions over the creation of an American episcopate. The life of the church at the parish level had been effectively dominated by the laity, and

[11] Jacob E. Cooke, ed., *The Federalist* (Middletown, Conn., 1961), pp. 352, 56–65. Anson Phelps Stokes and Leo Pfeffer, *Church and State in the United States*, rev. ed. (New York, 1964), pp. 188–250.

the church had never developed a satisfactory superstructure to bridge the gulf between the colonial parish and the sources of ultimate authority in England. Of course, the church in America had been nominally under the jurisdiction of the bishop of London. Though he exaggerated, William White of Philadelphia, who in 1787 became the first bishop of Pennsylvania, did not distort the essential reality when he wrote in 1782 that successive bishops had exercised their power "no farther than to the necessary purposes of ordaining and licensing ministers," and only on this basis had their authority found "a general acquiescence on the part of the churches," even though "destitute of legal operation." From 1689 the bishop of London had also designated commissaries to represent him in several of the colonies. These had functioned with mixed success, and whatever authority they exercised was as much the result of the force of their personality as their position. After its foundation in 1701 the Society for the Propagation of the Gospel had appointed missionaries to the colonies and tried to keep them under an effective discipline, although it also paid attention to the weight of parish opinion. In addition, conventions of clergy, drawn from a single colony or several adjoining ones, had met on a basis that was sometimes regular, sometimes not, to deal with the various problems that confronted them. These constraints had to some extent held in check, but in no sense overcome, the essential parochialism of Anglicanism in America.[12]

---

[12]William White, *The Case of the Episcopal Churches in the United States Considered* (Philadelphia, 1782), p. 6. For the state of colonial Anglicanism, see especially Frederick V. Mills, Sr., *Bishops by Ballot: An Eighteenth-Century Ecclesiastical Revolution* (New York, 1978), pp. 3–154; Carl Bridenbaugh, *Mitre and Sceptre* (New York, 1962); and John F. Woolverton, *Colonial Anglicanism in North America* (Detroit, 1984). Also helpful are Simeon E. Baldwin, "The American Jurisdiction of the Bishop of London in Colonial Times," *Proceedings of the American Antiquarian Society*, new ser. 13 (1899):179–222; Arthur L. Cross, *The Anglican Episcopate and the American Colonies* (New York, 1902); Elizabeth H. Davidson, *The Establishment of the English Church in Continental America* (Durham, N.C., 1936); Borden W. Painter, Jr., "The Anglican Vestry in Colonial America," Ph.D. diss., Yale University, 1965; Edgar L. Pennington, "Colonial Clergy Conventions," *Historical Magazine of the Protestant Episcopal Church* 8 (1939):178–218; and Alison G. Olson, "The Commissaries of the Bishop of London in Colonial Politics," in Olson and Richard

Together with the other problems it brought, Independence threatened to release the centrifugal forces inherent in colonial Anglicanism and dash any prospect of preserving church unity. William White, "the master mind in the whole movement for union," recalled in his *Memoirs* the fear that, as a result of the Revolution, the churches "in the different states, and even those in the same state, might adopt such varying measures as would for ever prevent their being combined in one communion." The events that averted this result have frequently been told and do not require extended narration here. From the early 1780s White and other leaders worked to erect a national church, a process that generated much heat and consumed much time. Although preliminary national conventions were held in 1785 and 1786, the failure of Bishop Samuel Seabury of Connecticut and his followers to attend undercut any claim that they were comprehensive bodies. If the Constitutional Convention of 1787 was the last chance to preserve national political union—as it seemed to many at the time—the same sense of urgency was felt in Episcopal circles. Its example put great pressure on the conflicting factions to compromise their differences so that the opportunity for church union might not be forever lost. By accepting constitutional and canonical formulas that papered over sectional and personal animosities and fudged deeply divergent positions on the role of bishops, clergy, and laity in the life and governance of the church, the national convention that met in 1789 sufficiently satisfied competing interest groups to permit the founding of the Protestant Episcopal Church in the United States of America.[13]

M. Brown, eds., *Anglo-American Relations, 1675–1775* (New Brunswick, N.J., 1970), pp. 109–24.

[13] William J. Seabury, *Memoir of Bishop Seabury* (New York, 1908), p. 312; William White, *Memoirs of the Protestant Episcopal Church in the United States of America*, 2d ed. (New York, 1836), p. 21. The period can be followed most easily in Mills, *Bishops by Ballot*, pp. 155–307, and Clara O. Loveland, *The Critical Years: The Reconstruction of the Anglican Church in the United States of America, 1780–1789* (Greenwich, Conn., 1956). See also Daniel D. Addison, "The Growth of the Laymen's Power in the Episcopal Church," *Papers of the American Society of Church History* 3 (1912):65–77, G. MacLaren Brydon, "New Light on the Origins of the Method of Electing Bishops Adopted by

These developments have commonly been discussed in terms of the creation of what had been an impossibility in the colonial period, an American episcopate. But equally important was another colonial impossibility, the empowerment of the laity formally to exercise a voice in church life above the parish level by its representation in the diocesan (state) and general (national) conventions that formed the new governing structures imposed on the individual parishes. By largely removing the Church of England from the internal contest for power in America, Independence forced competing groups to recognize the need to compromise their differences in ways that had not been necessary or possible earlier. The constitutional and canonical arrangements that eventually emerged from the 1780s so diffused and overlapped power throughout the governing bodies of the church that bishops, clergy, and laity had at least to moderate their disagreements if the authority of any or all was to have much effect. Bishops needed the consent of the clergy and laity as much as clergy and laity needed that of the bishops. Recogni-

---

the American Episcopal Church," *Historical Magazine of the Protestant Episcopal Church* 19 (1950):202–13, and Walter H. Stowe, "The State or Diocesan Conventions of the War and Post-War Periods," *Historical Magazine of the Protestant Episcopal Church* 8 (1939):220–56. Also extremely helpful are the records of convention proceedings, and constitutional and canonical changes. From the many relevant publications of William S. Perry, see *A Handbook of the General Convention of the Protestant Episcopal Church* (New York, 1881) and *Journal of General Conventions of the Protestant Episcopal Church,* 3 vols. (Claremont, N.H., 1874). The published records of the diocesan conventions are less easily consulted and for the most part must be tracked down in the relevant entries in Clifford K. Shipton and James E. Mooney, eds., *National Index of American Imprints through 1800: The Short-Title Evans,* 2 vols. (Worcester, Mass., 1969), and Ralph R. Shaw and Richard H. Shoemaker, eds., *American Bibliography: A Preliminary Checklist, 1801–1819,* 23 vols. (New York and Metuchen, N.J., 1958–83). See, however, *Journals of the Conventions of the Protestant Episcopal Church in the Diocese of Massachusetts, 1784–1816* (New York, 1890), *Journals of the Conventions of the Protestant Episcopal Church in the Diocese of Virginia from 1785–1787; 1789–1835* (New York, 1836), and *Proceedings of the Convention of the Protestant Episcopal Church in the State of New York, 1785–1791* (New York, 1791). On constitutional and canonical matters, see Edwin A. White, *Annotated Constitution and Canons for the Government of the Protestant Episcopal Church in the United States of America,* ed. Jackson A. Dykman, rev. 2d ed., 2 vols. (Greenwich, Conn., 1954).

tion that the price paid for a national church must be that no group could lay claim to ultimate power took place gradually and reluctantly, and it required the reinforcement of outside political events. However, once it arrived, even if only incompletely, it permitted the creation of a national church whose institutions were as obviously American as those of the nation's political life.[14]

For example, when the House of Bishops was created as a separate body in the national government of the church in 1789, it received the right to veto the legislation passed by the House of Deputies, which was composed of lay and clerical representatives. Its negative could be overridden only by a four-fifths vote of the other house. However, its institutional separation and veto power did not clothe it with sufficient authority to exempt it from having its actions rejected by a simple majority of the House of Deputies. In 1789 Bishop Seabury, as well as the clergy of Massachusetts and Connecticut, wanted the General Convention to permit the use of the Athanasian Creed in the worship of the church. Seabury won the concurrence of William White, the only other bishop present, but the House of Deputies, even after a joint conference, "would not allow of the creed in any form," which, White recorded, "was thought intolerant by the gentlemen from New England, who, with Bishop Seabury, gave it up with great reluctance."[15]

---

[14] For the subsequent history, see Percy V. Norwood, "Constitutional Developments since 1789," *Historical Magazine of the Protestant Episcopal Church* 8 (1939):281–95, and William H. Swatos, Jr., *Into Denominationalism: The Anglican Metamorphosis* (Storrs, Conn., 1979), pp. 73–93.

[15] White, *Memoirs*, p. 150. In its early years the House of Deputies normally conducted its business by a majority vote of those present or resolved itself into a committee of the whole to iron out differences. The constitution of 1789 provided for a more complicated voting procedure, one that in some respects imitated the Electoral College. At the request of a lay or clerical deputy the House was obligated to divide itself into lay and clerical orders, with each order having one vote per diocese and a majority of the votes of both orders required for a measure to pass. There was sufficient ambiguity about the process that the joint committee on canon law was charged in 1844 with the task of defining "what constitutes a majority of this House, voting by diocese and orders" (*Journal of the General Convention*

The bishops' right of veto remained a divisive issue for twenty years. Bishop Seabury and his adherents had wanted the House of Bishops to have an absolute veto in 1789, but had been forced to accept the four-fifths clause as a compromise because of the objection of Robert Andrews, a lay deputy from Virginia. He had expressed his "apprehension" that an absolute veto would wreck the union because it "was so far beyond what was expected by the church in his state as would cause the measure to be there disowned." Despite such sentiments the issue remained very much alive and continued to be pressed. In 1792 the Rev. John Bowdoin of Connecticut prepared *An Address to the Members of the Protestant Episcopal Church,* which advocated an absolute veto. It became widely known in Episcopal circles and provoked a critical southern response. In 1795 a printed circular letter from a "select committee, from a representation of seven churches" in South Carolina, threatened the secession of that state and Virginia from the national church if an absolute veto were enacted.[16]

The Rev. Henry Purcell, one of the leaders of the South Carolina protest, wrote a pamphlet, *Strictures on the Love of Power in the Prelacy,* in which his opposition to a veto and Bowdoin's *Address* became a basis for an attack upon the episcopate itself, whose integrity was still very much suspect in the South. After ranging widely through history, theology, and the Bible to prove the inherent corruption of the institution, Purcell concluded his essentially circular argument by asking whether bishops with the "artifice and guile" that necessarily characterized their behavior "ought to be gratified in their demands, and to have committed to them so dangerous . . . an addition of power as . . . a complete veto?" To give them one would erase the distinction between the Episcopal Church and Rome. It would "instantly" elevate bishops "to the chair of infallibility: for no greater could a pope enjoy."

---

of the Protestant Episcopal Church in the United States: 1844 [New York, 1845], p. 105; White, *Constitutions and Canons,* 1:38).

[16]White, *Memoirs,* p. 146; John Bowdoin, *An Address to the Members of the Protestant Episcopal Church in the United States of America* (New York, 1792). The text of the circular letter can be found in White, *Memoirs,* pp. 349–51.

For his freewheeling polemic Purcell narrowly escaped expulsion from the House of Deputies in the 1795 General Convention. In turn, once the convention had risen, he challenged the chief of his clerical detractors, John Andrews of Philadelphia, to a duel. He was restrained from carrying out his threat against Andrews by being bound over to keep the peace before the Pennsylvania courts.[17]

The capacity of the veto issue to inflame passions that at their extremes threatened both church unity and clerical lives prevented the General Convention from enacting an absolute veto until 1808, after it first submitted the proposal to the diocesan conventions for their consideration in 1804. Growing familiarity with the veto in its distinctly American, not British, guise had the effect over time of making the legislation less controversial and making the arithmetic of voting in the national convention better known. William White calculated in his *Memoirs* that the mathematics of convention opinion insured that the bishops already held a de facto right of absolute veto before 1808. Because a "proportion" of the House of Deputies would always "doubt the validity of a measure adopted without the episcopal sanction," he thought "it would be scarcely possible ever to carry a measure against the bishops," no matter what the provisions of the church's constitution. Granting an absolute veto to the House of Bishops simply gave constitutional recognition to the existing political reality.[18]

As the bishops were well aware, however, actually to exercise their power might well risk greater disruption than the process of acquiring it. Thus, when confronted with such controversial issues as the canon of induction, which arose in 1808, they continued their earlier practice of smoothing over disagreements with the House of Deputies whenever possible. In fact induction was charged with political dynamite for both deputies and bishops. Prodded by the example of the Diocese

[17] Henry Purcell, *Strictures on the Love of Power in the Prelacy* (Charleston, S.C., 1795), p. 66; White, *Memoirs*, p. 173; Perry, *Handbook of the General Convention*, pp. 85–87.

[18] White, *Memoirs*, p. 197; Perry, *Journal of the General Conventions*, 1:302, 312, 340–41, 352–53.

of Connecticut and pervasive clerical fears of unfair dismissals by parish vestries, the 1804 General Convention had required that newly elected clergy be inducted into their office, a practice that among other innovations limited the authority of vestries to dismiss them without the concurrence of their diocesan bishops. The change had been made without much consultation or even warning, itself an unusual event. By this attempt to impose its will on its constituent parts, the national church had invaded one of the most venerable customs and cherished lay prerogatives of its southern branches, whose origins lay in the colonial practice of regarding the tie between clergy and parish as essentially contractual, with clergy liable to dismissal at the will of the vestry.[19]

In Maryland this understanding had been enshrined in the state's vestry law, so the 1804 canon put the church on what might become a collision course with the state. Successive conventions of the Maryland diocese grappled with induction from 1805 to 1807. In 1805 it recommended in straightforward fashion that every parish induct its clergy into their office. By the 1806 meeting its members had discovered that the canon was in conflict with the constitution of the church in Maryland and proposed that the constitution be changed to conform to the canon. By 1807 it had learned that the canon violated the state's vestry law and sought to find a way out of its dilemma by instructing its delegates to the House of Deputies at its 1808 meeting to use their "endeavors" to have the canon reconsidered.[20] In South Carolina the church-state issue created by induction resulted from charters that antedated the Revolution and that gave its local churches their legal existence. A memorial of "sundry persons" to the diocese's 1805 convention claimed that "most, if not all . . . have at various periods been incorpo-

[19] Perry, *Journal of the General Conventions*, 1: 296, 298–301, 308, 312; Perry, *Handbook of the General Convention*, pp. 104–5; White, *Constitution and Canons*, 2:169–70.

[20] *Journal of a Convention of the Protestant Episcopal Church in the State of Maryland* (Baltimore, 1805), pp. 5–6; *Journal of a Convention of the Protestant Episcopal Church in the State of Maryland* (Baltimore, 1806), pp. 3–4, 8; *Journal of a Convention of the Protestant Episcopal Church in the State of Maryland* (Baltimore, 1807), p. 4.

rated; their charters limit their several powers and define their respective rights." In 1806 the diocesan convention, as one of its *Rules and Regulations,* enacted rule XIV, which provided that "no article, canon, rule, or other regulation of any general or state convention shall be obligatory on any Episcopal church within this state where the same shall be found to infringe on any of its chartered rights." The language of rejection was even blunter in 1807 as the convention voted that, because the requirement of induction was "obnoxious to several of the churches in the state," its delegates to the 1808 General Convention should work for repeal or modification.[21]

Questions about induction and church-state relations also arose in the New York diocesan convention in 1806. There they involved whether the inherent right of the church to require induction and to determine the qualifications of the members of its governing bodies without interference from the state was in conflict with the civil right of vestries to make binding contracts "on whatever terms they may deem proper" and to control parish temporalities. "With only a few dissenting voices," the convention dispatched the matter simply by voting that there was no conflict.[22]

Though the Maryland and South Carolina conventions remained isolated in voicing formal objection to induction, the members of the General Convention who assembled in Baltimore in 1808 knew from other sources that "complaints" had been made elsewhere about the canon. To extract the church from these difficulties, the House of Deputies resorted to a common ploy in any federal political system. It proposed to change the location where the church dealt with the matter so that what was insoluble at one level was transferred to another

---

[21] Quoted in Frederick Dalcho, *A Historical Account of the Protestant Episcopal Church in South Carolina* (Charleston, 1820), pp. 490, 495; *Rules and Regulations for the Government of the Protestant Episcopal Church in the State of South Carolina* (Charleston, 1807), p. 4; *Journal of the Proceedings of the Annual Convention of the Protestant Episcopal Church of the State of South Carolina* (Charleston, 1807), p. 7.

[22] *Journal of the Proceedings of the Annual Convention of the Protestant Episcopal Church in the State of New York . . . 1806* (New York, 1806), p. 17.

where it could be solved, or at least rendered less disruptive. The House of Deputies voted to rename the office of induction the office of institution, and to permit dioceses to dispense with it "where it interferes with the usages, laws, or charters of the church." In short, dioceses had the right to choose whether they wished to use the new office of institution, and the politics of choosing were to be conducted at the diocesan level as well. William White hinted in his *Memoirs* that, if the consequences of their action had been politically acceptable, he and the other bishop in attendance, Thomas J. Claggett of Maryland, might well have preferred to veto the proposed canon. It could be construed to weaken the authority of bishops and to produce greater disorder in the church, certainly in the relations between clergy and vestries. But, as White noted, he and Claggett could not simply consult their wishes. The divisive "consequences of rejecting the canon were so stated to them as to induce on their part the consenting to it."[23]

Toward the end of his life William White reflected that the resolution of the controversy over induction proved that "the art of governing consists in a great measure in not governing too much." Such a sentiment was a common one in antebellum America, and, of course, endures as a major theme in American political life. However, to state the significance of the episode solely in these terms subtly misstates the reality and obscures the way in which the creation of a federal system in the church had transformed its political culture from the colonial period. When confronted with the necessity of legislating on a deeply divisive issue, it had available a more complex set of institutional responses with which to react to the claims of competing factions and sections than the zero-sum choice that White's language implied. By converting induction into an issue that involved not simply whether but also where governance should take place, the General Convention

---

[23]White, *Memoirs*, pp. 195–96; Perry, *Journal of the General Conventions*, 1:347, 342, 345, 356–57; White, *Constitution and Canons*, 2:170–71. For the office of institution, see *An Office of Institution of Ministers into Parishes or Churches, Prescribed by the Protestant Episcopal Church in the United States of America* (New York, 1808).

sidestepped the threat that deciding the matter otherwise would have posed to the political peace and unity of the church.[24]

The Revolution was less traumatic for the Presbyterian Church than the Episcopal and did not require rejection of its institutional past in quite the same way, though selective erasure had a role to play here as well. In the analysis of Leonard J. Trinterud, whose *The Forming of an American Tradition* (1949) remains the best account of the Presbyterian Church's eighteenth-century history, organizational concerns became a pawn in the struggle for power of competing clerical groups—principally ones derived from New England and Ulster. Their escalating disputes drew practically all areas of church life into contention during the first decades of the eighteenth century. In the early 1740s the centrifugal strains became too great to be contained within the existing structure of governance, and the synodal unity first achieved in 1717 broke down. By 1745 Presbyterians were formally organized into two competing camps—the Old Side Synod of Philadelphia and the New Side Synod of New York. An uneasy reconciliation between the two occurred in 1758, but the principal solvent of old animosities was the growth in membership of the New Light wing. Its revivalism and theology of new birth brought it converts, put it in tune with the rising political aspirations of the patriot cause, and ensured that its version of Presbyterianism prevailed when the Presbyterian Church in the United States of America was formally created in 1788.

Recently variant readings of the history of these years have been given by Patricia U. Bonomi and Marilyn J. Westerkamp. Though in turn diverging from each other, their accounts of the political strains and stresses within colonial Presbyterianism differ from the one to be found in Trinterud principally in their emphasis on the centrality of the laity's assertion of power against the clergy. Nothing in either of their arguments, however, contradicts the conclusion to be

[24]White, *Memoirs*, p. 195.

drawn from Trinterud that before the Revolution the Presbyterian Church had already passed through and overcome the worst of the centrifugal threats that Independence created for Episcopalians. That result made the internal debate over organizational matters in the 1780s more moderate in Presbyterian than Episcopal circles and helped to spare Presbyterians the consequent threats to church unity.[25]

Regardless of the position one takes on these matters, one must recognize as well that the Presbyterian Church had not encountered the impediments to institutional innovation of the kind imposed on colonial Anglicanism by its British connections, though the legal limits the British placed on religious dissent had acted to retard its development in some areas. In general, then, Presbyterians had less catching up to do in an institutional sense than their Episcopal counterparts and for this reason, too, found the Revolution less intrusive in its effects. Yet for all its comparative freedom before Independence to determine its destiny without reference to British authority, Presbyterianism had been beset by a pervasive localism and milling factionalism in some respects as significant for its history as its more celebrated divisions over religious enthusiasm and the Great Awakening. These characteristics helped to make its colonial history different in degree but not essentially in kind from that of the Episcopal Church.

---

[25] Leonard J. Trinterud, *The Forming of an American Tradition: A Reexamination of Colonial Presbyterianism* (Philadelphia, 1949), is the standard account of early Presbyterianism. See also Patricia U. Bonomi, *Under the Cope of Heaven: Religion, Society, and Politics in Colonial America* (New York, 1986), especially pp. 133–60 and 187–216, and Marilyn J. Westerkamp, *Triumph of the Laity: Scots-Irish Piety and the Great Awakening, 1625–1760* (New York, 1988). Neither Bonomi nor Westerkamp provides, in a strict sense, a history of the Presbyterian Church, nor does Westerkamp's analysis extend to the Revolutionary era. However, their conclusions do not contradict the view that Presbyterianism had confronted and overcome the most serious of the centrifugal challenges of the colonial period before the American Revolution. Also useful are Elwyn A. Smith, *The Presbyterian Ministry in American Culture: A Study in Changing Concepts, 1700–1900* (Philadelphia, 1962), and Fred J. Hood, *Reformed America: The Middle and Southern States, 1783–1837* (University, Ala., 1980).

The origins of the Presbyterian Church in colonial America can be traced to what was, in the most literal sense of the term, a voluntary association. With Francis Makemie assuming the lead, a small group of like-minded clergymen came together in 1706 to form its first American presbytery. In its early years the continued existence of the church depended on the voluntary maintenance of this initial association, a parentage that helped to ensure that its governing apparatus both within and above the congregation, although unevenly elaborated, was essentially the creature of its clergy as well. By a gradual process this pattern of largely personal governance by the clergy was altered at the local level so that by 1770 lay authority was deeply and almost uniformly rooted there in the form of sessions of elders, elected by their congregations, who shared duties and responsibilities with their ministers. But no equivalent development took place in the evolution of the upper reaches of the church. Ruling elders had had the right to attend presbyteries and synods ever since the second meeting of the Presbytery of Philadelphia in 1707. But they never formed a distinct bloc in the deliberations of these bodies. Clergy-lay clashes could be commonplace events in the life of local churches, even in the relations of congregations with presbyteries and synods, but they did not echo, at least in any systematic way, within the meetings of presbyteries and synods. In fact, elders often did not attend them with regularity or in significant numbers, in part because of the difficulty and expense of travel but in part because of the equivocation that underlay their politics, which was dominated anyway by issues that most immediately affected the clergy. Initially the presence of elders had been intended to reinforce the authority of ministers, not to represent congregations or the laity, and their participation during the colonial period never completely shed its legitimating role to reveal a wholly representative one. In this context, for elders not to appear offered one way to assert independence. In most respects, then, the higher judicatories of the church resembled benches of clerical magistrates, with an admixture of elders, which possessed overlapping legislative, judicial, and executive functions. Although acknowledging some commonality, each could be jealous of the individual and collective prerogatives of its members and reluctant to admit the authority or supremacy of other benches. Yet in all of them the clergy retained their original dominance.[26]

At the level of practice the church suffered from much the same political and institutional bifurcations as colonial Anglicanism, with the prevailing shortage of clergy acting in both instances as a kind of cement to bind their parts together. In Presbyterianism the effects of the shortfall on local churches could be ambiguous. One can find instances of congregations moderating their quarrels with offending clergy because of the difficulty of finding replacements, although the process could operate in reverse, too, as clergy moderated their quarrels with offensive congregations because of lay control of the power of the purse. That inadequate salaries forced most ministers to work at other occupations to support themselves further confused the situation. Above the local level, however, the consequences of the shortage of clergy were much clearer. It undercut the centrifugal tendencies implicit in the laity's acquisition of power within the congregation by underlining the need for individual churches to maintain ties with presbyteries and synods, which had a monopoly of the supply of qualified clergy. For example, during the schism of 1745–58 the Synod of New York crushed its Old Light rival in Philadel-

---

[26]For the origins of the Presbytery of Philadelphia, see Boyd S. Schlenther, ed., *The Life and Writings of Francis Makemie* (Philadelphia, 1971), pp. 20–21, and Jon Butler, *Power, Authority, and the Origins of American Denominational Order: The English Churches in the Delaware Valley, 1680–1730* (Philadelphia, 1978), pp. 52–64. Ministers were expected to attend all meetings of their presbyteries and synods, unless excused, and to bring an elder with them. Compelling the attendance of clergy, though not without difficulties, was easier to accomplish than that of elders. Efforts to enforce attendance in the Presbytery of Philadelphia and its successor synods can be followed in William H. Roberts, ed., *Records of the Presbyterian Church in the United States of America* (Philadelphia, 1904). See also Trinterud, *Forming an American Tradition*, pp. 205–11. Whether the elder should be ordained or recognized in some other way, or chosen for life or elected annually, was a point on which Presbyterian practice diverged for much of the colonial period. In part the assertion of lay authority at the local level took the form of insisting on a congregational role in the selection of elders.

phia in part because it was able to generate a larger pool
of candidates for the ministry. The institutions of colonial
Presbyterianism could not contain the religious enthusiasm
unleashed by the Great Awakening in ways that permitted
it to retain its unity. However, it was politically so circum-
stanced that those passions split the church into two competing camps, not a jumble of unrelated congregations. The
Great Awakening divided the church without destroying the
potential for its synods to be knit together again in the
future.[27]

When its fractured parts were rejoined in 1758, the resulting Synod of New York and Philadelphia represented in
institutional terms essentially a reversion to the status quo
ante schism. The Plan of Union, whose ratification by a joint
meeting of the synods of Philadelphia and New York effected
their coming together, compromised doctrinal differences to
some extent and promised to redraw presbytery boundaries
"in such manner as shall appear . . . most expedient," which
in practice meant in ways that did not rekindle old antago-
nisms. Implicitly, however, it assumed that the political and
institutional bifurcations of the past would persist in the reconstituted church but that this persistence would not endan-
ger the church's survival. To some extent these assumptions
were a political necessity, the result of continuing differences
for which no bridge had been found during ten years of negotiations about reconciliation, from their tentative beginnings
in 1749 in Trenton, when commissioners from the two synods
met for the first time, to the culminating events of 1758 in
Philadelphia. Thus the document recognized that reunion at
the local level required lay consent, given formally in a way
that was separate from that of the clergy. Though the procedures were not spelled out in detail, it presupposed that the
question of whether congregations divided by the revival
would join together again basically must be settled by the vote
of their members. But the place reserved for elders in the
higher judicatories of the church did not formally change; by

[27]Trinterud, *Forming an American Tradition*, pp. 203–4, 150–52; Westerkamp, *Triumph of the Laity*, pp. 212, 198–99.

its silence on the matter the plan did nothing to resolve the ambiguity of their presence.[28]

A literal interpretation of the language of the Plan of Union might leave the impression that the split of the 1740s had resulted not from institutional malfunction or doctrinal deviance but from the dysfunctional behavior of the clergy, which could be cured once they agreed about the conduct they would exhibit toward each other in the future. Many of its provisions can be read as an attempt to heal an estrangement between onetime clerical partners by laying out a code of manners that would govern their relations after they moved back into their former quarters. For example, the plan stipulated that a clergyman who disagreed with a majority vote of the new synod about matters "indispensable in doctrine or Presbyterian government" would either accept the decision or "peaceably withdraw from our communion, without attempting to make any schism." Presbyteries would no longer appoint clergy within the bounds of other presbyteries without their consent. That only fourteen elders were present in Philadelphia to ratify the plan—in contrast to the forty-two clergy in attendance—suggests the continuing ambiguity of their role. The clergy would take the lead in reforming their manners and reuniting the church above the local level.[29]

Fortunately for the survival of Presbyterianism, its higher judicatories did not act on the assumption that reformed manners alone could repair the breaks of the past or that their improvement could be insured by concurrence in a formal document. As before, the submission of individual churches to higher authority in the church rested ultimately on its monopoly of the supply of clergy. The power to license and ordain clergy remained in the hands of presbyteries, an arrangement that gave them a far more important and powerful role in the life of the church than the synod. The Plan of Union assumed that the synod would act principally as a

---

[28] Roberts, ed., *Records of the Presbyterian Church,* p. 287; Trinterud, *Forming an American Tradition,* pp. 144–51; Richard Webster, *A History of the Presbyterian Church in America* (Philadelphia, 1857), pp. 218–39.

[29] Roberts, ed., *Records of the Presbyterian Church,* pp. 285–87.

presbytery of the whole to resolve the differences that arose within and between presbyteries, a function it was able to perform with only limited success. This impairment reflected the reality that low clerical attendance at its yearly meetings always undercut its ability to speak for all the clergy of the church, much less the laity or its individual congregations. Leonard Trinterud calculated that "from 1758 to 1774 over half the clergy had been absent every year but 1761, when 56 out of 105 had been in attendance." More significant, however, were the limited powers the synod had to compel conformity to its will. When squabbles broke out within presbyteries, it could attempt to compose differences by redrawing their boundaries or creating new ones, as it did in 1762 when it permitted dissident Old Light clergy in the Presbytery of Philadelphia to withdraw into the specially formed Second Presbytery. Seven Old Light clergy in the Presbytery of Donegal, in Pennsylvania, refused to accept a similar accommodation in 1767 and separated into an independent presbytery. They returned in 1768 only when the synod permitted them to choose the presbyteries in which they would be placed. Because of its distance from the site of the annual meetings the predominantly New Light Presbytery of Hanover, in Virginia, in effect suspended relations with the synod for much of the period 1761 to 1774. In seven of these fourteen years no clergyman showed up from Hanover, in six years one attended, and in one year two were present. The situation of the Hanover Presbytery was by no means unique, and there was little the synod could do to effect change and restore full relations until the Hanover clergy were willing to make the effort. The situation of the synod was somewhat like that of the bishop of London in colonial Anglicanism: its authority did not extend much farther than its churches and presbyteries were prepared to accept.[30]

The parallel with the Episcopal experience can be extended into the American Revolution and its aftermath, which reinforced the localism of colonial Presbyterianism and

---

[30]Trinterud, *Forming an American Tradition*, pp. 281, 158, 165, 282; Roberts, ed., *Records of the Presbyterian Church*, pp. 321, 383–86; Bonomi, *Under the Cope of Heaven*, p. 260 n. 44.

threatened to fragment the church into more parts than the revivals of the 1740s. In areas where fighting took place, congregations and presbyteries sometimes stopped meeting, and clergy often scattered. Although the synod continued to meet annually, the war loosened its ties with many presbyteries, even ones that did not suspend their functions, and clerical attendance remained low. For example, the Presbytery of Hanover persisted in its errant behavior, and only the presence of Samuel Stanhope Smith, "late . . . of that presbytery," in 1780 permitted the synod, for that year at least, to learn the names of its clergy as well as those of its licensed candidates for the ministry. The end of the war held out the prospect of rebuilding, even expanding, the church at the local and presbyterial level, but it offered little promise of restoring vitality to the synod, where attendance improved only slightly. In both 1784 and 1785 only six elders and thirty clergy, "scarcely one fourth of the ministers" in the church, gathered in Philadelphia for its meeting.[31]

The failure of attendance to rebound triggered fears that the church might wither away from lack of interest in the synod. In the language of manners it often employed when attempting to overcome difficulties, the synod wrote three of its most delinquent presbyteries in 1785 about its apprehension that "the members of the body may become entire strangers to each other." As with the Episcopal Church, the prospect of Presbyterianism's "mouldering away" furnished the motive for reconstructing its institutions. The process began when an "overture" was presented to the synod in 1785 that it "be divided into three synods, and that a general synod, or assembly, be constituted out of the whole." To complete the task thus introduced required three years and the silencing of some internal opposition, whose nature is now difficult to recover. John Rogers of New York City seems to have played much the same role of clerical mastermind in these efforts that William White did in the Episcopal Church. By their annual meeting in 1788 the members of the synod were sufficiently agreed to be able to ratify the new constitution. On

---

[31] Roberts, ed., *Records of the Presbyterian Church*, p. 485; Trinterud, *Forming an American Tradition*, pp. 280–82.

May 27 they adopted a Form of Government, and on May 29 a Directory of Worship, a Confession of Faith, and Larger and Shorter Cathechisms. The synod concluded its work by voting to dissolve itself at the end of its business on May 29. Its sixteen presbyteries would henceforth be grouped into four synods and select delegates annually to represent them in the General Assembly of the Presbyterian Church in the United States of America, which would meet for the first time in 1789.[32]

That the discussion and debate lasted from 1785 to 1788 tends to obscure the underlying agreement that existed throughout about the structure of the new church. The institutional arrangements first proposed by a committee of the synod in 1786 were incorporated into the constitution of 1788 with fewer essential modifications than one might expect in such a situation. The document did not presume to tamper with the existing pattern of ministerial-sessional governance at the congregational level, and presbyteries remained the most powerful of the higher judicatories of the church by their control of the ordination of clergy. The functional distinction between the new synods and the General Assembly was only briefly sketched in. Their least ambiguous difference in some ways was representational. As in the past, synods were to serve as presbyteries of the whole for the presbyteries under their jurisdiction, with attendance expected of all clergy. The General Assembly was to be a representative body for clergy and elders, with delegates for both to be chosen annually by presbyteries in proportion to the number of ministers within each one. Although clergy and elders had the right to participate in equal numbers in both synods and the General Assembly, the constitution did not provide for any enlarged or distinctive role for the latter in them. In institutional terms it did nothing to resolve the colonial equivocation about their function.[33]

[32] Roberts, ed., *Records of the Presbyterian Church*, pp. 509, 513, 546–48; Trinterud, *Forming an American Tradition*, pp. 282–306.

[33] The drafting of the constitution can be followed in Trinterud, *Forming an American Tradition*, pp. 283–306, and in the relevant documents them-

The sharpest break with the past occurred in the organization of presbyteries. All clergy were, of course, expected to attend the meetings of the one to which they belonged. Churches with settled ministers could send the same number of elders as clergy. For example, churches with one minister had the right to be represented by one elder, collegiate churches could send as many elders as they had ministers, and churches that shared a minister also had to share an elder. However, the constitution stipulated that congregations without a settled minister but "able and willing . . . to support one" were also entitled to be represented by an elder. A possible motive for the insertion of this clause can be found in an extraordinary circular letter the Presbytery of Long Island sent in 1790 to all its churches, several of which lacked ministers, that held out the possibility of lay control as a reason for them to obey the new constitution. It argued that congregations now held "the balance of power against the ministers. . . . As the vacant churches share a right of representation in the higher judicatories, and as it is to be supposed that there will always be vacancies within the limits of every presbytery, it by these means becomes a fact that the balance of power is thrown into the hands of the churches." The New England background of the churches in the presbytery and the competition they faced from Congregationalists made them wary of changes that might subtract from their autonomy. Clearly the letter was intended to attract support for the constitution by quieting fears about its effect on local independence. In 1788 the Presbyterian Church had some 214 congregations with ministers and more than 206 without. If the latter, at least some of whom presumably met the constitutional qualification, had insisted on being represented in

---

selves: *A Draught of a Plan of Government and Discipline for the Presbyterian Church in North America* (Philadelphia, 1786), *A Draught of the Form of the Government and Discipline of the Presbyterian Church in the United States of America* (Philadelphia, 1787), and *Constitution of the Presbyterian Church in the United States of America* (Philadelphia, 1789). See also Richard W. Reifsnyder, "The Reorganizational Impulse in American Protestantism: The Presbyterian Church (U.S.A.) as a Case Study, 1788–1983," Ph.D. diss., Princeton Theological Seminary, 1984, pp. 57–133.

presbyteries, these might have become quite different bodies. There is little evidence, however, that congregations, whether vacant or settled, were much interested at this time in preserving their autonomy by asserting such rights. They preferred the older pattern of not attending, which accomplished much the same result politically at considerably less trouble and expense. Because presbyteries determined the legitimacy of an elder's qualifications, the power of the clergy to dominate their affairs remained considerable, even if numbers of vacant congregations had sent representatives. To some extent, of course, Presbyterian clergy benefited from the same calculus of probability in its higher judicatories that William White later noted at work for bishops in the Episcopal Church: a "proportion" of elders would always doubt the legitimacy of measures undertaken without their approval.[34]

Rather than resembling a new and more democratically designed model, the church in many respects had something of a jerry-rigged aspect to it. Its constitution retained as much of the former pattern of magisterial governance as possible and, where expedient to do so, adopted a more representative—but in no straightforward sense a more democratic—one, particularly where the laity were concerned. This impression is confirmed by the attendance at the synod of 1788. Half of the presbyteries did not bother to send members to Philadelphia, 38 of the 177 ministers in the church were present, and only 10 elders showed up. One could accurately describe the meeting as something of a clerical rump session, which imposed a new constitution on the church by implicit acceptance rather than formal ratification from the bottom up. A similar manner of proceedings had sometimes taken place in colonial Presbyterianism but never in a way that had permitted higher authority to assert its powers to an extent greater than its presbyteries and congregations had

[34]*Constitution of the Presbyterian Church*, p. 143; "A Circular Letter," *Presbyterian Magazine* 9 (1859):328; Trinterud, *Forming an American Tradition*, p. 306; Ezra H. Gillett, *History of the Presbyterian Church in the United States of America*, rev. ed., 2 vols. (Philadelphia, 1864), 1:368–76; Robert Hastings Nichols, *Presbyterianism in New York State* (Philadelphia, 1968), pp. 28–32, 45–47, 87–88.

been prepared to accept, which was the case in this instance as well.[35]

The question of what might happen under the new plan of government if such an attempt were made in a sustained way did not become contentious until the early 1800s. As in the Great Awakening, it took the shape of a dispute over revivals, this time in the Synod of Kentucky. It eventuated in Barton W. Stone and five colleagues forming independent Christian churches in 1805 and, more important to the success of Presbyterianism in the South, members of the Cumberland Presbytery breaking away in 1810 to found what would become the Cumberland Presbyterian Church. Although receiving more attention at the time as well as later, the secession of Stone and his associates in the aftershocks of the Cane Ridge revival posed less of a threat to the church than that of Finis Ewing, Samuel King, and William McAdow, the clerical triumvirate that provided the nucleus of the independent Cumberland Presbytery. As the rejection of the Calvinist system by Stone and his fellow rebels gained momentum after the momentous events at Cane Ridge in 1801, it proved too radical to gain the support of other Presbyterian clergy or to attract converts from the sources from which Presbyterianism ordinarily drew its recruits. The future of the movement, in its early years at least, lay more among the Freewill Baptists and Shakers. In fact, its escalating extremism—by Presbyterian standards—persuaded two of the original Cane Ridge secessionists, Robert Marshall and John Thompson, to return to the Presbyterian fold in 1811. Rejecting the authority of

---

[35] The constitution provided that any standing rules of the General Assembly intended to "be obligatory on the churches" must first be transmitted to all the presbyteries and not be put into effect until approved by a majority of them in writing. By this standard the constitution was an illegal creation (*Constitution of the Presbyterian Church*, p. 148).

In 1796 the Synod of Philadelphia voted that the annual meetings of the General Assembly made its yearly meetings seem almost unnecessary and urged triennial meetings for the latter. Of course, with few exceptions the General Assembly met in Philadelphia each year, which made any distinction between its business and that of the synod particularly difficult to sustain (Gillett, *History of the Presbyterian Church*, 1:291 n. 1).

the Synod of Kentucky was one thing, that of the whole of the Calvinist tradition, quite another, even in the supercharged atmosphere of Kentucky Presbyterianism in the early 1800s.[36]

The challenge presented by the Cumberland Presbytery to the unity of the church, however, was far more substantial. It involved that unstable mix of theological differences and accusations of clerical malconduct that had split it apart in the 1740s. In America, as elsewhere, Presbyterians have made an extraordinary effort to spell out in detail the doctrinal standards, with their consequences for church life, to which members are expected to adhere. In practice, however, they have tolerated more divergence—or perhaps more accurately, ambiguity—about such matters than the compulsion to theological correctness that lies behind such an expenditure of energy might seem to suggest. The language of manners in the Plan of Union in 1758 was no accident of the Presbyterian tradition. As others before and after, the members of the synods of New York and Philadelphia could only paper over their divisions in perfunctory fashion. However, because the uproar of the revival had dimmed, if they could now manage to be civil to each other in spite of their differences, then they might manage to coexist in the same church. In the midst of the disorders set loose by the revival in Kentucky in the early 1800s, the members of the Synod of Kentucky and its Cumberland Presbytery accepted the necessity of correct standards but could neither agree about definitions nor avoid discharging their rancor at each other any more than their predecessors in the 1740s. Thus the issue became one of whether the institutions of the reconstructed Presbyterianism of 1788 could any better maintain its unity under these troubled conditions than those of the synodal church in the Great Awakening. The answer was that the new church by the addition of the General Assembly offered the possibility of prolonging the politics of the appellate process as charges and

---

[36]The literature on the Kentucky revivals is both voluminous and contentious. Superb guides to it, as well as the revivals themselves, can be found in Paul K. Conkin, *Cane Ridge, America's Pentecost* (Madison, Wis., 1990), and John B. Boles, *The Great Revival, 1787–1805* (Lexington, Ky., 1972).

countercharges between disputants could be shunted between four layers of its judicatories rather than the previous three. It thus offered greater time for tempers to cool and multiplied opportunities for reconciliation—in short, for mutually satisfactory understandings to be reached. However, the longer duration could also strengthen the resolve to resist and permit the forming of alliances that united in a common cause those who might otherwise have found themselves uncertain and isolated, and possibly more inclined to compromise.

Precisely this result took place in Kentucky and produced the Cumberland Presbyterian Church. The events that led to its foundation can be simply stated. The Synod of Kentucky had created the Cumberland Presbytery in 1802 out of the overlarge Transylvania Presbytery. The preponderance of a prorevival faction among its clergy provoked an inquisitorial visit in 1805 by an investigating commission dispatched by the synod with full synodal powers. Its head, John Lyle, had become a staunch opponent of what he considered to be the excesses of the Kentucky revivals and was determined to detect and root out even the suspicion of any doctrinal irregularity in the presbytery. Lyle's domination of the commission insured that its behavior was as highhanded as any feared by Henry Purcell in 1795 from a corrupt bishop in the Episcopal Church and as much resented by the local supporters of the revival. No one would even board its members when they held their hearings in early December. Suspensions of suspect ministers followed, with appeals to the General Assembly, which in 1809 came down on the side of the synod. Rather than submit to the dictates of Lyle and the synod, three of the Cumberland ministers, the minimum necessary to form a presbytery, came together in 1810 to constitute the independent Cumberland Presbytery, which by 1813 had more than sixty congregations.[37]

[37] Events in Kentucky can be followed in two opposed narratives—the prosynod one in Robert Davidson, *History of the Presbyterian Church in the State of Kentucky* (New York, 1847), and the sympathetic account of one of the founders of the Cumberland Church in Franceway R. Cossitt, *The Life and Times of Rev. Finis Ewing* (Louisville, Ky., 1853). Davidson's *Presbyterian Church in Kentucky* contains extracts from the relevant synodal minutes. Pro-

Its creation had an air of inevitability. As the dispensation of 1788 extended the appellate process in the Presbyterian Church in the United States of America, it also added to the fault lines that had separated the governing bodies of American Presbyterianism from its origins in 1706. The possibility of their becoming unstable under stress had always threatened to fracture its unity. No matter whether General Assembly, synod, or presbytery, the higher judicatories of the post-1788 church still resembled prickly benches of clerical magistrates, although sometimes with a larger admixture of elders than earlier. If the political dilemma of the Episcopal Church was to make the veto of bishops acceptable to those who opposed it, then that of the Presbyterian Church was to add the authority of shifting majorities in its General Assembly to those of synods and presbyteries, in spite of their conflicts and contradictions, and to extract acceptance of their decisions from the bodies beneath them in its governing hierarchy. That the General Assembly was a representative institution, in a way that synods and presbyteries were not, did not change the reality that the capacity of inferior groups to resent and resist unwanted intrusions was considerable. In peaceful times the friction of their interaction could ordinarily be dissipated, or at least contained, by the tolerance of some ambiguity and the practice of compromising politics, no matter how reluctantly, often under the rubric of manners. Whenever disagreements about the content of Presbyterian standards made clerical tempers run high, however—such as in the revival—compromise, ambiguity, and manners could easily go out the window. The inability of higher judicatories otherwise to take drastic corrective action of the kind that the situation seemed to demand invited the excesses of clerical majoritarianism that resulted in the heresy hunt of the Kentucky synod among the members of the Cumberland Presbytery. Absent any countervailing force on the synod, which the General Assembly was quite unable and unwilling to provide, the prorevivalists among the Cumberland clergy thought they

---

ceedings in the General Assembly can be followed in *Minutes of the General Assembly of the Presbyterian Church in the United States of America, 1789–1830* (Philadelphia, 1847).

had no alternative but to submit or withdraw into an independent church. Although the synod was clearly willing to compromise on some issues it regarded as less important, its readiness was a matter of too little, too late, from the point of view of the Cumberland dissidents. Their success in the revival strengthened their conviction of their rightness, and, among other sources of loyalty, their ability inexpensively to supply their converts with an adequate number of clergy—which the Synod of Kentucky could not—insured the support of the laity.[38]

To borrow from the language of John Calvin about the significance of works in human salvation, the creation of the Cumberland Church was the price American Presbyterianism paid for being able to live "not without . . . yet not through" the revival in the early 1800s. Although the consequences for Presbyterian unity of the separation of the Cumberland Presbytery have sometimes been decried, the reverse argument is probably more compelling. Its departure reduced the pressures on the institutions and clergy of both churches to a level that they could sustain. It permitted the Cumberland Church to get on with its chosen business of evangelizing the frontier without distraction, yet without its growth posing a threat to the unity of the rest of Presbyterianism. The periodic fractures of American Presbyterianism have probably acted to give its constituent churches an internal stability they would have otherwise lacked. Because the dispute among Kentucky Presbyterians was about the content of their standards, not the necessity of adhering to them, it separated quarreling clerical factions in the church into different bodies, not individual congregations, and preserved the possibility of reunion when the passions of the moment had cooled. In 1906 most of the Cumberland Church rejoined the Presbyterian Church in the United States of America, more or less on the Cumberland Church's terms, the same political formula that had permitted the 1758 healing of an earlier split over revivals.[39]

[38]Conkin, *Cane Ridge*, pp. 150–62.

[39]John Calvin, *Institutes of the Christian Religion*, ed. John T. McNeill, trans. Ford Lewis Battles, 2 vols. (Philadelphia, 1960), 1:798.

In some respects the necessity of adhering to a correct ecclesiology has played the same role among American Baptists that the acceptance of correct standards has for Presbyterians. In both instances the emphasis has acted to obscure the ambiguity, even divergence, that has existed in practice. In the case of the Baptists it has resulted in a slighting in their historiography—viewed as a whole—of analysis of the role of associations among their formally independent churches, beyond their obvious utility in sustaining unity and helping to make possible extraordinary growth. Perhaps more important, it has reinforced a tendency, present in most denominational studies, to assume the Baptists' colonial history and many subsequent developments to be different in kind from that of other churches, whereas in fact the discrepancy may sometimes be simply one of degree. Certainly this is the case with associations. The Particular, or Regular, Baptists lagged behind the Presbyterians by only a year in organizing a local federation of churches—the Philadelphia Association, organized in 1707. Because years of informal working together preceded its creation, one might argue that the matter of affiliating in some way beyond the individual congregation had greater urgency for Baptists than Presbyterians, whose Philadelphia Presbytery lacked this pattern of antecedent cooperation. The sparse historical record does not shed light on whether this coincidence in time concealed some causal connection. Possibly the common Calvinist heritage of Regular Baptists and Presbyterians propelled them in the same direction at roughly the same time. Yet the churches of the two other major doctrinal groupings among colonial Baptists also gathered themselves into associations. The Arminian General, or Six Principle, Baptists established a yearly meeting in Rhode Island, the area of their concentration, though the date of its founding is not clear. It may have taken place before the Philadelphia Association; it was certainly in being by 1717. Some of the Separate Baptists, who split away from New England Congregationalism in the upheavals of the Great Awakening, migrated to North Carolina, where one of their leaders, Shubal Stearns, organized the Sandy Creek Association in 1758, only three years after arriving there. By 1775 the Baptists had, by one computation, 494 churches in

America and had organized eleven associations. In institutional density their accomplishment was not far different from that of the Presbyterians, who at the same time had 588 churches and eleven presbyteries.[40]

Of course, the functional gamut of Baptist associations ran further than that of Presbyterian organizations. The meetings of Separate Baptist groups resembled the extended communion assemblies of Scots-Irish Presbyterians in America rather than the more magisterial proceedings of the Philadelphia Association. Yet, even with this wider range, the overlap of Baptist and Presbyterian bodies was considerable throughout the eighteenth century. Among other common activities, they exhorted and admonished wayward individuals and churches, disciplined and supplied clergy, and sought to define correct doctrine and practice. Whether Baptist or Presbyterian, no matter how peremptory their tone, they were usually very much aware that the authority of their decisions depended ultimately on the willingness of others to accept them. The experience of the Charleston Association in 1788 testifies to the quandaries this circumstance could create and the diplomatic dexterity that sometimes had to be displayed. It also

[40]This account draws heavily on Walter B. Shurden, *Associationalism among Baptists in America: 1707–1814* (New York, 1980). See also his "The Associational Principle, 1707–1814: Its Rationale," *Foundations* 21 (1978):211–24, Elliott Smith, *The Advance of Baptists across America* (Nashville, 1979), A. D. Gillette, ed., *Minutes of the Philadelphia Baptist Association, from A.D. 1707, to A.D. 1807* (Philadelphia, 1851), Robert T. Handy, "The Philadelphia Tradition," in Winthrop S. Hudson, ed., *Baptist Concepts of the Church* (Chicago, 1959), pp. 30–52, Robert G. Torbet, *A Social History of the Philadelphia Baptist Association: 1707–1940* (Philadelphia, 1944), Richard Knight, *History of the General or Six Principle Baptists* (Providence, 1827), and George W. Purefoy, *A History of the Sandy Creek Baptist Association* (New York, 1859). To permit comparison, the number of Baptist and Presbyterian churches in 1775 is taken from Marcus Jernegan's calculations in Charles O. Paullin, *Atlas of the Historical Geography of the United States*, ed. John K. Wright (Washington, D.C., 1932), p. 50. The figure for Baptist associations is that given for 1770 in Robert G. Gardner, *Baptists of Early America: A Statistical History, 1639–1790* (Atlanta, 1983), p. 139; for presbyteries, the number functioning in 1775 has been obtained from the list in Trinterud, *Forming an American Tradition*, pp. 312–14. See also Lester J. Cappon, ed., *Atlas of Early American History: The Revolutionary Era, 1760–1790* (Princeton, 1976), pp. 36, 71, 117.

underlines that agreement about manners and decorum could have as important an effect in determining the prevailing temper in Baptist circles as in the judicatories of the Presbyterian Church. In October 1788 some members of the High Hills (South Carolina) church took "considerable offense" at the more refined "dress and appearance" that Richard Furman, their former minister, had adopted since moving to Charleston some months before. They then complained to the association about "the strange fashion of apparel which come up among us." Without offending anyone, the association managed nimbly to dodge the trap that the High Hills' complainants wanted it to spring on one of its most prominent members by blandly observing that "both extravagance and neglect should be avoided" in dress, with "due respect . . . paid . . . to the customs of the place we reside." To the extent that views on church polity governed their behavior, Baptist meetings, of course, always had the option of not joining, or dropping out of, associations, whereas Presbyterians did not. At the level of practice, however, it is difficult to see a striking difference in the strength of the bonds that tied congregations to larger groupings in either church.[41]

The trajectory of Baptist associations diverged from that of their Presbyterian and Episcopal counterparts after the Revolution in that, although leaders in the Philadelphia Association, for example, made the same sometimes despairing efforts to develop a national hierarchy among Baptists, their efforts did not bear fruit. In fact, as early as 1766 Samuel Jones, who later became president of the Philadelphia Association, had written on its behalf to those organizing the Warren (Rhode Island) Association and suggested the value of a national body to incorporate all Baptist groups. The suggestion was obviously premature, and the outbreak of war made the issue moot until its end. Moreover, during the 1780s Baptists proved immune to the pressures that the triumph of political federalism placed on Episcopalians and Presbyterians.

[41] Letter of Richard Furman to Sarah Haynsworth, Oct. 29, 1788, and Minutes of the Charleston Baptist Association, Oct. 29, 1788. Both are quoted in James A. Rogers, *Richard Furman: Life and Legacy* (Macon, Ga., 1985), pp. 84–85.

In 1799, however, the Philadelphia Association invited "the different associations in the United States to favor them with their views on the subject" of a general conference, "to be held every one, two, or three years." Its invitation attracted so little support that by 1802 the association conceded that holding one was not "likely to be accomplished."[42]

In 1775 the Warren Association had marked out what might have become an alternate, though more narrowly constructed, road to national cooperation. It called for a consultation of Baptist groups on religious freedom. Even though the call received an eager response, particularly from Virginia Baptists, the planned meeting never took place. The Revolution created as many problems for the assembly of Baptist bodies as it did for Presbyterian and, of course, transformed the political situation in which they found themselves. The importance of religious freedom in Baptist ecclesiology and the centrality of that ecclesiology in defining Baptist identity invite speculation about possible consequences had the consultation occurred. It might have become a natural vehicle to establish some wider unity among Baptists, in much the same way that answering similar calls put patriot leaders on the path that led from the Continental Congress to the Constitutional Convention. But the opposite view is probably more sound. For example, during the debate from 1787 to 1788 over ratifying the Constitution, various newspapers reported "we hear that the Baptist societies in general, in the eastern, as well as the middle states, are much in favor of the new Federal Constitution." Yet the "favor" of Baptist opinion arrayed itself differently in Massachusetts. While a delegate to its ratifying convention in 1788, Isaac Backus calculated that of the "above twenty" Baptists in attendance only he and Elder Samuel Stillman from Boston voted for the Constitution, "with twelve Congregational ministers . . . though doubtless with very different views." In spite of a common ecclesiology and presumably a commitment to expressing their belief in religious liberty and the separation of church and state by appropriate ballots, Baptist delegates to the Massachusetts con-

---

[42]Gillette, ed., *Minutes of the Philadelphia Association*, pp. 343, 349; Shurden, *Associationalism among Baptists*, pp. 221–22.

vention could hold quite contrary views about ratifying the Constitution, whereas the very different religious views of Backus, Stillman, and the twelve Congregational ministers could persuade them to support it. The division among Baptists about the Constitution suggests the limits of appeals to religious liberty as a device to obtain national cooperation. Though agreed on the absolute necessity of adhering to a correct ecclesiology—a view that can admittedly forge unity under oppression—Baptists in less severe times have had just as many difficulties with the implications of their beliefs for political action and church-state relations as Presbyterians have had with interpreting their standards in the midst of revivals.[43]

In any event the Revolution brought more religious opportunity than oppression to Baptists. No matter what its adverse consequences for national unity, it did stimulate two other tendencies already present among Baptist associations— it added substantially to their number and to their utility for undertaking political action at the state level, where agreement could sometimes be easier to achieve because of specific local conditions. The associations began to grow more rapidly after the Great Awakening, and the removal of the constraints that British rule had placed on Baptist expansion was one of several factors that increased the rate of their formation, once past the immediate disruption of the war. From 1780 to 1814 at least one new association was founded almost every year; by 1800 they numbered 48, by 1814, 125.[44]

The withdrawal of the British also mobilized Baptists to conduct the final phase of the campaign they had begun in the colonial period to get rid of political restrictions on the practice of their beliefs. The movement for Independence altered the dynamics of the political process in the two locales—

[43]The newspaper quotation can be found in Robert J. Dinkin, *Voting in Revolutionary America* (Westport, Conn., 1982), p. 146. McLoughlin, ed., *Diary of Backus*, 3:1221 n. 1; Shurden, *Associationalism among Baptists*, p. 226. For the limitations of explaining political behavior by reference to religious beliefs, see Richard L. McCormick, *The Party Period and Public Policy: American Politics from the Age of Jackson to the Progressive Era* (New York, 1986), pp. 47–55.

[44]Shurden, *Associationalism among Baptists*, p. 39.

Virginia and New England—where they continued to suffer from the most serious oppression, and, consequently, those who opposed them there could only mount what was, in the long run, a series of rearguard actions in a conflict they must finally lose. The most prominent institutional participant in New England, was, of course, the Warren Association, which joined the fray through its Grievances Committee, first established in 1769 to collect "well attested grievances" against the "standing order" from "all the oppressed Baptists in New England." The availability of the Warren Association to disseminate intelligence, coordinate resistance, and apply political pressure was as significant for the eventual overthrow of the New England establishment as the appointment of Isaac Backus as its agent in 1772. Backus labored so effectively in part because the network of churches in the association could be honed into an instrument to protest religious oppression that was very similar to the committees of correspondence Sam Adams and other patriot leaders wielded against British political tyranny. Although certainly less bloody than the patriot contest, the Baptist struggle in New England took much longer to win. Massachusetts was the last of its states to abolish the vestiges of religious establishment, an event that did not take place until 1833. Almost three decades earlier, however, in 1805, the Warren Association had reappointed members to the Grievances Committee for the last year. It owed its demise to a significant decrease in the incidence of grievances, an accomplishment that was perhaps as important a milestone for Baptists in the struggle for liberty in New England as the ratification by the voters of Massachusetts in 1833 of the Eleventh Amendment to its constitution, which provided that "no subordination of any one sect or denomination to another shall ever be established by law."[45]

The organization of the General Association of Separate Baptists in Virginia in 1771 marked one beginning of an ef-

---

[45]McLoughlin, ed., *Diary of Backus*, 2:732–33; Shurden, *Associationalism among Baptists*, pp. 209–16. For Backus, see William G. McLoughlin, *Isaac Backus and the American Pietistic Tradition* (Boston, 1967), and Stanley Grenz, *Isaac Backus: Puritan and Baptist* (Macon, Ga., 1983). The attack on the standing order in New England can be followed in William G. McLoughlin, *New England Dissent, 1630–1833*, 2 vols. (Cambridge, Mass., 1971).

fective campaign there against its ecclesiastical establishment, as the formation of the Grievances Committee had two years before in New England. Although his activities cannot be documented in the same detail, the popular preacher John Leland played much the same role among Virginia Baptists as Isaac Backus in New England. Certainly he and other Baptist leaders employed many of the same tactics. The Baptist situation in Virginia was obviously different, however, and, before victory could be achieved, required them to participate as one of several interested groups in a diverse, only loosely affiliated, political coalition. Nonetheless, Baptist associations could claim at least part of the credit for the signing in 1786 of Thomas Jefferson's Statute for Establishing Religious Freedom, with its famous promise that "all men shall be free to profess . . . their opinions in matters of religion, and the same shall in no wise . . . affect their civil capacities." Continuing Baptist pressure resulted in the General Assembly's reducing the property holdings of the Episcopal Church when in 1798 it repealed the state's glebe laws that had, in its awkward formula, permitted "the church established under the regal government to have continued so." At the same time it declared the language of liberty in Jefferson's bill to be "a true exposition of the principles of the [Virginia] bill of rights and constitution."[46]

Although the effort to entrench their interpretation of lib-

---

[46]*Acts Passed at a General Assembly of the Commonwealth of Virginia . . . 1785* (Richmond, 1786), p. 27; *Acts Passed at a General Assembly of the Commonwealth of Virginia . . . 1798* (Richmond, 1799), pp. 8–9; Shurden, *Associationalism among Baptists,* pp. 200–209. For Leland, see Lyman H. Butterfield, "Elder John Leland, Jeffersonian Itinerant," *Proceedings of the American Antiquarian Society* 62 (1952):155–242, and Edwin S. Gaustad, "The Backus-Leland Tradition," in Hudson, ed., *Baptist Concepts of the Church,* pp. 106–34. For disestablishment in Virginia, see Thomas E. Buckley, S.J., *Church and State in Revolutionary Virginia, 1776–1787* (Charlottesville, Va., 1977), and Buckley, "Evangelicals Triumphant: The Baptists' Assault on the Virginia Glebes, 1786–1801," *William and Mary Quarterly,* 3d ser. 45 (1988):33–69; Richard C. Osborn, "The Establishment of Religious Freedom in Virginia, 1776–1786," M.A. thesis, University of Maryland, 1975; and Rhys Isaac, "Evangelical Revolt: The Nature of the Baptists' Challenge to the Traditional Order in Virginia, 1765 to 1775," *William and Mary Quarterly,* 3d ser. 31 (1974):345–68.

erty in the institutions, laws, and constitutions of the new republic supplied Baptist churches and associations with a common task in which to sink as many of their differences as they could, the impetus for national union gained its first success from a quite independent source—foreign missions. Their significance for overcoming the jealousies, scruples, and internal divisions of disparate Baptist groups could not have been foreseen in 1776 or 1787, even in 1800. Yet by 1814 thirty-three Baptist leaders—twenty-five clergymen and eight laymen—gathered in Philadelphia from states from Maine to Georgia to found its first national body, the General Missionary Convention of the Baptist Denomination in the United States of America for Foreign Missions, more familiarly known as the Triennial Convention because it subsequently met every three years. The cause of missions, whether home or foreign, had never figured prominently in Baptist consciousness in America until the end of the eighteenth century. Whatever efforts had been undertaken before then had simply reflected the interests and sporadic initiatives of individual clergy and churches. For example, the steady increase in the Baptists' presence in Georgia from the time the first one or two landed with James Oglethorpe in 1733, indeed the spectacular growth in their numbers from the 1780s, had not translated into organized missionary efforts until 1801. At its October meeting that year the Georgia Association "unanimously and cordially approbated" "the propriety and expediency of forming a missionary society in the state, for the purpose of sending the gospel amongst the Indians, bordering on our frontiers." Its decision for home missions took place in the same decade as those of many associations, no matter where located.[47]

During the same period interest in foreign missions also began to spread, though more slowly. Initially it most commonly expressed itself in groups, often women's "mite" societies, organized to contribute to the English Baptist mission in

[47]The quotation from the Minutes of the Georgia Association can be found in Jesse Mercer, *History of the Georgia Baptist Association* (Washington, Ga., 1838), p. 40; *Proceedings of the Baptist Convention for Missionary Purposes; Held in Philadelphia, in May, 1814* (Philadelphia, 1814), pp. 6–7; Shurden, *Associationalism among Baptists*, pp. 160–70.

India that William Carey had started in 1794. The catalyst for American independence in this field was, of course, Luther Rice. Sent to India in 1812 as one of the first missionaries of the American Board of Commissioners for Foreign Missions, he there changed his "sentiment upon the subject of baptism" from that of the Congregationalists to the Baptists and returned home in 1813 to launch an extraordinary tour from Massachusetts to Georgia to promote foreign missions. Its effect among Baptists echoed that of the ones George Whitefield had made among the colonists in many of the same places in the Great Awakening. Wherever Rice went, he reaped converts to the cause of foreign missions. For example, before his arrival the Savannah River Association had formed a General Committee to encourage missions and itinerancy, without spelling out what that entailed. After a visit from Rice to Savannah in 1813, the committee at its next meeting knew very specifically what, it wanted to do. It changed itself into the Savannah Baptist Society for Foreign Missions in order "to aid in the glorious effort to evangelize the poor heathen in idolatrous lands." A broader gauge of Rice's achievement can be found in a report of a committee of the Triennial Convention in 1814. Charged with discovering the number of Baptist foreign missionary societies, its members had to confess to the convention that they had been unable "to obtain such exact information as could be desired." Nonetheless, they had been able to identify at least seventeen such bodies in the United States.[48]

Stimulating their growth to make possible a more extensive collective support of foreign missions than existing societies could accomplish individually had, of course, been an intended consequence of Rice's journey from its inception. To some extent the warmth of his reception had been prepared

[48] William H. Brackney, ed., *Dispensations of Providence: The Journal and Selected Writings of Luther Rice, 1803–1830* (Rochester, N.Y., 1984), p. 72; Minutes of the Georgia Association, 1814, quoted in Robert G. Gardner, Charles O. Walker, J. R. Huddlestun, and Waldo P. Harris III, *A History of the Georgia Baptist Association, 1784–1984* (Atlanta, 1988), p. 78; *Proceedings of Baptist Convention, 1814*, p. 34; James B. Taylor, *Memoir of the Rev. Luther Rice*, 2d ed. (Nashville, 1937), pp. 96–140; Clifton J. Phillips, *Protestant America and the Pagan World* (Cambridge, Mass., 1969), pp. 20–40.

by the lines of communication Baptist leaders, especially in the seaboard states, had opened with each other in previous years, mostly to exchange information about matters of mutual concern, which included news about missions. Before Rice, however, this network had lacked a central switchboard through which all could talk with each other more or less simultaneously. Many of those prominent in organizing the Triennial Convention—such as Richard Furman of South Carolina, Matthias Tallmadge of New York, and William Staughton of Pennsylvania—already had an interest in foreign missions. In effect, Rice's travels provided a spur and a mechanism to convert what had been a series of individual and discontinuous conversations about them into a collective and ongoing one, with broad support among Baptists, that was capable of arranging the details of a meeting in Philadelphia in 1814. Many of the particulars of this discussion can only be incompletely recovered, especially since much of the evidence comes from memories faded by distance from the events. For example, in later life William B. Johnson, one of the delegates to the convention and at the time minister of the First Church in Savannah, recalled that "our brethren at the north" had requested Rice "to travel through as many states as would be practicable to engage the Baptists to form societies, whose delegates would meet at Philadelphia in May, 1814, to organize a Baptist Foreign Missionary Society for the United States." However, when Rice's thoughts returned to the subject in a letter he wrote in 1835 to Jesse Mercer, editor of the *Christian Index,* he gave a different interpretation. Although his backers in Boston in the Baptist Society for Propagating the Gospel in India had been interested in promoting cooperation, the proposal to meet in Philadelphia had come from Johnson. When Rice had visited him in Savannah in 1813, he had engaged to go "as far as Philadelphia to attend . . . a meeting" to form "some general combination or concert of action" among Baptist foreign missionary societies. Rice had then immediately written "to all the other societies, stating that fact, and urging the importance of the meeting in Philadelphia, as proposed by Brother Johnson." The question of precedence in proposing the Philadelphia meeting is, of course, not nearly so important as the meeting itself—the agreement by Baptist leaders that accomplished in 1814 what their predecessors in America had never been able to do, the creation of a national body to deal with a matter of common concern. No ambiguity exists about its place in the order of precedence among such institutions.[49]

Once the delegates reached Philadelphia, however, the success of their venture was by no means assured. Drafting a constitution almost immediately became a sticking point. At their first meeting on May 18, 1814, a committee of fifteen members was appointed to "propose a plan of concert." For reasons now lost, its work proved unsatisfactory, and the next day it asked that its version "should be dispensed with." A new committee of five was then chosen. After discussion and amendment its proposals were adopted on May 21 as the "basis of union and . . . rule of conduct" for the convention. Among other provisions, the constitution stipulated that any Baptist body that contributed at least $100 per year to the general missionary fund had the right to send two delegates or proxies to the triennial meetings of the convention. In turn, it would elect a twenty-one-member Baptist Board of Foreign Missions—to meet at least once each year—that would "in general . . . conduct the executive part of the missionary concern." But the vision that inspired at least some of those at Philadelphia encompassed more than foreign missions. Richard Furman gave it substance in his presidential address to the convention by resorting to the language of manners to contemplate the consequences of this "delightful union," the result of Baptists' having ended their "ignorance of each other." Their improving acquaintance insured a thriv-

[49]William B. Johnson, "Reminiscences of Brethren in the Ministry and Others with Whom I Have Been Associated," quoted in Hortense Woodson, *Giant in the Land: A Biography of William Bullein Johnson* (Nashville, 1950), pp. 33–34; William H. Brackney, *The Baptists* (Westport, Conn., 1988), pp. 79–80. Rice's 1835 letter can be found in Ira M. Allen, ed., *The Triennial Baptist Register* 2 (1836):46–48. The burgeoning interest in a national meeting can be followed in the relevant issues of the *Massachusetts Baptist Missionary Magazine*. See, for example, "Remarks on the Foreign Mission" 3 (1813):353–55, and "Foreign Mission Societies" 4 (1814):5–7. For the question of precedence, see Earl E. Eminhizer, "The Rise and Fall of the Triennial Convention," M.T. thesis, Crozer Theological Seminary, 1956, pp. 26–32.

ing foreign mission enterprise and a future in which "the promotion of the interests of the churches at home" would "enter into the deliberations" of the convention, by which he principally meant aiding home missions and establishing a seminary.[50]

As Furman's address underscored, the interval between the beginning of Rice's tour in September 1813 and the ratification of the constitution in May 1814 had in some respects as much consequence for Baptists as that between the call of the Annapolis Convention in 1786 to render the Articles of Confederation "adequate to the exigencies of the union" and the Philadelphia Convention that redefined the principles and institutions of American governance in 1787. Although the details of the Baptist journey to Philadelphia are much more obscure than the Federalist one, its participants imitated their secular predecessors by ending their trip at a destination different from what could have been predicted with any confidence seven months earlier. In addition to whatever personal and political accommodations they had reached with each other along the way, they had located in the cause of missions a motive, and in the voluntary principle a language, that enabled them to contemplate something other than a straightforward confederation of independent societies intended solely to support foreign missions, which was all even the most zealous advocate of a national union could initially have expected to achieve. In 1814, however, missions had some of the significance for Baptist leaders that revivals had for southern Presbyterians before Cane Ridge. Bitter criticism and divisions loomed ahead, but in 1814 even those Baptists with reservations about foreign missions did not want to make those misgivings the basis of public opposition to them or to an expanding agenda for the convention, any more than their Presbyterian counterparts did revivals and camp meetings before the excesses of Cane Ridge became apparent.[51]

By conceiving of the convention as the voluntary creation

---

[50]*Proceedings of Baptist Convention, 1814,* pp. 3–4, 7–8, 37, 42.

[51]*Proceedings of the General Convention of the Baptist Denomination in the United States . . . 1817* (Philadelphia, 1817), pp. 136–37; Charles L. Chaney, *The Birth of Missions in America* (South Pasadena, Calif., 1976), pp. 196–99.

of the Baptist denomination in America, the delegates had found a way to testify to its legitimacy—and, implicitly, to that of their program—while skirting the questions about the parentage of any national organization that might lurk in Baptist ecclesiology. Like the Federalists before—as well as the Episcopalians and the Presbyterians—they exploited the potential of the language of liberty to attempt to impose on Baptists from the top down an order and direction they probably could never have achieved by ratification from the bottom up. Denominationalism also offered a formula to bridge differences of gender and explicitly to incorporate women's groups into the convention. Soliciting their participation had obvious importance as missions possibly held more attraction for women than for men. Because membership in the convention was open to any Baptist body without restriction, other than the one to contribute $100 each year, women's groups could claim representation in numbers limited only by their financial resources. By its 1817 meeting the Triennial Convention had nine delegates—all men—in attendance from "six female societies," out of a total of 43 societies, associations, and churches entitled to send representatives. In addition, another 144 Baptist bodies had contributed in some way to its activities, of which 104 were female societies.[52]

[52]Some sense of the dialogue among Baptist leaders about the purpose of the convention can be found in the relevant biographies in Brackney, *Baptists*. See also Rogers, *Richard Furman*, pp. 143–62; Robert G. Torbet, *Venture of Faith* (Philadelphia, 1955), pp. 26–30; Roger Hayden, "William Staughton: Baptist Educator and Missionary Advocate," *Foundations* 10 (1967):19–35; and Hayden, "Kettering 1792 and Philadelphia 1814: The Influence of English Baptists upon the Foundation of American Baptist Foreign Missions, 1789–1814," *Baptist Quarterly*, nos. 1 and 2 (1965):3–20, 64–72; James A. Patterson, "Motives in the Development of Foreign Missions among American Baptists, 1810–1826," *Foundations* 19 (1976):298–319; and Reginald S. Mills, "Robert Baylor Semple: A Study in Baptist Denominational Development, 1790–1831," Ph.D. diss., Southern Baptist Theological Seminary, 1986, pp. 72–75, 120–26. For antimissionism, see Harold L. Twiss, "Missionary Support by Baptist Churches and Associations in Western Pennsylvania, 1814–45," *Foundations* 10 (1967):36–49; Larry D. Smith, "The Historiography of the Origins of Anti-Missionism Examined in Light of Kentucky Baptist History," Ph.D. diss., Southern Baptist Theological Seminary, 1982; Harry I. Poe, "The History of Antimissionary Bap-

In fact, by the end of its 1817 meeting the broad support that the convention enjoyed made it seem poised to take off for the multiple destinations initially laid out by Richard Furman. But, just as in 1814, that result was not a forgone conclusion before the delegates assembled. From 1815 conflicts over personalities and mission policy had roiled the Board of Foreign Missions and threatened to divide its members into irreconcilable cliques. For a time Furman had even worried that its disputes might extend into the denomination and animate a "party" spirit among its churches, which in turn might lay "a foundation for discord and discouragement" at the 1817 convention. If it and the board did not present a common front to the churches, then their lack of unity might destroy the entire enterprise. Like the Founding Fathers, Furman feared faction and party, but the convention had no institutional means to protect itself from their destructive effects other than trying to avoid having disagreements among the members of its governing bodies reach into the churches at large. Disputes that arose within these two bodies, if they remained within, might be compromised, possibly by appeals to manners. But once they escaped, the Triennial Convention could do little to protect itself from their consequences. Fortunately for its survival, the withdrawal from the board of its two principal antagonists—Henry Holcombe of Savannah and William Rogers of Philadelphia—together with some adroit maneuvering by Furman, calmed matters sufficiently to permit the delegates to the 1817 convention to continue to implement an expansive agenda without interruption. Though Furman, once again elected its president, thought they might be proceeding too precipitately, they voted to amend the constitution to authorize the board to spend part of its funds on "domestic missionary purposes" and "to institute a classical and theological seminary" when enough money for one had been separately raised. The Board of Foreign Missions moved with equal quickness to appoint John Mason Peck and James E. Welch "to commence a . . . mission"

---

tists," *Chronicle* 2 (1939):51–64; and Ira Hudgins, "The Antimissionary Controversy among Baptists," *Chronicle* 14 (1951):147–64.

in the American West, to undertake the salvation of its "remote settlers and the Indians." Establishing a seminary took longer and for a while threatened divisions of the kind that Furman had thought might take place in 1817. However, the disputes over it stayed within the board and convention, and in 1822 William Staughton was inaugurated as the first president of their creation, Columbian College (now George Washington University), in Washington, D.C.[53]

The horizon of unmet needs that seemed to stretch before the Triennial Convention without limit caused many Baptist leaders to envisage its conversion into an economic and policy-making instrument of a kind that neither the Episcopalians nor the Presbyterians had at the time. They sought a national institution that would be the dominant voice in allocating the resources for missionary, educational, and other benevolent activities within the denomination. As those interested in promoting this development—such as Luther Rice, William Staughton, and Francis Wayland of Boston—were well aware, however, for it to transpire first required greater Baptist order at the state level—specifically, the organization of conventions composed of delegates from the associations within each state. In turn, these bodies would each elect delegates to a general (national) convention that would replace the Triennial Convention. For a time it seemed that this ambitious plan to transform the denominational superstructure that supported benevolent activities would be realized without significant opposition. In 1821 associations in South Carolina and New York joined in the first state conventions. By 1824 nine states had conventions, and their future growth, as well as the eventual creation of a general convention, seemed assured. Yet the Triennial Convention of 1826, the meeting intended to cap these preparatory labors by converting it into a general convention, had a quite different ending. Many of

---

[53] Letter of Furman to Edmund Botsford, Jan. 14, 1817, quoted in Harry T. Cook, *Biography of Richard Furman* (Greenville, S.C., 1913), p. 99; *Proceedings of Convention, 1817*, p. 131; "Instructions from the Board of Missions to the Rev. Mr. Peck and Rev. Mr. Welch," *American Baptist Magazine and Missionary Intelligencer* 1 (1817):189–90; Rogers, *Richard Furman*, pp. 169–96; David B. Potts, *Baptist Colleges in the Development of American Society, 1812–1861* (New York, 1988), pp. 32–38.

those who had formerly supported conventions—for example, Francis Wayland—had changed their minds, in part because they had come to appreciate how the arithmetic of representation in the new general convention would limit their influence in its decisions. Delegates from associations in the two states with the most to lose by the proposed arrangements, New York and Massachusetts, packed the meeting. Pursuing a strategy agreed upon in advance, their leaders first sought to discredit Luther Rice for irregularity in handling the funds of Columbian College—a charge his laxness and impetuosity in financial matters, which sometimes verged on irresponsibility, made easier to sustain. After he was censured for the "many imprudencies . . . properly attributable to him," the convention then moved to sever its connection with the college and transfer the headquarters of the Board of Foreign Missions from Washington, D.C., to Boston. On the next-to-last day of its meeting, it gave the coup de grace to the vision that had initially inspired Richard Furman and others in 1814 by amending the constitution to restrict itself in the future to the support of foreign missions among the "heathen." In some respects this retrenchment performed the same pressure-reducing function for the convention and Baptists that the creation of the office of institution had for Episcopalians and the secession of the Cumberland dissidents had for Presbyterians in the Kentucky revival: it reduced the conflicts among its delegates and member bodies to a level they could accommodate without the threat of further disruption.[54]

In a well-known and influential article in 1958 Winthrop S. Hudson, a prominent Baptist historian, characterized these events by his compelling choice of title, "Stumbling into Disorder." To trace the network of intrigue that he uncovered among Baptist leaders, with Francis Wayland as villain in chief of the effort to slay the unifying intent of the founders of the Triennial Convention, would extend this essay well beyond its

---

[54]*Proceedings of the Fifth Triennial Meeting of the Baptist Convention . . . 1826* (Boston, 1826), pp. 18–20, 7; Torbet, *Venture of Faith,* pp. 90–99; Eminhizer, "Triennial Convention," pp. 58–69; Hayden, "William Staughton," pp. 27–32.

proper limits. Petty jealousies, clerical wheeling and dealing, and the bare-knuckled exercise of raw political and financial clout can readily be found by any who want to look for them. But a case can be made that a more apt title for Hudson's article might have been "Stumbling into Order," with order defined in this instance as the more or less systematic pursuit of the Baptist evangelical imperative of the early 1800s through benevolent activities. For if one examines the convention movement in terms not of its place in the history of Baptist connectionalism but of its location in contemporaneous events, a quite different picture emerges. Together with other religious groups, Baptists were grappling with a variant of the problem that confronted American society as a whole at the time: what policies to follow in the often zero-sum task of developing its resources—with the process structured by the emerging party system, in which the political convention played a prominent role. That the language of the Baptists emphasized salvation, and the party system liberty, should not disguise the particularist battles both within and between churches, as well as political parties, that undercut most efforts to bring greater unity to the undertaking. Though the Presbyterians and Episcopalians struggled with essentially the same issues, it is an irony of American religious history that Baptist leaders, committed by their ecclesiology to local autonomy, aspired from 1814 to 1826 to impose a central direction on the benevolent activities of their denomination in many ways greater than that achieved by the other two bodies in the period. Their lack of success reveals less about Baptist peculiarities than it does about the particularism of American society and the limited, diverse, and even contradictory responses it made necessary in the practice of either benevolence or governance.[55]

If John Pintard had actually attended the three national gatherings that took place in Philadelphia in 1820 during his "ec-

[55] Winthrop S. Hudson, "Stumbling into Disorder," *Foundations* 1 (1958):45–71. For Presbyterian and Episcopal efforts to achieve national control of educational and missionary activities, see Paul M. Limbert, *Denominational Policies in the Support and Supervision of Higher Education* (New York, 1929), pp. 15–16; Clifton H. Brewer, *A History of Religious Education*

clesiastical week," one wonders what his impressions of them might have been. Would superficial observation alone have enabled even him to distinguish which was Episcopalian, Presbyterian, or Baptist? A devout Episcopalian with wide connections in Presbyterian circles, Pintard was an astute observer of the subtleties of contemporary religious life and presumably would not have been easily misled about matters of religious identity. The bodies that assembled in Philadelphia drew their character from doctrine, tradition, and history, among other sources, in ways that would have likely made their differences readily apparent even to a less perceptive watcher than Pintard. Yet also lodged in the institutions that shaped the collective behavior of their members were the consequences of their passage through the era of the American Revolution—most notably their resort to the federal patterns that affected religious governance as much as political.

Mimesis undoubtedly explains much of this parallelism. Certainly the movement for constitutional reform in the 1780s gave greater urgency to Episcopal and Presbyterian efforts to achieve national unity, at the same time that it provided a map for the road that Baptists would follow in the 1810s. The particularism and localism that characterized the internal life of these churches threatened to undermine these efforts and encouraged a resort to federal structures and limited congregational participation in devising them, just as it did in the political sphere. In effect, the governing institutions of all three were devised by coalitions of clergy, with an admix-

---

in the Episcopal Church to 1835 (New Haven, 1924), pp. 226–46; Arthur J. Brown, *One Hundred Years: A History of the Foreign Missionary Work of the Presbyterian Church in the U.S.A.* (New York, 1936), pp. 13–42; Lefferts A. Loetscher, *Facing the Enlightenment and Pietism: Archibald Alexander and the Founding of Princeton Theological Seminary* (Westport, Conn., 1983), pp. 121–38; Elwyn A. Smith, "The Forming of an American Denomination," in Russell E. Richey, ed., *Denominationalism* (Nashville, 1977), pp. 127–34; Powel Mills Dawley, *The Story of the General Theological Seminary* (New York, 1969), pp. 27–81; and Robert Prichard, *A History of the Episcopal Church* (Harrisburg, Pa., 1991), pp. 122–23, 125–28. Limited resources and denominational particularism undermined Presbyterian and Episcopal endeavors in much the same way they did Baptist. For the policy consequences of political particularism in American development, see McCormick, *Party Period*, pp. 197–227.

ture of lay allies, and were imposed on coreligionists from the top down, no matter what the formal procedures for their ratification. Yet this clerical dominance also helped to place limits on the authority that religious leaders could exercise in their creations. By giving veto power to the House of Bishops, the founders of American Episcopalianism had to concede, both formally and informally, greater authority to the laity in the deliberations of the General Convention than either Baptist or Presbyterian clergy in their national bodies. No matter what the church, acceptance of the authority of higher bodies was most easily achieved when it legitimated what local groups already intended to do and did not require them to make choices in which some won and others lost. As well, their power to reach down to affect life within their denominations was limited by their being principally legislative and judicial bodies. Above the local level churches lacked much administrative capacity until late in the nineteenth century, the same pattern that prevailed in American government. Even the Triennial Convention had to rely on the cooperation of its member groups, as well as that of British Baptists, to carry out its purposes. The stability of higher bodies was constantly at risk, not only from localist and particularist tendencies, but from cliques that might arise among their members. In some respects schisms, secessions, and threats of one or the other have been more of a constant in the life of America's churches than the revivals to which historians typically pay more attention. At the same time the patterns of institutional life adopted in the Revolutionary era have accommodated an extraordinary amount of conflict and endured to an extent no one could have predicted at the time.

These decisions about organizational structures also shaped the way churches participated in the religious expansion of the nineteenth century. Although sometimes conceived as a competition between churches, it was equally one within them about many matters—among them the raising and allocating of resources and the effects of growth on the power of existing clerical factions. In the early 1800s Presbyterians and Episcopalians imitated the Baptists by finding it easier to sustain national unity in the support of foreign missions than home missions and seminaries. Dealing with the consequences of growth abroad among the "heathen" was much less divisive than dealing with its implications at home, whether from missions or revivals. The governing institutions of America's churches were no more able than those of its state and national governments to raise and distribute resources rationally in the pursuit of expansion. The question of the efficiency with which they were able to do so and its effects on their growth remain largely unexplored, in marked contrast to the situation in American political history, where the consequences for economic development of democratic federalism have been more fully canvassed. Did the organizational structures within American denominations contribute to some of the same profligacy and disregard for future effects in religious expansion that existed in economic expansion? Or should the federal pattern in religion and politics be seen as producing responses within churches that were similar to those political parties made to opportunities for economic growth? Did federal structures simply provide alternative venues in which both religious and political leaders attempted to devise coalitions that governed by distributing benefits that their constituents valued and that permitted them to do so at a number of institutional levels and in sometimes contrary ways? Both characterizations seem apt, though at some point the parallels between churches and political parties, and between religious expansion and economic development, surely break down. Yet progrowth attitudes dominated both religion and politics in the nineteenth century. Translating these attitudes into action through the governing structures that prevailed in both spheres helped to insure responses that could be contradictory and ambiguous in their effects, as well as ones in which disorder often provided the principal source of order.

PAUL K. CONKIN

Priestley and Jefferson

Unitarianism as a Religion
for a New Revolutionary Age

IT IS CLEAR that Americans fought a successful War for Independence. But what will never be completely clear is how many Americans wished to subvert established authority. In some states, particularly Pennsylvania, and in many local areas, some semblance of a wider revolution did take place, and in other places the crusade for Independence helped stimulate new expectations and demands from aggrieved minorities. But what was usually missing in even these hints of popular rebellion was any broad or concerted attack upon the prevalent forms of Christianity or many challenges to the power or prerogatives of the clergy. Religious continuities outweighed the significant changes. In most areas of America, the clergy joined laymen of wealth and standing in supporting, even leading, the crusade for Independence. Thus, unlike the revolution in France a few years later, our Revolution, such as it was, spawned no anti-Christian religions. Those who thought seriously about an appropriate religion for the new republic usually thought in terms of a reformed Christianity. It is my thesis that the most radically reformed version of Christianity to compete for acceptance in newly independent America was the Unitarianism preached so earnestly by Joseph Priestley and embraced so eagerly by Thomas Jefferson. Here, if anywhere, was a new religion that was so thoroughgoing in its doctrinal revisions as to fit well an age of political radicalism.

Thomas Jefferson met Joseph Priestley in 1797 in Philadelphia where he attended a series of sermons by Priestley.[1] At about the same time he read Priestley's two-volume polemic, *An History of the Corruptions of Christianity*. This book had more impact on Jefferson's religious views than any other book he read in his whole lifetime. He completely embraced Priestley's Unitarian Christianity, and he retained this commitment until his death. Priestley rescued him from earlier ambivalence and for the first time clarified a type of Christianity that Jefferson could wholeheartedly embrace, that he could recommend with almost evangelical zeal to close friends, and that he believed was most consistent with American republican institutions.

Why did Jefferson so eagerly embrace Priestley's views? The answer to this question involves the complex, often securely private, religious pilgrimage taken by Jefferson. By the time he became an adult the versions of Protestant Christianity that he knew firsthand were simply unbelievable to him in most doctrinal details. Contacts with latitudinarian and humanistic Anglicans, and an appreciative reading of English Deists, reinforced his doubts. The seemingly defining or essential doctrines of orthodox Christianity, in the external, almost caricatured forms in which he grasped them, seemed mythical, cruel, irrational, and divisive. The whole Pauline scheme of salvation—the doctrines of human depravity, of undeserved grace, of a vicarious atonement—never made good sense to him. Neither did the Christian belief in a triune God, which he found obscure and unbelievable.[2]

Jefferson's distaste for all Calvinistic forms of Christianity, including the watered down version preached in his own nominal church, the Anglican, was so intense at times that he could scarcely restrain his denunciations. This distaste was matched, or more than matched, by his reaction to the mythi-

---

[1] Dumas Malone, *Jefferson and His Times*, vol. 3, *Jefferson and the Ordeal of Liberty* (Boston, 1962), pp. 449–50.

[2] Despite a growing body of literature on Jefferson's religious views, most of it remains superficial or doctrinally uninformed. An insensitive, external but extended survey is in Charles B. Sanford, *The Religious Life of Thomas Jefferson* (Charlottesville, Va., 1984). The main chronology is in the six volumes of Dumas Malone's *Jefferson and His Times*.

cal and superstitious forms of Catholicism that he confronted in France. But in America he appropriately aimed most of his denunciations at the latter-day disciples of Martin Luther and John Calvin. In a letter to John Adams written late in 1823, he argued that Calvin was "indeed an atheist" who did not acknowledge and adore the "Creator and benevolent governor of the world" but worshiped a demon of "malignant spirit."[3] Yet Jefferson acutely observed that reformed Christianity often led, for those who rebelled against its obscurities, to desirable forms of Deism, while rebels against a more authoritarian Catholicism usually became atheists, a backhanded compliment to Protestantism. While intellectually open to atheistic arguments, he never believed them. The design argument, the widely perceived need for a creator, was completely persuasive to him or, perhaps better stated, was an intelligible means for him to justify a belief so central as to be beyond any choice. And he felt keenly the social danger should the majority of Americans become atheists. Influenced by Benjamin Rush, an early Universalist, and other professed but liberal Christians, he came to believe that the very survival of the American republic depended upon a theistic belief system or upon what, for Americans, would in all likelihood continue to be some form of Christianity.

Jefferson's justifications of theism were usually moral. As a parent, as well as in his reactions to those outside his family, he was a stiff, puritanical moralist. He placed almost impossible demands upon himself and had unrealistic expectations of others. Divine authority, and perhaps also the hope of eternal rewards and the fear of punishment, seemed to him a necessary support, not for an inborn moral sense, but for its maturing into moral practice. Americans would not respect each other's liberties, he said, unless they believed they were from God. Even Calvinists and Catholics, despite all their superstitions, were often moral men and women. And, in some sense, their religions had been conducive to their moral education. He thus supported Christian training for his two daughters

---

[3]Thomas Jefferson to John Adams, Apr. 11, 1823, in Lester J. Cappon, ed., *The Adams-Jefferson Letters: The Complete Correspondence between Thomas Jefferson and Abigail and John Adams*, 2 vols. (Chapel Hill, 1959), 2:591–94.

and even believed it essential to their growth. Certain core beliefs of Christianity, or what he believed to be its universal content—a creator God, an objective moral order, and a future judgment—seemed the best foundation for moral development or for types of altruism, and thus for a just and free social order. In his minimalist theological beliefs Jefferson accepted one version of that loaded, almost useless label, Deism, but with no public acknowledgment.[4] He kept his personal religious beliefs private. He knew they were unconventional in America, sure to frighten the orthodox, dismay kinfolk, and possibly impede his political career.

Jefferson had another side, one often unremarked. He was unusually religious, at least by many definitions of that ambiguous word. He suffered many personal losses, including the death of a sister, the early death of his wife, and finally that of a beloved daughter. He was very sensitive and emotionally vulnerable, with constant migraine headaches. Behind the studied coolness, he was passionate in his involvements, often lacking in self-confidence, a bit paranoid about the intentions of others. Thus he turned often, and with a sense of compelling need, to personal meditation and to inspirational reading. He had a rich and complex devotional life and used it to help ward off depression. In this sense he was a religious seeker, always trying to find consolation, moral instruction, and even the strength, the self-confidence, to keep on living. This personal need led him back, again and again, to classical writers, to the great Stoic moralists, and above all to his favorite philosopher, Epicurus and his prescriptions for ease of body and tranquility of mind. Jefferson's need did not at first lead him very often to the Christian Bible, although he did, as everyone else, profess his admiration for Jesus. But his fullest appreciation of Jesus as a great moralist, even greater than Epicurus, awaited his conversion to Priestley's form of Unitarianism.

Joseph Priestley was born in England in 1733, into a dissenting, latter-day Puritan, still Calvinist family. Precocious,

---

[4]He used the word *Deism* frequently, but in most cases he meant by it a belief in a unitary God.

he early took up the classical languages and committed himself to the Christian ministry. Even as a young man he rejected all forms of Christian orthodoxy as then understood in Britain. After an early career of teaching and preaching, he moved in 1767 to a church in Leeds where he openly embraced Socinianism, or Unitarianism. With his close, lifelong friend and generous patron, Theophilus Lindsey, he helped establish a small British Unitarian movement. Meanwhile, he dabbled in scientific experiments, most involving electricity and the properties of air, all under the careful instruction of his friend, the by then famous Benjamin Franklin. His religious reforms and his scientific achievements made him a welcome member of a small circle of English radicals who gathered in London every winter, and which for several years included Franklin and another dissenting minister, Richard Price. Priestley soon gained world renown for his experiments—for separating carbon dioxide, for devising a machine to make soda water, and, above all, for isolating what we now call oxygen.

In 1781 Priestley moved to Birmingham to pastor the largest dissenting congregation in England. Here his tracts and books in defense of a reformed, Unitarian Christianity climaxed in the 1782 publication of his *Corruptions of Christianity*. This "scandalous" book, joined with his political radicalism—support both for American Independence and for the early French Revolution—provoked a bitter and eventually violent response from organized and officially sanctioned mobs in Birmingham. On Bastille Day, 1791, they burned his house, his church, and his laboratory, destroying most of his life's work. He fled to London. In the midst of increasing political tensions and under the danger of arrest, he decided in 1794 to emigrate to America. He was enthusiastically greeted at New York as a martyr to the cause of liberty.[5]

Priestley well summarized his mature religious views in the *Corruptions of Christianity*. With an optimism that never deserted him even in the worst of times, he believed that Chris-

---

[5] F. W. Gibbs, *Joseph Priestley: Revolutions of the Eighteenth Century* (New York, 1967).

tianity, after the darkness of centuries, was finally reemerging in its early, pristine form. For good reasons, although not always apparent ones, the Supreme Governor of the Universe had allowed these corruptions to occur. Priestley believed completely in God's providence—all that took place in history had some good purpose, and all events reflected a type of necessity, a necessity that was, incidentally, fully consistent with the new, mechanistic science of Isaac Newton. Somehow, the ascendancy of all the corruptions, those that were at the heart of a purported orthodoxy, had prepared the way for the great reformation then in progress.[6]

Characteristically, Priestley began his study with the greatest corruption—the growth of Christian polytheism. He rested all his doctrines on one essential truth—the full unity of God—a doctrine anticipated by a few of the reformers, particularly Faustus Socinius, the founder of Polish Unitarianism. Priestley believed that this monotheism was the most important article of faith in both the Old and New Testaments, an article always affirmed by Jesus. It was also, he argued, clearly the doctrine of the earliest Church, particularly the Jewish Christians, the Nazarenes and Ebionites. To them, Jesus, who always identified himself as the son of man, was in all respects a man and nothing more than a man. As the promised Messiah, he had a special mission, one appropriate only to a person like ourselves—to clarify what God expects of humans, what are the requirements of salvation (essentially a life of virtue or selfless devotion and good works), what level of obedience God demands (to the point of martyrdom), and what God promises (a resurrection to eternal life for those who imitate Jesus). Priestley most emphasized resurrection. He rejected any idea of a separable soul, any possible form of immortality. Thus the promise of eternal life was a promise that a person, fully dead, would come back to life. This doctrine is not demonstrable by reason, neither self-evident nor evidenced. Consequently the great consoling hope of Chris-

---

[6]A convenient and short summary of Priestley's religious views is in *Memoirs of Dr. Joseph Priestley, to the Year 1795*, 2 vols. (Northumberland, Pa., 1806), 2:465–69.

tians rested upon the fact, one testified to by many reliable witnesses, that Jesus rose from the dead. Faith, to Priestley, was no more than belief in the reliability of these early witnesses. The well-documented resurrection of Jesus was the only evidence that God could, and would, reconstitute the dead at the time of Jesus' promised return to earth. He who first breathed life into bodies was quite capable of doing it a second time.[7]

Priestley spent fully half of his religious writings defending the simple humanity of Jesus against two opposing views—orthodox trinitarianism, which makes Jesus a God equal to the father, and Arianism, which accepts the subordinate status of Jesus but still views him as a preexistent, divine savior. Priestley's *Corruptions of Christianity* and even more his later *History of Early Opinions concerning Jesus Christ* (Jefferson also read this three-volume work) contained almost every conceivable argument then available in favor of Jesus' full humanity and an overwhelming body of historical arguments about how corrupting trinitarian theories developed in the Western church. To Priestley all such doctrines were pagan imports, most tied to the great Antichrist of antiquity, Plato. I cannot here summarize his arguments or evaluate them; my own view is that the Gospel of John and Paul's Epistles clearly support belief in a preexistent Christ or logos, and thus an Arian view. Priestley had to resort to ingenious arguments to overcome this counterevidence, arguments that were almost, but not quite, as loaded as those of his orthodox antagonists. His best arguments involved early Jewish Christians, but his evidence about them was too fragmentary for definitive judgments. His Unitarianism is most consistent with the synoptic Gospels, and this is where he placed his greatest reliance.[8]

[7]The views in this paragraph, and the following summary of his doctrines, are all drawn from Joseph Priestley's *An History of the Corruptions of Christianity*, 3d ed., 2 vols. (Boston, 1797).

[8]Priestley's views led to numerous refutations from orthodox spokesmen, but from none more able, or persevering, than Bishop Heneage Horsley. Soon the two wrote numerous tracts or polemics in a controversy that went on for years and became famous in Britain. The flavor of the debate, and the best arguments by orthodox Biblical scholars, are preserved in *Tracts in Controversy with Dr. Priestley, upon the Historical Question, of*

Priestley did not take scriptural evidence as in any sense infallible—it, too, derived from human sources, and in the case of Paul was a source he often believed unreliable. Priestley wrote extensively on the development of a New Testament canon and often gave greater credence to the tidbits of patristic information about the Jewish Christians than to the writers of New Testament books. In brief, he felt that the only directly inspired sections of the Bible were the clearly prophetic ones—the law as given to Moses, the reforms initiated by the prophets, the oral witness of Jesus, and, perhaps surprisingly, the apocalyptic books. But even these most inspired writings had to filter down to us through human scribes and were thus subject to errors or interpolations. Above all, he deferred to the words assigned to Jesus by Mark, Matthew, and Luke, or those words that seemed to be a consistent expression of Jesus' character and mission (obviously, Priestley used his own conception of Jesus to make these judgments, and thus the circularity of his arguments). He took as completely unreliable many of the often conflicting biographical details about Jesus and rejected out of hand the two contradictory and clearly mythical stories about Jesus' birth, including the notion of a virgin birth.

Priestley's second most daring doctrinal position, unlike his Unitarianism, had fewer earlier advocates. This was his rejection of any possible version of the atonement, of the doctrine that, in some sense, Jesus' death was an atoning sacrifice necessary to cancel the deserved penalties of human sinfulness. The logic here is that only a fully righteous person, perhaps only a divine being, could atone for the magnitude of human pride and guilt, and that only the imputed righteousness of such a savior could justify humans before Jehovah. In Priestley's day the arguments ranged over complete versus conditional atonement, but almost all Christians accepted some version of this doctrine and seemingly did so on the best scriptural grounds, ranging from the sacrificial image in Deutero-Isaiah to the powerful logic of Paul's Epistle to the Romans. In fact the doctrine of the atonement was central to the re-

the Belief of the First Ages, in Our Lord's Divinity, ed. Samuel Horsley, bishop of St. Asaph, 1st American ed. (Burlington, N.J., 1821).

forms of Luther and Calvin, inseparably linked to the doctrine of human depravity or Original Sin, to their belief that unaided humans are inherently unable to love God fully, and thus to the necessary role of divine grace in salvation.

Priestley saw the atonement doctrine as an early corruption in the church and dismissed all the sacrificial motifs in the New Testament as figurative. He saw, correctly, that the atonement doctrine lost much of its meaning if one denied the divinity of Jesus. Thus a consistent Unitarian had to reject or modify the doctrine. But his view also reflected his belief in a benevolent God, one always ready to forgive any penitent sinner. It struck Priestley as absurd, a cruel superstition, that such a God would have to allow his only son to die in order to pardon humankind. It made Jesus' death necessary for the wrong reasons—to appease a wrathful God's demand for justice. His scriptural proof was largely negative—the doctrine is ignored in most of the New Testament, and many passages in the New Testament seemed to him inconsistent with an atoning sacrifice. I cannot develop the controversy here. I believe that his orthodox opponents bested him in these debates, particularly if one accepts Paul as authoritative. Priestley, in his earliest writings against the atonement, seemed to realize this and simply said Paul erred. Later he backed away from this, used Paul as an authority on other issues, and thus tried to finesse Paul's language, not very convincingly.

I will discuss only one other of Priestley's central doctrines, for it helps clarify both his Unitarianism and his antiatonement stance. This is what became known as soul sleep. Priestley believed that the early church, corrupted by pagan mysticism and Platonic idealism, soon lost the early, essentially Jewish view of humans as holistic beings. The imported, pagan conceptions of immaterialism or spiritual substance led to the belief in a separable mind or soul and in the separate existence of disembodied spirits in paradise or purgatory. In his work on psychology, Priestley was persuaded by early forms of sensationalism and associationism that all of the phenomena of thought and self-consciousness can be fully accounted for as functions of the brain. The word *mind* refers not to an immaterial entity (nonsense to Priestley) but to certain functions of a special type of matter. Thought in humans is comparable to gravity in inanimate matter. We can describe these functions, but Priestley believed that their only possible explanation is that God made them so—the position taken by Newton about the laws of gravity. By denying a separable soul, Priestley not only destroyed any incarnation doctrine, any belief in an ethereal Christ that assumed a human body, but also made a mockery of all the later angels and saints that constituted the most numerous idols in the Catholic tradition. Purported saints, if they are fully dead in the ground, if their souls sleep until the resurrection, cannot intercede with God in behalf of living humans. Neither can Mary. And neither could Jesus if God had not already raised him from the dead and reconstituted him as a person. This corporealism, or materialism, was not original. Thomas Hobbes argued it persuasively, as did several disciples of Newton.

Beyond these most critical doctrines, Priestley identified literally hundreds of other corruptions in the church. He found no scriptural authority or early traditions to support sacramentalism—that is, any mysteries with saving efficacy. He rejected completely the Protestant doctrines of Original Sin, election to salvation, and the perseverance of saints. He endorsed the simple worship service of the earliest churches—songs, prayer, teaching, and, in memory of Jesus, the Lord's Supper, which he celebrated weekly. He denied all else—holy days, festivals, altars, holy waters, consecrations, liturgies, signs of the cross, incense, antique languages, processions, robed clergymen, formal and ornate sermons, and cathedrals. He denied any ecclesiastical authority to the clergy. He supported church discipline only by democratic congregations and then only for immoral behavior, never for heretical beliefs. He was England's most eloquent advocate of the complete separation of church and state and the most courageous enemy of the Anglican establishment. He repudiated monasticism or any form of asceticism, since Christians, above all people, should be happy. But he joined Roman Catholics in basing doctrine and practice on both scripture and tradition. The most dangerous idol of Protestants was their elevation of human-derived books into unimpeachable authorities. This invited dishonesty, for even the Gospels contained contradictory details that allowed no full harmonizing. No honest student of the Bible could claim that all parts of it were infallible.

Priestley eloquently summarized the purified Christianity that would outlive all these identified corruptions. It was all so simple. The great Parent of humankind commissioned the man, Jesus, to invite all people to the practice of virtue and made clear his intent to raise to eternal life and happiness all people who were virtuous and good. Priestley at first thought that the wages of sin would be permanent death but in later years adopted a Universalist view—God will grant eternal life to all, but those who have been wicked will have to suffer the consequences, before or after the resurrection. Jesus, by his miracles, proved his power and his mission, and by rising from the dead anchored all human hopes of a resurrection. Converts to this Christianity were to submit to baptism as a symbol of their commitment to the church, eat bread and drink wine in remembrance (Jesus invited everyone, including children, to the table), and live righteously. That is all. All other doctrines, all other rituals, were corruptions, borrowed from the heathen world and from false immaterial philosophies, with the greatest single key to subsequent corruptions in the church being the pagan belief in a separable soul. Abuses in church government reflected the designs of worldly men and power seekers, including a power-hungry clergy. But, unlike Jefferson, Priestley did not blame every abuse on the clergy. After all, he was a clergyman himself.

What Priestley wanted to exclude from Christianity should not blind one to his positive doctrines and to his fervor in preaching the Gospel as he understood it. Christianity was still, to him, a great miracle, a great truth, and a great promise. Without it, life would not be worth living. With it, Priestley remained until death an almost irenic optimist. He believed literally that all works together for the good for those who love the Lord. He died serenely, in the confidence that, in what would seem only an instant to him, he would come back to life to join his loved ones and share in the promised kingdom. Or, better phrased, he believed in that great new republic that Jesus would establish on earth. Priestley rarely used the word *kingdom;* it did not fit his politics and he could not believe it fit Jesus'.

Priestley's arguments were eye-opening to Jefferson. One who knows Jefferson will quickly recognize why. Not that Priestley persuaded him to accept any new doctrines; he simply reinforced most of what Jefferson had believed all along. Jefferson already believed in a single creator God. Much earlier he had relegated not only the atonement doctrine but most specific doctrines of the church to the level of human creations. Because of several intellectual influences (Epicurus, the seventeenth-century French priest and apologist for Epicurus and atomism Pierre Gassendi, and several materialistic French philosophes), he was already a corporealist.

What Priestley did was change Jefferson's definition and understanding of Christianity. He did this by what, for one as untutored as Jefferson in the historical criticism of the Bible, seemed an awesome and fully persuasive display of scholarship. Jefferson now realized that the orthodox versions of Christianity, what he had taken to be the real product, were all spurious and that his limited and essential beliefs were the real thing. This major semantic conversion amounted almost to a revelation. Jefferson could now rejoice that the Jesus he had always admired, the one who spoke so sublimely in the synoptic Gospels, was the only real Jesus, an examplary man with a great mission to the simple people of Galilee. Paul, whom Priestley treated with kid gloves, was to Jefferson no longer the ideal typical Christian but simply the first of many corrupters of Christianity. Even Jesus' seeming claims of divine status, sprinkled about the Gospels, were human distortions or later interpolations. In brief, what Priestley did was allow Jefferson to take his own undoubted doctrines, graft on to them the moral teachings of Jesus, and call the product Christianity.

After Jefferson heard Priestley's sermons in Philadelphia in the spring of 1797, the two men became collaborators. Not that they were personally close. They met only this once and corresponded sporadically. But they had a common goal—to convert Americans to Unitarianism. Jefferson did not embrace all of Priestley's doctrines. He never openly rejected any of them but, with his easy eclecticism, simply ignored several emphases, including soul sleep and the centrality of the resurrection. Jefferson never understood Priestley's necessitarianism, and when John Adams branded it another, equally unacceptable form of predestination, Jefferson simply professed his ignorance of it.[9]

Priestley found anything but a utopia in America. In this final decade of his life, he lost a beloved son and then his wife. He suffered tormenting illnesses, sorrowed over the escapades and emotional instability of another son, and faced at least some of the same diatribes from orthodox ministers that he had suffered in England. He could not resist becoming involved, on the side of liberty, during the controversies over the Alien and Sedition Acts, and he saw his close friend and houseguest Thomas Cooper jailed for sedition. Save for the intervention of John Adams he would undoubtedly have been prosecuted himself. He spent most of his scientific efforts defending an outdated and erroneous doctrine about phlogiston. He eventually built a new house at Northumberland, Pennsylvania, on a failed land venture launched by his sons. He knew a type of peace only in his last four years (from 1800 to 1804).

Priestley rejoiced in the election of his friend Jefferson to the presidency and had unbounded hopes for the new American republic, but many of his dreams remained unfulfilled.[10] Hopes of building a great academy at Northumberland collapsed. His reformed or Unitarian Christianity was not as appealing in America as he had anticipated. He held services in his home at Northumberland and celebrated the Lord's Supper, but only a handful of people ever attended. His first lecture series in Philadelphia in the spring of 1796 seemed very promising. An admiring Vice-President John Adams attended every talk, many members of Congress came, and President George Washington had him to tea and at least ex-

[9]See Adams to Jefferson, July 18 and 22, 1813, in Cappon, ed., *Adams-Jefferson Letters*, 2:361–63.

[10]Anne Holt, *A Life of Joseph Priestley* (Westport, Conn., 1970), pp. 186–216.

pressed an interest in his doctrines. Before the lectures ended, Priestley helped establish an enduring Unitarian congregation, the first with that title in America. But his health would not allow him to serve as its pastor (lay readers had to suffice), and he had to turn down a proffered chemistry professorship at the University of Pennsylvania. A second lecture series in 1797 (the one Jefferson attended) was less well received. He gave no more.

In 1803, the aging and ill Priestley published a little pamphlet, *Socrates and Jesus Compared.* Despite their mutual greatness and courageous martyrdoms, Priestley tried to prove that Jesus was much the greater person, with a more altruistic and universal message. President Jefferson read it with delight and wrote an appreciative note to Priestley. He so admired the comparative approach that he considered it for himself. But, swamped with work, he asked Priestley to extend the technique and to compare Jesus' moral teaching with that of his beloved Stoic and Epicurean moralists, particularly Epicurus. A flattered Priestley tried to comply and in the last year of his life wrote the first volume of such a comparison, a heavy, rambling, scholarly work that did not at all fulfill Jefferson's expectations. Even before publication, the great Priestley was dead; from this point on Jefferson would take every opportunity to eulogize him. But now only Jefferson could complete the comparison.[11]

Jefferson never did this, although he outlined the appealing doctrines of Epicurus. He also clarified his version of Christianity in a brief syllabus he sent to Rush: "I am a Christian," he said, in the only sense in which Jesus "wished any one to be; sincerely attached to his doctrines, in preference to all others; ascribing to himself every human excellence, and believing he never claimed any other." He professed his opposition to all the corruptions of Christianity and briefly outlined the basis of his contention that Jesus was a better

[11]This story is best told in Eugene R. Sheridan, introduction to Dickinson W. Adams and Ruth W. Lester, eds., *Jefferson's Extracts from the Gospels: "The Philosophy of Jesus" and "The Life and Morals of Jesus,"* The Papers of Thomas Jefferson, 2d ser. (Princeton, 1983), pp. 20–23; Jefferson's admiring acknowledgment to Priestley is in the appendix of this excellent compilation as Jefferson to Joseph Priestley, Apr. 9, 1803, pp. 327–29.

moralist than the classical philosophers. Classical moralists excelled in self-discipline but lacked Jesus' strong sense of social obligation. Jesus also taught a belief in the afterlife as a means of encouraging virtue in this life.[12] Jefferson sent this syllabus of Christian doctrine to family members and friends and seemed to want it to leak out to the larger public, perhaps to make clear that he was not an infidel, as so often charged, but the most reformed of Christians. This effort also led him to write a compendium of Jesus' teachings, taken directly from the Gospels, that he called "The Philosophy of Jesus." The text did not survive, but the editors of *The Papers of Thomas Jefferson* have carefully reconstructed the contents.[13]

In 1816, after he retired from politics and had joined in his long, often religiously oriented correspondence with Adams, Jefferson completed a much longer New Testament anthology, "The Life and Morals of Jesus." Since a text of this has survived, it is now often referred to as Jefferson's Bible. It contains a carefully screened selection of Gospel material about Jesus, as well as most of his own words. Even more cavalierly than Priestley, Jefferson selected what he thought authentic, that is, consistent with his view of Jesus' real character, and left out all else. With a gesture to scholarship, and as an impressive display of his classical learning, he copied the Gospel passages in four languages, beginning with the Greek original.[14]

In his last years, as he collected the good news from Adams and others, Jefferson rejoiced in the New England Unitarian movement. This led in 1825 to the forming of an American Unitarian Association, only a year before the simultaneous death of Jefferson and Adams. Adams, to the envy of Jefferson, was a member of one of these Unitarian congregations and was buried in its churchyard at Quincy. But to the despair of New England Unitarians, Jefferson refused to offer his imprimatur publicly to the growing movement. He craved peace

---

[12] Jefferson to Benjamin Rush, Apr. 21, 1803, ibid., pp. 331–36.

[13] Ibid., pp. 55–122.

[14] A carefully edited and annotated edition of "The Life and Morals of Jesus" is ibid., pp. 125–314.

and still had a morbid fear of attacks from the orthodox. Thus he worked only in the background, privately, a closet Unitarian. But he corresponded with Jared Sparks, historian and Unitarian clergyman at Baltimore, and praised the work of William Ellery Channing and other liberal ministers.[15]

All this led to his misplaced optimism about the future of this purified Christianity in America. In his last years Jefferson lamented that Unitarianism was not yet preached in the South, but he was sure it would quickly win broad acceptance in Virginia and "drive before it the foggy mists of Platonism which have so long obscured our Atmosphere." He asked New Englanders to send missionaries to Virginia. Such Unitarian visitors might be excluded by "our hierophants from their churches" but would be greeted in the fields by whole acres of hearers and thinkers. Thus he wrote in 1822 that Unitarianism, the belief in the "pure and simple unity of the creator of the universe is now all but ascendant in the Eastern states; it is dawning in the West, and advancing towards the South; and I confidently expect that the present generation will see Unitarianism become the general religion of the United states."[16]

Jefferson could see no reason why Unitarianism would not prevail in a country that had divorced religion from all civil authority. Political liberty and a reformed Christianity seemed twins, sure to develop in tandem. In 1824, only two years before his death, Jefferson read some Unitarian sermons and rejoiced in efforts "to restore us to primitive Christianity, in all the simplicity in which it came from the lips of Jesus." Unfortunately, until now the "metaphysical abstractions of Athanasius, and the maniac ravings of Calvin, tinctured plentifully with the foggy dreams of Plato, have so loaded it with absurdities and incomprehensibilities, as to drive into infidelity men who had not time, patience, or opportunity to strip it of its meretricious trappings." Thus, he exulted, the same private

[15] Jefferson to Salma Hale, July 26, 1818, to Jared Sparks, Nov. 4, 1820, and to Timothy Pickering, Feb. 27, 1821, ibid., pp. 385, 401–4.

[16] Jefferson to Thomas Whittemore, June 5, 1822, to Benjamin Waterhouse, July 19, 1822, and to James Smith, Dec. 8, 1822, ibid., pp. 404, 406–10.

judgment that gave us our political reformation would soon extend its effects to religion.[17]

Jefferson had no real doubts about the religion's future. In 1822, after listing the three simple doctrines of Jesus (one perfect God, a future state of rewards and punishments, and the duty to love God and one's neighbor as oneself), Jefferson announced that, had these doctrines been preached as purely as they came from Jesus' lips, the whole civilized world would already be Christian. He thus rejoiced that, in this blessed country of free inquiry and belief, which surrendered conscience neither to kings nor priests, the genuine doctrine of one God was reviving. He trusted that "there is not a *young man* now living in the US. who will not die a Unitarian."[18] Unfortunately, Jefferson was not only too sanguine, he did not appreciate how different most New England Unitarians were from his beloved Priestley. In fact, most of them were Federalists in politics, some were closer to Arianism than to true Unitarianism, almost none accepted materialism and soul rest, and lurking on the fringes of the young movement were the first extreme Platonists in America, the Transcendentalists.

In retrospect, other ironies abound when one reflects on the beliefs and the hopes of Priestley and Jefferson. Contrary to what they expected, their drastically simplified, demythologized, and moralized version of Christianity had very limited appeal. Jefferson, who found in Jesus' words the diamonds in what he regarded as a veritable dunghill of obscurities and abstractions, would have been dismayed to learn that it has been what he viewed as the dung, not the diamonds, that has continued to console and inspire American Christians. In other words, the depth and scope of Christianity's appeal has rested on its particularizing features, on the rich and psychologically pregnant doctrines of sin, guilt, and grace, and on all the rituals and liturgies and saints and angels. Granted, these particularities are human creations, most with pagan roots, but unlike Priestley and Jefferson we know that even

[17] Jefferson to John Davis, Jan. 18, 1824, ibid., pp. 413–14.

[18] Jefferson to Waterhouse, June 26, 1822, ibid., pp. 405–6.

their minimal or essential doctrines—a creator God, his demands for virtue, and judgment in an afterlife—are also human creations, neither meaningful nor believable in some cultures or even in some major historical religions.

The other great irony lies in what happened to Priestley's beliefs. They did not gain their enduring fulfillment among American Unitarians, many of whom eventually moved away from even the minimal doctrines of Christianity to the very infidelity that Priestley spent a lifetime trying to forestall. Rather, his Jewish-colored metaphysics—corporealism, soul sleep, a literal resurrection, a redeemed earthly republic, no eternal torment—became the core doctrines of American Adventists. I often hear the clearest echo of Priestley from Seventh Day Adventists, or even from the Mormons or Jehovah's Witnesses who come proselytizing to my door. Priestley's other doctrines—the unity of God, a rejection of the traditional atonement doctrine, the need to restore the simple worship described in Acts, faith as belief in witnesses—gained their fullest expression and broadest appeal in the early reforms of Barton W. Stone and the Christian movement, although Stone's later alliance with the Campbellites led him to retreat from his early quasi Unitarianism and his unorthodox conception of the atonement. But in the churches of the Christian Connection these doctrines lived on into the twentieth century. These Adventist and Restorationist sects, the ones most consistent with Priestley's doctrines, have often fervently supported the separation of church and state, but otherwise remain among the most conservative branches of Protestantism. How far removed they seem from the daring political and religious radicalism exemplified by Priestley and Jefferson.

RUTH H. BLOCH

Religion, Literary Sentimentalism, and Popular Revolutionary Ideology

NOT SINCE THE disputes of Progressive and consensus historians more than two decades ago have the dividing lines between scholars interpreting the ideology of the Revolution been so clearly drawn. To summarize a complex historiography in admittedly oversimple terms, the central debate concerns conflicting judgments about the relative strength of classical republican and liberal ideas in American Revolutionary ideology. Those historians stressing classical republicanism have situated American patriots in a framework of an older civic humanism and have highlighted their commitment to checks and balances and their fear of change.[1] Those

I wish to thank Robert Abzug, Joyce Appleby, and especially Daniel Howe for their helpful readings of earlier drafts of this essay.

[1] For example, J. G. A. Pocock, *The Machiavellian Moment: Florentine Political Thought and the Atlantic Republican Tradition* (Princeton, 1975); Bernard Bailyn, *The Ideological Origins of the American Revolution* (Cambridge, Mass., 1967); Gordon S. Wood, *The Creation of the American Republic, 1776–1787* (Chapel Hill, 1969); Lance G. Banning, *The Jeffersonian Persuasion: Evolution of a Party Ideology* (Ithaca, N.Y., 1978); Drew R. McCoy, *The Elusive Republic: Political Economy in Jeffersonian America* (Chapel Hill, 1980).

emphasizing liberalism have, to the contrary, underscored the Revolution's newfound optimism about the prospects of a society of free individuals regulated only by a minimal government.[2] In different ways each interpretation has challenged both the early twentieth-century Progressive theories about ideology as a simple reflection of economic interest and the later neowhig views about the importance of rational legal principles in the Revolutionary movement. Despite impressive recent efforts to reassert the centrality of constitutional rights in patriot arguments, the main thrust of contemporary scholarship has been to downplay the specialized legal issues of concern to some Revolutionary leaders and to emphasize instead the broad social and economic values underlying the public debate over the Revolution.[3]

What has divided those historians who stress the importance of classical republicanism from those who insist on the emergence of liberalism is essentially a disagreement over the substance of these broad underlying values. Classical republicanism has been associated with an ethic of civic or community-mindedness, in particular its celebration of public-spirited individuals willing to sacrifice their own interests on behalf of the common good. Such model citizens, according to the classical republican ideal, would display their virtue through service to the state, chiefly as statesmen and soldiers. Liberalism, on the other hand, has been identified with the promotion of free trade and arguments for limited government. Whereas for classical republicans the realization of liberty depended on disinterested, harmonious citizens acting within the state, for liberalism it depended on self-interested, competitive individuals acting outside the state in the market economy. The central question posed by recent historians of the American Revolution

[2] See, for example, Joyce Appleby, *Capitalism and a New Social Order: The Republican Vision of the 1790s* (New York, 1984); Isaac Kramnick, "Republican Revisionism Revisited," *American Historical Review* 87 (1982):629–64.

[3] John Phillip Reid, *Constitutional History of the American Revolution: The Authority of Rights* (Madison, Wis., 1987).

is which of these two ideological tendencies predominated.[4]

One reason for the intensity of the debate is that the flexible concept of "ideology" has been stretched to embrace far more than ideas about government per se. Looking beyond patriots' specific discussions of legitimate rule, political systems, duties to the state, and constitutional rights, historians frequently have found broader meanings pertaining to other important aspects of American social life. What has especially concerned such scholars as J. G. A. Pocock and Joyce Appleby, who have argued about the relative strengths of liberalism and republicanism, is the relationship between political ideas and attitudes toward economic development. Their contrasting perspectives on the economy have been phrased in terms of alternatively communitarian or individualistic values: the historians of classical republicanism have pointed to communal values harkening back to a precapitalistic past, those of liberalism to the economic individualism of the commercial market.

In following this historical debate, one is repeatedly left asking how, if at all, Americans of the Revolutionary generation reconciled these conflicting social values. Part of the answer, to be sure, is that even some of the most articulate ideological spokesmen—such as Thomas Jefferson—were, to our minds, often frustratingly contradictory, perfectly capable of entertaining seemingly opposite sets of convictions at the same time. Another way to address this problem is to note that the political elite and public commentators were internally divided along regional and partisan lines, with some inclining more toward classical republicanism (most typically Federalist New Englanders) and others more toward liberalism (Demo-

[4]The main lines of this debate can be followed in Pocock, *The Machiavellian Moment*, Appleby, *Capitalism and a New Social Order*, and James T. Kloppenberg, "The Virtues of Liberalism: Christianity, Republicanism, and Ethics in Early American Political Discourse," *Journal of American History* 74 (1987):9–33. In challenging the "republican synthesis" Joyce Appleby has not only pointed to the importance of a different set of values but questioned the usefulness of attributing any one dominant cultural understanding to the Revolutionary period. See especially her "Republicanism and Ideology," *American Quarterly* 37 (1985).

cratic-Republican Philadelphians, New Yorkers, some southern planters). Whatever these internal logical inconsistencies, regional differences, and political disagreements among the Revolutionary political leadership, however, the interpretive debate among historians over the relative importance of liberalism and republicanism has given surprisingly little attention to the transmission of such conflicting sets of values outside of explicitly political arguments. By concentrating on the ideological convictions of those most centrally engaged in the numerous political debates between the 1760s and the 1790s, historians of classical republicanism and liberalism have scarcely begun to explore the permeation of these basic ideological orientations into other dimensions of cultural life in the Revolutionary period.

Working on the periphery of the central debate about the political economy of republicanism, some historians have injected arguments about the ideological importance of contemporary commentary about religion and the family. Although when compared to the subjects of politics and economics these topics may appear somehow less "public," religious and familial values pervaded the popular understanding of public life. Far from merely reflecting the ideological convictions of either classical republicanism or liberalism, moreover, the social values expressed in popular writings about religious and domestic life embodied the competing strains of individualism and communalism in ways that significantly muted the conflict between them. Only by looking beyond the explicitly political debate of the period can we come to appreciate better the manner in which these seemingly opposite sets of values were both absorbed and at least partly resolved on the level of popular ideology.

Whereas most historians of Revolutionary ideology have focused on the public debates about British imperial legislation, Independence, the Constitution, and the partisan struggles of the 1790s, historians concentrating on religious and familial issues have dug deeply into the popular literary forms of published and unpublished sermons, domestic advice books, novels, and periodical fiction. There is little doubt that the audience for such works was extensive throughout the Revolutionary period. Indeed, among the imported books listed in late eighteenth-century northeastern library and booksellers' catalogues, both Samuel Richardson's novel *Pamela* and Thomas Newton's *Dissertations on the Prophecies* were held in far greater numbers than either of the two basic texts articulating classical republican and liberal perspectives on government, John Trenchard and Thomas Gordon's *Cato's Letters* and the *Independent Whig* and John Locke's *Treatise on Government*.[5] Cheaper, unbound sermons by American clergymen and lay religious exhorters spoke to an even wider public and, since some of these works were originally delivered orally, they might therefore have reached the illiterate as well as the educated. Literacy was high, in any case, especially in the Northeast where the popular Revolutionary movement was strongest, and it is doubtful that there was a wide gap between oral and print cultures. Plenty of inexpensive broadside, pamphlet, and periodical publications spoke to high and low alike. Even the first American magazines, which were certainly expensive by modern standards, were distributed through a remarkably broad spectrum of northern urban society.[6] While there were certainly components of the culture of the educated elite that were not shared by ordinary Americans—perhaps including an understanding of some of the more complex constitutional issues at stake in the struggle with Britain—the reverse is less true. With few exceptions, the popular culture of Revolutionary America was .popular more in the sense of being widely shared than in the sense of being the distinctive culture of the illiterate. And this popular culture was particularly preoccupied with both religious and domestic concerns.

Arguments for the centrality of religion to American Revolutionaries have a long history, of course. Before the emer-

---

[5] Ruth H. Bloch, "The Social and Political Base of Millennial Literature in Late Eighteenth-Century America," *American Quarterly* 40 (1988), esp. pp. 385–86. Also see Robert B. Winans, "The Growth of a Novel-Reading Public in Late Eighteenth-Century America," *Early American Literature* 9 (1975):267–75; David Lundberg and Henry F. May, "The Enlightened Reader in America," *American Quarterly* 28 (1976):262–71.

[6] David Paul Nord, "A Republican Literature: A Study of Magazine Reading and Readers in Late Eighteenth-Century New York," *American Quarterly* 40 (1988):42–64.

gence of the current republicanism-liberalism debate, as formidable a spokesman as Perry Miller insisted on the fundamental connection between Puritan covenant theology and the Revolutionary pronouncements of patriot clergymen.[7] The earliest formulations of the republican perspective by Bernard Bailyn were, indeed, written in part to challenge this religious interpretation.[8] Since then several works have appeared that further clarify the relationship of religious ideas to the ideology of the Revolution. Taken together these present a broad range of arguments for the basic affinity of American Protestantism to classical republicanism, for an implicit connection between religion and liberalism, and for the independent ideological contribution of religious beliefs.[9] So far, no one has attempted to untangle the strands of individualism and communitarianism within the dominant forms of Revolutionary religious expression, however, or to relate them to other currents within popular culture.

The case for the importance of religion to the American Revolution builds on a long history extending back to the seventeenth century. Among patriot New Englanders, especially, and to a lesser extent among Presbyterians and Baptists elsewhere, connections between religion and revolution can be traced to the English revolutionary Puritanism of the seventeenth century. Whereas in England the radicalism of the 1640s and 1650s was driven underground after 1660, in

[7] Perry Miller, "From the Covenant to the Revival," in Miller, *Nature's Nation* (Cambridge, Mass., 1967). Also see Alan Heimert, *Religion and the American Mind from the Great Awakening to the Revolution* (Cambridge, Mass., 1966).

[8] Bailyn, *Ideological Origins*, pp. 6–7, 32–33; idem, "Religion and Revolution: Three Biographical Studies," *Perspectives in American History* 4 (1970):85–169.

[9] See especially Nathan O. Hatch, *The Sacred Cause of Liberty: Republican Thought and the Millennium in Revolutionary New England* (New Haven, 1977); Ruth H. Bloch, *Visionary Republic: Millennial Themes in American Thought, 1756–1800* (New York, 1985); Harry S. Stout, *The New England Soul: Preaching and Religious Culture in Colonial New England* (New York, 1986); David S. Lovejoy, *Religious Enthusiasm in the New World: Heresy to Revolution* (Cambridge, Mass., 1985); Patricia U. Bonomi, *Under the Cope of Heaven: Religion, Society, and Politics in Colonial America* (New York, 1986).

America many ideas associated with the English Revolution stayed closer to the surface, gaining a kind of legitimacy among orthodox Protestants. American writings of the eighteenth century suggest that even the memory of Oliver Cromwell was not entirely tarnished by the shift to the right after the Glorious Revolution.[10] Transforming the promonarchical English holiday of Guy Fawkes Day, New England's alternative of "Pope's Day" annually ritualized hatred for both Catholics and the Stuart kings.[11] Meanwhile milder and more conventionally whig formulations about the blessings of English liberty had already found their way into Congregational sermons in the wake of the Glorious Revolution.[12]

On the level of religious belief, other elements of the English revolutionary tradition were sustained in the colonies— criticisms of sacerdotal authority, the idea of an elect nation, expectations of a millennial future—even though they did not always take an explicitly political form.[13] In the middle of the eighteenth century, the religious revivals of the Great Awakening reinforced and further disseminated these themes in many parts of the colonies.[14] It is no accident that popular support for the American Revolution came disproportionately from the Congregational, Presbyterian, and Baptist de-

[10] Alfred F. Young, "English Plebian Culture and Eighteenth-Century American Radicalism," in Margaret Jacob and James Jacob, eds., *The Origins of Anglo-American Radicalism* (London, 1984), pp. 195–97. It is clear from Young's reliance on evidence from leading clergymen and other prominent figures that this tradition was not, however, as "plebian" as he otherwise suggests.

[11] Young, "Plebian Culture and American Radicalism"; Peter Shaw, *American Patriots and the Rituals of Revolution* (Cambridge, Mass., 1981).

[12] Stout, *New England Soul.*

[13] See, for example, Bonomi, *Under the Cope of Heaven;* Stout, *New England Soul;* Bloch, *Visionary Republic.*

[14] There has been a fruitful historical debate about the connection between the Great Awakening and the Revolution. My own view is that the connection was subtle and indirect, but significant nonetheless. For opposing views, see Heimert, *Religion and the American Mind;* Lovejoy, *Religious Enthusiasm;* Jon Butler, "Enthusiasm Described and Decried: The Great Awakening as an Interpretive Fiction," *Journal of American History* 69 (1982):305–25.

nominations most powerfully affected both by the Puritan past and by the evangelical movement of the mid-eighteenth century. Of course influential nonrevivalist Congregational and Presbyterian ministers—such as Charles Chauncy, Jonathan Mayhew, and John Witherspoon—also joined in the religious attack on British tyranny, similarly drawing on a long history of New England and Scottish mistrust of English rule that was rooted in the revolutionary seventeenth century.

An appreciation of the familial themes in Revolutionary ideology is more recent among scholars, related above all to the rise of interest in the history of the family and the history of women.[15] This ideological dimension emerges most clearly in the debate of the 1780s and 1790s over female education and in the emerging genre of popular sentimental fiction. As a leading literary historian has recently argued, the American Revolution coincided with the onset of another, "reading," revolution.[16] Not only were Americans, especially women, becoming increasingly literate, but popular literary taste was shifting away from purely devotional religious literature to sentimental fiction.[17] Standing somewhat between these two genres and also in great demand in the late eighteenth cen-

[15]On these developments see especially Edwin G. Burrows and Michael Wallace, "The American Revolution: The Ideology and Psychology of National Liberation," *Perspectives in American History* 6 (1972):190–214; Linda K. Kerber, *Women of the Republic: Intellect and Ideology in Revolutionary America* (Chapel Hill, 1980); Mary Beth Norton, *Liberty's Daughters: The Revolutionary Experience of American Women, 1750–1800* (Boston, 1980); Jay Fliegelman, *Prodigals and Pilgrims: The American Revolution against Patriarchical Authority, 1750–1800* (New York, 1982); Jan Lewis, "The Republican Wife: Virtue and Seduction in the Early Republic," *William and Mary Quarterly*, 3d ser. 44 (1987):689–721; Ruth H. Bloch, "The Gendered Meanings of Virtue in Revolutionary America," *Signs: Journal of Women in Culture and Society* 13 (1987):37–58.

[16]Cathy N. Davidson, *Revolution and the Word: The Rise of the Novel in America* (New York, 1986), pp. vii, 55–79.

[17]Winans, "Growth of a Novel-Reading Public"; David D. Hall, "The Uses of Literacy in New England, 1600–1850," in William L. Joyce, David D. Hall, Richard D. Brown, and John B. Hench, eds., *Printing and Society in Early America* (Worcester, Mass., 1983), pp. 1–47. Hall and Davidson disagree about whether this marked a shift from an "intensive" to an "extensive" reading style. See Davidson, *Revolution and the Word*, pp. 72–73.

tury were numerous conduct books written by English and Scottish moralists that prescribed the appropriate education, behavior, and demeanor of young women and men facing prospects of marriage. After midcentury, newly established American magazines such as the *Boston Magazine,* the *American Museum,* and the *New York Magazine* also featured innumerable sentimental short stories as well as pieces of practical domestic advice. French and English novels were imported into the colonies in growing numbers, and by the end of the century the prodigious production of indigenous American sentimental literature had begun.[18]

The themes of this fiction and didactic literature almost inevitably involved courtship and seduction. The stock characters of novels and short stories consisted of dictatorial fathers sabatoging the marital choices of their daughters and sons, aristocratic rakes bent on exploiting maidens deceived by false promises, and, of course, the innocent, common young women and men themselves who were egalitarian and trusting, representative of simple, bourgeois virtue. What united the bulk of this literature and gave it an implicitly revolutionary meaning was its protest against the arbitrary control of fathers and the decadence of an hereditary elite.[19] Building on the model of Richardson's *Clarissa,* which along with his *Pamela* was one of the best-sellers of Revolutionary America, story after story either written or reprinted in late eighteenth-century America told of the cruelty of authoritarian, status-seeking fathers forcing their sacrificial offspring to reject true love or to accept odious suitors against their will.[20] So pervasive was this basic narrative structure that a character in one novel proclaims, "I hate almost all fathers in novels, because

[18] Herbert Ross Brown, *The Sentimental Novel in America, 1789–1860* (Durham, N.C., 1940); Davidson, *Revolution and the Word.*

[19] Fliegelman, *Prodigals and Pilgrims;* Lewis, "Republican Wife"; Davidson, *Revolution and the Word.*

[20] A few of the many examples include, *Fidelity Rewarded, or, The History of Polly Granville* (Boston, 1796); Samuel Relf, *Infidelity, or, The Victims of Sentiment* (Philadelphia, 1797); "Arria: Forced Marriage," *American Museum* (Sept. 1789); "Maternal Affection," *Boston Magazine* (Jan. 1784); "Honour Eclipsed by Love," *Boston Magazine* (Aug. 1785).

their poor daughters must suffer so much for their stubbornness."[21]

Such protests against oppressive patriarchal authority were seconded by equally strident objections to corrupt and artificial manners associated with aristocratic fashion and foreign taste. In fiction, innumerable foppish rogues like the character Dimple in Royall Tyler's play *The Contrast* or Montraville in Susanna Rowson's *Charlotte Temple* illustrated the moral dangers hidden within seductive genteel refinement. The prescriptive literature written by popular moralists also repeatedly warned against the dissipated pursuit of frivolous fashionable amusements at the expense of the simple virtues of domestic life. "If I wished a lady's picture to appear to advantage, it should not be taken when she was dressing for an assembly, a levee, or a birth night," counseled the English clergyman John Bennet in the many American editions of his instructive *Letters to a Young Lady*. "She should be holding *one* lovely infant in her arms, and presenting a moral page, for the instruction of *another.*"[22] The goal of female education, he insisted, was not the showy, polite accomplishments of foreign languages, musical skills, or learned conversation, but "the culture of the heart."[23]

The readers of this fictional and prescriptive literature about family life were no doubt typically more educated, genteel, and religiously liberal than the evangelical Protestants, but the messages of evangelical religion and sentimental literature were in many respects similar. Both endorsed expressions of emotion and both criticized traditional authority in its ecclesiastical and patriarchal forms. The fact that prominent

[21] Martha Read, *Monima, or, The Beggar Girl* (New York, 1802), p. 255.

[22] John Bennet, *Letters to a Young Lady, on a Variety of Useful and Interesting Subjects*, 2 vols. (New York, 1796), 2:94. Also see *The Lady's Pocket Library* (Philadelphia, 1792), pp. 10–18; John Cosens Ogden, *The Female Guide* (Concord, N.H., 1793), pp. 39–41; Thomas Gisborne, *An Enquiry into the Duties of the Female Sex* (Philadelphia, 1798); John Burton, *Lectures on Female Education and Manners* (Elizabethtown, N.J., 1799); Benjamin Silliman, *Letters of Shahcoolen, a Hindu Philosopher* (Boston, 1802), pp. 49–62; Thomas Branagan, *The Excellency of the Female Character Vindicated* (New York, 1807).

[23] John Bennet, *Strictures on Female Education, Chiefly As It Relates to the Culture of the Heart* (Philadelphia, 1793).

clergymen launched a vigorous campaign against novel reading is often regarded as evidence of a gap between the worlds of religion and literature.[24] Yet this very competition also suggests that these worlds considerably overlapped.[25]

No less an orthodox New Light than Jonathan Edwards took notice of favorable reviews in the British press of recent romances by Fenelon, Fielding, and Richardson, and found the writing of the last, in the words of his son, "wholly favourable to good morals and purity of character."[26] Ebenezer Parkman, a theologically conservative minister from Westborough, Massachusetts, similarly read both volumes of *Pamela* with great interest, expressing in his diary his intention to "draw up . . . some Remarks" on the work.[27] Nor were these instances of novel reading on the part of eighteenth-century American clergymen exceptional. The innumerable foreign and domestic variations on Richardsonian tales of innocent virtue pitted against worldly vice, with their characters ineluctably led from moral temptation to repentance and reform, met with widespread clerical approbation. In Samuel Miller's *Brief Retrospect of the Eighteenth Century* this New York Presbyte-

---

[24] Terrence Martin, *The Instructed Vision: Scottish Common Sense Philosophy and the Origins of American Fiction* (Bloomington, Ind., 1961); Davidson, *Revolution and the Word*, pp. 13, 41–50, 53–54.

[25] David Reynolds has drawn this connection in a different way. See his "From Doctrine to Narrative: The Rise of Pulpit Story-Telling in America," *American Quarterly* 32 (1980):479–98.

[26] Thomas H. Johnson, "Jonathan Edwards' Background of Reading," *Publications of the Colonial Society of Massachusetts* 28 (1931):193–222; idem, "Jonathan Edwards and the 'Young Folks' Bible,'" *New England Quarterly* 5 (1932):37–54; Terrence Erdt, *Jonathan Edwards: Art and the Sense of the Heart* (Amherst, Mass., 1980), pp. 78–79; Sereno E. Dwight, *The Life of President Edwards* (New York, 1830), p. 601. Erdt notes that Dwight wrongly reports that Edwards had already read Samuel Richardson's *Sir Charles Grandison* before leaving Northampton; the novel Edwards's son was referring to might well have been *Pamela*, which appeared earlier and which Edwards definitely owned by the mid-1750s. See Ola Elizabeth Winslow, *Jonathan Edwards, 1703–1758* (New York, 1940), p. 287.

[27] Francis G. Walett, ed., *The Diary of Ebenezer Parkman* (Worcester, Mass., 1974), pp. 138–39.

rian offered an extensive survey of contemporary novels in which he scrupulously distinguished between the commendable writings of Richardson, Fielding, Goldsmith, Henry MacKenzie, Fanny Burney, and Charlotte Smith and the objectionable works of such writers as Smollett, Sterne, Diderot, and Voltaire.[28] Characterizing the prevailing "morbid appetite" for fiction as a disease, Miller nonetheless recommended the reading of selected novels, acknowledging that fiction is "one of the most powerful means of exciting curiosity, of awakening sympathy, and of impressing the understanding and the heart."[29] On the liberal end of the theological spectrum, the Universalist minister Enos Hitchcock, while similarly expressing reservations about most novels, himself wrote a work of didactic sentimental fiction on the themes of domestic harmony and childhood education.[30] Much of the imported literature offering advice on education, including the popular Mrs. Chapone's *Letters on the Improvement of the Mind* as well as other well-known works by the respectable Scottish clergymen James Fordyce and Hugh Blair, reconciled an emphasis on piety with the approval of certain moralistic works of fiction.[31]

The conflicting religious attitudes of hostility and sympathy toward the novel stemmed, in part, from the clergy's own growing preoccupation with domestic themes similar to those found in fiction. Not since the seventeenth-century Puritans had so many ministers preached and written about the sub-

[28] Samuel Miller, *Brief Retrospect of the Eighteenth Century* (New York, 1803), pp. 158–67.

[29] Ibid., p. 173.

[30] Enos Hitchcock, *Memoirs of the Bloomsgrove Family*, 2 vols. (Boston, 1790), 2:82.

[31] Hester Chapone, *Letters on the Improvement of the Mind* (Boston, 1783), pp. 205–6. James Fordyce's *Sermons to Young Women* (Boston, 1796) and Hugh Blair's *Lectures on Rhetoric and Belles Lettres* (Philadelphia, 1784), both of which took this position, each went into several editions in late eighteenth-century America. On the Scottish clergy's openness to a type of sentimental fiction, see John Dwyer, *Virtuous Discourse: Sensibility and Community in Late Eighteenth-Century Scotland* (Edinburgh, 1987), pp. 141–67.

jects of child-rearing and family life.[32] And, like many of the novelists they so vociferously condemned, they too preached about the dangers of illegitimate pregnancy and the morally beneficial effects of feminine sensibility on men.[33] For all the animosity occasionally unleashed by clergymen against fiction, the culture of domestic sentimentality was religious as much as literary in its inspiration and form.[34] The clerical attack on the novel at the end of the eighteenth century can be seen in many ways as a quarrel among siblings, each committed to similarly sentimental conceptions of personal morality and the larger social good.

Just as the religious works and sentimental literature of the late eighteenth century were complementary components of the same larger culture, each bore directly on popular political understanding. Despite their seemingly apolitical content, many of the same themes that dominated religion and sentimental literature permeated the ritual activism and the polemical literature of the American Revolution. Biblical and familial imagery saturated Revolutionary arguments, especially in appeals aimed at a large popular audience. The pa-

[32] See, for example: Joseph Buckminster, *Heads of Families, to Resolve for Their Households, No Less Than for Themselves, That They Will Serve the Lord* (Boston, 1759); John Witherspoon, "Reflections on the Married State," *Pennsylvania Magazine* 1(1775):408–13, 543–48, 2(1776):109–14, 319–23; Timothy Dwight, "Reflexions on Second Marriages of Men," *American Museum* 6 (Dec. 1789):437–39; Benjamin Bell, *The Character of a Virtuous Woman, Delineated* (Windsor, Vt., 1794); Amos Chase, *On Female Excellence, or, A Discourse in Which Good Character in Women Is Described* (Litchfield, Conn., 1792); Ogden, *The Female Guide;* George Strebeck, *A Sermon on the Character of the Virtuous Woman* (New York, 1800); Eli Forbes, *A Family Book* (Salem, Mass., 1801).

[33] For example: Joseph Lathrop, "Female Honour," *American Museum* 8 (Dec. 1790):280–82; Thomas Barnard, *A Sermon Preached before the Salem Female Charitable Society, July 6th, 1803* (Salem, Mass., 1803), p. 17; Daniel Chaplin, *A Discourse Delivered before the Charitable Female Society in Groton, Oct. 19, 1814* (Andover, Mass., 1814), pp. 8–10; Samuel Worcester, *Female Love to Christ* (Salem, Mass., 1809), pp. 8–10.

[34] For an account of later Unitarian thought that elaborates upon such a connection between religion, literature, and sentimentalism, see Daniel Walker Howe, *The Unitarian Conscience: Harvard Moral Philosophy, 1805–1861* (Middletown, Conn., 1988), pp. 174–204.

triot movement repeatedly dramatized a religious perception of Great Britain as the agent of the Antichrist, beginning as early as the Stamp Act crisis of 1765 and continuing into the Revolutionary War. Colonial crowds, for example, hanged British ministers in effigy alongside the devil and turned the traditional anti-Catholic holiday of Pope's Day into a celebration of the American cause.[35] The polemical pamphlet and newspaper literature of the Revolution repeatedly associated the British with the Antichrist and the Americans with the ancient Israelites resisting tyrannical oppression.[36] One of the most widely reprinted Revolutionary pamphlets of the entire period, the lay Baptist John Allen's *Oration upon the Beauties of Liberty*, modeled its plea for resistance directly on that of the Old Testament prophet Micah.[37] With increased frequency as the colonists moved toward Independence, patriot literature portrayed the Americans not only as oppressed Israelites but as the historical forces of Christ destined by Providence to usher in the glory of the millennial kingdom of God.[38]

Often such explosive religious imagery was combined with equally emotional references to the dynamics of family life. Thomas Paine's best-selling *Common Sense* wove into its argument for independence both an appeal to the Old Testament prophets' indictment of monarchy and a characterization of America as a stifled, overprotected adolescent coming of age.[39] In an influential printed sermon of 1776, the Boston minister Jonathan Mayhew even more thoroughly mixed together religious and familial metaphors in his argument for American independence: Liberty was "a celestial Maid, the daughter of God, and, excepting his Son, the firstborn of heaven."[40] The conception of America as a virtuous youth

[35] Shaw, *Patriots and Revolution.*

[36] Bloch, *Visionary Republic,* esp. pp. 53–74.

[37] John Allen, *An Oration upon the Beauties of Liberty* (Boston, 1773).

[38] Bloch, *Visionary Republic,* esp. pp. 75–93. Also see Stout, *New England Soul;* Hatch, *Sacred Cause of Liberty.*

[39] Thomas Paine, *Common Sense,* ed. Isaac Kramnick (New York, 1976), pp. 83–84, 107.

[40] Jonathan Mayhew, *The Snare Broken* (Boston, 1776), p. 36.

was, of course, encoded in the name of the early patriot organization, the Sons of Liberty, and later on applied as well by the female Daughters of Liberty. Conversely, just as Great Britain assumed the diabolical stature of the Antichrist, the mother country and the king were both repeatedly cast in the image of oppressive, cruel parents.[41] By no means coincidently, at the conclusion of the Revolution its consumate symbol of authority and stability, George Washington, became known as the benign father of the nation, the good parent replacing the bad.[42]

On the one hand, this religious and familial imagery can be seen as the means through which Revolutionary leaders conveyed their political message to ordinary colonists. Whereas Americans outside the educated elite might have had some difficulty commiting themselves to the constitutional issues underlying the patriot cause, most Americans were Protestants well versed in a providential understanding of history and were also members of families familiar with the generational struggles between parents and children. The implication of such an interpretation is that the religious and familial symbolism was itself politically neutral, only to be infused with Revolutionary meaning by effectively drawing analogies to the imperial struggle at hand. This point of view would suggest that the ideological power of this symbolism was emotional rather than substantive, that it lacked political content of its own and served primarily as a rhetorical flourish conveying Revolutionary ideas to an unsophisticated public.

On the other hand, the religious and familial images that so often appeared within Revolutionary arguments need to be understood within the broader context of religious and literary culture. For the underlying ideological meanings embedded in the use of this imagery were more thoroughly articulated in religion, domestic advice literature, and fiction than in the explicitly political polemic itself. From this perspective, seemingly apolitical symbolism takes on a new significance as the source as well as the carrier of political outlooks. Many of the deeper social and psychological issues confronted by the

[41]Burrows and Wallace, "The American Revolution."

[42]For an analysis of this transition, see Fliegelman, *Prodigals and Pilgrims.*

Revolutionary generation—issues of authority, equality, autonomy, and interpersonal moral obligation—were central themes in religious exhortations about salvation and in sentimental and didactic writings about family life.

The relationship between communal and individualistic values comprises one of these basic themes, and it is also an issue at the heart of the current debate over the ideology of the American Revolution. Just as the political literature of the Revolutionary elite displays elements of both ideological tendencies—with communitarianism typically associated with classical republicanism and individualism with liberalism—one can find both tendencies within religious and sentimental literary culture. Yet the ways that communitarian and individualistic elements were combined within religion and fiction significantly deviates from both the liberal and the classical republican understandings of the political culture of the Revolution. A look at this broad cultural context reveals a fundamentally different way in which these core values of Revolutionary ideology may have been understood by this wider public. The simultaneous commitment to individualism and to the community appears from this perspective to be not so much contradictory as complementary. For while popular religious and sentimental culture incorporated aspects of both the classical republican and liberal points of view, a relatively cohesive social vision emerged despite the tension that existed within more explicitly political ideology.

Religion in eighteenth-century America is usually, if not exclusively, understood as communitarian, as wedded to a backward-looking ideal of social cooperation as opposed to the competitive individualism of the modern, secular, commercial world. It is well known that in popular evangelical exhortations, especially, the selfish pursuit of personal wealth and social prestige were repeatedly denounced as terrible sins. Revivalists preached on the superior morality of Christian self-sacrifice and loving benevolence. The religious awakenings of the mid-eighteenth century were themselves collective events, the first truly mass conversion rituals of American religious history, and the shared experience of the revivals bound evangelicals together in community against the unregenerate foes. Adherence to codes of simple dress and conspicuous abstension from frivolous entertainments were among the many ways that evangelical Protestants shaped what has been called a "counterculture" of opposition to the worldliness of the elite.[43] These communal characteristics of popular religious culture found repeated expression in the identification of the patriot cause with the united forces of Christ and in the definition of Revolutionary virtue as ascetic self-sacrifice on behalf of the whole. As the Connecticut army chaplain David Avery phrased his millennial hopes for the Revolution, while simultaneously denouncing selfish sinners who succumbed to the temptations of avarice and covetousness, "Should pure and heavenly love pervade through all these states, quicken all our hearts, and unite us in the glorious interest of the REDEEMER'S KINGDOM; should we love our neighbors as we love ourselves . . . then *America* will become IMMANUEL'S *land*."[44]

Yet there were individualistic elements to American religious culture as well, and they were more compatible with liberal notions of natural rights than with classical republican appeals to public virtue. Core doctrines of Reformation Protestantism had always upheld the primacy of the individual believer's relationship to God, and in the early American colonies church covenants were formed out of essentially contractual relationships among individuals. In different ways both the Arminian liberals and the Calvinist evangelicals of the eighteenth century developed this individualistic side of colonial Protestantism. In their emerging critique of the Calvinist assumption of human depravity and their increased emphasis on the power of individuals to effect their own salvation, the so-called liberal Protestants such as Chauncy, Mayhew, and Alexander Garden were in harmony with the individualism of political and economic liberal theory if not necessarily with its acceptance of material self-interest or its belief in limited government. Evangelical Protestantism also had its individualistic features, based on its very emphasis on conversion,

[43]Rhys Isaac, *The Transformation of Virginia, 1740–1790* (Chapel Hill, 1982).

[44]David Avery, *The Lord Is to Be Praised for the Triumphs of His Power* (Norwich, Conn., 1778).

which accorded primary value to individual spiritual experience as opposed to either sacerdotal or secular authority. During the Great Awakening, moreover, the conflicts between revivalist and nonrevivalist clergymen meant that many individuals were confronted for the first time with a choice between competing religious alternatives. In her recent history of colonial religion Patricia U. Bonomi has gone so far as to suggest that the Great Awakening produced "a new spirit of defiant individualism" in the face of the collapse of the unitary religious ideal.[45] Other historians have presented evangelical culture as uneasily balanced between contradictory individualistic and communitarian tendencies, as implicitly sanctioning the rise of a complex market economy and rising standard of living while at the same time offering a critique in the name of a primitivistic communal ideal.[46] Whereas the latter tendency merged with the classical republican plea for self-sacrificial virtue, the revivalists' defense of minority rights against religious establishments provided religious reinforcement for the more general liberal rights theories of the Revolution.

Just as religion contained both individualistic and communitarian elements, so did sentimental literature. Whereas the religion of this period is generally associated with communal solidarity, however, the fiction and domestic advice literature are usually described as individualistic. One reason for the religious reaction against the novel, argues a recent literary critic, is that it enabled readers individually to interpret the printed word without the intervention of clerical middlemen.[47] The same might well be said about the proliferation of domestic advice books, including even the many that were written by clergymen. Not only were individual consumers of literature thus freer to make their own judgments about the didactic messages being delivered to them, but the moral pre-

[45] Bonomi, *Under the Cope of Heaven*, p. 158.

[46] See, for example, Richard Bushman, *From Puritan to Yankee: Character and the Social Order in Connecticut, 1690–1765* (Cambridge, Mass., 1967); Rhys Isaac, "Radicalised Religion and Changing Lifestyles," in Jacob and Jacob, eds., *Origins of Radicalism.*

[47] Davidson, *Revolution and the Word*, p. 44.

dicaments presented in this literature were typically those faced by individuals with little or no protection from family or community. The images of young women and men encountering the temptation of a dissipated high life, or of impressionable virgins confronting deceptively charming seducers, encapsulated a social vision in which the self-contained individual is pitted against a turbulent, competitive, and self-interested world. A standard interpretation of the rise of the novel links the emergence of sentimental literature to the rise of the liberal bourgeoisie.[48] Not only were aristocratic rakes a common target of this fiction, but the theme of youthful rebellion against patriarchal authority expressed the Lockean values of individual autonomy as against filial obedience.[49] Both the class and the generational dynamics of this fiction, then, seem to celebrate a kind of liberal, antiauthoritarian individualism.

Yet at the same time the culture of sentimentality insisted on the necessity of human interaction and extolled the virtues of domestic life partly in the interests of the greater social good.[50] Even in fiction the gender dynamics illustrated in these plots reveal both the authors' sympathies and the hapless heroines victimized by male vice and their simultaneous inability to endorse female self-assertion.[51] Clarissa's rebellion leads her to ruin. Pamela, for all her heroic assertiveness, speaks in the name of cross-class mutual responsibility and familial bonds. Similarly, in one of the best works of American

[48] Ian Watt, *The Rise of the Novel* (Berkeley, 1957); also see Terry Eagleton, *The Rape of Clarissa* (Oxford, 1982).

[49] See, for example, "Directory of Love," *Royal American Magazine* (Apr. and May 1774); "Honour Eclipsed by Love," *Boston Magazine* (Aug. 1785); "Reflections on Parental Care and Filial Duty," *Christian Scholar's and Farmer's Magazine* (Feb. 1790); "Reflections on Marriage Unions," *New York Magazine* (Oct. 1790); "Parental Authority," *Ladies Magazine* (Oct. 1792). Also see Fliegelman, *Prodigals and Pilgrims*.

[50] This position is powerfully argued for the case of Scotland in Dwyer, *Virtuous Discourse*. Many of the Scottish texts he discusses were popular in America as well.

[51] This duality is explored in Davidson, *Revolution and the Word*.

fiction in this period, Hannah Foster's *The Coquette*, the sympathy one feels for the plight of miserable Eliza, who holds out for love and is deceived by the false charm (and false riches) of Sanford, is balanced by the subplot of the successful, sentimental marriages of her more sensible friends Lucy Freeman and the Richmans.[52] While freer to act than the women, even the men portrayed in sentimental fiction were ultimately bound to the conjugal unit, dependent on women and marriage for the realization of their virtue.[53] No less popular than the plot of the pathetic young woman destroyed by status-seeking parents and predatory men was that of the selfish rake reformed by triumphant female purity.[54] Even the didactic literature on courtship and marriage, while occasionally warning against the adage "a reformed rake makes the best husband," urged women to "civilize" their suitors and husbands, "in spite of early vicious habits, [to] compel them to a behavior of tenderness and love."[55] Nor were children depicted as ideally independent of all parental authority: good parents—like Richardson's triumphantly maternal Pamela or the crestfallen parents of Rowson's disobedient Char-

[52]A brilliant analysis of this novel, which argues that Eliza's inability to achieve the republican synthesis of independence, virtue, and happiness embodied developing tensions within American ideology, is Carroll Smith-Rosenberg, "Domesticating 'Virtue': Coquettes and Revolutionaries in Young America" (Paper presented at the Eightieth Annual Meeting of the Organization of American Historians, Philadelphia, April 1987).

[53]Lewis, "Republican Wife."

[54]The prototype is, again, found in the work of Samuel Richardson, in this case *Pamela*. Also see, for example: "Conjugal Prudence," *New York Magazine* (Mar. 1791); "Regrets on the Loss of Domestic Happiness," *New York Magazine* (Mar. 1793). Nonfictional magazine essays frequently delivered the same message. See, for example, "Panegyrick on the Fair Sex," *Boston Magazine* (Feb. 1785); "Advantages of Society of Virtuous Women," *Boston Magazine* (Aug. 1785); "Female Influence," *New York Magazine* (Apr. 1795).

[55]Hugh Smith, *Letters to Married Women* (Philadelphia, 1792), p. 123; *The Lady's Pocket Library*, pp. 10–12; James Fordyce, *Sermons to Young Women*, pp. 17–23; Gisborne, *Duties of the Female Sex*, pp. 8–9; Chaplin, *Discourse Delivered before the Charitable Female Society*, pp. 8–10; John Gregory, *A Father's Legacy to His Daughters* (Boston, 1779).

lotte—exercised benign and legitimate authority over their young.[56] In all these ways, then, the fictional endorsement of individualism was partial—qualified by its concurrent celebration of the solidarity, interdependence, and even the gender and generational hierarchy of what was portrayed as the ideal family.

Upon first impression, these images drawn from the religion and sentimental literature of the Revolutionary era seem a jumble of contradictions. One might be tempted to conclude that fundamentally irreconcilable tendencies collided within popular culture, with individualistic tendencies supporting a liberal ideological outlook and communitarian tendencies supporting a classical republican view. Surely the coexistence of these values was, in part, an expression of tension. However, from another perspective these contradictions can be resolved, at least to a point. Rather than being simply torn between liberal and classical republican values, Revolutionary popular culture defined the relationship between individualism and communitarianism in a significantly different way. The individualism of evangelical religion and sentimental literature was not that of economic liberalism. Far from endorsing the competitive free market, this was an individualism opposing the arbitrary authority of state churches and coercive fathers in the name of personal spiritual and emotional experience. It surely upheld the freedom of individual choice, but the choices described within these religious and sentimental frameworks were not those of individual autonomy but of identification with the communal groups of the church and family. Evangelicals insisted on the "right" of individuals to join churches without the consent of their families or their social superiors, but they also assumed the "right" of converts to regulate the behavior of their families and fellow church members.[57] Similarly, sentimental fiction accorded adolescents the "right" to resist tyrannical patriarchal authority,

---

[56]This is a central point of Fliegelman, *Prodigals and Pilgrims*. The novels are Samuel Richardson, *Pamela* (first American ed., Philadelphia, 1744), and Susanna Rowson, *Charlotte Temple* (1794), ed. Cathy Davidson (New York, 1986).

[57]Isaac, "Radicalised Religion."

but at the same time it sanctioned the authority of truly loving parents and husbands and celebrated the virtues of emotional interdependence within a family life that was deemed the foundation of social order itself. Thus, an anonymous essayist writing on love in a 1791 issue of the *New York Magazine* linked the individual romantic emotion to the collective good: "Perhaps, in the moment of its highest power, it may occupy the whole soul: But the moment of delirium will pass. . . . The lover becomes a husband, a parent, a citizen."[58]

Nor was this ethic of social solidarity the same as public spirit in the classical republican sense. The church and the family, unlike representative government or the military, were institutions located outside the republican state. Yet increasingly in the 1780s and 1790s, clergymen and educators claimed that these institutions were the moral foundation of the American republic. Good citizenship or patriotism, so the argument went, depended less on direct political participation than on the personal self-discipline and the emotional identification with the American republic taught in churches and families.[59]

Communitarianism and individualism can thus be interpreted as compatible as well as antagonistic themes within American Revolutionary ideology, particularly if one looks beyond explicitly political debate to the level of religious and literary popular culture. The dominant political language that emerged within American religion and sentimental literature was neither of public service nor of individual self-interest; rather, it spoke of diffuse patriotic sentiment. This sentiment was perceived to be rooted in interdependent social relationships symbolized by church and family. Ideally these institutions were at once internally communitarian while separate from the collective order of organized political life—private and increasingly voluntary while set apart from the competition of the market economy.

Rather than simply reflecting either classical republican or liberal political ideologies, these themes within Revolutionary popular ideology anticipate the emergence of nineteenth-

---

[58]"On Love," *New York Magazine* (June 1791):311.

[59]I have explored these themes in my "Gendered Meanings of Virtue."

century voluntary, benevolent, and social reform associations, groups with extensive support among white middle-class Protestants that also drew heavily upon the language of religion and sentimental domesticity. Movements espousing a variety of causes ranging from temperance to the abolition of slavery profoundly shaped the course of American history while typically remaining critical of both competitive capitalism and partisan politics. Alexis de Tocqueville recognized this peculiar mixture of antistatist individualism and social communitarianism when he described Americans as both libertarian and conformistic.[60] One can see this peculiar juxtaposition of values already in much of the popular ideology of the American Revolution. The religious and familial symbolism within Revolutionary discourse at once helps to explain popular allegiance to the patriot cause and suggests ways that important tendencies within Revolutionary popular culture—significantly different from both the liberal and the classical republican traditions—shaped the future development of American democracy. However useful the categories of liberalism and classical republicanism have proved in the analysis of Revolutionary political debate, these ideological tendencies were not polar opposites but overlapping parts of a cultural whole that historians have misleadingly torn asunder.[61]

[60]Alexis de Tocqueville, *Democracy in America,* 2 vols. (New York, 1945).

[61]Other recent works taking a similarly synthetic position, although confining themselves to an internal analysis of political ideology, are Kloppenberg, "Virtues of Liberalism," and Bailyn, *Ideological Origins,* rev. ed. (Cambridge, Mass., 1992).

Contributors
Index

Contributors

RUTH H. BLOCH is on the faculty of the department of history of the University of California, Los Angeles, where she teaches American colonial and Revolutionary history, women's history, religious history, and intellectual history. Her publications on the topics of the American Revolution, religion, and gender definitions include *Visionary Republic: Millennial Themes in American Thought, 1756–1800* (1985), "The Gendered Meanings of Virtue in Revolutionary America" (1987), "The Social and Political Base of Millennial Literature in Late Eighteenth-Century America" (1988), "Religion and Ideological Change in the American Revolution" (1989), and "Women, Love, and Virtue in the Thought of Edwards and Franklin" (1993).

PATRICIA U. BONOMI is professor of history at New York University. She is the author of *A Factious People: Politics and Society in Colonial New York* (1971) and *Under the Cope of Heaven: Religion, Society, and Politics in Colonial America* (1986). She is currently completing a biography of Edward Hyde, Viscount Cornbury, governor of New York and New Jersey from 1702 to 1708.

M. L. BRADBURY is a member of the history department at the University of Maryland, College Park. His interests combine the history of medicine and religion. Most recently he edited, with James B. Gilbert, *Transforming Faith: The Sacred and Secular in Modern American History* (1989). Currently he is completing a study of man midwifery in eighteenth-century Britain.

JON BUTLER is the William Robertson Coe Professor of American History at Yale University and is the author of numerous publications, among them *Awash in a Sea of Faith: Christianizing the American People* (1990).

ROBERT M. CALHOON is professor of history at the University of North Carolina at Greensboro. He is author of *The Loyalists in Revolutionary America, 1760–1781* (1973), *Revolutionary America: An Interpretive Overview* (1976), *Evangelicals and Conservatives in the Early South, 1740–1861* (1988),

CONTRIBUTORS

The Loyalist Perception and Other Essays (1989), and *Dominion and Liberty: Ideology in the Anglo-American World, 1660–1801* (1993).

PAUL K. CONKIN is a Distinguished Professor of History at Vanderbilt University. Before coming to Vanderbilt, he taught at the University of Southwestern Louisiana, the University of Maryland, and the University of Wisconsin. His scholarship and teaching are generally in the fields of American intellectual history, recent American history, and the philosophy of history. He has published books on the New Deal, utopian communities, American philosophy, American political and economic thought, Vanderbilt University and the Vanderbilt agrarians, American religion, and the philosophy of history.

ELAINE FORMAN CRANE is professor of history at Fordham University. She is the author of *A Dependent People: Newport, Rhode Island, in the Revolutionary Era* (1985) and the editor of *The Diary of Elizabeth Drinker* (1991). Her current research interests include a study of the social implications of physical pain in the eighteenth century and a monograph entitled *In the Beginning: Urban Women in Colonial New England*.

SYLVIA R. FREY is professor of history at Tulane University. Her published works include *The British Soldier in America: A Social History of Military Life in the Revolutionary Period* (1981), *New World, New Roles: A Documentary History of Women in Pre-Industrial America* (coeditor, 1986), *Water from the Rock: Black Resistance in a Revolutionary Age* (1991), and a number of scholarly articles. She is presently coauthoring a history of African-American Christianity before 1830.

EDWIN S. GAUSTAD is emeritus professor of history at the University of California, Riverside. Since retirement in 1989, he has been visiting professor at Princeton Theological Seminary and Auburn University. Major publications include *Historical Atlas of Religion in America* (1962; rev. ed., 1976), *A Religious History of America* (1966; rev. ed., 1990), and *Liberty of Conscience: Roger Williams in America* (1991). Current research includes a religious biography of Thomas Jefferson.

STEPHEN A. MARINI is professor of religion at Wellesley College, Wellesley, Massachusetts, and adjunct professor of church history at Andover Newton Theological School, Newton Centre, and Weston School of Theology, Cambridge. He is the author of *Radical Sects of Revolutionary New England* (1982) as well as numerous essays on religion in Revolutionary society, most recently "The Religious World of Daniel Shays" in Robert A. Gross, ed., *In Debt to Shays: The Bicentennial of an Agrarian Rebellion* (1993). He is currently completing two books, a comprehensive interpretation of American religion from 1764 to 1792 tentatively entitled *The Government of God: Religion in Revolutionary America* and a study of religion and music in contemporary America.

RONALD SCHULTZ is associate professor of history at the University of Wyoming. He is the author of "The Small-Producer Tradition and the Moral Origins of Artisan Radicalism in Philadelphia, 1720–1810" (1990), *The Republic of Labor: Philadelphia Artisans and the Politics of Class, 1720–1830* (1993), "Alternative Communities: American Artisans and the Evangelical Appeal, 1790–1830" (forthcoming), and coeditor, with Gary B. Nash, of *Retracing the Past* (1993). He is currently working on two books, *God and Workingmen: Popular Religion and the Creation of the American Working Class, 1730–1830*, a study of working-class religion in the early Republic, and *The Age of Transition: American Society, 1720–1830*, an interpretative study of America's change from a small-producer to an early capitalist society.

Index

337

INDEX